THEORY AND PRACTICE OF MUSLIM STATE IN INDIA

By the same author

History of the Khaljis, 1950, 1967, 1980
Twilight of the Sultanate, 1963, 1980
Studies in Medieval Indian History, 1966
Studies in Asian History (edited), 1969
Growth of Muslim Population in Medieval India, 1973
Early Muslims in India, 1984
The Mughal Harem, 1988
Indian Muslims: Who are they, 1990, 1993
The Legacy of Muslim Rule in India, 1992
Muslim Slave System in Medieval India, 1994
Growth of Scheduled Tribes and Castes in Medieval India, 1995

Theory and Practice of Muslim State in India

K.S. LAL

ADITYA PRAKASHAN
New Delhi

First Published: 1999
Second Reprint 2020

ISBN: 978-81-86471-72-2

Published by Aditya Prakashan, Delhi – 110 009
and printed at Replika Press Pvt. Ltd.

"I would not care whether truth is pleasant or unpleasant and in consonance with or opposed to current views... I shall bear in patience the ridicule and slander of friends and society for the sake of preaching truth. But still I shall seek truth, understand truth, and accept truth. This started by the firm resolve of a historian."

Jadunath Sarkar

Contents

Preface

My first article, "The Spirit of Muslim Government in India", was published in the Annual Bulletin of the Nagpur University Historical Society, No. 2, October 1947. It was revised and published under the title *Muslim State in India* by Vichar Prakashan, Allahabad, in 1950 in the form of a small book. Chapters on Muslim administration and government are also included in my *History of the Khaljis* (1950), *Twilight of the Sultanate* (1963), *Studies in Medieval Indian History* (1966), *Early Muslims in India* (1984), and *The Legacy of Muslim Rule in India* (1992).

Now fifty years after my first brochure on the subject, I present before the scholars my latest book entitled *The Theory and Practice of Muslim State in India.* Its *raison d'etre* is that in my earlier endeavours, no attempt had been made to trace the relationship between the injunctions contained in Islamic religious literature and the attitudes and actions of Muslim kings and conquerors. Ordinarily, historians writing on medieval Indian history refer to Muslim chronicles and histories as their only source materials. The study of Islamic scriptural literature like the Quran, the Hadis, the Biographies of the Prophet and the Shariat is ignored in historical studies as it is considered to belong to the domain of religion rather than to that of history. However, the study of this literature reveals that Muslim invaders and rulers were not cruel or fanatical by themselves as such, but they became so by pursuing the malevolent ideology as projected in the Quran and the Hadis against the non-Muslims. That is why the study of the 'moral and spiritual' literature of Islam becomes so important for the study of its history also.

Muslim invaders and rulers of India belonged to different races and different countries. There were Arabs, Turks, Uzbegs, Pathans, Africans, Persians and what are called the Mughals. They belonged to different sects like the Shias, Sunnis, Wahabis, etc. Their rule extended for about a thousand years from the eighth to the eighteenth century in various parts of the country. Their chronicles are written in different languages like Arabic, Persian and Turki. But their behaviour follows a uniform pattern. Even those rulers and nobles who had converted to Islam from Hinduism, behaved with their erstwhile co-religionists like any Afghan or Turk or Mughal. They considered their bloody acts against Hindus or non-Muslims as acts of righteousness. The source of this uniformity of action is the Quran, the Hadis and the Sunnah which they quote with pride. That is why the theory part of the Muslim state in India assumes so much importance. These scriptures do not belong only to the past. They are in operation even now. Hate words like Jihad, Kafir, and Mushrik are as current today as when they were first used about fourteen hundred years ago. Pious Muslims in long robes and pious Muslims in European dress (western dress does not make one modern in thought), in all places and at all times seek or provoke Jihad with an appeal to the Quran. Regular wars (Arab-Israel, Iraq-Iran, Afghanistan), terrorist activities (India, Algeria, Egypt, even America), and communal riots (India) are all called and fought in the spirit of Jihad. Such is the important place given to violence in Islam that when there are no non-Muslims to fight, the Muslims call one another Kafir and fight Jihad. Consequently, all over the world Jihadic terrorism seems to be a major Muslim activity even today, whether it is carried on in Muslim or non-Muslim majority countries.

Hence the importance of both the theory and practice in the study of Muslim state in India. The theory part is traced to the Quran, the Hadis and the Sunnah or the Biographies of the Prophet; the Practice part to the principal activities of Muslim rulers in India as narrated by their chroniclers. The Quran of course is all important in Islam. But no less important is the Hadis. One is complementary to the other. The Biographies of the Prophet are equally important.

In the Urdu preface (*ibtidaia*) of Sahih Muslim's translation by Maulana Wahid-uz-Zaman, Bashir Ahmad Naumani says that there are six authentic collections of Hadis — Bukhari, Muslim, Nasai, Abu Daud, Tirmizi and Ibn Majah. Urdu translations of these, together with the original text in Arabic, have been published by Aitqad Publishing House, Delhi. Mr. Sita Ram Goel was good enough to lend them to me for study. He also made available to me the Holy Quran's Urdu and Hindi translations with Arabic text published from Rampur. Thus I have been able to consult the most authentic translations of Islamic scriptures done by Muslims themselves and not by Western scholars who are sometimes accused of interpreting Muslim scriptures with a bias. And I do not speak myself, but let the Muslims speak, giving extensive quotations from their classical authors.

The most accepted biography of Prophet Muhammad is by Ibn Ishaq. Its English translation has gone through many reprints in Pakistan alone. *The Life of Mahomet* written by William Muir and *Mohammed and the Rise of Islam* by D.S. Margoliouth are equally authentic. These are based on primary source materials including Hadis and I find that the accusation of these authors being prejudiced is not correct.

So far as evaluation of medieval Muslim chronicles is concerned, it has been done by me earlier in most of my books. There is no need to repeat what has been written about them earlier. Also the present study covers only the overall polity of medieval India; it does not deal with the provincial or regional Muslim States like Bengal, Malwa, Gujarat, the Bahmani kingdom or Kashmir. However, wherever Muslim rule prevailed, the basic principles of governance were the same. In short, 'Muslim State in India' represents the theory and practice of all states in India ruled by Muslims.

This book has three parts. Part I deals with the Muslim state in medieval India, its obligations, its income and expenditure, its Jihad, its justice in historical perspectives. Part II is entitted Politics, for Muslim state in India has not ceased to exist even in modern times and Indian Muslims on account of Islamic laws and separate identity almost form a separate state within the Indian State. Part III is a Reposte on reviews of some of my books, carrying reiteration of some of my statements which have been challenged only with a motive to challenge.

K.S. Lal

Abbreviations used in References

For complete titles of works see Bibliography

Afif	:	*Tarikh-i-Firoz Shahi* by Shams Siraj Afif
Ain	:	*Ain-i-Akbari* by Abul Fazl, trans. by H. Blochmann
Akbar Nama	:	*Akbar Nama* by Abul Fazl, trans. by H. Beveridge
Babur Nama	:	*Memoirs of Babur*, trans. by Ms. A. Beveridge
Badaoni	:	*Muntakhab-ut-Tawarikh* by Abdul Qadir Badaoni
Barani	:	*Tarikh-i-Firoz Shahi* by Ziyauddin Barani
Bernier	:	*Travels in the Mogul Empire* by Francois Bernier
C.H.I.	:	*Cambridge History of India*
E.D.	:	*History of India as told by its own Historians* by Henry Elliot and John Dowson, 8 volumes
Farishtah	:	*Gulshan-i-Ibrahimi* or *Tarikh-i-Farishtah* by Muhammad Qasim Hindu Shah Farishtah
Foster	:	*Early Travels in India*, edited by William Foster
Ibn Battutah	:	*Rehla of Ibn Battuta*, trans. by Mahdi Husain

Isami	:	*Futuh-us-Salatin* by Khwaja Abdullah Malik
Khafi Khan	:	*Mutakhab-ul-Lubab* by Khafi Khan
Lahori	:	*Badshah Nama* by Abdul Hamid Lahori
Manucci	:	*Storia do Mogor* by Niccolao Manucci
Minhaj	:	*Tabqat-i-Nasiri* by Minhaj Siraj Jurjáni
Pelsaert	:	*Jahangir's India* by Francisco Pelsaert
P.I.H.C.	:	*Proceedings of the Indian History Congress*
Tuzuk	:	*Tuzuk-i-Jahangiri*, trans. by Rogers and Beveridge
J.A.S.B.	:	*Journal of the (Royal) Asiatic Society of Bengal*
J.R.A.S.	:	*Journal of the Royal Asiatic Society of Great Britain*

Part I

HISTORY

I
Introduction

1.1. THE RISE OF ISLAM

Professor R.P. Tripathi begins his famous monograph entitled *Some Aspects of Muslim Administration*, by writing that the Muslim "invaders gradually wormed themselves into the heart of India, and finally assumed the role of the earlier Hindu Empire-builders like Chandra Gupta, Samudra Gupta and even Harsha... The Muslim Sultan, however, differed from the earlier Hindu sovereigns in two respects. He did not belong to the country over which he had come to rule... Secondly, he believed in a religion whose outlook on social and political questions was very different from that of the Hindus. He did not come... simply for conquest. With him he had brought a well-defined religion, a highly developed civilization, and a set of institutions to which he clung with all his faith. Indeed, it was an avowed principle with him to maintain their purity and to establish them in lands under his sway."[1]

This statement of R.P. Tripathi lays stress on the following points: that Muslim invaders assumed the role of earlier Hindu empire-builders like Chandra Gupta, Samudra Gupta and Harshavardhan; that they did not belong to the country over which they had come to rule; that they believed in a religion which was very different from that of the Hindus; and that the invaders and rulers had not come just to conquer but also to establish Islamic religion and institutions in all their purity in this country.

We shall elaborate on these points to give an idea of what the present work is all about. It has been correctly said that the Muslim invaders and rulers did not belong to Hindustan. Muhammad Ghauri, Iltutmish and Balban ruled with the help of Muslim soldiers from abroad. The Khaljis and Tughlaqs may be considered Indian, but they also regularly recruited warriors from outside India for extending their dominions and spreading Islam in India. Many Muslim rulers depended upon the caliphs of Baghdad or Cairo for moral support. The Mughal invader Babur did not belong to India. He was forced by circumstances to march into Hindustan. His officers and soldiers disliked the country and clamoured to return home to Afghanistan. Babur himself had no love for the country and as per his wishes his body was taken and buried in his homeland. Akbar and Jahangir were regarded as Indians but not the other Mughals. As late as the seventeenth century the French physician Francois Bernier while on a visit to India asserted that "the *Great Mogol* is a foreigner in *Hindustan*, a descendent of *Tamerlane*, chief of those Mogols from Tartary who, about the year 1401, overran and conquered the Indies, consequently he finds himself in a hostile country, or nearly so..."

These alien rulers could not assume the role of earlier Hindu emperors. Although they gradually wormed themselves into the heart of India and built up large empires, they could not rule like Chandra Gupta, Samudra Gupta or Harshavardhan. The two belonged to two different religious streams. The Muslim sultans reigned according to the dictates of the Shariat, the Hindu emperors on the principles of Dharmashastra. Their rules of war and governance were poles apart. The Quran does not permit the existence or continuance of other faiths and their religious practices. Of the 6236 *ayats* in the Quran about 3,900 are directly or indirectly related to Kafirs, Mushriks, Munkirs, Munafiqs or non-believers in Allah and his Prophet. Broadly speaking these 3,900 *ayats* fall into two categories — those relating to

Muslims who for their faith will be rewarded in this as well as the world hereafter, and those relating to Kafirs or non-believers who are to be punished in this world and are destined to go to Hell after death. The Quran reads like a manual of war on mankind rather than a charter of brotherhood for all mankind. For people of other faiths, Jihad or permanent war was the command of the Quran and order of the day. Islam recommends Jihad or perpetual war on adherents of other religions — to lay hold of them, bind them, strike off their heads and burn them in the fire of hell. This makes Islam a totalitarian and terrorist cult which it has remained ever since its birth.

On the other hand, Indian kings waged wars according to humane rules which have been elaborately described in the Dharmasutras and Dharmashastras, the Ramayana and Mahabharata, and the Arthashastra treatises of Kautilya, Kamandaka, and Shukra. Even during the medieval period, as has been observed by K.M. Munshi: "Whatever the provocation, the shrine, the Brahman and the cow were sacrosanct.... War being a special privilege of the martial classes, harassment of the civilian population during military operations was considered a serious lapse from the code of honour. The high regard which all Kshatriyas had for the chastity of women, also ruled out abduction as an incident of war."[2] Moreover, never in this country was a war psychology developed for aggressive ends. The whole nation was never trained for purposes of war. Only one caste — the Kshatriya — was set aside for purposes of defence against foreign invasions and protection of life and property from internal dissensions. It is another matter that against the no-holds-barred Jihadists, all castes, all sections of Hindu society joined to fight the invaders and proselytizers, but fighting was the duty primarily of the Kshatriya.

In war and in peace, the Muslim rulers of Hindustan followed, as far as lay in their power, the injunctions of the Quran and the Hadis, the Shariat and the Sunnah. They had no knowledge of the scriptures and institutions followed by Chandra Gupta, Samudra Gupta or Harshavardhan. They could not and did not rule like Hindu kings. It is often said that all religions are alike. People may follow different paths but they all lead to the same God. If that were so, there was no need of any quarrel among peoples of different faiths. But strife among followers of different creeds is common. Therefore all religions are not similar. It is the fundamental teachings of a creed that mould the character and determine the conduct of its followers. Therefore it has been rightly pointed out by Tripathi that Muslim invaders and rulers believed in "a religion whose outlook on social and political questions was very different from that of the Hindus". The growing awareness that Muslim religion and Muslim rule were impositions and that Indians belonged to a different religious and political tradition, has not escaped Hindu consciousness of medieval history. It does not accept the Ilbaris, the Khaljis, the Tughlaqs, the Bahmanis, the Sharqis, the Lodis and the Mughals as indigenous dynasties on par with the Mauryas, the Guptas, the Cholas, the Pandyas, the Sangamas, the Marathas, the Sikhs, and the Jats. Its heroes are Prithviraj Chauhan, Vikram Pandya of Madura, Harihar and Bukka and Krishnadevaraya of Vijayanagar, Maharanas Kumbha, Sanga and Pratap, Maharajas Shivaji and Ranjit Singh and not Muhammad Ghauri, Alauddin Khalji, Sikandar Lodi or even Shahjahan.

It was the erudite Alberuni who, after describing the atrocities inflicted by Sabuktigin and Mahmud of Ghazni, declared that "the antagonism between them (the Hindus) and all foreigners receives more and more nourishment both from political and religious sources". Muslim invaders and rulers, had come not only to conquer but also to impose the Islamic religion. And the gulf created by the phenomenon has not been bridged. For, Islam is an imposition on India. Worse, it has been imposed through conquest. Ralph Borsodi, an American educationist and social thinker, in his

The Challenge of Asia observes that "everywhere in the world except in Asia Minor, the three great Semitic religions — Judaism, Christianity and Islam — are intruders; that indigenous Asia is Brahmanist, Confucianist, Buddhist, Taoist; indigenous Europe is pagan; that in Europe, Christianity is a superimposition; in Asia, Islam is."[3] The achievements of Muslim conquerors and rulers in India consist of the pursuit of their political and religious policy of superimposing Islam on India. This is clearly borne out by the writings of medieval Muslim chroniclers like Hasan Nizami, Minhaj Siraj, Ziyauddin Barani, Shams Siraj Afif, Farishtah, etc. It is by going through their works that one can appreciate the spirit of how Islam was made to spread in India. As against the modern apologists, they take pride in the fact that Islam spread in India through the sword and through methods laid down in Quran and Hadis.

Many educated Muslim rulers of medieval India had mastered the Quran and were familiar with other literature on Muslim religion and jurisprudence. The uneducated kings employed ulema to familiarize them with the Islamic lore. For an Alim and a Maulana, Quran was the first must among the works he studied. Its *Surahs* (chapters) and *ayats* (verses) are often quoted and its phraseology freely used by them while writing the chronicles of their kings. There are two sorts of Muslim historians — the dry annalists, and the pompous and flowery rhetoricians. But both of them use the language of their scriptures — a style more natural to their ideas and sentiments. Therefore, present-day scholars working on medieval Indian history should acquaint themselves with this literature to know what Islam stands for. It is necessary to know Islam in order to understand the spirit of Muslim rule in India. The religion and theology of Islam are based on four great works – (1) The Quran, (2) the Hadis, (3) the *Sirat-un-Nabi* or the Biography of Muhammad, and (4) the Shariat or Islamic law as elaborated in the *Hidayah*. The word 'Quran' literally means recitation, lecture or discourse. Muslims consider it to be the word of God conveyed to His prophet Muhammad through the angel Gabriel. The Quran is not only the heart of the religion but it is still "considered by one-eighth of mankind as the embodiment of all science, wisdom and theology".[4] The Quran is the principal scripture revealed by Allah to Prophet Muhammad. Consequently, its injunctions become commands of God. With the Prophet becoming inalienable part of it, he is also bestowed with unquestionable authority on each and every theory and practice of Islam.

The study of Quran and the necessity of expounding it gave rise to that most characteristically Muslim literary activity, namely, the books of tradition or Hadis, literally meaning "narrative". It is the compendium of the doings, sayings, reservations and judgements of Muhammad. Muslim theologians make no distinction between Quran and Hadis. To them both are works of revelation or inspiration. "In the Quran, Allah speaks through Muhammad; in the *Sunnah* [Hadis], He acts through him... No wonder that the Muslim theologians regard the Quran and the Hadis as being supplementary or even interchangeable'."[5] Within three hundred years of the death of Muhammad, the Hadis acquired substantially the form in which it is known today. Imam Bukhari (d. CE 870) compiled 'authentic' traditions from a plethora of voluminous traditions. Next in importance are the collections of Imam Muslim (d. 875) and Imam Tirmizi (d. 892). These are well known and oft-quoted. In the series of original collectors of Hadis, Imam ibn Majah's name is equally important. Born in 209 H/824 CE, he died in 273/886. He collected traditions at his home in Qazwin and by travelling abroad in Khurasan, Iraq, Hijaz, Egypt and Syria. In every *hadis* in his *Sunan ibn Majah* he quotes the copious authorities from whom he got his information.

Sunan ibn Daud by Imam Abu Daud Sijistani is a compilation of 4,800 *ahadis* selected from five lakh *ahadis*. In the preface to the work published from Delhi, the publisher rightly emphasizes that the Quran and Hadis are supplementary, that "without Hadis, it is not possible to practise the (injunctions) of the Quran and without Quran, Hadis is incomplete". *Mishkat-ul-Sharif* also is a collection of more than 6,000 *ahadis* selected by Abdullah al-Khatib al-Umari (d. 743/1342 CE), from the works of Bukhari, Muslim, Tirmizi, Abu Daud and many others. He quotes their authority at the end of each *hadis* cited.

Equally important guide for the Muslims in the performance of their duties is the life-story of Muhammad. Apart from several *maghazi* books dealing with the Prophet's campaigns, his first authentic biography too was ready in the eighth century. Its author Ibn Ishaq was born at Medina in 85 H and died in Baghdad in 151 H (704-768 CE). He wrote the *Sirat Rasul Allah*.[6] Other biographers of note who succeeded him were al-Waqidi, Ibn Hisham, and at-Tabari. Muslims try to mould their lives after the model of Muhammad. As advocated by Bukhari, I, p. 623, *ahadis* 1578ff, "No one regarded by any section of human race as the perfect man has been imitated so minutely."[7] In short, anything derived from the Quran and the Hadis is the Shariat or Islamic jurisprudence; anything derived from Hadis and history of the prophet Muhammad by and large constitutes the Sunnah. There is no aspect of life which does not receive guidance from Islamic scriptural literature. It deals with government and administration, payment of taxes, crime and punishment, buying and selling, treatment of women and slaves, baths, prayers and fasts, marriage, divorce and sex. Nothing is missing. Islam is complete in all matters of do's and don'ts for Muslims. A Muslim need not think at all — all his problems find a ready answer in Quran and Hadis.

Essentialism of Islam

Jihad is the highest duty of a Muslim. Jihad means attacking, killing, enslaving or converting non-Muslims even when they have done no harm to the Muslims, even when they are unarmed. Jihad is waged for the sake of Allah; war and worship in His service are the same. Shirking Jihad is the greatest sin; obtaining glory through Jihad is the highest grace. Islam suffers from the ego of triumphalism. It says that it should triumph over others, because it alone is true and all others are false. Not all exclusivists belong to the militant extreme, but all are convinced that their religion alone is true. This is Islamic fundamentalism. Fundamentalism is belief in the inerrancy of the scriptures of one's religion. Fundamentalism is not accidental but essential to Islam. What Islam always meant by "knowledge" (*ilm*) was religious knowledge by "revelation", the logic that all that is in Islam is right. It sees unchangeability as strength. That is why the word reform is so abhorrent to Muslim thinkers and religious leaders. In Islamic scriptures there are commands, directions and orders. There is no mention of discussions or consensus arrived at. This was the practice in Arabia after its conquest by Muhammad and this was the practice wherever Muslim armies marched. In Islam, truth is established by the sword, not through argument. Image breaking is a contribution of prophetic religions. In Islam, iconoclasm is important, but it is more important that the shrines of non-Muslims are desecrated and destroyed rather than spared through agreement or in exchange for wealth. (What Mahmud of Ghazni declared at Somnath according to Attar, is the gist of the true spirit of Islam).

The Quran and the Hadis provided the foundation upon which theology and law of Islam were raised. Totalitarian nature of Islam permits no separation of state and church. "Law in Islam is more intimately related to religion than to jurisprudence as modern lawyers understand it."[8] Named after their founders Abu Hanifa (c. 699-767), Abu Abdullah Muhammad bin Idris (c. 767-820), Ahmad Bin Hanbal (c. 780-855) and Malik bin Anas (c. 715-795) — the four *mazahib* or schools of Islamic law named Hanafi, Shafii,

Hanbali and Malaki respectively, had come into being in the eighth-ninth century. The Hanafi law is followed in India. If at all anything was wanting with regard to Muslim law, it was provided by *Hidayah* or Guidance.[9] The *Hidayah* is a voluminous treatise based on Sunni law composed by Shaikh Burhanuddin Ali who was born at Marghinan in Transoxiana about 530 H and died in 593 H (1135-1196).[10] Burhanuddin claims to have studied all earlier commentaries on the Quran and the Hadis belonging to the schools of Malik, Shafi and Hanbal besides that of Abu Hanifa.[11] The other outstanding work of this kind is the *Kanz-ud-Daqaiq* of Maulana Abdullah Nasafi.

Muslim law in its ultimate form was thus available to the conquerors and sultans who established their rule in India in the thirteenth century. True, there were no printed editions of these works. But beautiful hand-written copies were always available, at least to distinguished conquerors and kings and their counsellors. Muslim law is definite, clear and universal. This law was the actual sovereign in Muslim lands; no one was above it and all were ruled by it.[12]

Muslim state in India was administered according to this law. Muslims and non-Muslims were all governed by it. For Muslim sultans and governors in India, it provided examples, precedents and judgements by the learned in the law in other Muslim lands. It helped them in taking decisions in any matter of importance. Qazis and Muftis were there with them to render advice and interpretation on complicated matters. In short, the functioning of the Muslim state in India, its history and polity, cannot be correctly understood without a working knowledge of Islamic scriptures and law.

1.2. THE SPREAD OF ISLAM

Muhammad, the prophet of Islam (full name Abu al-Qasim Muhammad ibn Abdullah ibn Abdul Muttalib ibn Hashim) was born in Arabia in or around 570 CE and died in 632. In 622 he had to migrate from Makkah to Madinah (called *hijrat*) and this year forms the first year of the Muslim Hijri calender. During his life time, Muhammad made Arabia a land exclusively adherent to Islam. After his death, the Arabs embarked on a series of territorial expansions and made themselves masters of Syria, Palestine, Egypt and Persia within a short span of twenty years, or, in the rhetorical words of Earnest Barker, Arab Islamism "Spreading with the rapidity of an electric current from its power house in Mecca, it flashed into Syria, it traversed the whole breadth of north Africa; and then, leaping the Straits of Gibralter it ran to the Gates of the Pyrenees."[13] Such unparalleled feats of success were due to their proud feeling of Arabicism, their zeal for the new faith, and the material gains brought through holy war or Jihad. The ponderosity of the Jihad gave them the energy and the rapidity of electric current. And Islam came to be what the world has ever since recognized it to be — a militant religion, a creed of aggression and violence.

Islam originated in the land of the Arabs. The rise of Arabs as a political power has been elucidated by a large number of writers on Islam. T.W. Arnold observes that the expansion of the Arabs was due not so much to the religious spirit as to their desire to obtain the lands and goods of their neighbors who were richer and more fortunate than themselves.[14] Most Arabs of the days of prophet Muhammad were poor. They needed a reformer to improve their economic condition. There are two ways of alleviating poverty and gaining economic well-being. One way is to work hard and raise one's resources through labour and sweat. The other is to attack and rob others and thereby grow rich. The early indigent Arab Muslims could either be persuaded to make a living by working hard, or encouraged to attack and plunder the others. Islam resorted to the second alternative as ordered by Allah. Recruits, mainly from among the slaves or lower classes, began to swell the ranks of the believers, or in the flowery words of Edward Gibbon, the shepherds were turned into robbers and robbers were collected to form an army of conquest. "Soldiering was not only the noblest and most pleasing professions in the sight of Allah but also most profitable."[15]

Anwar Shaikh analyses the expansion of Arab power in the following words: "The prophet Muhammad divided humanity into two sections — the Arabs and the non-Arabs... The Arabs are the rulers and the non-Arabs are to be ruled... Islam is the means to realize this dream... Islam has caused more damage to the national dignity and honour of non-Arab Muslims than any other calamity ... Yet they believe that this faith is the ambassador of 1. Equality and 2. Human Love. This is a fiction."[16] Creation of a pure (Muslim) nation, demanded that the Jews must be expelled from Arabia. So, they were treated mercilessly. Finally, the policy of ethnic cleansing was adopted, and the Jews were banished.[17]

As the Quran is in Arabic, this must be the preferred language of the Muslims everywhere. Translation of Quran in fact is not Quran. The real Quran is the one that has been revealed in the Arabic language.[18] Besides, *"no place on earth has ever exacted such a tribute of reverence from mankind as the Kaaba. Respect to the Kaaba means, respect to Mecca, respect to Mecca means respect to Arabia, and respect to Arabia means respect to Arabs, the dwellers of Arabia"*. (italics by the author).[19] Everything about Arabia is superior, says also the Hadis. Mecca is Allah's best land and most beloved of God. Muhammad decreed that Muslims everywhere must prostrate five times a day facing Makkah. When Muslims die, they must be buried facing Mecca which is the guarantee of their salvation. Keeping one *roza* in Makkah brings benediction (*sawab*) of one lakh *rozas.*[20]

Muhammad made Hajj to Arabia an obligatory ritual for his followers. As prophet of Allah, Muhammad was aware of his power and influence over Muslims. If he had said that Hajj should be performed every year, it would have become obligatory on Muslims to go for Hajj every year.[21] He knew their limitations and therefore made one Hajj at least good enough in one's lifetime. Mecca was declared Allah's own land and it became a centre of pilgrimage of Islam and of all Muslims; Hajj impressed upon Muslims the sanctity of Arabia. Besides for the old, the weak and women, Hajj is their Jihad.[22] Hajj created an everlasting source of income for the Arabs.[23] Ruben Levy notes that "the largest amount of space devoted in the Quran to any of the four duties is then given to the pilgrimage".[24]

Anwar Shaikh dwells on this early period of Arab glory. "The Arabs made a profession of robbing and murdering the non-Muslims in the name of Allah, but they called it Jihad. Egypt and Iran were the early casualties. It was the pillaged wealth and abducted daughters and sisters of the foreign nations which lent the golden touch to this Arab era."[25] "After their spectacular conquests, the Arabs were unwilling to concede equality to the non-Arab converts to Islam, despite Islamic doctrine that expressively forbade discrimination. But for the Arabs there were the conquered and the conquerors... The Arabs ruled as a sort of conquistador tribal aristocracy", to which only "true Arabs" could belong...[26] Later on the same was done by the "true Turks". The Turks took concubines from the conquered people, but their children and their slave women were heavily discriminated against and were not considered full Turks.

To sum up, Islam spread through unparalleled feats of armed might. Some Muslim merchants spread their creed by peaceful means also by making their employees and other beneficiaries join their faith. Peaceful propagation of Islam was ruled out by the fact that the majority of early Arab Muslims were not educated enough to discuss, debate, argue and convince. Hence they were not trained for spreading the new creed through any missionary endeavour. They could only wield the sword very well. Hence Muslim historical literature repeatedly mentions that Islam spread through military conquests when the vanquished were offered the alternative of Islam or death. They accepted Islam because they had hardly any other choice. Death is no choice because nobody chooses death, so they chose Islam.

In view of this it is difficult to agree with the view that Islam was hailed by people living under "despair and frustration" and that its "success should be sought, not so much in the strength of Muslim armies, as in the revolutionary impact of the principles of the new social order which Islam preached and strove to establish".[27] It is true that Muslims believe Islam to be a religion of equality and love. This idea of equality and love may not be a total fiction, but it is meant not for all the people; it is confined to Muslims only.

There are one or two passages in the Quran evincing tolerance like: Your religion to you, my religion to me; or, there is no compulsion in religion. "All passages preaching tolerance are found in Meccan, i.e., early Suras, and all the passages recommending killing, decapitating, and maiming are Medinan, i.e., later toleration has been abrogated by intolerance. For example, the famous verse 9.5, "Slay the idolaters wherever you find them," is said to have cancelled 124 verses that dictate toleration and patience.[28]

Islam has two sets of principles of morality, ethics and justice: One for Muslims and the other for non-Muslims. Sincerity, well-wishing and brotherhood are for the believers and faithful. For non-Muslims the principles and standards of behaviour are different. The differences are elaborately defined in the Quran, the Hadis and the Sunnah. Subversion of many ancient civilizations by Islam is a historical fact. Welcome reception of the new creed by other people because they were living in frustration in their old order, is only an assumption.

This assumption is disproved by a patent fact. Islamic armed creed projected through war, achieved quick success only in small countries with small populations (beginning at home with Arabia itself), not in large countries with large populations. In 622 CE "when the Muslims took up arms they had little more than a tiny existence. In 632 the Muslims had conquered the whole of the Arabian Peninsula. It was conquered at the cost of only 150 men killed in the battle-field on the enemy side."[29] For the same reason, it could accomplish its aim of spreading Islam in Egypt, Syria, Iraq, Iran and North Africa. According to Colin Clarke's estimates the population of Egypt about the middle of the fourteenth century was three million, of the rest of North Africa two million, of Asia Minor, Syria and Cyprus eleven million, and of other countries of South-West Asia also eleven million.[30] The fighting force of these countries in the seventh and eighth centuries would have been very small — too small to withstand the armed might of the invading Arabs. Hence these were overrun and Islamized speedily. Big countries with large population and hoary civilizations like India, China, Russia and Europe rejected Islam. Not that Islamic armies did not try to penetrate them, but they were persistently resisted and Islam was not accepted by them as their national creed or culture. India is the most appropriate example of this phenomenon. Here a thousand years of Islamic rule, terror and vandalism failed to impress the people about the Islamic revolution. Islam was not welcomed as harbinger of a revolution promising a new world order because it was not believed to be so by those who were subjected by it. If today some Muslim countries like Saudi Arabia and Iran take pride in the achievements of Islam and dream of furthering Pan-Islamism, they do not care or dare to remember the point of time when their original religions and civilizations were subverted; they do not desire to recapitulate how their ancestors had felt at the sudden trampling of their cherished values through violence. Of course some countries like Egypt, Turkey and Algeria which were similarly Islamized in medieval times now want to rid themselves of Islamic fundamentalist shackles.

1.3. THE ADVENT OF MUSLIMS IN INDIA

Arab invasion of Sindh: The Arab and later Turk Muslims spread into India through three major waves of invasions, but it took them five hundred years to do so. After the conquest of Iran by 643 CE, the boundaries of the Caliphate touched the frontiers of India. India, known to early Arabs as Hind wa Sind, too could not escape Muslim expansionist designs, and they sent their armies into India both by land and sea. They proceeded along the then known (trade) routes — 1. from Kufa and Baghdad, via Basra and Hormuz to Chaul on India's west coast; 2. from West Persian towns, via Hormuz to Debal in Sindh; and 3. through the land route of northern Khurasan to Kabul via Bamian. But progress of Muslim arms and religion in India was slow, very slow. For, the declarations of the objectives of Muslim invaders had not taken into account the potentialities of Indians' stiff and latent resistance. Caliph Umar (634-44 CE) had sent an expedition in 636-37 to pillage Thana. It was followed by some attempts on the part of Caliphs Usman and Ali. But in vain. The four 'pious' Caliphs of Islam died without hearing of the conquest of Sind and Hind.

The first full-fledged Arab invasion of Sindh was launched by Muhammad bin Qasim in 712 on the command of Hajjaj bin Yusuf on behalf of the Caliph. By the irony of circumstance, the majority of the Sindhi population at that time was Buddhist. They were averse to fighting. But there was no difference between them and Brahmans with regard to resistance to the invader.[31] Debal, the fort-temple town, was attacked first. When the siege of Debal had continued for some time a defector informed Muhammad about how the temple could be captured. Thereupon, the Arabs, planting their ladders, stormed the citadel-temple and swarmed over the walls. As per Islamic injunctions, the inhabitants were invited to accept Islam, and on their refusal to do so, all adult males were put to the sword and their wives and children were enslaved. The carnage lasted for three days. The temple was razed and a mosque built on its site and with its debris. Muhammad laid out a Muslim quarter, and placed a garrison of 4,000 in the town.

The result of the destruction of Debal, the venerated shrine of Sindh, was that the Jats, who perhaps had earlier shown indifference if not jubilation on the arrival of the new comers, turned enemies of Muslims for all time to come.[32] Most of the major cities of Sindh were captured, their temples broken, their men massacred and their women and children enslaved. Muhammad bin Qasim was permitted to remain in Sindh only for a little over three years but Muslims and Islam came to stay in Sindh permanently. A dent had been made in India's social fabric, and its wealth looted. Foreign and newly converted Muslims remained confined mostly to cities, particularly Multan. Multan, according to al-Masudi (writing about CE 942), remained one of the strongest frontier places of the Musalmans. Ibn Hauqal who finished his work in CE 976 says, "The Muslims and infidels of this tract wear the same dresses, and let their beards grow in the same fashion. They use fine muslin garments on account of the extreme heat. The men of Multan dress in the same way. The language of Mansura, Multan and those parts is Arabic and Sindian..." This, in brief, was the social change brought about in Sindh after the introduction of Islam there.

Two points in the destruction of Debal need be taken note of. First, the carnage there lasted for three days. The conquering Muslim army is generally allowed three days of pillage. This three day pattern is repeated in many Muslim massacres, e.g., Timur's massacre in Delhi (1399) or Sultan Muhammad's in Constantinople (1453). The lust for slaughter used to assuage in this period and it sufficed the soldiers to gather captives and precious objects. The second is the destruction of the temple of Debal. Iconoclasm represented Quwwat-ul-Islam. Muslims destroyed Hindu temples because of 'dominance urge'. But they did more harm to themselves than they visualized. Besides earning permanent Hindu hostility, they harmed their own maritime trade and commerce. For example, Hindu temples on the seaboard like Debal on the west coast and Jagannath Puri on the east, served as light houses for the sailing ships.[33] Muslims destroyed all. They themselves suffered in the long run. They became weak on the sea so that even the might of Akbar's empire could not prove equal to the small number of Portuguese who dominated the Indian seas.

Mahmud of Ghazni's Campaigns in Punjab

A more terrifying wave of Islamic invasion came with Mahmud of Ghazni, three hundred years after the Arab invasion of Sindh. During this period Islam was spreading in various regions outside India with varying degrees of success. Furthermore, the newly converted Turks, the slave protectors of the pious Caliphs, had carved out their own kingdoms at the expense of the Caliph's "empire". Alaptigin and Subuktigin belonged to this class of slaves. They made frequent inroads into Hindu Shahiya territories of Afghanistan and Punjab. But when Subuktigin's son Mahmud delivered his first attack in the year 1000 CE, he let loose hell in the region.

Mahmud could launch forth seventeen expeditions during the course of the next thirty years. He fulfilled his promise to the Caliph of carrying out yearly campaigns against the non-Muslims of Hindustan both in letter and spirit of Islamic theology. For this he has been eulogized sky-high by Muslim poets and Muslim historians. He was always careful to include the Caliph's name on his coins, depict himself in his *Fateh-namas* as a warrior for the faith, and to send to Baghdad presents from the plunder of his Indian campaigns. The Caliph al-Qadir Billah in turn praised the talents and exploits of Mahmud, conferred upon him the titles of *Amin-ul-millah* and *Yamin-ud-daula* (the right hand) after which his house is known as Yamini Dynasty.

Mahmud Ghaznavi was very successful in the usual fields of Islamic expansionism — conversions of Hindus to Islam, destruction of temples and acquisition of wealth. The sack of Somnath in particular came to be considered a specially pious exploit because of its analogy with the destruction of the idol of al-Manat in Arabia by the Prophet. This "explains the idolization of Mahmud by Nizam-ul-Mulk Tusi,[34] and the ideal treatment he has received from early sufi poets like Sanai and Attar, not to mention such collectors of anecdotes as Awfi."[35] It is indeed noticeable that after the Somnath expedition (417H/1026 CE), "a deed which had fired the imagination of the Islamic world", Caliph al-Qadir Billah himself celebrated the victory with great éclat. It is also significant that Mahmud now issued his coins for the first time from Lahore.

Alberuni writes that "Mahmud utterly ruined the prosperity of the country... by which the Hindus became like atoms of dust scattered in all directions... Their scattered remains cherish.. the most inveterate aversion towards all Muslims... Hindu sciences have retired far away from those parts of the country conquered by us, and have fled to places which our hand *cannot yet reach* (italics ours), to Kashmir, Benaras and other places."[36] Later chroniclers write with a tinge of pride that fourteen Ghaznavids ruled at Lahore and its environs for nearly two hundred years. But there was progressive deterioration in their administration. However, the importance of occupation of most part of the Punjab lies in the fact that Muslims had come to stay in India. And these Muslims helped in the third wave of Muslim onrush which swept northern India under Muhammad Ghauri.

Muhammad Ghauri's Invasion of India

Muhammad Ghauri was not as valiant and dashing as Mahmud, but his knowledge about India and about Islam was much better. He now possessed Alberuni's *India* and

Burhanuddin's *Hidayah*, works which were not available to his predecessor invader. Alberuni's encyclopaedic work provided to the Islamic world in the eleventh century all that was militarily advantageous to know about India. Equally important was the *Hidayah*, the most authentic work on the laws of Islam compiled by Shaikh Burhanuddin Ali in the twelfth century. These and similar works, and the military manuals like the *Siyasat Nama* and the *Adab-ul-Harb*, made the Ghauris and their successors better equipped for the conquest and governance of non-Muslim India. There need be no doubt that such works were made available, meticulously studied and constantly referred to by scholars attached to the courts of Muslim conquerors and kings.

Muhammad Ghauri led his first expedition to Multan and Gujarat in 1175 and 1178. In 1191 he attacked Prithviraj Chauhan ruling at Ajmer and Delhi but was defeated and forced to beat a hasty retreat. Next year he again started from Ghazni towards Hindustan with full preparations and with a force of one hundred and twenty thousand Turks, Persians and Afghans. On reaching Lahore, he sent an ambassador to Ajmer and invited Prithviraj to make his submission and accept Islam. The arrogant message met with a befitting retort, and the armies of the two once more encamped opposite each other on the banks of Saraswati at Tarain, 588 H/1192 CE. The Rajput army was far superior in numbers. Prithviraj had succeeded in enlisting the support of about one hundred Rajput princes who rallied round his banner with their elephants, cavalry and infantry. To counter such a vast number Muhammad Ghauri "adopted a tactic which bewildered the Rajputs" and they were defeated.

With the defeat and death of Prithviraj Chauhan, the task of the invader became easy. Sirsuti, Samana, Kuhram and Hansi were captured in quick succession with ruthless slaughter and a general destruction of temples and their replacement by mosques. The Sultan then proceeded to Ajmer which too witnessed similar scenes. In Delhi an army of occupation was stationed at Indraprastha under the command of Qutbuddin Aibak who was to act as Ghauri's lieutenant in Hindustan. Later on Aibak became the first Sultan of Delhi. That is how the Muslim state was established in northern India.

Muslim conquest of Sindh and Punjab is an old story. It has been graphically described by early medieval Muslim chroniclers like al-Kufi, Utbi, al-Biladuri, Ibn-ul-Asir, Hasan Nizami, Minhaj Siraj, etc. Mahmud of Ghazni's extraordinary exploits fired the imagination of Muslim historians and they praised him sky-high for his achievements. He was their model, their hero. In all spheres of Islamic piety he excelled over all other Muslim conquerors. His iconoclastic zeal, in particular his sack of Somnath, won him unlimited praise from poets and historians, contemporary and later. Mahmud was hailed throughout the Islamic world as a second Muhammad and his destruction of Somnath was lauded by the sufi poets Attar, Sanai and Umar Khayyam. These poets equated Somnath with the temples of the Goddess al-Manat smashed by Muhammad in Arabia. As the *Dictionary of Islam* says, Muslim writers are "unanimous in asserting that in the time of the Prophet... the only choice given to the idolaters of Arabia was death or reception of Islam". Breaking of temples and forcible conversions at the point of sword were achievements of all Muslim invaders and most Muslim rulers. Their Jihad spread Islam in the infidel land of Hindustan and filled the coffers of Muslim conquerors with immense wealth. However, some modern Muslim apologists express a view contrary to what has been said by contemporary chroniclers of the medieval period. Probably they are shocked at the barbarous conduct of their medieval brethren and want to salvage the reputation of Islam, although whatever was done was done in accordance with the canons of their creed. Muslim historians of the medieval period honestly state that non-Muslims were converted to Islam through force; modern Muslim apologists claim that conversions were effected through peaceful means. Medieval chroniclers take pride in the iconoclastic zeal and achievements of their heroes; modern apologists plead otherwise. Medieval historians credit Muslim invaders with fighting Jihad for spreading Islam; modern Muslim writers say that their motive was economic — that the invaders were interested in loot and plunder and had little to do with religion. It needs to be emphasized that the truth here does not lie midway. It lies on the side of the medieval chroniclers. Still, the apologists complicate matters by contradicting the versions of their own co-religionists who were closer to and more intimately associated with events about which they wrote than our modern apologists. The idea of a secular Muslim state is an innovation of a few modern "progressive" writers who wish to bracket Muslim civilization with tolerant civilizations. They should remember that there is a difference between the spread of Islam and, say, spread of Buddhism and no amount of jugglery of words and "interpretations" can prove that the spread of Islam was peaceful. All Hadis, and all chroniclers discriminate between Muslims and non-Muslims, and Islam spread in India through the exertions of Muslim heroes like Mahmud of Ghazni and through Jihad as recommended by Islamic scriptures.

As Dr. Ali Issa Othman, for some years adviser to UNRWA (United Nations Relief and Works Agency) on education said: "The spread of Islam was military. There is a tendency to apologize for this and we should not. It is one of the injunctions of the Koran that you must fight for the spreading of Islam."[37] The successes achieved in this fight for spreading of Islam is also the main story of the medieval Muslim chronicles. The importance of 'force' in Islam should be acknowledged rather than minimized. The denial of force as a means of spreading Islam by a few modern apologists, like Aziz Ahmad and Muhammad Mujeeb[38] cannot alter the basic truth about the history and philosophy of Islam, nor the spirit behind words like Kafir, Jihad, Jiziyah, etc.

II
The State

Muslim rule in India has been conveniently divided into two periods, the Sultanate of Delhi (1206-1526) and the Mughal empire (1526-1707). It continued up to 1857, though in the later stages only nominally. When the Sultanate was established, it carried with it the experience gained by the Arab rule in Sindh and the Ghaznavid rule in Punjab of about two centuries. Meanwhile a well-developed statecraft had sprung up in Muslim countries during the seventh to the twelfth centuries. This was mainly due to the universality of Islamic law. The Ghazni and Delhi sultanates cannot be isolated from the rest of the Muslim states particularly in the functioning of their institutions. There were parallel and sometimes identical institutions under the kingdoms of Ghazni and Delhi. The Sultanate of Delhi may not have possessed uninterrupted political continuity; its boundaries also constantly changed. As political entity, however, the Sultanate received sustenance from the evolution of institutions abroad and at home. The Mughal empire too in its early years lacked stability. But from Akbar (1556-1605) onwards there was undisturbed one dynasty rule. Its geographical boundaries also expanded and there was further growth of Islamic administrative institutions.

2.1. NIZAM-I-MUSTAFA

For an Islamic state, the Quran, the multiple Hadis collections and the administrative acts and principles of the Prophet had set up rules for a 'purified' system of governance. Muhammad was not only the founder of a faith, he was also the ruler of Arabia. He personally participated in war. He delivered judgements, he executed prisoners of war. He entered into treaties with tribal leaders within and potentates outside Arabia. Since everything was done at the behest of Allah which was conveyed to Muhammad in the form of revelations, his ministration is known as Nizam-i (Muhammad) Mustafa, meaning a regulated and purified system of governance based on the commands of God. Nizam-i-Mustafa is rightly translated into the English language as a theocratic administration both in letter and spirit.

Thus the state the Muslim invaders and rulers set up in India was a theocracy. This is the conclusion also arrived at by Jadunath Sarkar,[1] R.P. Tripathi,[2] K.M. Ashraf,[3] T.P. Hughes,[4] *The Encyclopaedia of Islam*[5] and many others. "All the institutions that the Muslims either evolved or adopted were intended to subserve the law,"[6] observes Tripathi. On the other hand, I.H. Qureshi says that the "supremacy of the Shara (Islamic law) has misled some into thinking that the Sultanate was a theocracy."[7] Qureshi's contention may not be taken seriously, because he tries to eulogize every aspect of Muslim rule in India.[8] But when Mohammad Habib declares that "it (Muslim state in India) was not a theocratic state in any sense of the word" and that "its foundation was, non-religious and secular",[9] his statement calls for an appraisal.

Theocracy envisages "direct intervention and authorship of God through revelations in government of society", or "that constitution of a state in which the Almighty is regarded as the sole sovereign, and the laws of the realm as divine commands rather than human ordinances..."[10] Prophet Muhammad envisaged only a theocratic state for Islam. From the very beginning it had been so conceived. As P.K. Hitti points out, "Hitherto (Battle of Badr 624 CE) Islam had been a religion within a state; in al-Madinah after Badr, it passed into something more than a state-religion — it itself became the state."[11] "The history of the political structure of Islam, its system of government, laws and institutions, virtually starts from that date."[12] D.De Santillana, another recognised authority on Islamic law and society, says that "Islam is the direct government of Allah, the rule of God, whose eyes are upon his people. The principle of unity and order which in other societies is called *civitas*, *polis*, state, in Islam is personified by Allah: Allah is the name of the supreme power, acting in the common interest. Thus the public treasury is the treasury of Allah, the army is the army of Allah", even the public functionaries are "the employees of Allah."[13] According to Dr. Qureshi himself, the Shara "is based on the Quran which is believed by every Muslim to be the word of God revealed to His Prophet Muhammad... on these two rocks — the Quran and Hadis (the Prophet's interpretations, traditions) is built the structure of Muslim Law... This law was the actual sovereign in Muslim lands."[14] "The protection of Shara," writes Ibn Hasan, "has two aspects: The propagation of the knowledge of Shara and its enforcement as law within the state. The one implied the maintenance of a class of scholars devoted to the study, the teaching and the propagation of that knowledge, and the other the appointment of one from those scholars... as an adviser to the king in all his acts of state. The scholars devoted to that knowledge are called Ulama and the one selected from among them is termed Shaikh-ul Islam."[15] The Shaikh-ul-Islam was the representative of the ulema and it was his duty to bring "to the notice of the King what he thought detrimental or prejudicial to the interest of his religion, and the King had little option in acting upon such an advice".[16] Their advice was the establishment of the Nizam-i-Mustafa or a *theocratic* state.

In short, the law which obtained in medieval India under Muslim rule was the Shara which was based not on human experience but on divine revelation. It was not a secular law. Muslim state could not be a secular state. In fact Islam and secularism are mutually exclusive. One has only to read the Quran and a few Persian chronicles of medieval times to realise the extent to which the Muslim state in India was theocratic both in spirit and in action.

The fundamental basis of the Islamic polity is the attainment of complete religious uniformity, to root out heresy and to extirpate infidelity. Under it, populations everywhere were to be converted into true believers.[17] The Quranic injunction is: "And when the sacred months (Ramzan) are passed, kill those who join other deities with God, wherever you shall find them. But if they shall convert... then let them go their way."[18] The prophet of Islam who had accorded some sort of religious toleration to the Jews of Medina, expelled them afterward to bring about a complete religious uniformity in that city, while Caliph Omar I (CE 634-644) expelled the Jews and Christians from the whole of Arabia.[19]

Hindu Influence on the Muslim State

This could not be done in India. The country was too vast and the resistance of the people against Islamization of the country too determined.[20] Here Islam could not be forced down the throats of the people despite persistent desire and efforts of Muslim invaders and rulers. And so during the twelve centuries of Muslim rule some compromises had to be made.

Twelve centuries is a long period to have kept the Muslim conquerors and rulers isolated from the majority population of the Hindus. In every sphere of life and activity, the Hindu fertile thought and vision influenced the rigid Muslim attitudes. In art and architecture the conquerors were inevitably impressed by the achievements of the Hindus and there came into being what is known as the Indo-Saracenic architecture. So was the case with painting and music. In classical and folk music the Hindus were past-masters, and the music that the Muslim rulers patronized in India was mainly Hindu. Similar was the case with polity. The concept of the theocratic Islamic state was not unoften influenced by the secular and tolerant traditions of Indian rules of governance although this did not change the theocratic nature of the Muslim state. Side by side the Muslim Sultanate and regional Muslim Kingdoms, there were Rajput States and the Vijayanagar Empire whose nature of administration would have been constantly watched by the Muslim kings. It is well known that Hindu kings on the western coast built mosques for the convenience of Muslim traders and settlers in India. In the fifteenth-sixteenth century Vijayanagar rulers treated their Muslim subjects with a consideration which was alien to the Islamic Shariat. For instance, Deva Raya II (1419-1449) "gave orders to enlist Mussulmans (as soldiers) in his service, allotting them estates, and erecting a mosque in the city of Vijayanagar. He also commanded that no one should molest them in the exercise of their religion, and moreover, he ordered a Koran to be placed before his throne on a rich desk."[21] This policy continued throughout. Under Krishna Deva Raya (1509-1530), "great equity and justice was observed.,." During the reign of Ram Raja (1542, 1556-1570), when, on one occasion, the Muhammadans sacrificed a cow in a mosque in the 'Turukvada' area, the excited officers and nobles, led by the king's own brother Tirumala, made a representation to the king. But he did not yield to them saying that it would not be correct to interfere in their religious practices and declaring that he was the master of the bodies of his soldiers, not their souls.[22]

Many Muslim scholars and rulers did not fail to notice this freedom in Hindu society and religion. To Babur, a conqueror, India provided a completely new environment. "Hindustan is a wonderful country," writes he. "Compared with our (Muslim) countries it is a different world... Once the water of Sindh is crossed, everything is in the Hindustani way... people and horde, opinion and custom."[23] This was due to the traditional Hindu tolerance. In spite of what the Muslims had always done to the non-Muslims in pursuance of their scriptures, the Vijayanagar kings allowed, according to Duarte Barbosa "that every man may come and go, and live according to his own creed without suffering any annoyance, and without enquiring whether he is a Christian, Jew, Moor or Heathen. Great equity and justice is observed by all."[24] Abul Fazl extols the Hindus in his *Ain-i-Akbari* in the following words: "The inhabitants of this land are religious, affectionate, hospitable, genial and frank. They are fond of scientific pursuits, inclined to austerity of life, seekers after justice, contented, industrious, capable in affairs, loyal, truthful and constant... They one and all believe in the unity of God, and as to the reverence they pay to the images of stone and wood and the like, which simpletons regard as idolatry, it is not so." In a footnote Jadunath Sarkar adds that "the same things were observed by the Chinese pilgrim Yuan Chwang in the 7th century: 'The ordinary people ... are upright and honourable... They are faithful to their oaths and promises... In their behavior there is much gentleness and sweetness.'" And of the Marathas: "The disposition of the people is honest and simple... to their benefactors they are grateful; to their enemies ruthless. If they are asked to help one in distress, they will forget themselves in their haste to render assistance."[25] Even Badaoni concedes that freedom and tolerance existed among Hindus. He writes that "Hindustan is a nice large place where everything is allowed, and no one cares for another (i.e. interferes in the affairs of others) and people may go as they may".[26]

It stands to reason that in such an environment the Muslim mind, fanaticised by the commands of the Shariat, would have been occasionally dented by the Hindu spirit of tolerance, to breathe in freedom with a people who did not believe in one imposed version of God, one Book and one Prophet. Perhaps the first king who realised what India was, was Iltutmish, who tackled his orthodox ulema in his own way. Alauddin Khalji (1296-1316) even thought of founding a new religion which was believed to be in contravention of Islam (and the Shariat) for the Muslims were apprehensive that its enforcement would entail slaughter of a large number of Musalmans. Alauddin was illiterate and lacked the genius of taking any revolutionary step. But it appears that he recognised the fact that the rule of the Shariat was not entirely feasible in India and declared that "I know not whether these laws (his *zawabits* or regulations) are sanctioned by our faith or not, but whatever I conceive for the good of the state, that I decree".[27] His contemporary chronicler confessed that if the Muslim kings followed the tradition of the Prophet, kingship and governance would be impossible for them in India. It was probably the experience of such rulers that prompted Ziyauddin Barani to advocate that if the enforcement of the Shariat was impossible or impracticable, new laws should be enacted by rulers. "It is the duty of a king," says he, "to enforce if he can, those royal laws which have become proverbial owing to their principles of justice and mercy. But if owing to the change of time and circumstances he is unable to enforce the laws of the ancients (Muslim rulers), he should, with the counsel of wise men..., frame laws suited to his time and circumstances and proceed to enforce them. Much reflection is necessary in order that laws, suited to his reign are properly framed, so that *they in no way contravene the laws of Islam*" (italics added).[28] These laws Barani calls *zawabits*. Barani does not necessarily contradict himself. He knows the difficulties in the enforcement of the Shariat in India. Hence his advocacy of framing new laws. He also knew that the Shariat could not be superseded by any other law. Hence on every page of his *Tarikh* and his *Fatawa-i-Jahandari* he calls upon Muslim rulers to crush the Hindus in every possible manner according to the tenets of Islam.

Barani wrote in the fourteenth century. But right up to the middle of the sixteenth century no king made any laws of the kind, and the Shariat continued to be the supreme law prevalent in the Turkish, Afghan and Mughal times. They ruled with all the excesses that Islamic theory envisaged. It was late in the sixteenth century that emperor Akbar promulgated a number of regulations for "the real benefit of the people". That is, he removed to some extent the disabilities imposed on the majority of the population. Akbar was an administrative genius. His reforms cover all areas of religion and society, and their number runs into hundreds. However, we shall take note of only those major measures which were considered to be in contravention of the Shariat and the Sunnah to see how far his government was secular or theocratic.

Akbar's Deviation

The first revolutionary step of Akbar was the abolition of the Jiziyah, the hated discriminatory tax paid by Hindu Zimmis. The Hindus, as Zimmis, had become second class citizens in their own homeland and were suffered to live under certain disabilities. One of them was that each adult must pay a poll tax called Jiziyah (about this later on in detail). The Zimmis also had to suffer in respect of their mode of worship, payment of taxes, and on account of certain sumptuary laws. Death awaited them at every corner, because, being idolaters, they could be given a choice only between Islam and death. The state rested upon the support of the military class which consisted largely of the followers of the faith. They were treated as the favoured children of the state while various kinds of disabilities were imposed upon the non-Muslims.

Jiziyah was an outcome of Jihad and was an inalienable part of the Muslim theory of taxation. It brought great income to the state. But it was an emblem of inferiority for the Hindus who were held down by sheer force through this financial burden. All earlier Muslim kings had imposed it in its true religious connotation. With its abolition in 1564, Akbar brought Hindus on par with Muslims as common citizens of the state rather than treat them as second class citizens. In an Islamic state it was prohibited to treat infidels and idolaters as equal to the people of the faith. But "in spite of the disapproval of statesmen, and of much chatter on the part of the ignorant, (this) sublime decree was issued... Which might be regarded as the foundation of the arrangement of mankind."[29] Akbar removed restrictions on the public religious worship by non-Muslims. He abolished pilgrim tax on Hindus (1563) and removed all restrictions on the building of places of worship of non-Muslims. This led to the building of churches by Christians[30] and temples by Hindus. A church was built in Agra itself; others were constructed at Lahore, Cambay and Thatta. Many Rajas built temples dedicated to their favourite Gods. Raja Mansingh built a temple at Brindaban at a cost of 5 lakh rupees and another at Banaras.[31] Christians were People of the Book, but granting permission to build temples of idolaters was against the injunctions of the Shariat. Akbar did not stop at that. He allowed his Hindu spouses to perform Hindu worship inside the palace. A full Hindu temple built in his Allahabad fort still exists. Apostasy is punishable by death in Islam.[32] Under earlier kings conversion of Muslims to other faiths was not allowed. Such apostates paid with their lives for their "falling off from grace".[33] Akbar issued orders permitting those Hindus who had been forcibly converted to Islam earlier, to reconvert to Hinduism.[34] He also prohibited making slaves of prisoners of war. All this did not conform with the Quran and the Shariat.

Akbar's 'Infallibility decree' also falls under "anti-Islamic" measures. Although the document was written by the principal ulema and presented to Akbar for the glory of God and propagation of Islam, it was deemed to confer on the Emperor final powers of decision over conflicting opinions of the Mujahids. According to Badaoni, Akbar challenged the doctrines of Islam itself, and this made the author of *Muntakhab-ut-Tawarikh* rave. He writes: "At the religious discussion meetings held by Akbar, 'at which every one... might say or ask what he liked,' the emperor examined people about the creation of the Quran, elicited their belief, or otherwise, in revelation, and raised doubts in them regarding all things connected with the Prophet and the imams. He distinctly denied the existence of *Jins*, of angels, and of all other beings of the invisible world, as well as the miracles of the Prophet."[35] In the history of Muslim rule in India, it was for the first time that freedom of thought and critical appraisal of Islam was witnessed in the Court circles. In this atmosphere, the people also got busy collecting "all kinds of exploded errors, and brought them to his Majesty, as if they were so many presents... Every doctrine and command of Islam as the prophetship, the harmony of Islam with reason... the details of the day of resurrection and judgement, all were doubted and ridiculed."[36] "Bir Bar..., Shaykh Abul Fazl and Hakim Abul Fateh... successfully turned the emperor from Islam and led him to reject inspiration, prophetship, the miracles of the Prophet and of saints and even the whole law."[37]

There were many factors responsible for such an attitude of Akbar, for such a change of mind and heart. We need not enumerate all of them here. But one reason is the most prominent – Akbar's association with Hindu scholars. His sympathetic and receptive mind willingly accepted the goodness that Hindus possessed and Hindu men of learning successfully conveyed to the King. Some earlier monarchs like Muhammad bin Tughlaq had also associated with Hindu saints and yogis but they had remained fundamentalists. It was Akbar's genius that grasped the finer points of Hindu civilization "skilfully represented" by learned Brahmins and he built up a political edifice on the oft-quoted principle of *Sulehkul*, or peace with all.

In India, Muslim sultans and padshahs came across a civilization which was different from theirs in many ways. It is another matter that many of them were not educated and the goodness of Hindu civilization was appreciated by only a few savants and kings like Alberuni and Akbar. About emperor Akbar, Abdul Qadir Badaoni says that he used to invite learned Hindus for discussion. "As they (the Brahmins) surpass other learned men in their treatises on morals, and on physical and religious sciences, and reach a high degree in their knowledge of the future, in spiritual power and human perfection, they brought proofs based on reason and testimony..., and so skilfully represented things as quite self-evident... that no man could now raise a doubt in His Majesty."[38] Also, "His majesty, on hearing... how much the people of the country prized their institutions, commenced to look upon them with affection."[39] He also believed that it was wrong to kill cows, which the Hindus worship.[40] The custom of Rakhi, celebration of Diwali for similar reasons, became quite common. Jahangir also participated in all major Hindu festivals. He describes the Ramlila and dwells on the Hindu caste system and the four *Varnashrams* without any criticism. Jahangir even performed the *shraddha* of Akbar.[41] Akbar was by nature tolerant. But he also felt that the sentiments of the vast population of the Hindus had to be respected if a strong and stable national state was to be built up.

What sentiments of the Hindus Akbar respected; what aspects of Hindu philosophy impressed Akbar? In Islam truth is established by the sword. "Fight against them (the *mushriks*) until idolatry is no more, and Allah's religion reigns supreme," says the Quran *Surah* 2, *ayat* 193. In Islam all dissent is treated as heresy and stamped out as infidelity. In Hinduism truth is sought to be arrived at through introspection and soul-searching, through argument and discussion (*shastrarth*). Dissent is not only tolerated but even encouraged and no one is declared a heretic. Buddhism and Jainism started as non-conformist movements. But in course of time Mahavir and Buddha were absorbed in the Hindu pantheon as their own 'Gods'. On their part, Buddha and emperor Ashoka did not indulge in any campaign to destroy other sects; they advocated promotion of all sects.[42] In Hinduism all kinds of ideas are welcome for reflection, all kinds of gods emanating from these ideas are worshipped. To call such people by the derogatory epithets of polytheists and Kafirs is the height of arrogance and ignorance. As Ibn Warraq points out, "Implicit in all kinds of monotheism is the dogmatic certainty that it alone has access to true God, it alone has access to truth."[43] Akbar tried to understand the spirit of India in a spirit of accommodation. He got the Ramayana and the Mahabharata translated into Persian. And what did the Mahabharata say on this point? *"Dharmam yo badhate dharmo na sa dharmah prakirtitah; avirodhat tu yo dharmah sa dharmah satyavikarmah"* (a religion which opposes another religion is not a true religion. True religion is that which does not come in the way of another religion). Akbar subscribed to such a view. As professor Toynbee has said: "Islam, like the other two religions of the Judaic family, is exclusive-minded and intolerant by comparison with the religions and philosophies of Indian origin. Yet the influence of India on Akbar went so deep that he was characteristically Indian in (his) large-hearted catholicity."[44]

In short, Akbar's policy of *Sulehkul* (secularism?) could go no further, looking to the times and exigencies of the state. Jahangir ordinarily continued Akbar's toleration. His memoirs, the *Tuzuk-i-Jahangiri*, as a book reveals a non-religious secular outlook. Shahjahan may not have been as tolerant as his two predecessors, but it appears that his ardour for Islam was tampered by the love of his deputy, son, and heir-apparent Dara Shukoh.

The main principles of Muslim administration are known to all students of medieval Indian history. They were known to Mohammad Habib. The one reason why Habib and many others like him say that Muslim rule in India was not theocratic in any sense of the word and that its foundation was non-religious and secular, is that when they conjure up the vision of Muslim rule in India they only think about the one hundred years of Mughal rule between 1556 and 1658. But one hundred years rule of three Mughal emperors — Akbar, Jahangir, and Shahjahan — does not make more than a thousand years of Muslim rule in India secular.

Record of Mughal Secularism

The first king of the Mughal dynasty was Zahiruddin Muhammad Babur. He conquered and ruled as a normal Muslim king. He inherited his religious policy in India from the Lodis. Sikandar Lodi's fanaticism[45] must have been the norm of officials who continued to serve when Babur came to power. Babur himself was an orthodox Muslim. His ideas are reflected in his memoirs. Before engaging in battle with Rana Sanga, he wrote: "I made public the resolution to abstain from wine. (My) servants... dashed upon the earth., the flagons and the cups... *They dashed them in pieces as, God willing! soon will be dashed, the gods of the idolaters*"[46] (italics added). Babur and his officers broke Hindu temples in many parts of the country.[47] He raised towers of skulls of the slain infidels. Babur is said to have been a secular king on the basis of his alleged Will admonitioning Humayun to behave liberally towards the Hindus. But the Will has been found to be a non-genuine document.[48]

In short, Babur was content to govern Hindustan in the orthodox fashion. Humayun had not much chance of developing any distinct religious policy of his own, although he was liberal towards the 'heretic' Shias. Sher Shah Suri too was neither liberal nor fanatic. He devotedly believed in the Shariat and said that "it behoves kings not to disobey the commandments of God, to inscribe the pages of their history with the characters of religion, that their servants and subjects may love religion; for kings are partakers in every act of devotion and worship which proceeds from the priests and the people."[49] "If Muslim chroniclers do not praise him for his religious fanaticism as they do Alauddin, Feroz Shah (Tughlaq), or Sikandar Lodi, they simply bring him to the level of the general run of Muslim rulers."[50] The hundred years (1556-1658) of Mughal rule comprising the reigns of Akbar, Jahangir and Shahjahan were a shade different. But for their fits of rage, Akbar and Jahangir were kind kings. About the former Abul Fazl says, "The compassionate heart of his majesty finds no pleasure in cruelties or in causing sorrow to others; he is ever sparing of the lives of his subjects, wishing to bestow happiness upon all."[51] But as said earlier a hundred years of religiously less oppressive administration does not make the twelve centuries of Muslim rule secular. These three Mughals proved an exception when they, more or less, left the religious beliefs of their subjects alone. Else Aurangzeb's militant policy of religious persecution, as advocated by the Islamic scriptures, was the norm of Muslim rule in India. A Muslim state could only be Islamic in character. Muslim state could not but be a theocracy as the ideology of Islam was more important than thoughts and actions of a few individual 'secularist' kings.

Shariat a Must

For, no Muslim monarch including the three Mughals mentioned above, could move away from the ideology of Islam, from the laws of Islam, from the practice of the Shariat. Akbar abolished Jiziyah in 1564. In all probability many of his 'devout' officers in far off regions, did not care to enforce this anti-Islamic measure. Therefore, ten years later he once again issued orders for its abolition. Badaoni tells us that it was customary "to search out and kill heretics" (Shias), let alone non-Muslims as late as 1574. Hemu's father, when captured, was offered his life if he turned Muslim. Abdun Nabi executed a Brahman for blasphemy on the complaint of a Qazi. Husain Khan, the governor of Lahore (died 983H/ 1575-76) ordered Hindus to stick patches on their shoulders so that no Muslim could be put to the indignity of showing them honour by mistake, nor did he allow Hindus to saddle their horses. Jihad was practised as usual, massacre at Chittor was done in true Jihadist spirit. "The *Akbar Nama*, the *Ain-i-Akbari* and Badaoni are all agreed that prior to 1593, some Hindus had been converted to Islam forcibly." In 1581 some Portuguese captives at Surat were offered their lives if they turned Muslim. Even iconoclastic zeal did not disappear under Akbar. Kangra was invaded in 1572-73, and even though Birbal was in joint command, the umbrella of the Goddess was riddled with arrows, 200 cows were killed and Muslim soldiers threw their shoes full of blood at the walls and doors of the temple. A Mughal officer, Bayazid, converted a Hindu temple into a Muslim school. Jain idols in Gujarat could not escape vandalism. "Such seem to have been and continued to be the popular prejudices against the Hindus", under Akbar and his successors as per the obligations of the Shariat and practice of Sunnah, writes S.R. Sharma.[52] In his letters to Abdullah Khan Uzbek written in 1586 Akbar definitely declares himself a Muslim and proudly boasts that on account of his conquests Islam had now spread to territories where it had not been heard of before and the temples of the non-believers had been converted into mosques. "He also roundly declares that the institutes of the Prophet and revelation of God have always been his guides."[53] Jahangir, when a prince, at one time intended demolishing some of the Hindu temples at Banaras but desisted therefrom on Man Singh's intervention. In his reign conversions to Islam were encouraged, conversions back from Islam to Hinduism were punished. When he visited Kangra, he celebrated the Muslim occupation of the fort by desecrating its famous temple. At Pushkar he broke the image of Varaha and a bull was sacrificed to signify the victory of Islam over idolatry.[54] In his reign Muslims began to behave as bullies once again.[55] Under Shahjahan, Akbar's *Sulehkul* was almost reversed. During his reign temples were destroyed in Gujarat, Banaras and Allahabad, and at Orcha. Like Jahangir he stopped marriages between Muslim girls and Hindu men. Apostasy from Islam again became a capital crime in accordance with the tenets of the Shariat. During the reign of Shahjahan titles in use among Khalifas and Ghaznavids were revived. Whenever the Muslim state used to show signs of 'secularist' weakness, the glorious memory of Mahmud of Ghazni used to inject a sense of pride in its polity. The title of Yaminuddaula (right hand of the state) was bestowed by the Khalifa al-Qadir Billah on Mahmud of Ghazni. This title was once again conferred by Shahjahan on Abul Hasan Asaf Khan (IV), the father of Mumtaz Mahal.[56] Mir Jamaluddin Inju was also promoted by Jahangir to the title of Azududdaula (arm of the state).[57] The bestowal of the title of Yaminuddaula on Asaf Khan itself points to the direction in which the state was reshaping itself. All that Islam advocated was more or less continued under all the Mughal monarchs. Akbar and Jahangir, like Babur and Shahjahan, adopted the title of Ghazi. Muslim nobles and ulema would not let the Muslim kings stray away from the path of Islam. Any deviation was sought to be corrected at the first opportunity. Immediately after the death of Akbar, "Mulla Shah Ahmad, one of the greatest religious leaders of the age, wrote to various court dignitaries exhorting them to get this state of things altered in the very beginning of (Jahangir's) reign because otherwise it would be difficult to accomplish anything later on."[58] Aurangzeb openly claimed to have fought "the apostate" Dara to re-establish the law of Islam.

There was nothing new in this. At the close of the Khalji regime, Ghiyasuddin Tughlaq declared himself as a champion of the faith, because the ulema had been dis-satisfied with Alauddin's rule and Ghiyasuddin with the activities of the neo-convert Nasiruddin Khusrau. Therefore according to R.P. Tripathi, "The slogan of 'Islam in danger' so common yet so effective in the history of the Muslims, was started."[59] And this slogan helped Ghiyasuddin Tughlaq in winning the throne. The ulema were equally dissatisfied with Muhammad bin Tughlaq. On his demise, Shaikh Nasiruddin Chiragh obtained from Firoz a promise "that he would rule according to the tenets of justice and law". Firoz Shah Tughlaq proved true to his word and "made religion the basis of his government".[60] A little later Amir Timur openly claimed to have attacked Hindustan with the avowed object of destroying idolatry and infidelity in the country.[61] Akbar's tolerance had exasperated the Muslim divines, and a promise was obtained from his successor, Jahangir, that he would defend the Muslim religion. Liberal Muslims like Shaikh Mubarak and his sons Faizi and Abul Fazl had to pass many years underground. When they became close to Akbar and were supposed to influence his ideas, they were squarely abused by the true Muslims. "Some bastards such as the son of Mulla Mubarak," writes Badaoni about Abul Fazl, "wrote treatises in order to revile and ridicule our religious practices. His majesty liked such productions and prompted the authors."[62] Thus whether we consider the influence of the Muslim religious class (the ulema), the application of the law of Islam (*Shara*), or the activities of the kings, it is clear beyond doubt that the medieval state was a theocratic state. No wonder that many contemporary and later Muslim writers praise the deeds of Aurangzeb with great gusto. The name of Akbar is obliterated; it does not find mention by a single Muslim chronicler after his death.

The law which prevailed in India under Muslim rule was the Shariat. "This was the actual sovereign in Muslim lands."[63] It was not a secular law. Muslim state was not a secular state. If in this scenario two or three individual Muslim monarchs behaved in a less orthodox fashion, they did not as they could not make the Muslim state in India non-theocratic. The ideology of Islam does not permit practice of secularism. It refuses compromise with other faiths. It tries to dominate over them. It teaches Muslims that they are the rulers, that they must convert or destroy those who do not accept Islam, that those who do not subscribe to Islam are enemies of Allah. Islamic jurisprudence is based on this basic assumption. Islamic economy is based not on capital formation by multiplication of interest through investment, but on loot and extortion from non-Muslims through Ghanaim, Khams and Jiziyah. Islamic Shariat advocates annihilation of all creeds except that of Islam — 'Islam in its pristine purity'. This phenomenon has created unsurmountable problems in all countries of the East ever since the birth of Islam. It is now permeating in the West also. It stares in the face of those Muslim countries which try to step into secularism and modernity like Egypt, Algeria, Turkey and some others. India's problem is unique. It is one country which could not be converted to Islam, "although there were mass (forcible) conversions".[64] This phenomenon baffles Indian Muslims to this day — why could India not be made a Muslim country despite the exertion of more than a thousand years. The apologists try to explain it by 'discovering' that Muslim state was a secular state. They do not attribute it to persistent Hindu resistance, nor to the continuance of the great Hindu civilization to which should go the real credit.

2.2. THE GOVERNMENT

By the quick conquest of the lands of Persia and Egypt the Arabians came into possession of the earliest seats of civilization in the whole world. "In art and architecture, in philosophy, in medicine, in science and literature, in government, the original Arabians had nothing to teach and everything to learn." The Arabs were an observant race. With sharp curiosity these Muslim Arabians, with the help of their subject peoples turned Muslim, began to assimilate, adopt and reproduce the latter's intellectual and aesthetic heritage. In Damascus, Jerusalem and Alexandria, they admired and copied the work of the architect and the artisan. "Throughout the whole period of the Caliphate the Syrians, the Persians, the Egyptians and others as Moslem converts or as Christians and Jews, were the foremost bearers of the (Islamic) torch of enlightenment and learning." Even India acted as an early source of inspiration, especially in wisdom, literature and mathematics. But Persian influence pinned down Arab Islam as it were. Gradually Persian titles, Persian wines and wives, Persian ideas and thoughts won the day. The Caliphate became a replica of Iranian despotism.[65] In two fields only did the Arabian hold his own: Islam remained the religion of the state and Arabic continued to be the official language. Belief in the paramount superiority of the Arabic language is an article of faith among Muslims.

Evolution of Administrative Institutions

The administrative system of Islam had evolved gradually. In Arabia, in its earliest stages, the problem was to provide the new converts to Islam with subsistence. They were indigent and poor, and to help them, poor tax (*zakat*), voluntary contributions, and war booty (*ghanaim*) formed the revenue of the state at the start. Muhammad was followed (632 CE) by a succession of Caliphs at Madinah.[66] According to Mawardi (who wrote in the fifth century of Islam), the Imamate, or Caliphate, was divinely ordained and the Caliph inherited all the powers and privileges of the Prophet.[67] The institutions which developed under the Caliph became models of governance in the world of Islam. The Caliph Muawiyah (661-89 CE) transformed the republican Caliphate into a monarchy and created a governing class of leading Arab tribes.[68] These two institutions — kingship and nobility — became an integral part of Islamic polity.

After the Umayyad came the Abbasid Caliphs. They established their capital in the newly built city of Baghdad. The Abbasids came under the irresistible influence of superior Persian culture and Persian institutions. The Abbasid dynasty lasted for full five centuries (752-1258 CE) and under it different branches of administrative machinery were greatly elaborated and new departments and offices created. The Quran contained almost nothing that may be called civic or state legislation. So also is the case with Hadis. There are very few references to government and administration in the Hadis. This lacuna was filled by Persian theories and practices. Persian court etiquette, Persian army organisation and administrative system were all adopted and developed under the Abbasids.

The Turks brought these institutions into India, adding some more offices and institutions while keeping the core intact. Muslim administration had evolved in Muslim lands through centuries and was highly developed before it was brought to India by the Turkish sultans. At the head was the monarch or Sultan. He appointed and was assisted by a number of ministers. A brief list of ministers and officers will give an idea of the framework of the central administration. At the top were four important ministers (and ministries) which formed the four pillars of the State.[69] These were Wazir (Diwan-i-Wazarat), Ariz-i-Mumalik (Diwan-i-Arz), Diwan-i-Insha and Diwan-i-Rasalat. The Wazir was the Prime Minister who looked after the revenue administration. Ariz-i-Mumalik or Diwan-i-Arz was head of the army. He was known as Mir Bakhshi under the Mughals and was the inspector-general and paymaster-general of the army. Diwan-i-Insha was incharge of royal correspondence, and Diwan-i-Rasalat of foreign affairs and pious foundations. Sadr-i-Jahan, also called Sadr-us-Sudur, was the Chief Qazi. Under him was placed the Justice Department. There were officers of the royal household like Wakil-i-Dar (Chief Secretary), Amir-i-Hajib (Master of Ceremonies) and Barbak, 'the tongue of the sultan', whose duty it was to present petitions of the people to the king. There were dozens of other officers and hundreds of subordinates both in the Central administration and in the *Subahs* or provinces.

The Central government was formed on the Persian model. As seen above, the Prime Minister was called Wazir and his ministry Diwan-i-Wazarat. All Muslim political thinkers attached great importance to this office. Abu Daud says that a good wazir is an asset. When Allah wants to destroy some ruler, he gives him a bad wazir.[70] Fakhr-i-Mudabbir and Ziyauddin Barani who were scholars of Islamic scriptures, say the same thing.[71] The main business of the Wazir who presided over Diwan-i-Wazarat was finance, although he oversaw most of the affairs of the state. "Agriculture, Building, Charitable institutions, Intelligence Department, the Karkhanas and the Mint were all directly or indirectly under the Diwan-i-Wazarat.[72] Next in importance was the Diwan-i-Arz under the Ariz-i-Mumalik. He was the controller-general of the military department.[73] Muslim state introduced two new elements in Indian polity. It brought in a new law — the Shariat law. Secondly, it was based on military force. Formerly, under Hindu kings, state power was subject to numerous customary and constitutional restraints. Muslim state in India found its support solely in military force. Its Chief Commander was the King; its administrative commander was the Ariz-i-Mumalik (Mir Bakshi of the Mughals). As said earlier, the Diwan-i-Insha dealt with the correspondence between the Sultan and the local governments, including all correspondence of a confidential nature. The Diwan-i-Rasalat, as the term indicates,[74] looked after diplomatic correspondence, and as such this ministry was a counterpart of the present-day foreign office.

The Diwan-i-Qaza, or the Department of Justice, was presided over by the Chief Qazi. Administration of Islamic justice was given a special place of importance in the Muslim state. We have devoted a separate chapter to it. One department of considerable importance was that of the Barid-i-Mumalik who was the head of the State Information Bureau. Through this department, the centre was kept informed of all that was happening all over the empire.

A network of news agents or intelligencers was spread out in all localities. They acted both as secret information agents as well as open news reporters. There were also a large number of spies in every place and chiefly in the houses of the nobles to report their affairs to the Sultan. Espionage played a very important role in Islamic autocracy.

The king's court, palace and household also had an elaborate administrative set up of its own.[75] The provincial government was a miniature replica of the central. The governors were called Walis and Muqtis. An expert in accounts called Sahib-i-Diwan was appointed in each province. He kept the local revenue records and submitted them to the Wazir. The army maintained by the governors and garrison commanders was subject to control and inspection by the provincial Ariz, who was responsible to the central government. Similarly, administrative arrangement of *parganas*, *shiqqs* and later *sarkars* was also clearly laid down. During the Mughal period, some new offices were created while nomenclatures of some others were changed.[76] The administrative system also got the stamping of the Chingezi *Yasas* and the Institutes of Timur.[77]

But the core of administration remained Islamic. Just as the administrative system implanted in India had evolved in Iran and adjoining Islamic countries, important administrators also came from these regions to run it. This rendered the administration exotic and prompted Bernier to declare that the Mughal was a foreigner in India. The Mughal empire brought into existence and maintained for a century and a half (1556-1707) a bureaucracy, mainly Mughal, Turk and Afghan, and partly Rajput, with strong vested interest in Mughal imperialism. During this period and thereafter, the disparity in standards of living not only between the higher and lower strata of the ruling class but also between the higher officials and average citizens, became so pronounced that a deep gulf yawned between the people and the bureaucracy, isolating the latter and turning it into a separate class essentially alien and foreign in outlook from the masses.

The Sovereign

The sovereign in the Muslim state was called Amir, Sultan, Badshah or Shahanshah. He personified the will of the Muslim people, a people who have been one of the greatest empire builders. It is said that during the time of the Prophet the word sultan was never used in the sense in which it is used or understood today. In the Quran the term sultan is vague and occurs in the abstract sense of "Power, Authority".[78] Since the institution of sultan or king came from Persia, there is not much in the Quran about it. But there are quite a few *ahadis* which mention the institution of sultan and advocate unflinching loyalty to him. Quoting a *hadis* from Muslim, al-Khatib-ul-Umari, the author of *Mishkat-ul-Sharif* writes that "the Rasul said if one obeys me, he obeys Allah; if he disobeys me, he disobeys Allah; one who was obedient to the Amir was obedient to me and one who was disobedient to the Amir was disobedient to me".[79] There should be affection and respect between the Hakim and his subjects. Those who create dissensions between the community and the ruler and between ruler and ruler should be killed.[80] No community can remain coalesced without a leader. Such was the importance given to the leader by the Prophet that he ordained that if three men were going on a mission, they should choose one of them as the leader.[81] In course of time as the numbers of Muslims increased, obedience to the leader became an imperative necessity and there are many *ahadis* advocating unflinching loyalty to the sultan who alone could be leader of warriors engaged in expansionist wars (glorified as the Holy Jihad). The idea of this loyalty is elaborately expounded in many *ahadis*. It is laid down that even if a Habshi *ghulam* is appointed as the Hakim, even if he be a mutilated *ghulam* whose ears and nose have been cut off, is appointed as the ruler, he is to be given unflinching obedience. A *hadis* says: "One who obeys me (the Prophet) obeys God; one who shows insubordination to me shows disobedience to Allah."[82] Such declarations frightened the poor, ignorant Muslims. "Badshah is the shadow of God on earth." Every oppressed person looks to him for justice. He is responsible for the well-being of his subjects. When the king is unjust and he commits a sin, his subjects should be patient towards him. They should not curse him but obey him without demur.[83] Because if a Muslim strays away from the community even a wee bit, he will be destroyed. The Muslims should stay together as a group (*jamaat*), as a community, under the leadership of the king.[84] For a Muslim king was not only expected to be a true Muslim himself; he was required to see that all his subjects were true Muslims and the dignity of Islam and Islamic laws was upheld by them.

When this model of sultan came in contact with Persian Sassanid polity, writes K.A. Nizami, "many servile forms of Sassanid court were adopted as legitimate substitutes for the earlier democratic practice of *bay't*". But the fact is that contrary to the assertion of Nizami, *ahadis* were not "manufactured to cast a halo round the person of the sultan."[85] The idea of Commander, Leader, Hakim or Sultan is many times given by all collectors of Hadis. Besides, there is no democracy involved in *bay't*. It is true that early Muslims ate with Muhammad, they prayed with him in the mosque. However, the relationship thrown up throughout the works of Hadis, is that of master and suppliant; there was not to question why; there was but to do as directed. There is no word for 'democracy' in Islam. In modern times the Arabs use the Greek word *dimuqraatiya*. Following upon the Muslim tradition the monarch was known as sultan during the early Muslim rule in India. This appellation was continued till it was replaced by Babur who took the title of Padshah. Thus sultan was the accepted title when the Turks conquered and set up a Muslim state in Hindustan. Before this Muslims had set up empires in many parts of the world. Empire building and ruling effectively in accordance with the precepts of the Shariat was in the logic of the history of Islam and this could be accomplished only by a sultan. The sultan was usually a strong warrior, often without a peer in strength. He gathered a strong army, collected taxes and contributions and was surrounded by counsellors. They bestowed upon him attributes of divinity, upon his subjects those of devilry, thus making his presence in the world a sort of a benediction necessary for the good of mankind. Once man was declared to be bad and the king full of virtues, there was hardly any difficulty for political philosophy and religion to recommend strict control of the people by the sultan.[86]

In the *Siyasat Nama*, Nizm-ul-Mulk Tusi stressed that since the kings were divinely appointed, "they must always keep the subjects in such a position that they know their stations and never remove the ring of servitude from their ears."[87] Alberuni, Fakhr-i-Mudabbir, Amir Khusrau, Ziyauddin Barani and Shams Siraj Afif repeat the same idea.[88] As Fakhr-i-Mudabbir puts it, "If there were no kings, men would devour one another."[89] Even the liberal Allama Abul Fazl could not think beyond this: "If royalty did not exist, the storm of strife would never subside, nor selfish ambition disappear. Mankind (is) under the burden of lawlessness and lust...".[90]

In this context it would be pertinent to point out that there were monarchs both in the West and the East and in both autocracy reigned supreme. Still in the West they could wrest a Magna Carta from the king as early as in 1215 CE and produce thinkers like Hobbes, Locke, Rousseau, Montesqueue and Bentham who helped change the concept of kingship in course of time. But in Islam, a rigid, narrow and limited scriptural education could parrot-like repeat only one political theory — man was nasty, brutish and short and must be kept suppressed. So that when in England they wrested power by executing the king after a long civil war (1641-49), in India Shahjahan, a contemporary of Charles I, ruled as an autocrat and his reign is called a 'golden age'. The history of Islam is witness to the fact that autocracy and Islam are more natural allies than democracy and Islam. "The glitter of gems and gold in the Taj Mahal or the Peacock Throne," writes Jadunath Sarkar, "ought not to blind us to the fact that in Mughal India, man was considered vile; – the mass of the people had no economic liberty, no indefeasible right to justice or personal freedom, when their oppressor was a noble or high official or landowner; political rights were not dreamt of... The Government was in effect despotism..."[91] Consequently, medieval Muslim political opinion could recommend only repression of man and glorification of king.

The king was divinely ordained. Abul Fazl says: "No dignity is higher in the eyes of God than royalty... Royalty is a light emanating from God, and a ray from the sun, the illuminator of the universe."[92] Kingship thus became the most general and permanent of institutions of medieval Muslim world. In theory Islam claims to stand for equality of men, in practice it encourages slavery and imposes an inferior status on non-Muslims. In theory Islam does not recognize kingship; in practice Muslims have been found to be servile to authority. Muhammadans themselves were impressed with the concept of power and glamour associated with monarchy. The idea of despotism, of concentration of power, penetrated medieval mind with facility, and obedience to the ruler was advocated as a religious duty.

The duties and obligations of a Muslim monarch were clearly laid out for him by religious and political works, traditions and precedents. The Shariat, the four schools of Islamic law, works of political theorist like al-Mawardi's *Ahkam-us-Sultaniyah* and Nizamul Mulk Tusi's *Siyasat Namah*, the actual working of the Abbasid Caliphate running into more than five centuries, and the exploits of Muslims from Prophet Muhammad to Mahmud of Ghazni, had combined to lay down a code of private and public conduct for Muslim monarchs. Works of Indian Muslim political theorists and historians like Fakhr-i-Mudabbir's *Adab-ul-Harb*, Ziyauddin Barani's *Fatwa-i-Jahandari* and *Tarikh-i-Firoz Shahi* and later on *Fatawa-i-Alamgiri* and similar other works too constantly repeat the principles and ideals to be followed by a Muslim king.

In his personal life, the Muslim king was expected to be God fearing and pious. He was to say his prayers five times a day and observe the fasts of Ramzan. According to Barani he was expected to live the life of a common soldier, drawing from the public treasury the same salary as he gave to his soldiers (elsewhere he recommends him to live with magnificence and keep a large harem which would add to his dignity). By his words, acts and movements, his personal qualities and behaviour he was to appear to live and also enable people to live according to the laws of the Shariat.[93] In public life, the Muslim monarch was enjoined to discharge a host of civil, military and religious duties. The sultan was expected to be the refuge of the suffering and the oppressed. He was to impart justice in accordance with the requisites of the Shariat. He was to levy taxes according to the law and appoint honest and efficient officers "so that the laws of the Shariat might be enforced through them."[94] At times he was to enact *zawabits* (regulations) to suit a particular situation, but while doing so, he could not transgress the Shariat nor "alter the law".[95] His military duties were to defend Muslim territories, to guard its frontiers by garrisoning the forts, make preparations for war, and to keep his army well equipped and ever on the alert for conquest and extension of the territories of Islam.[96]

Thus religious and political thinkers had gone on multiplying the duties of a Muslim monarch, presenting him with an unmanageable agenda. Obviously the king could not possibly follow all their injunctions. In such a situation there was adjustment and accommodation between precept and practice. If a sultan could not follow these behests in their entirety, this in no way compromised his status or weaken his position. The rulers who tried to live like true Muslims, are highly praised by their contemporaries. But those who did not, are not blamed or decried. Often the ulema overlook; many even justify their not-so-Islamic actions and habits. Ziyauddin Barani is very liberal with regard to such aberrations. He says: "If the king's faith in the religion of the Prophet is firm and unshakable, then there is no harm if he is not excessively given to his religious devotions and cannot fulfil the supererogatory duties prescribed with regard to fasting and prayer." Similarly, "If there is no fault or defect in the religious beliefs of the king, the enjoyments and pleasures in which he indulges as a human being are forgiven to him out of consideration for his firm faith...(and) the sins due to his human nature are erased from the records of his life."[97] Not only enjoyments and sins due to human nature were forgiven, the ulema, chroniclers and clericals, indeed all custodians of medieval publicity media, admired the large harems, the extravagance, the grandeur and the magnificence of the monarch. This mode of living raised his stature and strengthened his position in public eye. But in this the ulema went too far and exhibited a vacuum in the process of their thinking. While drinking of wine by a monarch was perhaps rightly overlooked, there was no redressal suggested even when he turned out to be a tyrant. There was no remedy recommended except to pray for change of his heart.

In short, the mainspring of Muslim regime was monarchy. Individual rulers may have been unsafe, but the institution was permanent; no other kind of system was envisaged.[98] Since the institution was not vulnerable, kingship tended to be despotic, and even tyrannical. Within this framework it had variables. However, by and large, royalty was autocratic, and imperialistic, tempered only by revolution or fear of revolution. Cruelty and terror, strength and force, conquest and annexationism, glory and grandeur were its hallmarks.

What does Barani mean by statements like "If the king's

faith in the religion of the Prophet is firm," or "If there is no fault in the king's religious beliefs," to earn him immunity from punishment for all sinful acts? It means *that* Muslim monarch who subserves the interests of his religion in its true spirit. In the Islamic religion human beings are divided into two distinct entities — Muslims and infidels. Citizenship rights are given to Muslims only, non-Muslims at the most can be given the status of Zimmis or second class citizens. For, Allah raises some people (*qaums*) and he degrades others.[99] Momins are favoured by God and infidels are denounced. Muslims should always help one another. Protection of life and property of one momin is incumbent upon another momin. Abusing or killing of a Muslim by another Muslim is *kufr*. Hadis exhort the Muslims: "Do not loot another Muslim". "One who will kill another Muslim, Allah will throw him in Perdition face down."[100] But the treatment meted out to an infidel should be just the opposite of it, because the two are different from one another in the eyes of Allah and his prophet. The Hadis say to Muslims: If you meet fire-worshippers and idolaters, do not wish them. If an infidel falls ill, do not visit him to enquire about his health; if he dies, don't accompany his bier.[101] A Kafir dies. His heir becomes Muslim. This Muslim is not to honour the *wasiat* (wish/will) of his Kafir father.[102] The Zimmi cannot be a witness against a Muslim; he cannot be the guardian of his child who is a Muslim.[103]

"In the words of the Hanafi jurist Sarakhsi (d. 483/1090) the word of a dishonest Muslim is more valuable than that of an honest dhimmi."[104] Muslim religious literature and sufi hagiography overflow with such ideas. As if this discrimination was not enough, there are many *ahadis* and *ayats* of the Quran asking Muslims to kill Kafirs outright. Islamic scriptures recommend setting Muslims against non-Muslims, believers against infidels – to defend Islam and destroy unbelief. Individual and group killings of Kafirs are encouraged. One who kills a Kafir is given the latter's property. Khalid bin Walid said that the Prophet ordained that the property of the killed belonged to the killer; [it was not to be taken into account for khams]. In the Battle of Hunain, Abu Talha killed twenty Kafirs and got their goods.[105] There are still more bloody instructions about group killings of Kafirs, but of this in the next chapter on Jihad.

A Muslim monarch was expected to carry out all these directions of the Quran and Hadis. In Islamic scriptures the primary duty of every good Muslim king, indeed of every devout Muslim, is to fight religious war or Jihad against the infidels. But the duty of propagating Islam and carrying on Jihad mainly devolved on the sultan. Since there is Jihad till idolatry is destroyed, Jihad was the monarch's most important duty.[106] It is a great sin for a Muslim to shirk the battle against non-believers — those who do will roast in hell. Ziyauddin Barani had this idea of a good religious Muslim monarch — the sultan even if he was unable to extirpate infidelity he must at least keep the enemies of God and his prophet dishonoured and humiliated.[107]

III
Obligations of the State

According to Ruben Levy, "the functions which the lawyers and theorists lay down for the Caliphate, the duties of the ruler in Islam are four" – (1) Judgement (or justice), (2) Taxation, (3) Friday service and (4) Jihad.[1] We shall take up Jihad first.

3.1. ISLAMIC WAR OR JIHAD

War against non-Muslims is called Jihad in Islamic scriptures. The first Jihads were fought in Arabia against the Pagans, Jews and Christians. Later on they were fought wherever Muslims went to spread their religion. Jihad is fought to serve Allah. According to a Pakistani army scholar, Brigadier S.K. Malik,[2] "the fountain-head of the Quranic dimensions of war lies in the fact that war is waged for the cause of Allah... To those who fight for this noblest heavenly cause, the Book promises handsome heavenly assistance. The index of fighting for Allah's cause is Man's total submission to his Will. Those who fail to submit themselves fully and completely to the Will of God run the risk of incurring heavenly wrath... Fighting involves risk of life and property that must be accepted willingly and cheerfully."[3] Said the Book, "Not equal are believers who sit (at home) and receive no hurt, and those who strive and fight in the cause of Allah with their goods and their persons. Allah hath granted a grade higher to those who strive and fight with their goods and persons than those who sit (at home)." "The central theme behind the causes of wars, as spelt out by the Holy Quran, was the cause of Allah... In the pursuit of this cause, the Muslims were first granted the *permission* to fight but were later *commanded* to fight in the way of God as a matter of religious obligation and duty."[4]

Inspiring terror into the hearts of the enemy was a part of the tactics of Jihad. Talking of Badr, Almighty Allah addressed the Prophet thus: "I am with you: give firmness to the Believers: I will instil terror into the hearts of the Unbelievers."[5] In the battle of Uhud, Allah identified the causes of the Muslim defeat, provided divine guidance, and held out a promise: "Soon shall we cast terror into the hearts of the Unbelievers."[6] The Quran referred to the treachery of Banu Quraiza, "Allah did take them down from their stronghold and cast terror into their hearts, (so that) some ye slew, and some ye made prisoners. And he made you heirs to their lands, their houses, and their goods..."[7] "Terror struck in the hearts of the enemies is not only a means, it is the end in itself. It can be instilled only if the opponent's faith is destroyed. Psychological dislocation is temporary; spiritual dislocation is permanent... To instil terror into the hearts of the enemy it is essential, in the ultimate analysis, to dislocate his faith."[8] This is exactly what the Muslim invaders and rulers tried to do in India.

The Holy Quran spelt out the divine war against Paganism when it commanded the Muslims to take recourse to fighting. "And fight them on," ruled the Book, "until there is no more tumult or oppression, and there prevails justice and faith in Allah." Similar instructions were repeated after the battle of Badr, about a year later. "And fight them on," the Holy Quran directed on that occasion, "until there is no more tumult or oppression, and there prevails justice and faith in Allah altogether and everywhere."[9]

Three ideas are central in the above postulation. There have been wars but the wars fought by the Muslims are in the service of Allah. This gives Islamic belligerency divine sanction, and terrorism becomes a divine command. The second idea put forward is that Paganism is tumult and oppression while Islam is justice and faith in Allah. This is what the Muslims are taught to believe. And thirdly participation in this divine war is a must; there is reward for the participants and punishment for non-participants. Jihad in a word is total war.

Jihad is for ever

"The origins of Jihad lie in the desire for the expansion of Arab power and the spread of the Islamic religion first in Arabia and later on in the whole world. Muhammad knew that his people could not rule the world until they were welded into an effective fighting force against the unbelievers for taking over their countries, personal possessions and women, and subjugating them to the Arabian hegemony... Since Jihad is against the unbelievers, the Prophet created unlimited opportunities for holy wars by declaring other religions false and ungodly."[10] Thus Jihad is Allah's command to the Muslims to destroy the non-Muslims. It is not at all necessary that the non-Muslims should have wronged the Muslims; their true crime is that they do not believe in Islam. The aim of Jihad is to make them believe in Islam through the power of the sword.

The *Dictionary of Islam* defines Jihad as "a religious war with those who are unbelievers in the mission of Muhammad. It is an incumbent religious duty, established in the Quran and the traditions as a divine institution and enjoined specially for the purpose of advancing Islam..."[11] The Quran says in *Surah* (Chapter) 2 *ayat* (injunction) 193, "Fight against them (the *mushriks*) until idolatry is no more, and Allah's religion reigns supreme." The command is repeated in *Surah* 8 *ayat* 39. In *Surah* 69 *ayats* 30-37 it is ordained: "Lay hold of him and bind him. Burn him in the fire of hell." And again: "When you meet the unbelievers in the battlefield strike off their heads and when you have laid them low, bind your captives firmly" (47:14-15). "Cast terror into the hearts of the infidels. Strike off their heads, maim them in every limb"(8:12).[12] And "Fight and slay the pagans wherever you find them, and seize them, beleaguer them and lie in wait for them in every stratagem till they respect and establish regular prayers and practise regular charity" (11:8). Such commands, exhortations and injunctions are repeatedly mentioned in Islamic scriptures — the Quran and Hadis. The main medium through which these injunctions were to be carried out was the holy Jihad. The Jihad or holy war is a multi-dimensional concept. When it comes to Jihad, no two Muslims can disagree on this basic concept. It means fighting for the sake of Allah, for furthering the cause of Islam, for converting people to the 'true faith', for killing them if they resist, for seizing their property and their women and children, and for destroying their temples. Iconoclasm and razing other people's temples is central to Islam; it derives its justification from the Prophet's Sunnah or practice. Muhammad had himself destroyed Pagan temples in Arabia and so set an example for his followers. Without Jihad there is no Islam. Jihad is a religious duty of every Muslim.

It is remarkable that all the injunctions about Jihad, a war against non-Muslims for all time, occur in the al-Madinah *Surahs*. These were revealed after Muhammad had established himself as a paramount ruler, and was in a position to dictate terms to enemies. Verses revealed in Mecca (609-622 CE) begin as a hesitant call to arms for the defence of "mosques, churches and synagogues", and end by being transformed in Madinah into a violent call for all round destruction of non-Muslims. There is nothing surprising about it. One important fact regarding Quran is that each revelation is suited to the exigencies of the Prophet's policy or passion.

That being so, there are rules laid down for carrying on Jihad. These rules are given more elaborately in the Hadis.

Muslim theologians make no distinction between the Quran (the Holy Book) and the Hadis (Traditions). Both are works of revelation and inspiration, the one supplementing the other. The leaders of Jihad were told to offer their enemies, that is those who disbelieved in Allah, three options: 1. Invite them to accept Islam; if they do so, then invite them to migrate from their lands to the land of Muhajirs (Madinah in the early days of Muhammad, Darul Islam in later days). If they refuse to migrate, tell them that they will be subjected to the commands of Allah like other Muslims, but they will not get any share in rewards or spoils of war. But if they participate in Jihad they would be entitled to their share. 2. If they do not accept Islam, demand from them the Jizyah. If they accept to pay the Jizyah, do not rob or kill them because as Zimmis, they should be left unharmed. 3. But if they refuse to pay the Jiziyah tax, then seek Allah's help and fight them.[13]

Fair enough. But patience for such negotiations and agreements was not quite feasible in the midst of war with prospects of gainful plunder. One should have normally invited the infidels to embrace Islam before attacking them, but if the Musalmans did attack them before offering them Islam and slay them, even women and children, and take possession of their property, no punishment, expiation or atonement was due on the part of such Muslims. For, according to the Prophet "war is stratagem", "war is deceit".[14] Inspired Mujahids did deeds of valour, of horror and of terror. Muslim chroniclers have written about such achievements of the heroes of Islam with zeal and glee. The Mujahids were encouraged to embark on Jihad because they were promised handsome rewards in this world as in the world to come. That is how Jihad and prayer became equal in beneficence. That is why a Jihadist sought *shahadat* (martyrdom).[15] In this world, the property and possessions of the infidel killed by a Musalman became the reward of the latter — wife, children, animals, wealth. "The man who kills the infidel, even the one who kills a wounded infidel, shall have the right to retain what he had taken from the man he killed — that booty will not be subject to the one-fifth deduction customary for booty in general. He shall also of course get in addition his share of the general spoils."[16]

Paradise as Reward of Jihad

In the next world is Paradise for the Mujahid. Whether he survives in battle against an infidel, or is wounded or is slain, Paradise is ensured for him after his death. The spiritual merits of participating in Jihad are equal to all other religious duties like keeping fasts, standing in prayer constantly and obeying Allah's commands in Quran.[17] Jihad for the spread of Islam is the most meritorious gateway to Paradise. "Paradise is under the shadow of the swords," the Prophet told his followers.[18] The Paradise in the Quran provided "Rest and passive enjoyment; verdant gardens watered by murmuring rivulets, wherein the believers... repose (quaffing) aromatic wine such as the Arabs loved from goblets placed before them or handed round in silver cups resplendent as glass by beautiful youths... 'Verily! for the pious is a blissful abode; Gardens and Vineyards, and damsels with swelling bosoms, of an equal age, and a full cup...' These damsels of paradise are introduced as *'lovely large-eyed girls resembling pearls hidden in their shells, a reward for that which the faithful have wrought... 'Verily! we have created them (the houries) of a rare creation; We have made them virgins, fascinating, of an equal age'*."[19] In Paradise the souls of the Mujahids will roam about at will like the free birds who have their nests in brightly lighted chandeliers. They will be wedded to houries and live in gardens with golden pillars studded with precious stones. There will be seventy thousand golden gates at each of which a beauty (hourie) will await their arrival.[20] And all their sins will be forgiven."[21] "A man came to Allah's Apostle," the Hadis records, "and said, 'Instruct me to such a deed as equals Jihad (in reward).' He replied, 'I do not find such a deed.'"[22] In consequence of such rewards there was a keen desire on the part of the Mujahids "to fight in the way of Allah and be killed, to fight and again and be killed, and to fight again and be killed."[23] It is significant that a detailed description of Paradise attainable through Jihad is repeated and restated at the end of *Sunan ibn Majah*.[24] Muslim students in Madrsas are instructed in the Quran and Hadis from an early age. Books of Hadis are read and re-read by devout Muslims. The closing pages of a book always leave a lasting impression on the reader's mind. The description of Jihad and Paradise at the close of the collections of Hadis inspires the Muslim to an everlasting zeal for Jihad and for entering the tempting Paradise.

However, in spite of the clear injunctions in the Quran and the Hadis, T.P. Hughes writes that "the mystics speak of two Jihads: Jihadul Akbar or 'the greater warfare', which is against one's own lusts; and al Jihadul Asghar, or, the lesser warfare, against infidels."[25] There is no Jihad of the former type mentioned in the Quran or Hadis. There is also no defensive Jihad. As M. Mujeeb says, "The *Hidayah* is quite explicit about the legality of *Jihad* (holy war) against infidels even when they have not taken the offensive."[26] As Hughes himself quotes from Burhanuddin Ali's *Hidayah*, to the latter Jihad or "war is permanently established until the day of Judgement".[27]

The above discussion shows that the difference between ordinary and Islamic war lies in the latter's essence of malevolence and savagery. The encouragement to loot and obtain booty in this world and the promise of Paradise in the next packs the Jihadists with cruel zeal to plunder and kill no end. Jihad's brutalization of war is writ large on the pages of medieval history. The Turks and Pathans were mainly Hindus and Buddhists before they were converted to Islam. Their record of war and atrocities before they became Muslims is normal. But once they went over to the new faith they were brutalized, and what the Arab armies did in Syria, Iraq,

Iran, Egypt, North Africa, Spain and Sindh, bears close resemblance to what the Turks and Pathans did in India. Not only outsiders but even those Hindu rulers or zamindars who became Muslim (e.g. in Afghanistan, Kashmir or Gujarat) became hard-hearted and brutalized and treated their erstwhile co-religionists with the same fanaticism as was practised by foreign invaders or resident Muslim rulers. Their zeal was also kept alive by works written in India on the merits of Jihad. From Fakhr-i-Mudabbir's *Adab-ul-Harb* and Ziyauddin Barani's *Fatwa-i-Jahandari* to Aurangzeb's *Fatawa-i-Alamgiri*, all are works on Muslim politics. Aurangzeb's *Fatawa-i-Alamgiri* truly mentions that the noblest occupation for Muslims is Jihad. This meant that military service provided the best career for a Muslim, and it was the business of the kings and commanders to declare every war a Jihad. The practice of the military profession was made identical with the fulfilment of a religious duty.[28]

Jihad in India

The sanguine psychology produced by Jihad is evident in the behaviour of some of the greatest names in Indian Muslim history. Muhammad bin Sakifi had been sent to invade Sindh by al-Hajjaj. Hajjaj had earlier been appointed Governor of Mecca by Caliph Abdul Malik in 73 H (692 CE) where he built the holy Kaba.[29] It was a pious performance; his other great achievement was, as he claimed, that he had killed 100,000 men with his own sword.[30] The ambition and boast of killing one lakh or a hundred thousand human beings was shared by many Muslim Caliphs, invaders and rulers. Khalid bin Walid was known as "the Sword of Allah," Abul Abbas, the first Caliph of the Abbasid line was renowned as "The blood pourer" and Alauddin Husain was called "*jahan soz* (world burner)".[31] He carried fire and sword through the kingdom of Ghazni (1151 CE). Such titles had a pride of place in the history of Islam.

In India Muhammad bin Qasim killed by thousands, but Mahmud of Ghazni surely killed by lakhs,[32] and took pride in the fact. This becomes clear from just two instances. In his attack on Thanesar, "the blood of the infidels flowed so copiously that the stream was discoloured, and people were unable to drink it". Similarly, in the slaughter of Sirsawa near Saharanpur, "the Musalmans paid no regard to the booty till they had satiated themselves with the slaughter of the infidels."[33] The temper of a people armed against mankind was surely influenced by the licence of rapine, murder and revenge as recommended by their creed. The story is told of how once Mahmud of Ghazni went on cutting down victim after victim with his sword. In the process his fingers got jammed on the sword-hilt. His grip had to be relaxed by douching his hand in hot water. Like Hajjaj, Mahmud was a scholar of Quran.

Jihad under Turks

The chroniclers of the early Turkish rulers of India take pride in affirming that Qutbuddin Aibak was a killer of lakhs of infidels. Leave aside enthusiastic killers like Alauddin Khalji and Muhammad bin Tughlaq, even the "kind-hearted" Firoz Tughlaq killed more than a lakh Bengalis when he invaded their country. Timur Lang or Tamerlane says he killed a hundred thousand infidel prisoners of war in Delhi.[34] He built victory pillars from severed heads at many places. These were acts of sultans. The nobles were not lagging behind. One Shaikh Daud Kambu is said to have killed 20,000 with his dagger.[35] The Bahmani sultans of Gulbarga and Bidar considered it meritorious to kill a hundred thousand Hindu men, women and children every year.[36] These wars were fought in the true spirit of Jihad — the total annihilation or conversion of the non-Muslims. It was in this spirit that some ulema requested Sultan Iltutmish (1210-1236) to confront the Hindus with a choice between Islam and death.

He advised them patience as dictated by the compulsions of the situation. Iltutmish fought against Nasiruddin Qubacha and Tajuddin Yaldoz. But his wars against them are not called Jihad. Jihad was against non-Muslims. Hence the insistence of the ulema on this religious duty. In a hundred years time Muslim ambition paved the way for confident optimism. During the reigns of Nasiruddin Mahmud and Ghiyasuddin Balban (1246-86) extensive campaigns in southern Uttar Pradesh, Bundelkhand and Baghelkhand as well as Gwalior, Narwar, Chanderi and Malwa were undertaken. In Katehar and Mewat there were systematic massacres of Rajputs and Mewatis in the true spirit of Jihad. While the numbers of the enslaved boosted Muslim demography, massacres were ordered on selective basis — only of Hindus.[37] Similar scenes were witnessed during Alauddin Khalji's invasion of Gujarat in 1299, where massacres by his generals in Anhilwara, Cambay, Asavalli, Vanmanthali and Somnath earned him, according to *Rasmala*, the sobriquet of *Khuni*. Also in Chittor, where Alauddin ordered a massacre of 30,000 Hindus. The comment of Amir Khusrau on this genocide (keeping in mind the population of the period) is significant. "Praise be to God"!, writes he in his *Khazain-ul-Futuh* (completed in 1311 CE) "that he (the sultan) so ordered the massacre of all the chiefs of Hindustan out of the pale of Islam, by his infidel-smiting sword, that if in this time it should by chance happen that a schismatic should claim his right, the pure Sunnis would swear in the name of this Khalifa of God, that heterodoxy has no right."[38] Shorn of its verbosity his comment on the horrible massacre only points to the fact that except for Sunni Muslims no other people could be permitted to live in India. Four years later he wrote in his *Ashiqa* — "Happy Hindustan, the splendour of Religion, where the Law finds perfect honour and security. The whole country, by means of the sword of our holy warriors, has become like a forest denuded of its thorns by fire... Islam is triumphant, idolatry is subdued. Had not the *Shariat* Law granted exemption from death by the payment of poll-tax, the very name of Hind, root and branch, would have been extinguished."[39] Ziyauddin Barani, a contemporary of Amir Khusrau, writes in a similar spirit. He quoted the disposition of Qazi Mughisuddin before Alauddin that the Hindus were the greatest among the enemies of God and the religion of the Prophet[40] and so needed to be eliminated. It is in a similar vein that he advocates an all-out Jihad against the Hindus in his *Fatawa-i-Jahandari*.[41] So whether it was a sufi of the stature of Amir Khusrau about whose liberal credentials every secularist swears, or it was an orthodox Maulana like Ziyauddin Barani, the position of the Hindu idolaters in the Islamic law was given by them fairly correctly.[42] They deserved to be exterminated through Jihad. If the sultans conceded to the Hindus the status of Zimmis, it was because of the compulsion of the Indian situation.

That is how wars against Hindus were no ordinary wars, casualties no common casualties, and massacres were massacres of extermination. This thirst for extermination was also whetted by the resistance of "the enemies of God" with their determination for survival. The rite of Jauhar killed the women, the tradition of not deserting the field of battle made Rajputs and others die fighting in large numbers. When Malwa was attacked (1305), its Raja is said to have possessed 40,000 horse and 100,000 foot.[43] After the battle, "so far as human eye could see, the ground was muddy with blood". Many cities of Malwa like Mandu, Ujjain, Dharanagri and Chanderi were captured after great resistance. The capitulation of Sevana and Jalor in Rajasthan (1308, 1311) were accompanied by massacres after years of prolonged warfare. In Alauddin's wars in the South, similar killings took place, especially in Dwarsamudra and Tamil Nadu.[44] His successor Mubarak Khalji once again sacked Gujarat and Devagiri.

Under Muhammad Tughlaq, wars and rebellions knew no end. His expeditions to Bengal, Sindh and the Deccan, as well as ruthless suppression of twenty-two rebellions, meant only depopulation in the thirteenth and first half of the fourteenth century.[45] For one thing, in spite of constant efforts no addition of territory could be made by Turkish rulers from 1210 to 1296; for another the Turkish rulers were more ruthless in war and less merciful in peace. Hence the extirpating massacres of Balban, and the repeated attacks by others on regions already devastated but not completely subdued. Bengal was attacked by Bakhtiyar, by Balban, by Alauddin, and by all the three Tughlaqs — Ghiyas, Muhammad and Firoz. Malwa and Gujarat were repeatedly attacked and sacked. Almost every Muslim ruler invaded Rantambhor until it was subjugated by Alauddin Khalji (1301, again temporarily). Gwalior, Katehar and Avadh regions were also repeatedly attacked. Rajputana, Sindh and Punjab (also because of the Mongol invasions), knew no peace. In the first decade of the fourteenth century Turkish invaders penetrated into the South, carrying death and destruction. Later on Bahmani and Vijayanagar kingdoms also came to grips with each other. Mulla Daud of Bidar vividly describes the war between Muhammad Shah Bahmani and the Vijayanagar King in 1366 in which "Farishtah computes the victims on the Hindu side alone as numbering no less than half a million."[46] Muhammad also devastated the Karnatak region with vengeance.[47]

Jihad under Mughals

The Mughals came with new weapons and new strategy of war, but their religious ideology of Jihad and zeal remained as of old. This is borne out by the difference in Babur's attitude and actions in his two wars, one against the Muslim Ibrahim Lodi and the other against the Hindu Rana Sanga. Babur's war against Ibrahim Lodi was only a war, against Rana Sangram Singh it was Jihad. After the defeat of the Lodi Sultan in the First Battle of Panipat in April 1526, according to

Ahmad Yadgar, Babur praised the slain King, and his corpse was given a decent burial at the command of the victor.[48] On the other hand, the story of the Battle of Khanwa against Rana Sanga in March 1527 has been described in the royal memoirs in an entirely different idiom. In it Rana Sanga is repeatedly called a pagan (Kafir) with studied contempt. His nobles and soldiers are similarly abused repeatedly. On account of Sanga's large army and reputation for bravery, Babur renounced wine as a measure of seeking God's grace. And how? — cups and flagons were "dashed in pieces, as God willing! soon will be dashed the gods of the idolaters."[49] The whole narrative of Babur as well as Shaikh Zain's *Fateh Nama* is laced with quotations from the Quran for wishing victory against the infidels, for "adequate thanks cannot be rendered for a benefit than which none is greater in the world and nothing is more blessed in the world to come, to wit, victory over most powerful infidels and dominion over wealthiest heretics, '*these are the unbelievers, the wicked*'." All the Hindu chiefs killed in battle "*trod the road to Hell from this house of clay to the pit of perdition*". When they were engaged in battle, they were "*made to descend into Hell, the house of perdition. They shall be thrown to burn therein, and an unhappy dwelling shall it be.*"[50] In Babur's memoirs his narrative of Jihad is laced with quotations from the Quran in dozens which shows that he was, like Mahmud Ghaznavi, a scholar of Quran and Hadis and no simple secular warrior.

After the victory over Rana Sanga, Babur took the title of Ghazi or victor in holy war. As trophy of victory "an order was given to set up a pillar of pagan heads."[51] Similar tower of pagan heads was piled up after the success at Chanderi against Medini Rai. "We made general massacre of pagans in it. A pillar of pagan heads was ordered set up on a hill north-west of Chanderi (and) converted what for many years had been a mansion of hostility, into a mansion of Islam."[52] Such language is used, such towers of heads of the slain are piled up, only in the case of Hindus. Similar ideas and actions are not found in Babur's description of wars against the Muslims in India. The language betrays the psychology developed by the ideology of Jihad contained in Islamic scriptures. The ideology is not of universal brotherhood. Its brotherhood is confined to Muslims only.

Even in emperor Akbar's 'secular' reign the religious spirit of Jihad was not lost. Abdul Qadir Badaoni who was then one of Akbar's court chaplains or imams, states that he sought an interview with the emperor when the royal troops were marching against Rana Pratap in 1576, begging leave of absence for "the privilege of joining the campaign to soak his Islamic beard in Hindu infidel blood". Akbar was so pleased at the expression of allegiance to his person and to the Islamic idea of Jihad that he bestowed a handful of gold coins on Badaoni as a token of his pleasure.[53] It may be recalled that as an adolescent, Akbar had earned the title of Ghazi by beheading the defenseless infidel Himu. Under Akbar and Jahangir "five or six hundred thousand human beings were killed," says emperor Jahangir.[54] The figures given by these killers and their chroniclers may be a few thousand less or a few thousand more, but what bred this ambition of cutting down human beings without compunction was the Muslim theory, practice and spirit of Jihad, as spelled out in Muslim scriptures and rules of administration. Under Aurangzeb every chronicler avers that wars against infidels were fought in the spirit of Jihad. In short, Jihad was never given up in India from the time of Muhammad bin Qasim to that of Aurangzeb and beyond, so long as Muslim rule lasted.

We may close this discussion on the theory and practice of Jihad by pointing out that the prophet of Islam was a very practical man. He advocated Jihad or aggressive wars against non-Muslims till eternity because he did not visualize a world without Kafirs and people of other faiths. But he could not be sure of success always. Muhammad himself sometimes got Muslim prisoners of war released by giving in exchange beautiful slave girls to the strong adversary at Medina.[55]

Therefore, in many *ahadis* he recommended that if infidels harass the Muslims, and offer them peace in return for property the Imam must not accede thereto as far as possible, as this would be a degradation of the Muslim honour. But if destruction is apprehended, purchasing peace with property is lawful, because it is a duty to repel destruction in every possible way.[56] Muslims also repelled destruction *in this wise* in Hindustan from the time of Iltutmish to that of Aurangzeb. Aurangzeb, ever keen on Jihad as stressed in his *Fatawa-i-Alamgiri*, used to surrender forts to the Marathas when destruction stared him in the face. Rajputs too used to recover their forts and properties from Muslim rulers throughout the medieval period. But Jihad was a religious duty for Muslims till eternity for the annihilation of non-Muslims. It was carried out in India to the best of the competence and strength of Muslim invaders and rulers throughout the medieval period.

3.2. JUSTICE

The Daily Mail, London, published a series of articles on India between April 1933 and April 1934 by many eminent British administrators. These articles were later published in the form of a pamphlet which cost one penny. The articles are full of imperialist love for India — a love also shared by the earlier Muslim imperialist power. Islam has all the ingredients of imperialism found anywhere in the world in any age. In one of the aforesaid articles Rothermere asserts that "The plain fact is that India is as indispensable to Britain as Britain is to India" in the same vein as today it is claimed that India is as indispensable to Muslims as Muslims are to India. In another article Sir Michael O'Dwyer, formerly Lieutenant Governor of the Punjab, wrote: "The essentials of a good government in every country are: (1) External and internal security, (2) Impartial justice (3) Progressive and efficient administration and (4) Light taxation."[57] According to Ruben Levy, as noted earlier, "the duties of the ruler in Islam are (also) four" — Judgement or Justice, Taxation, Friday service and Jihad. We have already dealt with Jihad which also took care of external and more so of internal security. We shall take up the study of taxation later on. Here we shall concentrate on Justice and Friday service under Muslim rule.

Justice by the King

In Islam, justice has to be done in accordance with the Quran. If solution is not found in the Quran it should be done as per the Sunnah. If Sunnah also fails to provide an answer, then it should be done according to *ijtihad* (or individual judgement).[58] But justice must be done. Justice — Islamic justice — has a very important place in a Muslim state.

"Justice is the balance in which the actions of people, good or bad, are weighed," says Ziya Barani.[59] "According to the ancient political ideal... the sovereign is the fountain of justice and it is his duty to try cases personally in open court."[60] Like their Hindu counterparts, past and contemporary, Muslim kings in India like Iltutmish, Balban, Alauddin Khalji and Muhammad Tughlaq, followed this ideal and personally administered justice in open court. So did the Mughals. While the emperors attended to ordinary cases every day in open *darbar*, they had fixed one day in the week specially for cases requiring evidence of witnesses and their cross-examination. Akbar's day of administering justice was Thursday, Jahangir's Tuesday, Shahjahan's Wednesday and Aurangzeb's also Wednesday. Besides kings, the princes, commanders of armies, and other high officers of the state also decided cases, expert opinion on law being provided by judicial officials possessing knowledge of the Shariat.

The law courts under Muslim rule were located in administrative units of the empire, in Parganas, Sarkars, Subahs and the capital of the empire. The *adalat* of the Pargana Qazi was the lowest court under the Mughals.

Appeals were preferred to higher courts, to the Qazi-i-Subah and the emperor. The emperor's court was the highest court in the empire. He tried both civil and military cases. He also sat as the final court of appeal within the empire. In deciding cases, he had the assistance of a Mufti or Mir Adl. There was a hierarchical cadre of officials like Qazi-ul-Quzzat or Lord Chief Justice, Qazis, Naib Qazis, Mir Adls and Muftis who expounded the law and gave opinion on complicated cases. The emperor's court was quite popular with the people who obtained redress from his impartiality.

Judiciary of Muslim State

But the emperor was not a Qazi or Mufti. Besides, he could not decide all the hundreds of cases that came up for hearing. These cases were dealt with by the judiciary. The chief court of the empire was located in the capital and was presided over by the Qazi-ul-Quzzat, or the Chief Justice of the realm. He was appointed by the emperor. He had the power to try original civil and military cases. He heard appeals from and supervised the working of provincial courts. He was assisted in his work by Qazis, Muftis, Muhtasibs. The Muhtasib was the chief custodian of public morals. It was his duty to see that there was no infringement of Islamic law in the public as well as private lives of the people. He used to enquire into the conduct of the people and so instilled a sense of fear in them. The office of the Muhtasib was instituted by Caliph al-Mahdi (775-785) to see that the religious and moral precepts of Islam were observed and that the offenders were detected and punished. Muhtasib was like the Christian Inquisitor without the latter's licence of cruelty and torture. The office of Muhtasib was an integral part of the administrative set up of the Muslim state. There were Muhtasibs during the Sultanate period and in the Mughal empire. They were there in the capital as well as the headquarters of the provinces and their subdivisions.

Islamic Justice

Justice has one meaning for the ruler, another for the ruled. What was impartial justice for the British was imperialist oppression for the Indians. What was impartial justice for the Muslims was the imposition of the Islamic Shariat on the Hindus because Muslim law was full of discrimination against non-Muslims. Muslim law on crime and punishment is complicated and cruel. Where imprisonment of a month or two would be considered sufficient, say for pilferage or theft, in Islam it is visited with cutting of hands and feet. A Hadd (pl. Hudud) comprises punishments that are prescribed in the Quran and the Hadis. These include stoning to death for adultery; one hundred lashes for fornication,[61] and eighty lashes for drinking wine. When a woman is to be stoned a chest deep hole is dug for her, so that her nakedness is not exposed and the modesty of the watching multitude is not offended. No such hole need be dug for a man. The stoning is begun by the witnesses followed by the Imam or Qazi, and then by the participating believers. Cutting off the right hand is prescribed for theft,[62] and cutting off feet and hands for highway robbery. In the cases of murder the right of revenge (*qisas*) belongs to the victim's heir. But the heir can forgo this right of death for murder and accept blood-price in exchange. For the death of a woman, Jew or Christian, only half of the blood-price is due. "As slaves and unbelievers are inferior in status to Muslims they are not entitled to *qisas* according to most Muslim *faqihs* (jurists)."[63] In all such cases, a woman's testimony (*shahadah*) has half the weight of a man's.

It is a very great crime to apostatize from Islam (*irtidad*) and its punishment is death. The Quran gives the broad outline of these punishments, all Hadis collections provide many details of the same. Both Quran and Hadis are specific about punishment of death for giving up Islam.[64] One can accept Islam freely; one can be forcibly converted or could be captured in war and made a Muslim, but once converted, one cannot abjure Islam. Once a group of men apostatized from Islam. Ali burnt them to death. Eight men of the tribe of Ukl became Muslims. They went to Madinah, but away from the control of the Prophet, they turned away from Islam. The Prophet sent twenty Ansars after them. They were captured and brought back. The Holy Prophet "got their hands cut off and their feet, and put out their eyes, and threw them on the stony ground until they died". Another *hadis* adds that "while on the stony ground they were asking for water, but they were not given water."[65] The rules are so strict that if a Muslim does not deny Islam, if he adheres to all injunctions but denies one single principle, he becomes Kafir and deserves to be killed.[66] There was no effective law to hinder the infliction of many other forms of cruel punishment according to the caprice of the local official. For example, killing a man by making a snake bite him became a common Muslim punishment in India.[67]

Men have been punished in war and peace in all countries through the ages. But severe flogging, mutilation of limbs, amputation of hands and feet and noses and ears, putting out eyes by piercing them with red hot iron, nailing of hands and feet, flaying alive, hamstringing and decapitating were Islamic specializations. Add to this pouring molten lead into the throat, crushing the bones with mallets, burning the body with fire, driving nails into the hands, feet and bosom, cutting the sinews, sawing men asunder — these and many similar tortures were common. With this background, with this ideology, with this set of punishments, justice in medieval India under Muslim rule could only be barbarous in nature, content and cruelty. There were cruel kings and kind kings, there were corrupt Qazis and honest Qazis, but so long as punishments remained barbaric, there was little hope for the accused or the victim. In Islamic conception the state belongs to God. Hence a violation of public right becomes an offence against God. As a result punishment for injury done to God's authority has to be visited according to the rules laid down by God and his Prophet as contained in the Quran and Hadis.

In India in the Sultanate period such punishments continued to be awarded as the chronicles of Barani and Afif show. Under Alauddin Khalji and Muhammad bin Tughlaq punishments became more severe. Cutting of hands and feet was sanctioned by the Shariat. Alauddin added to it slicing off flesh from the haunches of the defaulting shopkeepers.[68] Since "God Almighty himself in the Quran commended the complete degradation of the non-Muslim (*yan yad yaham saghrun*),[69] slaying, plundering and imprisoning of the Hindus became routine. For a handful of *tankahs*, revenue officials were clamped in jails for many years receiving blows and kicks,[70] while the Hindus in general had no gold or silver left in their houses. Muhammad Tughlaq confined Shaikhzada Jami in an iron cage leading to his death.[71] Under him punishments laid down by the Shariat were scrupulously awarded. The mother of prince Masud was ordered by the Sultan to be stoned to death for adultery, the verdict having been pronounced by Qazi Kamaluddin. Ibn Battutah relates that on one occasion he himself as Qazi gave eighty stripes to one Razi of Multan for making himself drunk and stealing five hundred *dinars*. He also says that during Muhammad Tughlaq's reign people used to admit uncommitted crimes and courted death to escape torture. When the royal order was issued for the execution of any person, he was executed at the gate of the palace where his corpse remained for three days.[72] The Diwan-i-Siyasat worked vigorously and every day hundreds of culprits were brought for punishments.[73] Sultan Firoz Tughlaq writes in his *Fatuhat* that he appeased by means of gifts the heirs of those who had been deprived of a limb, nose, eye, hand or foot in the time of his late lord and patron Sultan Muhammad Shah. Firoz Tughlaq is known for his kind-heartedness but, according to Shams Siraj Afif, he killed one lakh 80 thousand Bengalis in war. Towers of skulls of the killed were erected. The chronicler adds, "Firoz

Shah was near the mound of skulls with all magnificence and glory and was inspecting the counting of the heads.

In India, in course of time and under the influence of Hindu environment the violence of punishments was mitigated to a great extent. Under Akbar, "the compassionate heart of His Majesty finds no pleasure in cruelties or in causing sorrow to others; he is ever sparing of the lives of his subjects, wishing to bestow happiness upon all..."[75] So that, by the time of Akbar and Jahangir, "No person was to suffer, for any offence, the loss of nose or ear. If the crime were theft, the offender was to be scourged with thorns, or deterred... by an attestation on the Koran."[76] In his *Tuzuk*, emperor Jahangir asserts that "I forbade the cutting of the nose or ears of any person, and... made a vow... that I would not blemish any one by this punishment."[77] This statement, however, inadvertently shows that mutilation of this type was quite prevalent before him. Perhaps the digressions from the letter of the law prompted Aurangzeb to restate once more and clearly, the basic canons of Islamic law in his *Fatawa-i-Alamgiri*, completed in 1670.[78] Aurangzeb also issued a *farman* to the Diwan of Gujarat in June 1672 giving a gist of his penal code. In theory and practice mutilation and decapitation was continued under Aurangzeb, but there was greater emphasis on repentance, and flogging was more often resorted to. But that was also to give time to the accused to see the merits of the 'bright religion' and become its adherent. Those who did not show subservience were meted out cruel punishments. In northern India, Gurdwara Sisgunj in Chandni Chowk, Delhi, stands witness to Aurangzeb's idea of punishment to non-Muslims. Here the Sikh Guru Tegh Bahadur was called upon to embrace Islam, and on his refusal was tortured for five days and then "beheaded on a warrant from the emperor" (December 1675). In South India when the Maratha King Sambhaji and his minister Kavikalash were taken prisoner, "that very night his (Sambhaji's) eyes were blinded and the next day the tongue of Kavikalash was cut out. After a fortnight's torture their limbs were hacked one by one and their flesh thrown to the dogs" (March 1689).

Fate of the Mutilated

What was the fate of those who were mutilated? It would be euphemistic to say that they lived a miserable life. One case gives a glimpse of the plight of such people. Pietro Della Valle was in western India in 1623-24. In Cambay, where "the people are most part Gentiles", he saw "a famous Hospital of Birds" and another of animals like goats, sheep, and calves. "Among the beasts there was also a thief, who having been taken in theft had both his hands cut off. But the compassionate Gentiles that he might perish miserably now (that) he was no longer able to get his living, took him into his place, and kept him among the poor beasts, not suffering him to want anything."[79] So, the victims of Muslim justice could live like beasts after they had been mutilated. But many managed to survive. They probably got their food from the free kitchens run by the government.

There was probably another avenue of relief, perhaps rather than probably. Mutilation, blinding and beheading were common punishments as laid down by the Shariat. It stands to reason that some sort of remedy would have been sought to be applied in the case of persons who had lost a limb or the eyes. In India, the land of Charak, Shushrut and Dhanwantari, medicine and surgery had been in a developed state from ancient times. The art and science of surgery was widely practised even by some expert barbers, as for example, for doing circumcision of little Muslim boys and newly converted adults. Allama Abul Fazl and emperor Jahangir both write, but under the caption of magic and sorcery, whereby a man would be cut up in many pieces and then made to appear unhurt. Jadunath Sarkar in a footnote in the *Ain-i-Akbari* recounts the testimony of Ibn Battutah, Edward Melton, and many others about how dismembered limbs were joined together to form the living man once again.[80] Jahangir's *Tarikh-i-Salim Shahi* describes such a case of revival of a man.[81]

In emperor Jahangir's *Tarikh-i-Salim Shahi*, surgical operations by Bengalis, Portuguese and others are described at length along with the description of alchemy and magic.[82] But there may have been some remedy available to cure, to some extent at least, the disabilities of the mutilated. Jahangir talks of his expert, excellent and loyal physicians but they were not surgeons.[83] However, his own son Khusrau, who had been blinded had his eyes partially restored.[84] Similarly, slit noses could be repaired to look almost like the original through plastic surgery.[85] Niccolao Manucci gives a detailed description of such an operation of rhinoplasty during the Bijapur-Mughal war under Aurangzeb, when the Deccanis used to cut off noses of Mughal soldiers and send them bleeding to the Mughal camp.[86] But there is no case cited of one who had lost his hand or leg being restored to normal health in medieval India.

Jails

One thing not mentioned in Islamic scriptures is imprisonment of people. The Quran and Hadis do not speak of jails. The Hadis in particular speak only of beheading or mutilation. In India there were jails under Muslim rule. But these were few. The number of prisoners was not large, for the usual punishments were mutilation and death. In the fourteenth century "for (a default in collection of) five hundred or one thousand *tankahs*" revenue officials were clamped in jail for many years under Alauddin Khalji. Besides government officials, bootleggers and other criminals were fettered and thrown into underground jails, built specially for them. In these monstrous holes many offenders died, or survived with completely shattered health.[87] Amir Khurd, the author of *Siyar-ul-Awliya*, describes the horrible conditions prevailing in such prisons. He says that once his father Saiyyad Kamal was imprisoned by Sultan Muhammad Tughlaq in Bhaksi jail near Devagiri. It was reported about that place, says he, that no prisoner used to come out alive from it as it was full of rats and snakes.[88] The state hardly made any arrangements for "reformation" of the prisons, and the prisoners suffered of oppressions of local authorities.[89] By the sixteenth-seventeenth century there were jails in many Mughal forts. The jail in the Gwalior Fort was meant, besides others, for royal prisoners ever since the Sultanate period. The other prisons of note were Ranthambhor, Rohtas, Bhakkar, Junnair, Biana and Lahore. Gwalior was the most prominent fort and next to it in importance was Ranthambḥor. Jahangir released "not less than seven thousand individuals, some of whom had been in confinement for forty years," in the fort of Gwalior.[90] Similarly, he set free many prisoners, except murderers and rebels, from the fort of Ranthambhor on two occasions.[91]

Punishment for the Poor

The stern justice, the dire punishments, as happens in autocracies, were meant for the poor while the rich and influential remained untouched; the rich who could "put a few coins in the hands of the Qazi," got scot free. This was specially so, say, in the case of wine-drinking. Wine is prohibited in Islam, but in practice only for the poor.

Many Muslims cannot forgo the pleasure of drinking wine in this world when it is promised to them in the next. The description of Paradise in the Quran specifically mentions free flow of wine *(kasir-ut sharab* and *utuf-ul yeham)* as one of its blissful contents (*Surah* 38 *ayat* 51, also 37: 45-46). Prophet Muhammad in one verse of the Quran praises wines of different colours *(sharab-i-mukhtalif alwana)* as signs of God's grace to mankind and cure of many diseases (Quran 16:69). Nasai devotes many *ahadis* to the discussion of drinking in Islam. According to him Muslims drank wine of wheat and barley. They were advised by the Prophet to dilute strong wine with water and not to get intoxicated.[92] According to Bukhari many Muslims drank wine on the day of *ghazwah*.[93] However, as the early companions of the Prophet got drunk, Muhammad was obliged to show some disapproval. He found that drinking led to gambling, quarrelling and stealing and, worse still, to neglecting the namaz. Consequently, he forbade it outright (Quran 2:216; 5:90-92). Wine-drinking became punishable by eighty lashes, and according to some traditions drinking of wine is punishable by death.[94]

In medieval India Muslim ruling classes drank freely, at the same time punishing poor helpless Muslims for the "crime". For example, while Alauddin Khalji had prohibited wine-drinking, his own son Qutbuddin Mubarak drank hard and so drank his nobles. All Mughal emperors from Babur to Shahjahan drank hard, Jahangir drank the hardest. But since wine is prohibited in Islam, it was a matter of routine for rulers to put a stop to drinking by common people. Even orthodox sultans like Firoz Tughlaq and Sikandar Lodi drank secretly "to keep in good health".[95] Most of the Mughal nobles drank openly and "all princes drank in secret."[96]

In such a scenario, the responsibility of punishing the guilty fell on the Qazis or Muslim judges. Judges of medieval India were, generally speaking, not held in high esteem in high circles. Some lacked erudition, others integrity. Maulana Shamsuddin Turk, a theologian hailing from Egypt in the fourteenth century, complained "that ill-fated wiseacres of black faces sat in the mosques with abominable books and made money by cheating both the accuser and the accused..."[97] At home they were accused of being bereft of dignity and being altogether worthless.[98] The sultans even used to punish the Qazis quite often. European travellers visiting India during the Mughal period like William Finch, Edward Terry and Francois Bernier are also critical of medieval judicial officers. They are criticised either for ignorance of law or cruelty or corruption.[99]

The Qazis could be easily bribed. Qazi Abdul Wahab, the Chief Qazi of Aurangzeb's reign, had amassed a fortune of 33 lakhs of rupees besides much jewellery during the sixteen years he held office.[100] But the Qazi alone did not administer justice. The will of the king and his substitutes (subedars, nobles) "is the law".[101] For example, Shahjahan, like Sher Shah Suri, insisted on his police officers to any how produce the thief, else they themselves would be punished. Naturally a 'culprit' was produced if not the real thief. One good thing in the system was that the trial by the king, his officers and Qazis was quick, but executions were also as quick as the trials. All this was due to the fact that the quality of courts left much to be desired, as, "the judicial department stands in marked contrast in organisation, in status, and dignity to other departments of the central government which were highly organised and equipped with efficient men."[102]

However, in a society where slavery existed, where the Muslims were taught to "obey God, the Prophet and those in authority over you," and Hindu attitude of fatalism among the lowly generated slavish respect for all those who administered justice — kings, officers, qazis — the punishments, howsoever barbarous, were taken in their stride.

3.3. FRIDAY SERVICE

In every religion prayers have a place of importance. In Islam their place is much more important as they are said as many as five times during the day. In Islam, the liturgical mosque service is known as *Salat*. *Salat* is Arabic: its equivalent in Persian and Urdu is namaz. The following are the times of prayer: (i) *Fajr ki namaz*, *Salat-ul-fajr*, or morning prayer, is said from 5 a.m. to sunrise. (ii) *Zuhur ki namaz, Salat-uz-zuhr,* or midday prayer, between 1 and 3 p.m. (iii) *Asr ki namaz, Salat-ul-asr,* or afternoon prayer, from 4 to 4.30 p.m., or till sunset. (iv) *Maghrib ki namaz, Salat-ul-maghrib,* or sunset prayer, at 6 p.m. (v) *Isha ki namaz, Salat-ul-Isha,* or prayer when night has closed, at bed time, between 8 p.m. and midnight. These five times of prayer are obligatory(*farz*). Besides these are others known as 'traditional' (*sunnat*) and supererogatory(*nafl*) which are observed by more religious and devout persons.[103]

"The daily prayers are not necessarily congregational. They may be offered up by the worshippers singly or in companies, in the mosque, at home, or by the way. But at mid-day of Friday, the service took a more public form, at which the believers as a body, unless detained by sufficient cause, were expected to attend. The usual prayers were on this occasion followed by an address or sermon pronounced by Mohammad. This weekly oration was usefully adapted to the circumstances of the day and feelings of the audience. It allowed full scope for the prophet's eloquence... and helped rivet the claims of Islam."[104]

Friday, the day chosen for the congregational prayer, had a special significance. According to many *ahadis* Friday is the best day on which the sun rises, the day on which Adam was taken into Paradise and turned out of it. On Friday his sins were pardoned. He died on Friday. It will be the day of Resurrection (*Qiamat*). The Prophet made his first entry into Madinah on that day, and he appointed it as the day of public worship. A Muslim saying namaz on Friday has his supplication granted by Allah.[105] According to a conservative interpretation, "Friday was not indeed to be a Sabbath; for that institution he (the Prophet) had no desire to imitate, but it was to correspond with the sacred week-day of the other communities, and since the Christians had seized the day after the Saturday, he had no choice but to take the day before it."[106] The origins of Friday service may be traced to the early problems of Islam. In the beginning, Muslims were few. They were advised to remain together, in groups, in company, and in prayer to have a feeling of the strength of unity. It was decided to call them all to pray together in congregation.[107]

The Azan

In the absence of a time-knowing device, like the clock, the worshippers used to assemble for prayer at different times resulting in much confusion. It was felt necessary to call the congregational prayer at one appointed time. How could this be done? It was suggested that a flag should be raised on a high place. People will see it, inform one another and assemble for prayer. But the Hazrat did not approve of it. It was then suggested that the Jewish trumpet or the Christian hammer may be employed for calling the people to prayer. This too was not appreciated. The Prophet did not want any similarity with Jewish or Christian practice. Besides, in every masjid, there would have been need to keep a horn for blowing. Umar saw in a dream the principle of azan or "call to prayer". It was also revealed to Abdullah bin Zaid. The Prophet asked his black slave Bilal to summon the worshippers to prayer. Bilal had a loud voice. He called from some eminence, such as the roof of a barn. It was in the second year of *hijr* that this practice became regular in Madinah and began to be regarded as an institution of Islam.

Once this institution was established, no exceptions were made. Those who heard the call were ordered to come to join the congregation on pain of having their houses burned down, no excuse being permitted.[108] A blind old man living far from the congregational mosque asked the Prophet for permission to absent himself as he was blind and old — he could not see and could hardly walk. The Prophet asked him if he could hear the azan. On being told he could, he was denied permission for absenting himself from the congregation.[109] The *ahadis* declare that namaz said in congregation is twenty-five times superior to namaz said alone at home. Muhammad was very strict about attendance in congregational prayer.[110] It was obligatory for every Muslim, with the exception of four — ghulam, woman, boy and the sick.[111] Muhammad was very particular about Muslims staying together and eating together like brothers.[112] He exhorted them to pray together lest the Mushriks should harm them.[113] It became incumbent on one momin to protect the life and property of another momin. If a non-Muslim harms a Muslim, the whole community should join together to save the latter from harm.[114] "Muhammad is the Apostle of Allah; and those who are with him are strong against Unbelievers, (but) compassionate amongst each other."[115] The unity among Muslims for which the community is famous, was thus established from the very birth of the creed.

Friday Namaz a must

The Friday congregation service posed some problems which, however, were satisfactorily solved. Abu Daud tells how order for bathing on Friday was issued. Early Muslims were poor. They used to wear blankets (of camel wool). They had to do lot of physical labour and sweated profusely. The masjid (in Madinah) was small with low ceiling. Once in summer season, the bad smell of perspiration reached the Rasul. He observed that when such a day arrives (i.e., Friday) take bath, use oil and perfume you have. In course of time Allah made them rich (through Jihad). They began to wear other clothes besides the blanket. Their burden was also lightened (as they began to take work from slaves and slave-girls) and mosques also became spacious. The odour which inconvenienced one another was gone. That is how bath became customary on Friday. Bath is considered good but not "obligatory".[116] But it is obligatory that the service should be performed in Arabic and that the clothes and body of the worshipper should be clean.[117]

The Prophet was a strict disciplinarian, and a watch was kept on the Faithful about the observance of namaz. One who neglected namaz for three Fridays without reason, was marked out by Allah.[118] Even children were to say namaz. For boys it began at the age of seven, at 10 they were to be beaten up if they avoided it.[119] When there was Jihad, namaz was to be said in parts and by rotation.[120] It was inculcated in the minds of the Musalmans that the difference between a Musalman and a Kafir is that of namaz. There is a vow of namaz among the Muslims. One who renounced it did *kufr*, did *shirk*.[121] So far as the congregational prayer was concerned, attendance was compulsory. Compulsion inculcated a sense of awe and raised the number of devotees. People "could refuse this invitation or call at their peril, spiritual and physical. As his followers became more powerful, the peril became increasingly more physical."[122]

As the strength of the worshippers increased it was felt necessary to manage the crowd by making them stand in rows of straight files. First a long stick was used to see that the *jamaat* stood in linear array. Later on a line was drawn for the same purpose.[123] Men and boys stood in front rows, women in the last.[124] Men stood as close to one another as possible lest Shaitan should pass between them or Allah sow discord among them.[125] No one was allowed to pass in front of the congregation during prayer. If one did, the order was to fight him. In the days of the Prophet, a man once happened to pass on a donkey in front of the namaz. His feet were cut off.[126] The namaz during the early period was performed in privacy. Afterwards it was employed as a sort of military drill. "Whatever may be its origin, it is evidently a military exercise, intended to train soldiers *(mujahidin)* for endurance... "[127] In the early years of Islam the main features of the Friday service were prayer in congregation with worshippers standing in straight linear rows. Attendance was compulsory and military discipline was maintained. The sermon was like the order of the day; it comprised advice, reprimand and directions on the religious and political obligations for the faithful. A sense of awe pervaded — raising the number of worshippers. The occupation of Makkah (8 H/630 CE) had sky-rocketted the prestige of Muhammad. It was the Quraish who had declared war on the Prophet and opposed him. When Makkah was occupied, the Quraish became his subjects. Since they could no longer display enmity towards him they entered into God's religion, coming to him from all directions.[128]

Congregational Prayer and Iconoclasm

The tradition of Friday congregational prayer was followed wherever the Muslims went. In India in the early eighth century, Muhammed bin Qasim established many mosques in towns he took in Sindh, like Debal, Alor, Nirun and Multan and propagated the Islamic faith. Besides, there were some mosques in Gujarat and on Malabar coast where there were settlements of Muslim merchants. The Quwwat-ul-Islam Masjid was the first congregational mosque built in Delhi after the conquest of Hindustan by the Muslims. It was built, as per Arabian tradition and command, from the materials obtained from the places of idols. In this case the Mosque was built from the debris of 27 Hindu and Jain temples as per an inscription found carved on it. It had been ordained in the Hadis to construct mosques at places where idols were, and the tradition was scrupulously followed in Arabia. At Taif, for example, a masjid was built where there were idols of Mushriks.[129] It is related in some Biographies of Muhammad that while the siege of Taif was being carried on, some companions were ordered to destroy every idol they could find. "Thereupon Ali, the Commander of the Faithful... destroyed all the idols of the Bani Hoazan and Bani Thaqyf which were in that region."[130] No count of temples is available in the sources. They must have been many. Similar was the fate of other temples. There were 360 idols at Kaba. They were all destroyed. Hubal, the principal idol in the Kaba, was pulled down and used as a doorstep when the Prophet conquered Makkah. Having purified Makkah, the Prophet sent expeditions to those idols which were around and had them destroyed. These included al-Uzza, al-Manat, Suwa, Buana and Zulkaffan.[131] When Islam arrived in India, both the practices were religiously followed — building mosques at the sites and with the debris of Hindu temples and using idols as steps leading into the mosque. Just as it was commanded to fight the non-Muslims till they recited the *Kalima*,[132] it was also commanded to "make your Masjids as tall and magnificent as Jews and Christians make their synagogues and churches."[133] The Quwwat-ul-Islam Mosque in Delhi was erected in this very spirit — as symbol of unity and strength of Islam as other mosques had been built earlier by the invader Mahmud of Ghazni at many places. The congregational mosques in particular also stood as a challenge and an invitation to the people to convert to the new creed.

For example, at Kalinjar in 1202, "The temples were converted into mosques," writes Hasan Nizami, "and the voices of the summoners to prayer ascended to the highest heavens, and the very name of idolatry was annihilated."[134] Call to prayer five times a day with a loud voice carried an invitation and a message — join us, or else. This helped in the conversion of people to Islam.

Mosques came up in large numbers in towns and cities and even in villages as the Muslim rule spread. In any place the main mosque was known as the Jama Masjid or Friday Congregational Mosque. The Quwwat-ul-Islam Mosque in Delhi, the symbol of strength of the newly established Islamic state in India, served as the congregational mosque.

It was extended by Sultans Iltutmish and Allaudin Khalji. Alauddin nearly doubled the size of this Masjid and built a magnificent gate to its entrance known as the Alai Darwaza. This indicates swift rise in Muslim population in the proximity of the mosque. As per tradition *madrasas* were located in the Friday mosques. Alauddin's *madrasa* or college lies immediately to the southwest of the Quwwat-ul-Islam Mosque. He constructed many other mosques as well as some masjids in his newly built city of Siri.

Of the mosques of Alauddin Khalji constructed outside the capital, mention may be made of the masjid at Mathura[135] and the tomb of Shaikh Farid (built C 1300), which was probably a converted Hindu or Jain temple. There is another masjid built about the same time in Bharuch. It is also a converted Jain temple. In 1300 Alp Khan, brother-in-law of Alauddin and governor of Gujarat, constructed the Adinah mosque at Patan. It was built of white marble, and it is related "that it was once an idol temple converted into a mosque". The Adinah mosque no longer exists. After the conquest of Chittor in 1303, Alladin "constructed a congregational mosque. There was a temple lying in ruins."[136] In Biana there is the Ukha mosque belonging to the Khalji period. Many mosques were built during Alauddin's invasion of the South. Farishtah claims that a mosque was built as far away as at Rameshwaram and called Masid-i-Alai and that it was in existence when Farishtah lived.[137] The above examples clearly show that as per the dictates of the Quran and the injunctions of the Hadis and the Sunnah, mosques in India too were built on the sites of the idol temples and with the materials obtained from razing the shrines. Muhammad bin Tughlaq built the Begumpuri Masjid at Jahanpanah. It is an imposing mosque of great size. Firoz's Kali Masjid or Kalan Masjid built by Khan-i-Jahan II in 789 H/1387 CE., stands intact till today near the Turkman Gate of old Delhi.[138]

Congregational Prayer in India

Five times a day namaz was performed by all Muslim kings, nobles and others. From the early days of Islam in Arabia there was insistence on compulsory namaz for all Muslims. Sultans Iltutmish and Balban said it and presided at Friday prayers. In his *wasaya* (precepts) Balban exhorted both his sons, princes Muhammad and Bughra Khan, that a king should not neglect the worship of God and five-time prayers should be offered punctually and in congregation. In his turn Bughra Khan told his son Kaiqubad that namaz and *roza* are very important. One who does not observe namaz is no Muslim; to kill him is justified.[139] All this refers to converted Indians who swelled the Muslim numbers since the days of Muhammad bin Qasim.[140] They were nominally converted as, for example, Barwaris whose leader Nasiruddin Khusrau Shah created *fitna* during and after the reign of Qutbuddin Mubarak Shah (1320 CE). It appears that they did not care to observe five-time namaz and were dubbed as low born. Muhammad Tughlaq kept a strict watch on their attending the Friday prayers. According to Ibn Battutah: "His standing orders were to the effect that prayers must be recited in congregations... even the menials — those who held the animals of the staff — were punished when they missed the prayers. The sultan issued orders that the people (newly converted) should learn the principles of ablution and prayers as well as the fundamentals of Islam, and they were interrogated on these... In the course of a single day he once killed nine persons for neglecting that (prayers)."[141] As for Muhammad Tughlaq himself "the mottos and emblems of Islam are preserved by him, and he lays great stress on the performance of (the obligatory five prayers of the day)."[142] All Muslim sultans and officers participated in Friday service, although this obvious fact may not have been mentioned by chroniclers about each and every member of the ruling class.

Some innovations were introduced by Firoz Shah in the Friday Service. The Sultan 'invented' the *Tas wa Gharial* or the Big Bell or Clock. It was fixed at the top of the Kushak-i-Firozabad and people were amazed to see it. When the bell was struck people came to know about the time of day and night. It guided the *namaziz* about the *zuhr* and '*asr* prayers and the *roza-dars* about the time of *iftar* and *sehri*. In a way it was against the dictates of Islam in which any Jewish or Christian practice was taboo, and striking the bell or gong for calling the people to prayer was Christian. Still, the azan as usual was continued to call people for prayer and the *Tas wa Gharial* had many other uses also — Afif recounts seven benefits of the contraption.[143]

After the Friday services, Firoz Shah used to repair to his palace where parties of musicians, athletes, wrestlers and story-tellers assembled in groups from the four parts of the city. Their number used to swell about two or three thousand. The king listened to music and witnessed the performance of the dancers. He watched the wrestling feats of the pugilists and listened to anecdotes of the story-tellers. He passed his time in these entertainments till the time of the *asr* prayer. Then performers were handsomely rewarded. Every one present received some award, including the children present on the occasion.[144] Shams Siraj Afif writes about mosques of Firoz Shah Tughlaq thus: "From the *qasba* of Inderpat (present Indraprastha Estate) to the Kushak-i-Shikar (present Delhi University area), five *kos* apart all the land was occupied... There were eight Public Mosques and one private mosque... The Public Mosques were each large enough to accommodate 10,000 suppliants."[145] This also shows how Muslim population had grown in the capital city in the course of a hundred and fifty years.

Needless to repeat that mosques, and in particular Friday mosques, continued to be built throughout the medieval period throughout the country. When Muslim provincial dynasties came up, mosques of large size and built with local materials came up in Sindh, Kashmir, Gujarat, Maharashtra, Malwa, Jaunpur and the Deccan kingdoms in Karnataka and Andhra Pradesh. In the Sultanate of Delhi, Sikandar Lodi was by far the greatest builder in the fifteenth century. A devout Musalman, he is said to have built mosques throughout his kingdom,[146] like in Lahore, Karnal, Hansi and Makanpur (district Kanpur), besides many others in Delhi and Agra.[147] His notable structures in Delhi are the Moth ki Masjid and the mosque attached to the Bara Gumbad. The Lodi rulers, indeed all Afghan ruling elite, observed the five-time *namaz* and presided over Friday service.

Protest against Iconoclasm

Mughal kings, queens, princes and princesses, all built congregational mosques in many important places in the country. Most of these were constructed at the sites of old Hindu temples. Muslim rulers made it a point to construct large congregational mosques and idgahs after destroying magnificent Hindu temples found in places held specially holy by the Hindus. The smaller temples were replaced by ordinary mosques. Consequently we shall also confine our examples to a few well-known temples which were razed or turned into mosques. Somnath, a very famous temple on the west coast, was sacked by Mahmud of Ghazni and several other Muslim kings. Babur built the Babri Masjid at Ayodhya on the temple site of the birthplace of Lord Ram (Ramjanambhumi). In the reign of Akbar, a mosque was built in 975 H/1567-68 CE at Jaunpur. It merits mention because the details of the undertaking show how the owner was dispossessed of his property and how the officer completing the task was rewarded. The mosque was built by Nawab Mohsin Khan. The materials for the mosque were "taken from those of the temple of Lachman Das, Diwan of Khan-i-Zaman Ali Quli Khan... Akbar made over all the property of the Diwan to Nawab Mohsin Khan," for "thanks that by guidance of the Everlasting and Living (Allah), this house of infidelity became the niche of prayer (i.e. Mosque). As a reward for that the generous Lord, constructed an abode for its builder in paradise."[148] Akbar took great interest in conserving, repairing and adding to the Dargah of Muinuddin Chishti at Ajmer which is also built on a Dev temple.[149]

Jahangir was not wanting in the performance of his duty in this regard while Shahjahan was quite zealous. Of course the puritanical Aurangzeb chose the most renowned sites of Hindu worship to construct congregational mosques — Ayodhya, Mathura and Banaras. Saqi Mustaad Khan, the author of *Maasir-i-Alamgiri* writes: "His majesty, eager to establish Islam, issued orders to the governors of all the provinces (imperial *farman* dated April 9, 1669) to demolish the schools and temples of the infidels and put down with the utmost urgency the teaching and the public practice of the religion of these misbelievers." Soon after "it was reported that, according to the Emperor's command his officers had demolished the temple of Vishwanath at Kashi". "The reviver of the faith of the prophet, issued orders for the demolition of the temple situated at Mathura, famous as the Dera of Kesho Rai. In a short time by the great exertions of his officers the destruction of this strong foundation of infidelity was accomplished, and on its site a lofty mosque was built at the expenditure of a large sum." "Praised be the august God of the faith of Islam that... such a wonderful and seemingly impossible work was successfully accomplished. On seeing the strength of the emperor's faith... the proud Rajas were stifled... the idols, large and small... were brought to Agra, and buried under the mosque of the Begum Sahib (Jahanara Begum), in order to be continually trodden upon. The name of Mathura was changed to Islamabad."[150]

Friday service is an article of faith with Muslims. It has three components — congregational namaz, sermon by the imam and, under Muslim rule, an ever rising number of *namazis*. Congregational mosques could be built without destroying Hindu temples. But in Islam, breaking the shrines of the people of other faiths is advocated by Hadis and Sunnah. Provocative acts of iconoclasm were therefore freely indulged in India without any regard to the feelings of the non-Muslims. Muslim chroniclers have written dozens of accounts about how Hindu temples and monasteries were razed to the ground and how images of Hindu gods and goddesses were destroyed or desecrated. Commandments of Allah (Quran) and precedents set by the Prophet (Sunnah) are frequently cited by them in support of what the Muslim warriors did both in times of war and of peace. But they do not mention Hindu response to such malevolent acts. Hindu Rajas were not stifled; Hindu resistance never slackened. They did react for years, for decades and for centuries, as best as they could, under the circumstances. We shall confine our notice to the only four renowned temples — Somnath, Ayodhya, Banaras, and Mathura — held specially sacred by the Hindus. The bitter memories of their destruction still linger in the Hindu mind.

Somnath was sacked by Mahmud of Ghazni in 1026 in the reign of Bhim Deva (1022-64 CE). It was rebuilt by Raja Kumarpala (1143-74). Gujarat was again invaded by a general of Alauddin Khalji in 1299, and the temple sacked again. The wealth of the temple was seized, its idol broken and carried to Delhi on bullock carts where it was thrown at the steps of the Congregational Mosque to be trampled under the feet of the faithful. After the destruction of the temple by Ulugh Khan in 1299, Chudasena, the Raja of Junagarh (1270-1333), again restored the edifice. In the middle of the nineteenth century it stood in a mutilated form, but "the whole of the buildings are most elaborately carved and ornamented with figures single and in groups of various dimensions."[151] This shows that it had a chequered history of destruction and restoration from the eleventh to the nineteenth century. After about a thousand years of its first destruction, it has been rebuilt for the seventh time as a magnificent temple dedicated to Lord Somnath in the middle of this twentieth century.

In 1528-29 Mir Baqi, a Mughal official, by Babur's orders destroyed the temple at Ayodhya commemorating Lord Rama's birthplace, built a mosque in its place as attested to by an inscription on it.[152] But the Hindus continued to struggle to reclaim it and worship there. Aurangzeb destroyed it once again when, writes Niccolao Manucci, "all of them (temples at Hardwar and Ayodhya) are thronged with worshippers, even those that are destroyed are still venerated by the Hindus and visited by the offering of alms."[153] Finally Hindus, working on the principle that "revenge is a kind of wild justice," have destroyed the Babri structure on December 6, 1992 and are striving to build the Ramjanambhumi temple at its original site.[154]

The desecration and conversion of the temple of Bir Singh Bundela at Mathura built at a cost of thirty-three lakh rupees sent a wave of consternation in the contemporary Hindu mind. The idol was removed by its priests and taken to Rajasthan. Maharana Raj Singh of Mewar installed it in a tiny village of Sihar on 10 March 1672.[155] Sihar has now grown into an important town, which named after the deity, is now known at Nathdwara. At Banaras the temple of Bisheshwar was built by Rani Ahilya Bai of Indore near the place of the one converted into a mosque by Aurangzeb. Maharana Ranjit Singh of Punjab mounted a gold plate on its *shikhara*. Marathas, Sikhs, Bundelas and Jats joined the crusade against the Mughals. Like Somnath and Ayodhya, Hindus want to get back the temple sites of Banaras and Mathura also. It is a struggle in contemporary Indian politics and therefore we shall stop here.[156]

In the capital of the empire, generally the emperor used to lead the Friday prayer as was done by Akbar in March 1579. Citing the authority of Faizi Sarhindi, Sri Ram Sharma says that while playing the role of the imam, Akbar was only following in the footsteps of his predecessors.[157] So also did his successors. Elsewhere in the empire governors, military commanders, qazis and other high officers led the Friday prayers in congregational mosques. Akbar's famous Mahzarnama or the Infallibility Decree was issued in such a congregational assembly between August and September 1579. His policy of *Sulehkul* too would have found a mention in the Friday *Khutbas*. Similarly, Aurangzeb's reversal of this policy would have found a reflection in the Friday sermons. That is how one Friday when he went to public prayer in the Jama Masjid of Delhi, a vast multitude of Hindus thronged the road from the palace to the mosque, with the object of seeking relief (from the Jiziyah). The protest was crushed, but the emperor also got perturbed and stopped going to lead the Friday prayer at the congregation mosque. He prayed in the small mosque of marble inside the Red Fort called Moti (Pearl) Masjid, built for his private service. However, as said earlier, little is known about Friday sermons in the medieval period. But if the Friday sermons in present times reflect the trend, it can be surmised that in the medieval period also references would have been made to day-to-day political and religious problem. It has been found that these sermons result in working up the feelings of the *namazis*, and sabre-rattling and street riots generally take place on Fridays after the afternoon prayer.

Friday Service and Growth of Muslim Population

As said earlier, Friday service added to the number of worshippers because of many reasons. The rise in the number of Muslims in medieval India has been dealt with by us in a separate monograph.[158] We have seen how in the reign of Firoz Tughlaq two congregational mosques in Delhi could accommodate 10,000 worshippers each. Such was the rapid growth of Muslim population during Muslim rule. A pronounced feature of Muslim chroniclers is a description of how the Hindus were converted by force, how Hindu temples and monasteries were razed or converted into Muslim places of prayer. Very often the unlettered Hindu worshippers continued their prayers at these very spots. But now they prayed as Muslims at places that were so sacred to them but which had been converted into mosques. Today the descendants of these converts insist on their separate and different identity. As I have said elsewhere,[159] no community, however newly born, however weakly consti-tuted it may be, exists without a moral power which animates and directs it. After the passing of a few generations, Indian Muslims have forgotten the circumstances of their conversion, and developed a sense of oneness amongst themselves. With time, they began to insist on being considered a distinct and separate entity in Indian society. On the other hand, the Hindus were so well organized in their social and religious life,[160] that a few conversions had not even made a dent in their social organization, and gradually they would have tended to become indifferent towards those who had become Muslamans. As the influence of the parent society on them declined and the influence of Muslim regime and religion increased, the Indian Muslims began to look more and more to Muslim ruling and privileged classes abroad for guidance, help and protection and in return gave them their unflinching cooperation. Much more important than the recession of Hindu moorings and the ascension of Muslim beliefs and culture in their life and thought, is the fact that these Muslims are governed by a new set of laws — the Shariat. They pray in a different fashion now, in congregation and several times a day. They marry amongst themselves. The magic word 'Islam' gives them a unity of thought, interest and action. Of the three components associated with congregational prayer, two still adversely contribute to the political scene in India — the problem of minorities and the unforgettable vandalism of Muslim iconoclasm.

IV
Income of the State

One of the main functions of the state was collection of taxes. No scheme of conquest or defence or administration was possible without regular inflow of revenue. Muslim jurists divide the revenue of a Muslim state into two categories — religious and secular. The principal religious tax was Zakat and it was collected from the Muslims only. The secular taxes comprised Khams, Jiziyah and Kharaj; these were levied on the non-Muslims. So these were four major taxes — Khams, Jiziyah, Kharaj and Zakat. Besides these there were a few other sources of revenue. The importance of sound state finance was widely recognized by Muslim political thinkers and administrators. The financial system of the Muslim state was laid down by the Shariat and the Abbasid tradition. By the time the Muslim state was established in India, its revenue system had been carefully elaborated and its principles clearly set.

4.1. KHAMS

We shall take up Khams first. For there was conquest before setting up of any government or administration. In the age of Islamic conquests, Jihad was the most flourishing industry, and Khams flowed as a reward of military victory. Khams as the word indicates, was one-fifth share of the Muslim state of the war-booty (*ghanima*) obtained in Jihad. The remaining four-fifths was distributed among the warriors. The *mal* obtained from Kafirs without engaging in war was called *fay*. The law of one-fifth (*khams*) did not apply to it. The whole benefit of it went to Muslims at large — the orphans, the poor, travellers etc. The special thing about Khams *is that it was obtained through war with Kafirs.*[1] Loot in war is common. It was common in the medieval period. What is special about Khams is that in Islam robbing of the infidel enjoys religious legitimacy. It was the command of God. Amir Timur in his *Mulfuzat-i-Timuri* declared: "Plunder in war is as lawful as mother's milk to a Musalman."

The early Arab Muslims belonged to the poor, economically 'scum' sections of the society. They had to be provided for. There were two ways of doing it. One was to urge the needy neo-Muslims to work hard and earn livelihood through honest means. The other was to prompt them to attack non-Muslims and rob them of their possessions, and distribute the same among the faithful. Muhammad took with him 315 men to the battle at Badr. They were on foot. They had no clothes and no food. He prayed to God to give them all these. God gave victory to Muslims. When they returned from Badr, there was no man who had not brought one or two camels. They got enough clothes and sufficient food.[2] Khams provided an easy way of financially benefiting both the poor Muslims and their rich masters.[3]

Rules about Khams were laid down after the Battle of Badr. The Prophet's army had collected a motley spoil from the enemy camp. A diversity of opinion arose about its distribution. The contention was so sharp that Muhammad interposed with a message from heaven, and assumed possession of the whole booty. "It was God who had given the victory; and to God the spoil belonged." Shortly afterwards, the following ordinance which the Muslim law of prize recognises to the present day was given forth: "And know that whatsoever thing you plunder, verily one-fifth thereof is for God and for the Prophet, and for him that is of kin (unto the Prophet), and for the orphans, and the poor and the wayfarer..."[4] The procedure about distribution followed was like this. After an expedition, Muhammad used to ask his slave Bilal to announce three times to the faithful to bring whatever they had obtained in *ghanaim*. People brought their booty and Muhammad distributed the loot among Muslims as per the one-fifth rule. While surrendering the gains, no stealing or perjury was allowed. The Rasul, Abu Bakr and Umar used to beat the men who did not truthfully disclose their gains and set fire to their goods. Even thread and needle was to be surrendered and no embezzlement was allowed. There was fire of hell for such culprits, say many *ahadis* of Bukhari. Sometimes Muhammad used to give something extra to a Mujahid beyond his share, but one who disappeared from the battle got nothing. According to Abu Daud, no share was fixed for women, *ghulams* or *bandis*, but they were given something if they happened to be present at the time of distribution.[5]

In accordance with the divine command, the booty was divided in equal allotments, among the whole army, after the Prophet's one-fifth had been set apart. Muhammad obtained the camel of Abu Jahl and also selected the sword by the name of Zulfiqar, beyond his share according to a custom which allowed him, in virtue of his prophetic dignity, whatever thing might please him most before division.[6] In short, in the early years of Islam, every believer was given a share in the booty accruing from new religious wars that were becoming the order of the day; they also had a share in the large revenues coming from a fast expanding Muslim empire. Every Arab was drafted as a soldier of Islam and his name was put on payroll. Umar regularized the system. Every Arab was a partner in the revenues derived from the loot and exploitation of the newly conquered lands — Muslim brotherhood in action. The scales were fixed according to one's nearness to the Prophet. The widows of Muhammad received an annual allowance of 10,000 dirhams each every year; the famous Three Hundred of the Battle of Badr had 5,000 dirhams each; those of the Pledge of the Tree, received 4,000 each; every one who had converted to Islam before the Battle of Badr got annually 4,000 each, and their children 2,000 dirhams a year, and so they graduated downwards to 200 dirhams. Wives, widows, and children had each their share. Every Muslim had a share in this classification. Officers of the Arab Occupation Armies in different cantonment areas of the empire received yearly from 6,000 to 9,000 dirhams; and every boy, as soon as born, received 100 dirhams each; every Muslim had the title to be entered on the payroll, with a minimum allowance of ten pieces, rising with advancing age to its proper place.[7]

These stipends were hereditary and they created a class of people who lived on the fat of the land they occupied. It laid the foundation of a thorough imperialism which was more durable than any other the world had known in the past.[8]

The legitimacy of loot and provision of a share to the warrior attracted many volunteers for Jihad. It also encouraged the soldiers to follow their leaders unitedly through thick and thin. It formed the very basis on which Muslim brotherhood had been organised from the very beginning. Besides the soldiers and the rulers, sultans and nobles, the saiyads, sufis, ulema, poets, mullahs, maulvis, muftis, imams, qazis and hajis, who had been at one time or the other the warriors of Islam or sycophants at the courts also lived lavishly on war booty dished out to them in the form of *inams*, pensions or *madad-i-maash*. All these sections in turn prompted their rulers to more and more Jihad to obtain more and more Khams.[9] As a Zimmi the Hindu soldier had no share in the booty as he could not wage Jihad. Hindu women and children similarly had no claim. But Hindu troops were also paid something "in order to encourage them to fight and inferiority of their station be rendered manifest to them."[10]

Khams in India

The Muslim rulers of Hindustan followed the tenets and traditions of Islam. The one-fifth share, called Khams, of the Ghanimah obtained as booty in their campaigns, and one or two articles specially selected by the Muslim ruler, were also continued to be regarded as the share of the sultans of India. The rest was distributed to the army. It is another matter that the sultans tried to appropriate much more than their share of Khams. Another rule which became the norm in India was the general disposal of the acquisitions in war. It was also set in Arabia after an attack on the Jews. The expedition was against the Jewish tribe, the Banu Quraizah, which was led by Muhammad. The Jews were besieged and later compelled to capitulate. "Their fate was left to the decision of the Prophet's companion, Sa'd, whose sentence was that the male captives should be slain, the female captives and children sold into slavery, and the spoils divided among the army. The Prophet commended the cruel judgement of Sa'd, as a decision according to the judgement of God..."[11] In most campaigns in Hindustan after victory the Muslim sultans or their commanders also used to slay male captives, and enslave women and children. And like in early Islam, the Muslim rulers in India used the wealth obtained in war and through other means to the best of their enjoyment. They created a ruling class which lived on the fat of the land it occupied. They milked the people thoroughly and laid the foundation of Islamic imperialism which more or less survived for a thousand years.

In Hindustan, the income from Khams was considerable. An idea of the profits can be had from the account of the Arab invasion of Sindh by al-Biladuri. According to him Muhammad bin Qasim had forwarded to Hajjaj 120 million dirhams which represented only one-fifth of the total loot (of 600 million) which was paid into the Caliph's treasury according to the rule of Khams.

Economic historians are prone to believe that Muslim invaders of India were motivated mainly by material gains and they were not enthused by political motives or with zeal to spread Islam. It must be remembered that in human mind or human society social, political, and religious affairs cannot be separated from one another. All act and react upon one another. In the history of Islam, the three are interrelated and cannot be divided into watertight compartments. Still let us see how economic denudation of India led to its people losing their status in society and drifting into lower classes and castes.

From the sack of Debal to the end of Muhammad Qasim's stay in Sindh, the invaders had gained 600 million dirhams in money[12] and thousands in slaves (especially women) and distributed them liberally among the Muslims from the Caliph to the common soldier.[13] The economic life of Sindh had got completely unhinged during his campaigns. A large number of people and merchants had fled "to Hind" and abroad.[14] Most others had been sucked dry. Such was the erosion of demography and prosperity that after the capture of Brahmanabad, "all people, the merchants, artisans and agriculturists were divided separately into their respective classes, and (only) ten thousand men, high and low, were counted. Muhammad Qasim then ordered twelve dirhams weight of silver (i.e., twelve silver coins or their equivalent) to be assigned to each man (for rehabilitation), because all their property had been plundered."[15] The Brahmans, "the attendants of the temples were likewise in distress. For fear of the (Muslim) army, the alms and bread were not regularly given to them, and therefore they were reduced to poverty."[16] From the destruction of Debal to the end of the campaign temples had been broken with the zeal of an iconoclast and their *purohits* and other dependents had no employment, no income. "It was ordained (by Qasim) that the Brahmans should, like beggars, take a copper basin in their hands, go to the doors of the houses, and take whatever grain or other thing that might be offered to them, so that they might not remain unprovided for."[17]

Mahmud Ghaznavi also collected lot of wealth from Khams. A few facts and figures may be given as illustrations. In his war against Jayapal (1001-02 CE) the latter had to pay a ransom of 2,50,000 dinars (gold coin) for securing release from captivity. Even the necklace of which he was relieved was estimated at 2,00,000 dinars "and twice that value was obtained from the necks of those of his relatives who were taken prisoners or slain..."[18] A couple of years later, all the wealth of Bhera, which was "as wealthy as imagination can conceive," was captured by the conqueror (1004-05 CE). In 1005-06 the people of Multan were forced to pay an indemnity of the value of 20,000,000 (royal) dirhams (silver coin). When Nawasa Shah, who had reconverted to Hinduism, was ousted (1007-08), the Sultan took possession of his treasures amounting to 400,000 dirhams. Shortly after, from the fort of Bhimnagar in Kangra, Mahmud seized coins of the value of 70,000,000 (Hindu Shahiya) dirhams and gold and silver ingots weighing some hundred maunds, jewellery and precious stones. There was also a collapsible house of silver, thirty yards in length and fifteen yards in breadth, and a canopy (*mandapika*) supported by two golden and two silver poles.[19] Such was the wealth obtained that it could not be shifted immediately, and Mahmud had to leave two of his "most confidential" chamberlains, Altuntash and Asightin, to look after its gradual transportation.[20] In the succeeding expeditions (1015-20) more and more wealth was drained out of the Punjab and other parts of India. Besides the treasures collected by Mahmud, his soldiers also looted independently. From Baran, Mahmud obtained, 1,000,000 dirhams and from Mahaban, a large booty. In the sack of Mathura five idols alone yielded 98,300 *misqals* (about 10 maunds) of gold.[21] The idols of silver numbered two hundred. Kanauj, Munj, Asni, Sharva and some other places yielded another 3,000,000 dirhams. We may skip over many other details and only mention that at Somnath his gains amounted to 20,000,000 dinars.[22] These figures are more or less authentic as Abu Nasr Muhammad Utbi, who mentions them, was the secretary to Sultan Mahmud, so that he enjoyed excellent opportunities of becoming fully conversant with the operations and gains of the conqueror.

Besides gold and silver, the Ghaznavids collected in loot and tribute and Khams, valuable articles of trade like indigo, fine muslins, embroidered silk, and cotton stuffs, and things prepared from the famous Indian steel, which have received praise at the hands of Utbi, Hasan Nizami, Alberuni and many others. For example, one valuable commodity taken from India was indigo. From Baihaqi, who writes the correct Indian word *nil* for the dyestuff, it appears that 20,000 *mans* (about 500 maunds) of indigo was taken to Ghazni every year. According to Baihaqi, Sultan Masud once sent 25,000 *mans* (about 600 maunds) of indigo to the Caliph at Baghdad for "the Sultans often reserved part of this (valuable commodity) for their own usage, and often sent it as part of presents for the Caliph or for other rulers."[23]

Khams was collected not only on wealth captured in war but on all items of loot like animals and humans. Khams on animals was fixed according to rules of barter and exchange. For example, in the early days of Islam, according to a *hadis*, twenty goats were considered to be equal to one camel.[24] Of the humans captured, the policy was to kill all males who could bear arms and capture their women and children as per the rule laid down in Quran and Hadis.[25] The non-combatant men were made slaves and put on sundry duties in the king's palace, distributed among the nobles or sold in the markets in India and abroad. Women and children were the prize of the warriors, and as early as the days of Qutbuddin Aibak "even a poor Muslim householder (who was also a soldier) became owner of numerous slaves."[26] One-fifth, and often more of this item, was the share of the state or the monarch.

Women as Khams

An important item of Khams was women. "An idea of the number of slaves flooding the Muslim empire as a result of conquest may be gained from such exaggerated figures as the following: Musa took 300,000 captives from North Africa, one-fifth of whom he forwarded to the Caliph, and from the Gothic nobility in Spain he captured 30,000 virgins; the captives of one Muslim general in Turkestan alone numbered 100,000."[27] In India from the days of Muhammad bin Qasim in the eighth century to those of Ahmad Shah Abdali in the eighteenth, enslavement, distribution and sale of Hindu women and children was systematically practised by Muslim invaders and rulers of India. A few lakh women were enslaved in the course of Arab invasion of Sindh. In the final stages of its conquest, "When the plunder and the prisoners of war were brought before Qasim... one-fifth of all the prisoners were chosen and set aside (to be sent to Caliph through his agent Hajjaj); they were counted as amounting to twenty thousand in number... (they belonged to high families) and veils were put on their faces, and the rest were given to the soldiers."[28] In Muhammad Ghauri's invasion of Gujarat 20,000 prisoners were captured and in 1202 at Kalinjar 50,000 *kaniz wa ghulam.*[29] Under the Khaljis and Tughlaqs thousands of non-Muslim women were captured in never-ceasing campaigns.

As per the Hadis virgins were to be preferred[30] but if a married woman with husband still alive was taken captive and introduced into the sultan's harem, conjugal felicity with her was permitted by law. One such case is that of Kamla Devi, the consort of Raja Karan Vaghela of Gujarat, who was captured by Alauddin Khalji's generals and introduced into his harem. Sexual relations with a married woman whose husband was living was taboo, but in an *ayat* received by the Prophet from Allah when women with husbands living are captured in war and "you are their master," it is allowed to have conjugal relations with them.[31] Throughout the medieval period in the North, South, East and West women-capturing or purchasing was a major pleasure activity of the ruling class.[32] No wonder that mainly through this activity 2,000 women were inducted into the harem of a nobleman (e.g. Khan Jahan Maqbul, Wazir of Firoz Shah Tughlaq), another 2,000 into the harem of a prince (e.g. Alam Shah, son of Aurangzeb), and 5,000 into that of a king (e.g. Jalaluddin Muhammad Akbar). One example of such activity may be given to end the unhappy story. In the time of Jahangir, his general Abdullah Khan Uzbeg destroyed, in the Kalpi-Kanauj area alone, all towns and took all their women and children as slaves. He once boasted: "I made prisoners of five lacs of men and women and sold them. They all became Muhammadans. From their progeny there will be crores by the day of judgement."[33] Kafir women had a special place in the Muslim psyche. Gloating over the pleasures of Paradise, Ibn Majah writes on the basis of appropriate *ahadis*, that a Jihadist will be married to seventy-two beauties in Paradise of whom two will be *hurs* and seventy Kafir women obtained in *miras*, transferred from hell for his pleasure's sake.[34]

Thus the glories of Kufa, of Baghdad and of Ghazni, the glories of the empires of Islam everywhere like in Agra, Lahore and Delhi, comprising of magnificent palaces, spacious audience halls adorned with costly rugs, silken curtains and embroidered cushions, with hundreds of young charming maidens with shoes studded with precious stones, dancing and gyrating in unison, thousands of slave girls running about at the bidding of their master, about which the Muslim historians, poets and minstrels sing ceaselessly, were gifts of Khams, the state's share of the loot and plunder of the infidels.

Wealth obtained through Khams

Alauddin Khalji wanted to keep his treasury full and people poor. He disliked people from growing opulent.

Therefore, he appropriated four-fifths of the spoil as Khams. This proportion seems to have become the norm till Firoz Tughlaq changed this 'illegal' practice, as he calls it, and reverted to the sanctioned one-fifth of the loot of soldiers as share for the state treasury.[35] Sometimes to enthuse the soldiers all the individual plunder from the rebels was left with them to enjoy.[36] But one-fifth was the norm as per the law. Since Khams brought lot of wealth to the government and the soldiers it made both of them greedy. This situation led to many embezzlements and mutinies. The Prophet had repeatedly commanded the Muslims in the Hadis not to hide any gains in war and to declare their personal loot honestly.[37] But human nature asserted itself against the Shariat's demand. Only one example of this would suffice. Gujarat was invaded by Khalji forces in 1299. The soldiers sacked dozens of towns and looted a number of monasteries, palaces and temples there. The social practice of the times and especially the use of various kinds of gold ornaments by the Hindu families had made gold a household commodity. The Arab traveller Abdurrazzaq who visited the Deccan in the fifteenth century writes that "all the inhabitants of the country, whether high or low, even down to the artificers of the bazars, wear jewels and gilt ornaments."[38] Farishtah also says that even the poor in the Deccan put on gold ornaments and the high class people used to eat in gold and silver plates.[39] This was about the time when people in the North had already been divested of much of their gold and silver by waves of invaders and dynasties of rulers. Still the old habits had continued. The people of Gujarat, a rich kingdom with a flourishing trade, were continually attacked and robbed. In the words of Abdullah Wassaf "the Muslim army plundered gold and silver to an extent greater than can be conceived, and an immense number of brilliant precious stones, such as pearls, diamonds, rubies, and emeralds, etc., as well as great variety of cloths, both silk and cotton, stamped, embroidered, and coloured. They (also) took captive a great number of handsome and elegant maidens, amounting to 20,000 and children of both the sexes, more than the pen can enumerate."[40] They also exacted immense booty in bullion, jewels, and other valuables from the merchants and other rich men of the port-town of Cambay or Khambhat. Besides, "each soldier had plundered sufficient wealth for himself."[41] In the course of the return journey dispute arose regarding the quantum of Khams and various kinds of brutal punishments were inflicted upon the soldiers to extort confession from them with regard to their individual gains. They wished to part with only one-fifth of their loot as required by the rules of Khams, but Alauddin's orders were for collecting four-fifths.

According to the contemporary chronicler Ziyauddin Barani, harsh enquiries were made about the amount and items of loot. The commanders did not believe in the version of the soldiers and wanted to take the best out of everything from the lashkar of gold, silver, and other precious articles. There were many ticklish technicalities involved in the search operation. The army comprised of many "Hindus, Muslims, Amirs, and neo-Muslims (Mongols)."[42] According to law there was no share in the loot for the Mushriks joining the Jihad.[43] Then, according to Isami, the soldiers besides plundering what they could lay their hands on, dug out and carried away treasures hidden underground by the Gujarat people.[44] Khams was due on it if it belonged to non-Muslims. In Gujarat, however, there were many rich Muslims who had their hidden treasures ransacked. Khams was also not due if the property belonged to a person who had been killed by a trooper. In such a case his whole belongings went to the killer; no Khams was due on it.[45]

The case of Gujarat shows how loot in war fed the greed of both the soldiers and the commanders of the king. Resistance of the soldiers sometimes took the form of rebellion. But during the whole of the Sultanate period of more than three centuries, immense wealth was gathered by Muslims through loot and Khams. Rizqullah narrates one incident which is worth reproducing. During Sher Shah's time Champaran in

Bihar was attacked by his commander. The kingdom had escaped Muslim visitation during the last two hundred years, and all the riches and treasures which were amassed during that period were now looted by Mian Husain Farmuli's men. "The shoes of the infidels who lost their lives in this action... when melted down no less than 20,000 *mohurs* of gold were obtained from them."[46]

Khams during the Mughal Period

During the Mughal period, the quantum of such gains increased because of their exceptional success in war. Babur's gains were immense. As will be seen later on he distributed huge amounts of these to his ladies, princes and Begs. And if Humayun was not successful in this regard, Sher Shah and his successors made up for the deficiency. Akbar was victorious in almost every campaign and the extent of his success determined the quantity of loot, tribute and Khams during his reign of half a century. It is not necessary to catalogue all the monetary gains of Akbar through war. An example alone may suffice to give an idea of the same. In 1564 Asaf Khan I, the governor of Kara under Akbar, invaded the kingdom of Gondwana of Rani Durgawati on behalf of the emperor. "When the fort (of Chauragarh) was taken there fell into the hands of Asaf Khan and his men an incalculable amount of gold and silver. There were coined and uncoined gold, decorated utensils, jewels, pearls, figures, pictures, jewelled and decorated idols, figures of animals made wholly of gold, and other rarities. The coin was said to include a hundred large pots full of the gold *ashrafis* of Alauddin Khalji."[47] If a small kingdoms like Gondwana could bring in so much wealth, how much more would have been collected in loot and Khams from larger kingdoms can only be imagined. But it is not possible to go into the gains from all the enterprises of Akbar and his successors.

Khams did not mean just material gain or loss in war.

It meant ruination of the country as a whole as vouched by the Muslim chroniclers themselves. We have seen how immense were the gains of Muhammad bin Qasim and Mahmud of Ghazni in their campaigns. And Alberuni who was eye-witness to Mahmud's exploits in India, writes: "*Mahmud utterly ruined the prosperity of the country* (emphasis ours)... The Hindus became like atoms of dust scattered in all directions. This is the reason, too, why Hindu sciences have retired far away (to Kashmir, Benaras and other places)... Their scattered remains cherish, of course, the most inveterate aversion towards all Muslims."[48] Abdullah Wassaf wrote about the exploits of Alauddin Khalji's generals in Gujarat campaign (1299) between March 1300 and 1310. He repeats in the beginning of the fourteenth century what Alberuni wrote in the beginning of the eleventh. "*The Muhammadan army brought the country to utter ruin and destroyed the lives of the inhabitants and plundered the cities, and captured their offspring...* (emphasis added)..."[49] Similar was the result of Asaf Khan's sack of Gondwana.[50] Collection of Kharaj was circumscribed by the fear of the peasantry abandoning cultivation if pressured too far. Collection of Jiziyah was possible only where non-Muslim residents were too weak to resist. The stream of income from Khams never got dry as there were always infidel lands to subjugate and destroy.

Destruction Wrought by the Islamic Way

In the seventeenth century Francois Bernier, the French physician-savant wrote that wherever Muslims went and ruled, ruin followed. In his time the "present condition of *Mesopotamia, Anatolia, Palestine,* the once wonderful place of *Antioch*, and so many other regions anciently well cultivated, fertile and populous, but (are) now desolate... Egypt also exhibits a sad picture..." So happened in India. About here, writing in the glorious days of Islamic Mughal rule, he says that "most towns in Hindustan are made up of earth, mud, and other wretched material; that there is no city or town (that) does not bear evident marks of approaching death."[51] Hindustan reverted to British and Hindu rule and was by and large saved. But the once wonders of Hindu and Buddhist regions which remained with Muslims or got demographically dominated by them like Afghanistan and Kashmir set upon a path of decline. Once upon a time Afghanistan was a great centre of Gandhara art and culture. The sculptural art of Gandhara, under Kushan dynastic patronage, created the Bamiyan colossi of the Buddha carved from the living rock by nameless Kushan sculptors. The famous Chinese traveller Hiuen Tsang, passing through Bamiyan, on his way to the court of Harshavardhan and the University of Nalanda in 629 CE praised it as a centre of art to which sculptors, architects and painters flocked. Bamiyan Buddha is the tallest statue in the world. There are (or rather were) many wonderful pieces of architecture and sculpture strewn all over Afghanistan. Here flourished poets like Ashvaghosh, physicians like Charak and philosophers like Nagarjun. Here flourished trade which provides wealth which in time pipelines facilities into all creative activity. The violence of Islam destroyed all this in Afghanistan in course of time. Today Afghanistan is being ruled by the Taliban in accordance with the Islamic Shariat. And the whole world knows how it is being ruled.

Kashmir too was a centre of Hindu and Buddhist art and learning in the ancient period. The background of Muslim penetration is given by Alberuni. He writes: "In former times, Khurasan, Persis, Iraq, Mogul, the country up to the frontier of Syria, was Buddhistic,[52] but then Zarathustra went forth from Adharbaijan and preached Magism in Balkh (Baktra)... both by force and by treatise... The succeeding kings made their religion (i.e. Zoroastrianism) the obligatory state-religion for Persis and Iraq. In consequence, the Buddhists were banished from those countries east of Balkh..." India, as far as known to Alberuni was Brahmanic, not Buddhistic."[53] "But then came Islam... Muslims began to make inroads into their (Hindus') country. Muhammad Ibn Elkasim Ibn Elmunabbih (Muhammad bin Qasim) entered India proper and penetrated even as far as Kanauj, marched through the country of Gandhara, and on his way back, through the confines of Kashmir... All these events planted a deeply rooted hatred in their (Hindus') hearts... Mahmud Ghaznavi utterly ruined the prosperity of the country." The process of ruination of Kashmir was continued. Kashmir was gradually bereft of this 'Science' as sultans like Sikandar Butshikan and sufis of his ilk began to Islamize the region. By Abul Fazl's time much of Hinduism was gone and a little of Buddhism remained. For writes he, "The third time that the writer accompanied His Majesty to the delightful valley of Kashmir, he met a few old men of this persuasion (Buddhism), but saw none among the learned [Brahmans?]."[54] Emperor Jahangir found near Srinagar only "the remains of a place of worship for recluses: cells cut of the rock and numerous caves."[55] Kashmir Valley is today experiencing the full blast of Islamic cultural tradition. But when all these regions were first sacked loot and Khams were the motives of attack. If Khams resulted in ruination, Jiziyah brought in both economic loss and moral as well as mental degradation to the victims.

4.2. JIZIYAH

The levying of Jiziyah on non-Muslims has been regarded by most of the Muslim jurists as an important duty of the Muslim state as it was believed to be one of the most lawful taxes. The Quran prescribes Jiziyah in a verse revealed in the context of Jihad. Translated in English it reads thus: "Fight against such of those who have been given the scripture as believe not in Allah nor the Last Day... and follow not the religion of truth, until they pay the tribute readily, being brought low."[56] The Quran recognizes only two communities, viz. Jews and Christians, as scriptuaries. According to Imam Malik, one of the four great jurists, the verse of the Jiziyah is applicable to all non-Muslims excepting apostates. Abu Hanifa applies it even to idolaters excepting the idolaters of Arabia. In brief Jiziyah is primarily a Jihadic impost, not a fiscal one, as sought usually to be made out. It is a penalty for *kufr*, and alternative to killing, plunder, enslavement, ransom, forcible conversion. It is a badge of humiliation for being a non-Muslim, of utter servility to Islamdom.[57]

Spirit of the Tax

According to the *Encyclopedia of Islam* the Muslim state was a theocracy in which the non-Muslims were given the status of Zimmis. "They are not citizens of the Muslim state but are suffered to live under certain disabilities." One of the chief disabilities was that "each adult, male, free, sane Zimmi must pay poll tax, Jaziyah".[58] T.P. Hughes writes: "Theoretically, the inhabitants, together with their wives and children are considered as plunder and property of the state, and it would be lawful to reduce them to slavery. In practice, however, the milder course prevails, and by paying the stipulated capitation-tax the subdued people become, in the quality of Zimmis, free subjects of the conquering power, whose condition is but little inferior to that of their Muslim fellow subjects."[59] Similar is the opinion of N.P. Aghnides, an authority on Muslim theory of finance. According to him, "In return for Jaziyah the Zimmi was entitled to protection for life and exemption from military service. The Jaziyah was levied as the cash equivalent to the assistance which they would be liable to give if they had not persisted in their unbelief, because living as they do in a Muslim state, they must be ready to defend it... Moreover, the main object in levying the tax is the subjection of the infidels to humiliations... and... during the process of payment, the Zimmi is seized by the collar and vigorously shaken and pulled about in order to show him his degradation."[60] In its essence thus, Jiziyah was not just a tax. It was an instrument of humiliation of the non-Muslim. Its spirit kept the non-Muslim reminded that he was an inferior citizen of the Muslim state. If he felt the burden too great he could convert to Islam. Jiziyah was thus an instrument of conversion also.

In short, Jiziyah originated as an offshoot of Jihad. Jihad is to be fought with all resources, lives, possessions and tongues. It is said to have four forms — Jihad by heart, Jihad by tongue, Jihad by hand and Jihad by the sword.[61] Jihad presupposes that the world is meant for and belongs to the Muslim to the exclusion of all others, and therefore the Muslims can indulge in virtual liquidation of Kafirs.[62] But an alternative was offered by Jiziyah. Akida was a Christian king of the city of Duma. He was caught alive in Jihad. Muhammad asked him to pay Jiziyah. He paid it but later (because of economic pressure) converted to Islam.[63] Jiziyah remained an instrument of conversion and exploitation throughout the history of Islam.

The Quran gives no guidance about the rate of Jiziyah. It was Umar, the second Caliph, who settled three grades of Jiziyah — for the rich, the middle class and the poor (who included cultivators and artisans). He also exempted women, children, beggars, insane, blind and monks from the payment of Jiziyah. Many *ahadis* describe the collection of Jiziyah, for example, from the Persian fire-worshippers.[64] Muhammad's *'wasiat'* gives the essence of Jiziyah. His command was: Do Jihad in the name of God and way of God and kill those who are Munkirs. Do not steal from *ghanimat*. From those who do not believe demand Jiziyah. If they refuse, fight them.[65]

A few things are obvious from the above discussion. Jiziyah is a Jihadist impost. It is penalty for *kufr*, an alternative to forcible conversion or killing. It was imposed to humiliate the non-Muslim and to keep him reminded of his inferior status (of Zimmi) in the Muslim state. From the statement of Qazi Mughisuddin in the fourteenth century to those of Mulla Ahmad, Shaikh Ahmad Sirhindi and Shah Walliullah in later centuries, the burden of their assertion is the same — Jiziyah is meant for the humiliation of the non-Muslims. Of course, it is based on Islamic scriptures, the Quran and Hadis, so that the statement of one is repeated by the others. Here are some examples. Questioned by Sultan Alauddin concerning the position of the Hindu as a Khirajguzar, the Qazi of Bayana expounded the injunction of the Faith thus: "By the ecclesiastical law the term Khirajguzar is applicable to a Hindu only, who as soon as the revenue collector demands the sum due from him, pays the same with meekness and humility, coupled with the utmost respect. God Almighty himself (in the Quran) declares with regard to their being subjected to degradation... and *thus he expressly commands their complete degradation* in as much as these Hindus are the deadliest foes of the true Prophet. *Mustafa*, on whom be peace, *has given orders regarding the slaying, plundering, and imprisoning of them*, ordaining that *they must either follow the true faith, or else be slain and imprisoned, and have all their wealth and property confiscated. With the exception of the Imam-i-Azam* (Abu Hanifa)... *we have no other great divine as authority for accepting the poll tax* (Jiziyah) *from a Hindu*; for the opinion of the other learned men is based on the *hadis* (Tradition) 'Either death or Islam'."[66]

According to Mulla Ahmad, "the main object of levying of Jiziyah on them (the Hindus) is their humiliation... God established (the custom of realising) Jiziyah for their dishonour. The object is their humiliation and the (establishment of) prestige and dignity of the Muslims."[67] Shaikh Ahmad Sirhindi (1564-1624), who proclaimed himself as Mujaddid-i-Alf Sani or Renovator of the Second Millennium of Islam, wrote many books and several letters to the courtiers of Akbar and Jahangir. In one such letter he wrote that "the honour of Islam lies in insulting *kufr* and *kafirs*. One who respects the *kafirs* dishonours the Muslims... The real purpose of levying the Jiziyah on them is to humiliate them to such an extent that they may not be able to dress well and to live in grandeur. They should remain terrified and trembling." So also said Shah Walliullah (1703-1762) and many other respected Muslim ulema and sufis.[68] Those who blame the ulema for the cruelty and orthodoxy of Muslim rulers should remember that it was not possible for the ulema and sufis to give wrong interpretation of the scriptures before autocrats. They interpreted correctly and rendered correct advice. Muslim religion and its tenets are responsible for an iniquitous tax like Jiziyah and not its advocacy by the ulema. The denial to the entire non-Muslim people of the basic human right of freedom and equality of every man is internalised with Jiziyah. Muslims never tire of harping on equality of man in Islam, but this claim is belied by Jiziyah. This also refutes the claim of modern Muslim apologists that the Muslim state in India was a secular state.

Jiziyah in India

Jiziyah was imposed in India from the day the Muslims set foot in the country. After capturing Brahmanabad, Muhammad bin Qasim levied Jiziyah on the population according to three grades. The first was to pay silver equal to 48 dirhams, the second 24 dirhams and the lowest 12 dirhams.[69] According to Farishtah the Hindu Shahiya king Jayapala, when defeated by Subuktigin, offered to pay Jiziyah and Kharaj to him. It was levied under the so-called Slave Kings, "but there seem good reasons to believe that the term Jiziyah was not used exclusively in the sense of a capitation tax," says Habibullah.[70]

Curiously enough, Barani himself on two occasions calls land revenue as Jiziyah.[71] The earliest imposition of the tax in its true sense was by Firoz Shah Khalji (1290-96).[72] In the time of Alauddin Khalji the conversation between Qazi Mughisuddin and the Sultan has been given above and is well-known. The Qazi emphasised that the Hindu is a Kharaji, that his degradation is necessary, that except for Abu Hanifa all other jurists say that the choice to be given to such idolaters is Islam or death. So far as Alauddin is concerned, independently of what Qazi Mughisuddin or Ziyauddin Barani advocated, he suppressed the Hindus to the utmost by collecting all legal (and some illegal) taxes from the Hindus, and earned the approbation of a visiting Maulana — Shamsuddin Turk. Jiziyah continued to be collected throughout the Sultanate period. In the reign of Firoz Tughlaq those who paid the Jiziyah were divided into three classes. The first had to pay 40 *tankahs*, the second 20 and the third 10. In his reign for the first time Jiziyah was imposed on the Brahmans also. The Brahmans represented that its incidence weighed heavily upon them. The Sultan lowered the rate for them, and they were assessed at ten *tankahs* and fifty *jitals* for each individual.[73] K.R. Qanungo and R.P. Tripathi write on the authority of Abbas Sarwani that Sher Shah collected the Jiziyah and the pilgrim tax. The collection seems to have been continued by Babur and Humayun. Writing about the abolition of Jiziyah by Akbar, Abul Fazl says that in spite of its unpopularity it was imposed by Akbar's predecessors who "were girded up for the contempt and destruction of the opposite factions". Akbar considered Jiziyah as the greatest hurdle in the way of Hindu-Muslim integration and so abolished it in 1564. This was done "in spite of disapproval of the statesmen and of the (loss of) great revenue, and of much chatter on the part of the ignorant."[74] Jahangir and Shahjahan continued the policy of Akbar. Akbar gave a common citizenship to all his subjects, Hindus and Muslims alike. For a hundred years after this step was taken, the Hindus felt that the Mughal empire was their own, but after about one century this feeling was once again shattered. Aurangzeb reimposed Jiziyah in 1679. His *Fatawa-i-Alamgiri* recognizes two systems of collection of this tax: (i) Lump sum payment of an agreed upon amount by the ruler of a territory or the people thereof and (ii) Payment by individual tax-payers of amounts individually assessed in territories directly under Muslim rulers, governors etc. Sri Ram Sharma reproduces Aurangzeb's order about the imposition and collection of Jiziyah dated 26th July, 1696. It says that "Jiziyah lapses on death and on acceptance of Islam". During the course of the year some people used to die and some used to convert, but the amount of Jiziyah for the place remained unaltered. In view of this the first type of payment was disadvantageous to Hindus. The last paragraph of the order reads: "The non-Muslim should himself bring the Jiziyah; if he sends it through his deputy it should not be accepted. At the time of payment the non-Muslim should keep standing, while the chief should keep sitting. The hand of the non-Muslim should be below and that of the chief above it and he should say. 'Make payment of Jiziyah, O! non-Muslim' and should not say, 'O! infidel'." Aurangzeb thus imposed it in the true spirit and letter of the tax.

Resentment against Jiziyah

Such a hateful tax in which insult was added to economic injury, was resented by the Hindus more than any other imposition. Originally, Jiziyah applied to non-Muslim scriptuaries like Jews and Christians. The bigoted and fanatically inclined jurists hold that the idolaters do not come within the purview of Jiziyah, and the only alternatives open for them are either conversion to Islam or death.[75] However, the Sunni jurists Abu Hanifa and his disciple Abu Yusuf permit its imposition on the non-Muslims even if they be idolaters.[76] India was inhabited by idolaters primarily. Application of Jiziyah to them was, in a way, a matter of kind concession, from the Muslim point of view. But the Hindus resented it throughout. They knew that it was meant to humble and humiliate them. When Firoz Tughlaq (1351-1388 CE) levied Jiziyah on the Brahmans, they represented to the Sultan that they had never before been asked to pay it and to put up with the indignity attached to it. The Sultan, writes Shams Siraj Afif, "convened a meeting of the learned Ulama and renowned Mashaikh and suggested to them that an error had been committed: the *Jiziyah* had never been levied from Brahmans; they had been held excused, in former reigns. The Brahmans were the very keys of the chamber of idolatry, and the infidels were dependent on them (***kalid-i-hujra-i-kufr und va kafiran bar ishan muataqid und***). They ought therefore to be taxed first. The learned lawyers opined that the Brahmans ought to be taxed. The Brahmans then assembled and went to the Sultan and represented that they had never before been called upon to pay the *Jiziyah*, and they wanted to know why they were now subjected to the indignity of having to pay it. They were determined to collect wood and to burn themselves under the walls of the palace rather than pay the tax. The Sultan replied that they might burn and destroy themselves at once for they would not escape from the payment. The Brahmans remained fasting for several days at the palace until they were on the point of death. The Hindus of the city then assembled and told the Brahmans that it was not right to kill themselves on account of the *Jiziyah*, and that they would undertake to pay it for them."[77]

The protest of the Brahmans did succeed in getting some concessions from the king. He fixed their Jiziyah at a low rate although in status they belonged to the upper class. Secondly, he permitted other Hindus (shopkeepers and traders) to pay the tax on their behalf. But Aurangzeb (1658-1707) was more adamant because he himself knew the law well. His imposition of the Jiziyah provoked repeated protests. "On the publication of this order (reimposing the *Jiziyah*) by Aurangzeb in 1679," writes Khafi Khan, "the Hindus all round Delhi assembled in vast numbers under the *jharokha* of the emperor to represent their inability to pay and pray for the recall of the edict... But the Emperor would not listen to their complaints." Thereupon the Hindus resorted to Satyagrah as it were. One Friday, when Aurangzeb went to public prayer in the great mosque, a vast multitude of the Hindus thronged the road from the palace to the mosque, with the object of seeking relief. "Money changers and drapers, all kinds of shopkeepers from the Urdu Bazar, mechanics, and workmen of all kinds, left off work and business and pressed into the way... Every moment the crowd increased, and the emperor's equippage was brought to a standstill. At length an order was given to bring out the elephants and direct them against the mob. Many fell trodden to death under the feet of elephants and horses. For some days the Hindus continued to assemble, in great numbers and complain, but at length they submitted to pay the Jiziyah." Abul Fazl Mamuri, who himself witnessed the scene, says that the protest continued for several days and many lost their lives fighting against the imposition. People's resentments against Aurangzeb was also expressed in incidents in which sticks were twice hurled at him and once he was attacked with bricks but escaped.[78] There were organized protests against Jiziyah in many other places like Malwa and Burhanpur. In fact it was a countrywide movement "and there was not a district where the people... and Muqaddams did not make disturbance and resistance."[79]

People's demonstrations apart, protests came from higher quarters as well. During the reign of the stern Sultan Alauddin Khalji, the Hindu chiefs and landlords often did not care for the summons of the Diwan and did not call at his office. They were in no way inclined to show an attitude of servility. They evaded to pay any of the prevalent taxes including the Jiziyah.[80] In Aurangzeb's time, this odious tax is said to have evoked a protest from Shivaji in his famous letter to Aurangzeb.[81] In this letter Shivaji urged the impolity of the impost and appealed to Aurangzeb to think of the common

Father of mankind and the equality of all human beings. A similar letter is said to have been written by Rana Raj Singh as well. These Rajas dealt with the emperor on their own level. Aurangzeb, on his part, became more stiff and made the collection obligatory. All this led to many awkward situations. On one occasion a Mansabdar killed the *amin* who had gone to collect Jiziyah. The only punishment that was meted out to the Mansabdar was that he was degraded. On another, in a rather comic incident, the beard and hair of an *amin* were pulled by the people who sent him back empty-handed.[82]

A tax which created so much agitation in the empire, was bound to create controversy and flutter in the court circles. References to the times of Khaljis and Tughlaqs point to an active role of the ulema in persuading the sultans to impose Jiziyah on the non-Muslims. For the reign of Aurangzeb the *Mirat-i-Ahmadi* suggests that the theologians as usual took the initiative in the matter. They represented to Aurangzeb the anomaly of the non-believers being exempted from the payment of the Jiziyah under a king of Aurangzeb's piety.[83] But the ulema had a say during the reigns of weak kings; Alauddin and Aurangzeb were not weak monarchs. The fact was that Jiziyah was a regular Islamic (Jihadic) tax. Its importance in a Muslim state was well-known. The problem was that the Hindus were in such a great majority in India that here some thought was necessary before insistence on its imposition. That is why there were many in the court and palace who thought preservation of peace to be better than the enforcement of an explosive religious regulation which hurt the feelings of the majority of the population. Niccalao Manucci writes[84] that some highly placed and important persons at court opposed the imposition of Jiziyah. Jahanara Begum Sahib, the elder sister of Aurangzeb, opposed it. There was an earthquake some time after and some of the courtiers are said to have once again urged the emperor to retrace his step. "All the high-placed and important men at the court opposed themselves to this measure. They besought the king most humbly to refrain..."[85] But to the imperial bigot Jiziyah was all important. Besides earning religious grace, he could also spread Islam through economic pressure.

Jiziyah as a Means of Spreading Islam

It was Aurangzeb's intention to use Jiziyah for spreading Muslim religion among his subjects. Many writers on medieval Indian history find in the conversion of many low caste Hindus to Islam a hand of the oppression of Hindu upper castes, or the Hindu caste system itself, and the attraction of the "democratic spirit of Islamic brotherhood and equality". The fact is that the Hindus shunned conversion. But many among the poor classes turned to Islam in order to escape the Jiziyah. It was imposed on all non-Muslims — rich as well as poor — and collected in a humiliating manner. The poor sections of Hindus who mostly came from low castes and who could not afford to pay became Musalmans to escape both the economic burden and insults of the collectors. This is borne out by the delight expressed by Sultan Firoz Shah Tughlaq who writes in his *Fatuhat-i-Firoz Shahi*: "I encouraged my infidel subjects to embrace the religion of the Prophet. I proclaimed that every one who repeated the creed and became Musalman should be exempted from the Jiziyah. A great number of Hindus presented themselves day by day from every quarter and adopting the faith were exonerated from the Jiziyah."[86] Similar was the achievement of many other Muslim rulers. Equally happy was Aurangzeb in his success in this area. As the contemporary European courtier Manucci observed, "Many Hindus who were unable to pay (Jiziyah) turned Muhammadan to obtain relief from the insults of the collectors... Aurangzeb rejoices."

Jiziyah was not a good or bad 'gesture' on the part of Aurangzeb. It was a regular and important Islamic tax.

The problem was that the Hindus had enjoyed relief from it for more than a hundred years and were not willing to live with this oppressive imposition once again. The contention of M. Mujeeb that it was levied for economic reasons does not make Jiziyah a secular tax. And the question arises: What were the economic difficulties of Muhammad bin Qasim in Sindh? To sum up: There is a tendency to plead that people voluntarily converted to Islam without any resort to force. It would be rewarding to estimate the numbers who converted only to escape from the payment of Jiziyah. With Aurangzeb the Mughal empire started on a course of decline and fall. It would be interesting to make a critical study of how far Jiziyah was responsible for the fall of the Mughal empire.

Revenue from Jiziyah

As mentioned in the beginning, Jiziyah in India was meant to be applied to the Hindus only. It was imposed on the Hindus from the beginning of the Muslim rule. Their numbers were so large that the income from Jiziyah was substantial. But beyond this no further information is available about the rates applied to various sections of the people and the amount of revenue collected. Shams Siraj Afif tells us that the rates during the reign of Firoz Shah Tughlaq were forty, twenty, and ten *tankahs* from the rich, middle and poor persons respectively.[87] Under Aurangzeb, the assessees were roughly divided into three classes according as their property was estimated at not more than 200 dirhams ("the poor") between 200 and ten thousand dirhams ("the middle class") and above ten thousand ("the rich").[88] Shroffs, jewellers, money-changers, clothiers, land-owners, merchants, and physicians were placed in the high class. Tailors, dyers, cobblers, shoemakers and artisans in a hundred other crafts were counted as poor. Other sections and vocational groups formed the middle class. Women, children below fourteen, and slaves were exempted. Blind men, cripples and lunatics paid only when they were wealthy. But what was the total amount collected is not known.

What is known, and that in a general way, is that it brought good amount of revenue into the royal exchequer. Abul Fazl, writing about its abolition in the reign of Akbar, says that crores of rupees were lost, although he gives no exact figures. The quantum of Jiziyah according to Jadunath Sarkar was 4.42 per cent of the provincial revenues. The *Mirat-i-Ahmadi* suggests that it was 4 per cent in the province of Gujarat. Surely, its incidence on the people was not inconsiderable. "In violation of modern canons of taxation the Jiziyah hit the poorest portion of the population hardest, and annually took away from the poor man the full value of one year's food... as the price of religious indulgence. The tax yielded a very large sum. In the province of Gujarat, for instance, it was 5 lakhs of Rupees a year...".[89] It has, however, to be admitted that we do not get satisfactory figures indicating the total amount of income from this source. Stray references that Gujarat yielded 500,000 rupees and Burhanpur about 850,000 rupees, do not provide sufficient data to warrant any definite conclusions, except that whenever it was collected it brought in handsome revenue. It was a good source of income to the Muslim state in India. However, the imposition of Jiziyah has not to be judged by the money it brought in. It is an indication of the nature of Muslim rule in India and an indictment of the apologists who claim that it was not only secular but also popular.

4.3. KHARAJ

Kharaj was the land tax. In an agricultural country like India, it comprised the major source of the revenue of the state. The early Muslim invaders like the Arabs in Sindh and Turks in Hindustan were mainly soldiers. They were busy in conquest. They had neither the time nor the inclination to introduce any changes in the Hindu agrarian system prevailing in India. For about a hundred years of Muslim rule (c. 1200-1300), the sultans appear to have continued with the prevailing land tax system.

Land tax in pre-Muslim India

It is difficult to assess exactly the portion of produce taken by the state during the Hindu period. The country was vast and divided into a number of states. There could not have been a uniform rate of tax or a uniform method of collection throughout the country. Modern research, however, has been able to give us a tolerably correct picture of the pre-Muslim times. In the early Hindu period the king charged 1/6 of the produce as land tax. The tax was not rigid but flexible. According to the Hindu theories of finance as expounded in the Smriti and Niti the state demand could vary from 1/12 to 1/6 of the produce. Kautilya advocates even 1/4 if there were irrigation facilities. The king was entitled to a tax as he protected the people. Thus it was not actually a tax but a wage (*vetana*) given to the king by the people for protecting them.[90] But even those who did not pay anything were equally entitled to protection.[91] One fact to be remembered in this connection is that in all Dharma Sutras great emphasis is laid on the duty of the king as a protector of the people.[92]

In later Hindu India, say between the death of Harshavardhan and the conquest of Muhammad Ghauri (c. 650-1200 CE), again the Hindu theories and practices of taxation continued to prevail. Medieval writers and commentators on Smriti and Niti like Medhatithi and Shukra, however, permit a higher portion of the produce as the share of the state. Shukra even permitted up to 50 per cent if the lands were irrigated by canals, tanks and wells.[93] Chandreshwar, another medieval writer, says that the king should only take such an amount as is necessary for the needs of the government and may not be felt oppressive by the subjects.[94] These figures and statements show that the incidence of taxation on the people seems to have grown with the passage of time, but 1/6 was the ideal and any divergence from it did not do credit to the ruler. Alberuni, who had made a thorough study of the conditions in India, also mentions 1/6 as the revenue of the state.[95]

The theoretical aspect apart, there are some definite data available about this period. Hiuen Tsang testifies to the low incidence of land tax in Harsha's time (d. 647).[96] The Rashtrakutas (750-1000 CE) who ruled over a major portion of the Deccan peninsula and whose sphere of influence extended into the Malwa country stretching up to Prayag (Allahabad) in the north, took about 20 percent of the gross produce on land.[97] This tax included the *uparikara* or *bhogkara* which may safely be identified with the *khuti* (or collection charges) under the Sultanate. A refreshing reference in this regard is that 15 per cent of this revenue was returned to the village for its own needs.[98] Writing about the Rashtrakutas, al-Idrisi (12th century) says that the "Kingdom is vast, well-peopled, commercial, and fertile. It pays heavy taxes so that the king is immensely rich."[99] It is not known whether al-Idrisi meant the land tax to be high or the customs duties, as then trade flourished well in the Deccan and we know from Ibn Battutah that duties in the first half of the fourteenth century were as high as 25 per cent of the commodity. Farther south, in the Chola kingdom, the land tax together with tolls and octrois was 4/15 or about 25 percent on the gross produce in Rajadhiraj's time(1035-1053 CE).[100]

The above discussion focuses on a few salient features of taxation in the Hindu period. The fundamental principle was that the royal revenues should be collected diligently and prudently but without harshness, protecting the people and their welfare in every possible way. In the ancient or Hindu period there is no mention of peasants forsaking cultivation, abandoning their fields and escaping into forests because of excessive taxation as became common during the medieval period. Nor is there any evidence of people being reduced to such straits as to sell themselves and their families into slavery as bonded labourers, a phenomenon which had become common under Muslim rule.

Kharaj under early Sultans

The early invaders and rulers like Muhammad Ghauri, Qutbuddin Aibak and Shamsuddin Iltutmish carried on with the prevailing system of taxation. Iltutmish, however, divided the newly conquered kingdom into *iqtas* and distributed most of them among his nobles and soldiers for their maintenance keeping some portion for his personal expenses and that of his harem.[101] At this stage of the history of the Sultanate much wealth was obtained through Khams or the state's share of war booty and tribute from vanquished princes, and there was hardly any financial problem.

Sultan Ghiyasuddin Balban (1246-66-86) was faced with the task of encountering Mongol invasions. This menace on the one hand put a check on his expansionist ambitions curtailing income from war booty, and on the other his expenditure on the army was considerably increased. Balban used to say that "I have devoted all the revenue of my kingdom to equip my army, and I hold my forces ready and prepared to receive the (the Mongols)."[102] Even then Balban did not feel the need to tax the peasants heavily. He followed a moderate policy regarding collection of land revenue. He ordered that "excessive (tax) should not be tried to be levied from obedient and submissive *raiyyat*... In collecting Kharaj, a middle course should be adopted. Neither should the demand be so high that the agriculturists should become paupers, nor should it be so little that because of their easy life born of prosperity, they become prone to recalcitrance and disobedience... The king felt that the army and the *raiyyat* should be placed on equal footing so that, year after year, with the salary of the one class and cultivation by the other, they could live with frugality and contentment."[103] The inference is difficult to resist that during the first hundred years of the Sultanate, "the Muslim was merely a tax receiver and took little direct part in the production and increase of the country's agricultural wealth."[104]

According to Muslim law land tax collected from Muslims was called Ushr and that collected from non-Muslim was Kharaj.[105] The rate of Ushr was 10 per cent of the produce and for Kharaj it was 20 per cent. However, we find very few recorded instances of Muslim cultivators. Kharaj could be raised up to 50 per cent.[106] Under Qutbuddin Aibak land tax was 20 per cent.[107] We have no figures for the reigns of Iltutmish and Balban, but taking into account the rates prevailing in the times of their predecessor Aibak (20 per cent) and successor Alauddin Khalji (50 per cent) it may safely be presumed that it was around 33 per cent in their reigns.

A Grinding Tax Structure

The Sultanate of Delhi had completed about a hundred years when Alauddin Khalji ascended the throne. His problems were many. Most parts of the country were independent. Hindu Rajas were powerful and unsubdued. Muslim nobles were rebellious. The Mongols were knocking at the gates of Hindustan time and again. Alauddin Khalji needed a large army to deal with these problems. To maintain a large army he needed money and so this Sultan raised the land tax (Kharaj) to fifty per cent. Under his predecessors, it does not seem to have been above one-third of the produce. Furthermore, under Alauddin's system all the land occupied by the rich and the poor "was brought under assessment at the uniform rate of fifty per cent". This measure automatically reduced the chiefs practically to the position of peasants. Since his aim was to strike at the major source of power, the wealth, of the Hindus,[108] he also levied many other taxes like house-tax and grazing tax. According to the contemporary chronicler Ziyauddin Barani, all milk-producing animals like cows and goats were taxed. According to Farishtah, animals up to two pairs of oxen, a pair of buffaloes and some cows and goats were exempted.[109] This concession was based on the principle of *nisab*, namely, of leaving some minimum capital to enable one to carry on with one's work.[110] But it was hardly any relief, for trustworthy persons informed the chronicler Shams Siraj Afif that in former reigns (obviously a reference to Alauddin's days) if an Amil left one cow with the peasant (*raiyyat*), another used to take possession of that also.[111] The payment of Kharaj, however, did not entitle the Hindu peasant to protection of the state. For protection and safety he had to pay an extra tax, Jiziyah, as we have seen before. So besides Kharaj, there were taxes like *kari*, (derived from Hindi word *kar*), *charai* and Jiziyah. Poll tax, tax on cattle etc. defy classification because they are entirely arbitrary.

Muslim jurists knew that if the collectors were not satisfactorily paid they would resort to corrupt practices. Therefore Islamic scriptures made a provision for a fair payment to them. As per the Hadis an Amil (collector) could obtain from the *bait-ul-mal* (treasury) expenses of one wife, one servant if he did not have one of his own and a house (if he did not already possess one). Besides this if he took anything more "it is theft, embezzlement."[112] But the Amils in Hindustan collected much more than was actually due. The land revenue system was exceedingly complex. There was no uniformity either in the period for which the tax was assessed or in the basis of assessment. The basis of assessment in some cases was the "total assets" of an estate; in others, it was the economic rent, the net produce etc. The local official was allowed considerable discretion. The rent was always enhanced. It was common for jagir owners to exact miscellaneous payments and services from the peasants.

In short, a substantial portion of the produce was taken

away by the government as taxes and the people were left with the bare minimum for sustenance. For the Sultan had "directed that only so much should be left to his subjects (*raiyyat*) as would maintain them from year to year... without admitting of their storing up or having articles in excess". It is from this point of time that the Indian peasant was made to maintain himself and his family from one harvest to the next. In the coming years and centuries, there is repeated mention in the chronicles about the rulers' directives to protect the peasant from undue exactions which seems to have become the common practice. Sultan Alauddin's rigorous measures were taken note of by contemporary writers both in India and abroad. In India contemporary writers like Barani, Isami and Amir Khusrau were inclined to believe him to be a persecutor of the Hindus. Foreigners also gathered the same impression. Maulana Shamsuddin Turk, a divine from Egypt, was happy to learn that Alauddin had made the wretchedness and misery of the Hindus so great and had reduced them to such a despicable condition "that the Hindu women and children went out begging at the doors of the Musalmans."[113] The same impression is betrayed in the writings of Isami and Wassaf.[114] While summing up the achievements of Alauddin Khalji, the contemporary chronicler Barani mentions, with due emphasis, that by the last decade of his reign the submission and obedience of the Hindus had become an established fact. Such a submission on the part of the Hindus "has neither been seen before nor will be witnessed hereafter". In brief, not only the Hindu Zamindars, who had been accustomed to a life of comfort and dignity, were reduced to a deplorable position, but the Hindus in general were impoverished to such an extent that there was no sign of gold or silver left in their houses, and the wives of Khuts and Muqaddams (Zamindars) used to seek sundry jobs in the houses of the Musalmans, work there and receive wages.[115] The poor peasants (*balahars*) suffered the most. The fundamentalist Maulana Ziyauddin Barani feels jubilant at the suppression of the Hindus, and writes at length about the utter helplessness to which the peasantry had been reduced because the Sultan had left to them bare sustenance and had taken away every thing else in Kharaj (land revenue) and other taxes.[116]

But there was much greater oppression implicit in this measure. It was difficult to collect in full so many and such heavy taxes. "One of the standing evils in the revenue collection consisted of defective realization which usually left large balances,"[117] and unrealised balances used to become inevitable. Besides, lower revenue officials were corrupt and extortionate. To overcome these problems, Sultan Alauddin created a new Ministry called the Diwan-i-Mustakhraj. The Mustakhraj was entrusted with the work of inquiring into the revenue arrears, and realizing them.[118] We shall discuss about the tyranny of this department a little later; suffice it here to say that in Alauddin's time, besides being oppressed by such a grinding tax-structure, the peasant was compelled to sell every maund of his surplus grain at government controlled rates for replenishing royal grain stores which the Sultan had ordered to be built in connection with his Market Control.[119]

The contemporary chronicler Ziyauddin Barani writes that Alauddin Khalji was an ill-tempered and tyrannical king. He had no learning and he did not associate with the ulema. Sultan Balban respected the ulema and used to consult them often. After returning from Bengal he went to their houses personally and informed them of his success.[120] Firoz Tughlaq also used to visit them in their houses. But Alauddin Khalji did not associate with the clerics.[121] When necessary, he consulted with his nobles but not with the ulema.[122] Barani wrote in old age. Though his memory remained unimpaired, a little confusion with regard to chronology in his narrative was natural in advanced age. Alauddin's three most trusted nobles and counsellers, namely, Nusrat Khan, Zafar Khan and Ulugh Khan had died by 1301, while his draconian measures, euphemistically called "reforms" were brought into operation mainly between the siege of Ranthambhor and expedition to Chittor (1301-1303).[123] Therefore, he surely deliberated with the ulema in matters of law. A few scholars like Qazi Ziyauddin of Bayana, Maulana Zahir Lang and Maulana Mushayyad Kuhrami were nominated to be present at dinner time. Qazi Mughisuddin of Bayana also used to come occasionally.

During the days when taxes were being assessed and collected with great strictness. Alauddin once inquired of Qazi Mughisuddin about the status of the Hindus in a Muslim state, whether they were Kharaj-*guzar* of Kharaj-*deh, payers* or *givers* of Kharaj. The Qazi expositioned their legal status thus: "By the ecclesiastical law the term Kharajguzar is applicable to a Hindu only, who as soon as the revenue collector demands the sum due from him, pays the same with meekness and humility, coupled with the utmost respect... and should the collector choose to spit into his mouth, opens the same without hesitation, so that the official may spit into it. The purpose of this extreme humility on his part and the collector's spitting into his mouth, is to show the extreme subservience incumbent on this class, the glory of Islam and the orthodox Faith, and the degradation of the false religion.[124] God Almighty himself (in the Quran) expressly commands their complete degradation, in as much as these Hindus are the deadliest foes of the true Prophet. Mustafa, on whom be peace, has given orders regarding the slaying, plundering, and imprisoning of them, ordaining that they must either follow the true faith, or else be slain or imprisoned and have all their wealth and property confiscated. With the exception of the Imam-i-Azam (Abu Hanifa)... we have no other great divine authority for accepting the poll tax (Jiziyah) from a Hindu; for the opinion of the other learned men is based on the *hadis* 'Either death or Islam'."

Kharaj was originally applied to a land tax or tribute realised from non-Muslim tribes.[125] After the defeat of Jews at Khaibar (628 CE) they became "the first Zimmis, or members of a subject caste, whose lives were to be guaranteed, but whose earnings were to support the Believers."[126] These Jews were the first Kharajguzars in Islam. Later on Kharajguzars were found in whatever countries the arms of Islam conquered. The Kharajguzars were Zimmis who had submitted to absolute obedience to the Islamic state. As non-Muslims they were Kafirs who could not be accorded any rights. But as Kharajguzars they were/are granted some minimal rights solely in view of their accepting and submitting themselves to the suzerainty of Islam. Thus Qazi Mughisuddin described the status of Kharajguzars fairly correctly.[127]

This exposition of the Quranic injunctions happened to square so much with the steps which the Sultan had already taken, albeit totally in ignorance of the law, that he burst out into a laughter of approval of the Qazi's views and informed him with great gusto that "I have established laws... so that under the fears of my command they would all escape into a mouse hole; and now you tell me that it is inculcated in the Divine law that the Hindus should be made obedient and submissive in the extreme... Rest assured, that the Hindu will never be submissive and obedient to the Musalmans until he becomes destitute and impoverished..." So, as mentioned before, the Sultan made them destitute. Destitute to the extent that the peasants sometimes paid Kharaj by selling their wives and children.[128] It is one thing to raise taxes and be happy. But to gloat over the impoverishment of the Hindus, both by the kings and chroniclers, is because of the ideology which advocates degradation of non-Muslims. Barani is the first and probably the only Muslim chronicler in the fourteenth century to mention the sale of families for defraying land tax. As we shall see, in later centuries foreign travellers were so shocked at this inhuman cruelty that they mention the fact repeatedly. The sale of peasants meant that they were reduced to the position of bonded labourers as slaves for life. When they were free (whatever the extent of their freedom), the government got 50 to 75 per cent of their produce. When they became bonded labourers the sultan got cent per cent of the produce earned by their exertions. Of course some coarse grain was given to them to keep them alive to continue to work in the fields.

After Alauddin's death (CE 1316) most of his measures seem to have fallen into disuse, but the peasants got no relief, because Ghiyasuddin Tughlaq who came to the throne four years later (CE 1320) continued the atrocious practice of Alauddin. He also ordered that "there should be left only so much to the Hindus that neither, on the one hand, they should become arrogant on account of their wealth, nor, on the other, desert their lands in despair".[129] In the time of Muhammad bin Tughlaq even this latter fear turned out to be true. The Sultan's enhancement of taxation went even beyond the lower limits of "bare subsistence". For the people left their fields and fled. This enraged the Sultan and he hunted them down like wild beasts.[130] Still conditions did not become unbearable all at once.

The reign of Muhammad bin Tughlaq started off well so far as the collection of Kharaj was concerned. The contemporary chronicler writes with satisfaction that Kharaj of far-flung regions like Gujarat, Malwa, Devagiri, Telang, Kampila, Dwarsamudra, Malabar, Tirhut, Lakhnauti, Satgaon, Sunargaon was collected with as much ease as that of Doab and brought (after deduction) to the treasury located in Hazar Situn in Delhi. The *walis*, *iqtadars* and administrators were kept under strict watch so that they collected the Kharaj from Rais and Raigans in full. The officers and retainers of the latter were treated with rigour and not a *kouri* or dirham was condoned. In three or four years, however, the situation changed because of the dislike of the people for the Sultan so that except Devagiri and Gujarat no other region remained under full control. Kharaj could not be realised in full. There was rebellion everywhere. This was due mainly to the enhancement of Kharaj in the Doab to ten or twenty times, which obviously means 10 or 20 per cent. Production and realisation went down. The rich became recalcitrant and the poor became destitute. People of other regions, fearing the fate of Doab people, fled and hid themselves in the jungles.[131]

It is difficult to surmise if the condition of the peasants was better or worse when the ruler at the centre was strong or weak. Under strong kings like Alauddin Khalji and Muhammad bin Tughlaq, the people of course suffered. But their condition was no better, say, under the weak Saiyyads (C. 1400-1450) when revenue was regularly or irregularly collected through military expeditions.[132]

Kharaj under the Mughals

If Sher Shah was "considerate" to the agriculturists, Babur and Humayun, could give little time and attention to agrarian and fiscal matters. Like Alauddin Khalji in the Sultanate period, Akbar was the first Mughal emperor to introduce novel principles and improved practices in land revenue administration. During his fifty years of reign a number of measures were adopted from time to time. Some important ones were Todar Mall's settlement of Gujarat which was later extended to most of Northern India, the introduction of the institution of Karoris — the principles of ten years settlement, classification of lands (into *polaj, parauti, chachar, banjar*) for assessment of revenue and so on — but that was to get maximum from the peasantry. For in the Mughal period the condition of the peasantry became more and more miserable; if there was any progress it was in the enhancement of taxation. According to W.H. Moreland, who has made a special study of the agrarian system of Mughal India, the basic object of the Mughal administration was to obtain the revenue on an ever-ascending scale. The share that could be taken out of the peasant's produce without destroying his chances of survival was probably a matter of common knowledge in each locality. In Akbar's time, in Kashmir, the state demand was one-third, but in reality it came to two-thirds.[133] The Jagirdars in Thatta (Sindh) did not take more than half. In Gujarat, according to Geleysen who wrote in 1629, the peasant was made to part with three-quarters of his harvest. Similar is the testimony of De Laet, Fryer and Van Twist.[134] During Akbar's reign, says Abul Fazl, evil hearted officers because of sheer greed, used to proceed to villages and *mahals* and sack them.[135] But they alone were not to blame. The policy of the government was to exact land tax in full whatever the circumstances. There were no remittances, no concessions. For example, "When either from excessive rain or through an inundation, the land falls out of cultivation the husbandmen are, at first, in considerable distress. In the first year, therefore, but two-fifth of the produce is taken: in the second three-fifth; in the third, four-fifth and in the fifth, the ordinary revenue. According to difference of situation, the revenue is paid either in money or in kind. In the third year the charges of 5 per cent and one *dam* for each bigha are added."[136] Tables of various harvests in provinces meticulously prepared by Abul Fazl confirm his above statement. The burden of arrears went on multiplying and the peasant was crushed under it. Conditions became intolerable by the time of Shahjahan when, according to Manucci, peasants were compelled to sell their women and children to meet the revenue demand.[137] Manrique (1628-43) writes that the peasants were "carried off... to various markets and fairs, (to be sold) with their poor unhappy wives behind them carrying their small children all crying and lamenting..."[138] Bernier too affirms that the unfortunate peasants who were incapable of discharging the demands of their rapacious lords, were bereft of their children, who were carried away as slaves.[139] Here was also confirmation of the practice of bonded labour in India.

Collection of Kharaj was accomplished through many

other objectionable methods, some leading to great suffering to the people. From the allotment of Jagirs to *ijaradars* to the actual collection of taxes it is an unmitigated story of sordid corruption and tyranny for which both the tax collector and the king were equally responsible. Manucci describes the process thus: "When any hungry wretch takes it into his head to ruin the kingdom, he goes to the king and says to him: 'Sire; if your majesty will give me the permission to raise money and a certain number of armed men, I will pay so many millions. The king then asks how it is intended to raise the money. It is by nothing else than the seizure of everybody in the kingdom, men and women, and by dint of torture compelling them to pay what is demanded. Such financiers are hateful and avaricious men. The king generally consents to their unjust proposals, as he thereby satisfies his own greed; he accords the asked-for permission, and demands security bonds."[140] Elsewhere Manucci adds that "If the tax contractor pays twenty-five thousand rupees to the crown, he must have at least recovered one hundred thousand. They always keep back three-fourths for themselves and pay in one-fourth only to the royal treasury."[141]

On the allotment or transference of a jagir on the above lines, the allottee officer carried the royal *farman* to assume his charge. The *farman* bore the royal seal with the counter mark of the chief Wazir,[142] but by the time of Aurangzeb such *farmans* appear to have lost authority. For, when the allottee carried the letter of conferment, he was not given charge of the jagir until and unless a present or bribe was given to one already in possession of the land. Needless to say that the giver of the bribe collected the amount from the cultivator in course of time. As has been well said, the essence of imperialism is exploitation. It protects vested interests. The only interest that it does not protect is that of the masses, of the peasantry and the workers. To protect them can only mean to protect them against exploitation.

Imperialism, of which the essence is exploitation, cannot afford such protection.

The great lords and petty contractors (*iqtadars*, *jagirdars*, *faujdars*, and *ijaradars*) collected the land revenue through their retainers. These retainers or troopers were hired by the nobles for a temporary period and were known as *sih-bandis* (or irregular levy) under the Mughals.[143] They were not considered eligible for musters and were generally regarded with some contempt when compared with the regular soldiers or *tabinan*. These quasi-troops behaved like modern *dadas* employed by their dons and they went to any length in perpetrating atrocities on the peasants and the common people. They entered the houses of the ryots and in many cases occupied them. Often through them girls of the family were abducted and forcibly married to their masters. This marriage also entitled the master to inherit the property and thereafter he cultivated (another man's) land on his own behalf. Their cruelties were a common knowledge. Even the royal scribe Jahangir describes this process in *Tarikh-i-Salim Shahi*.[144] On accession to the throne emperor Jahangir promulgated his famous twelve ordinances. One of these said that a government collector or Jagirdar should not without permission intermarry with the people of the *pargana* in which he might be; that the Jagirdars should not forcibly take the ryot's lands and cultivate them on their own account and that they should not take possession of any one's house.[145] In candid language girls of the ryots were non-chalantly abducted mainly through the exertions of hired retainers. This was also possible because the Jagirdar sometimes paid his own soldiers and retainers by allotting them a share of his revenue. In a note in the English translation done by Henry Elliot, he says that "these perpetual repetitions of the same edicts shows either the very weak authority of the original promulgators or the vain-glory of their descendents, in assuming to themselves credit to which they were not entitled."[146] For as Manucci observed, the king knew how the money was intended to be raised. The retainers or *sih-bandis* were employed with his knowledge and permission, and the collection helped satisfy the king's own greed.

4.4. ZAKAT

Zakat or "*Zakah*" or alms tax can be defined as that portion of a man's wealth which is designated for the poor. The term is derived from the Arabic verbal root meaning "to increase", "to purify" and "to bless". It finds its origin in Allah's command to "take *sadaqah* (charity) from their property in order to purify and sanctify them (at-Taubah:103)... In this *ayat* "Purify means to purify them from stinginess, greed, and meanness... As an obligation upon Muslims, *zakah* is one of the essential requirements of Islam. If somebody disputed its obligation, he would be outside of Islam, and could legally be killed for his unbelief unless he was a new Muslim and could be excused for his ignorance." And as is usual in injunctions of the Quran and Hadis, there is a threat held out to those who refrain from paying Zakat. Both Bukhari and Muslim relate from Abu Hurairah that the messenger of Allah said: "No owner of a treasure who does not pay *zakah* will be spared, for his treasure will be heated in the Fires of Hell and then made into plates. His flanks and his forehead will be branded with them until Allah pronounces judgement on His servants during a day lasting fifty thousand years."[147]

In short, Zakat is a religious tax levied on the Muslims. By paying Zakat and thereby sharing his property with the needy a Muslim purifies himself of avarice. Generally speaking Zakat amounted to one-fortieth or two-and-half per cent of the property. But since it is an act of piety to pay Zakat, and since it is based on a clear injunction of the Quran, it must be realized by the imam. In fact it is the ruler's duty to take Zakat from the defaulter and rebuke him if he refrains from payment. Zakat is not levied on primary necessities of life like dwelling houses, clothes, utensils, slaves and animals used for ploughing or riding.[148] It is charged only on "apparent property" such as gold and silver, herds and merchandise, and only when such property exceeds a certain taxable minimum (*nisab*).

There are three conditions which qualify a man to pay Zakat. First, he must have reason and maturity, for there can be no responsibility without them. Second, he must live in Dar-ul-Islam, because the payment of Zakat is an act of worship and as such it can be rightly performed by Muslims only. Third, he must be a freeman, because a slave is not supposed to own property.[149] These conditions exempt infants, non-Muslims, lunatics, slaves and even debtors, that is, insolvent persons, from payment of Zakat tax.[150] The Zakat on the apparent property was collected by the state according to the fixed rate, but the Zakat on non-apparent property was given to the beneficiaries directly by the property owner according to his own discretion and judgement.[151] As explained in the article in the *Arab Times* referred to above, "Zakah must be paid by every Muslim who has a *nisab*, which is the minimum of one's holdings liable to *zakah*." *The nisab is conditioned by the following*:

1) *Zakah* should be paid on any amount of money remaining after meeting the expenses for such necessities as food, clothes, housing, vehicles and craft machines.

2) A complete year of Islamic calender should pass, starting from the very day of the *nisab's* possession, without any decrease during the year. In case of its decrease (being less than *nisab*), the year count (*hawl*) starts from the day of the *nisab* to completion.

Commenting on the issue, an-Nawawi said: "In our view and the views of Malik, Ahmad and the majority of scholars, the amount of property liable for payment of *zakah*, such as gold, silver, or cattle, is tied to the completion of *nisab* through the turn of a whole year. If the *nisab* decreases in any time of the year, (the counting of) the year discontinues."

Zakat was perhaps the most difficult to assess and

still more difficult to realize. It was levied on "apparent property". Now, we know that in the medieval times people used to hide their possessions lest the sultan should come to know of their wealth. Zakat could not be realized forcibly since "compulsion vitiates its character". Again, it could only be applied to a property held in possession by the owner for at least one year.[152] If a person just to avoid payment transferred his taxable property to someone else including his own wife, even a day before the date of payment, he escaped from paying.[153] On the other hand pious Muslims sometimes paid Zakat in advance for two or three years.

The Muslim jurists divide the revenue of a Muslim state into two categories — secular and religious. The secular taxes, consisting mainly of Khams, Kharaj, and Jiziyah were levied on non-Muslims.[154] The religious tax was Zakat levied on Muslims. In India it seems to have been shared by Hindus also as it included customs duties. The revenue derived from Zakat was expended for charitable purposes and the other taxes were earmarked mostly to satisfy secular demands.

There is a desire to equate Zakat with Jiziyah to emphasise the fairness of the Islamic fiscal system. The Muslims pay Zakat and the non-Muslims Jiziyah. But the analogy is fallacious. The rate of Zakat tax is as low as 2½ per cent and that on the apparent property only. All kinds of concessions are given in Zakat with regard to *nisab* or taxable minimum. In its collection no force is applied because force vitiates its character. On the other hand the rate of Jiziyah is very high for the non-Muslims — 48, 24 and 12 silver *tankahs* for the rich, the middling and the poor, whatever the currency and whichever the country. Besides, what is central to Jiziyah is the humiliation of infidel always, particularly at the time of collection. What is central in Zakat is that it is voluntary; at least it cannot be collected by force.

In India Zakat ceased to be a religious tax imposed only on the Muslims. Here Zakat was levied in the shape of customs duties on merchandise and grazing fee on all milk-producing animals or those which went to pasture, and was realized both from Muslims and non-Muslims. According to the Islamic law, "import duties for Muslims were 5 per cent and for non-Muslims 10 percent of the commodity." For, Abu Hanifa, whose Sunni school of law prevailed in India, would tax the merchandise of the Zimmis as imposts at double the Zakat fixed for Muslims.[155]

Mushroom Levies

Besides the four regular taxes, there were various kinds of local imposts levied. Alauddin Khalji imposed house tax and grazing tax (*ghari* and *charai*). He also levied a tax on all milk producing animals. These and many others like tax on selling flowers, on betel leaves, octroi duty on sale of grain and pottery, stall tax (*tah bazari*), tax on gambling, amusements and dancing girls mentioned by Afif continued till the time of Firoz Tughlaq. They were collected in the capital city and some other important cities. Firoz Tughlaq ordered their abolition in 777 H/1375 CE as they were considered to be not in accordance with the Shariat. This resulted in a loss of 30 lakh *tankahs* annually,[156] which shows that income from such imposts was not inconsiderable.

Such imposts, however, used to grow like mushroom; these were regularly pruned but also regularly collected from time to time so that with Jiziyah and Pilgrim Tax, Akbar also abolished duties on *gao-shumari* (each head of oxen), *sar-i-darakhti* (on each tree), *peshwar* (vocational tax on artificers), darogha's fees, tehsildar's fees, treasurer's fees, lodging charges, *hasil bazar* (market duties) and many more. These imposts were "equal in amount to the income of Hindustan."[157] So also did Jahangir. He also issued instructions forbidding levy of many such cesses. He writes in his memoirs that he prohibited collection of imposts "under the names of *tamgha* and *mir bahri* (river tolls), and other burdens, which the jagirdars of every province and district had imposed for their own profit."[158] Similarly a *farman* of Aurangzeb preserved in *Mirat-i-Ahmadi* "directed the jagirdars of the province of Gujarat not to realise cesses such as *rahdari, mahi, mallahi, tarkari, tah bazari,* etc., which had been abolished, from traders and merchants."[159] "Zekhaut, Sermohary and Tumgha had yielded to Akbar sixteen hundred Hindustani *manns* of gold, equal to sixteen thousand *manns* of Iraq," says Jahangir at another place.[160] These imposts brought profit to local officials if they did not always add revenue to the royal exchequer.

The discrimination and humiliation for non-Muslims in the Muslim state was not confined to the collection of Kharaj or other major taxes only. It extended to *tamgha* or customs duties also. These levies on Hindus used to be high, on Muslims often reduced or wholly rescinded. The government was unduly keen to exempt Muslims from the levy. Prior to the Battle of Khanua against Rana Sanga, Babur abolished "throughout all the territories" the customs duties or *tamgha* on Musalmans — though its yield was large and though it had been established and maintained by former rulers. "For it is a practice outside the edicts of the Prince of Apostles (Muhammad)."[161] Naturally in an Islamic state Muslims were treated with special favour. For Jahangir writes: "As I had remitted in my dominions customs duties amounting to krors, I abolished also all the transit dues (*sair-jihat*) in Kabul. From the provinces of Kabul and Qandahar large sums used to be derived every year from customs (*zakat*), which were in fact the chief revenue of those places. I remitted these ancient dues, a proceeding that greatly benefited the people of Iran and Turan."[162]

Jahangir also writes, "I had done away with the whole of the customs dues and charges of Kabul, and whichever of my descendants and successors should do anything contrary to this would be involved in the wrath and displeasure of God. Up to the time of my accession these were fixed and settled, and every year they took large sums on this account from the servants of God (the Muhammadan people in general). The abolition of this oppression was brought about during my reign."[163] Similarly, customs duties at Cambay were abolished. The Royal scribe writes that "in the time of the Sultans of Gujarat the customs of this part came to a large sum. Now in my reign it is ordered that they should not take more than one in forty," i.e. 2½ per cent. In other parts they collected 10 to 16 per cent. "In Jeddah, which is the port of Mecca, they take one in four (25 per cent) or even more." Jahangir claims to have "the grace to remit the whole of the customs dues of his dominions, which came to a countless sum, and the very name of customs (*tamgha*) has passed away from my empire."[164] But all this was Jahangir's wish and his good intentions. The customs duties were collected by officers who were corrupt and unrelenting. In fact, customs duties were also a source of oppression and exaction. Still as Edward Terry notes, the customs duties were "not high, that strangers of all nations" may have greater encouragement to trade with the Mughals.[165]

In conclusion a few points may be noted about the tax system in the Muslim state. Of the four major taxes sanctioned by Canon Law, viz. — Zakat, Khams, Jiziyah and Kharaj, only Zakat was obligatory on Muslims, while the other three were due from non-Muslims. The rate of Zakat was light. It was just two-and-a-half per cent or one-fortieth of taxable property. Besides, force could not be used in the collection of Zakat. On the other hand, in the collection of the other three major taxes taken from non-Muslims force was freely used. Medieval chronicles are replete with stories of oppression and torture in the collection of taxes from non-Muslims realised through war and terror. The Muslim state was run on the dictates of Islamic scriptures. Their main plank was discrimination between Muslims and others. In matters of taxes all concessions were given to the Muslims and all strictness and humiliation extended to the non-Muslims.

4.5. OTHER SOURCES OF INCOME

Taxes were collected from the people. From defeated Rajas and Zamindars huge amounts were extorted as war indemnities. When the capital city of a Raja or any other important city of his kingdom was attacked, the people were robbed, the temple treasures were raffled and the Rajas fleeced. Full advantage was taken of their helpless state. The wealth collected from these sources filled the treasuries of the sultans and badshahs. Punjab and Gujarat had surrendered wealth and treasure on many occasions to Mahmud Ghaznavi, Qutbuddin Aibak and Shamsuddin Iltutmish. But Alauddin Khalji's coffers overflowed with the wealth obtained from defeated princes. Before attacking Devagiri in 1296, Alauddin, as yet a prince, had learnt during his raid on Vidisha that Raja Ram Chandra of Devagir had inherited a huge treasure accumulated by his ancestors.[166] Marco Polo describing the treasures of the South says that "when the king dies none of his children dares to touch his treasures. For they say, 'as our father did gather together all his treasure, so we ought to accumulate as much in our turn'. And in this way it comes to pass that there is an immensity of treasure accumulated in this kingdom (Maabar)." The Venetian traveller describes at length the jewellery the king wore about his person as well as the ways in which they used to obtain "very fine and great pearls". The king desires to reserve all pearls for himself "and so in fact the quantity he has is something almost incredible."[167] About the Vijayanagar kingdom Abdurrazaq says that "In the king's treasury there are chambers with excavations in them, filled with molten gold, forming one mass."[168] Thus, the treasuries of the Deccan kingdoms were full of precious metals and precious stones. Ram Chandra was defeated in a surprise attack, and Alauddin collected from him "six hundred *man* of gold (a *man* was equal to 14 the then *ser*), seven *man* of pearls, two *man* of precious stones like rubies, sapphires, diamonds and emeralds, one thousand *man* of silver and four thousand pieces of silk and sundry articles the details of which are beyond computation". This detailed account is given by Farishtah; he is indirectly supported by the contemporary writers Barani and Amir Khusrau. Barani says that Alauddin brought so much money from the Deccan that despite the squandering of it by his successors much of it remained till the time of Firoz Tughlaq.[169] It is said that the wealth turned his head and he began to conceive of "absurdities and impossibilities", but in the end settled on furthering his conquests. Through these his treasuries got filled with gold to such an extent that his coins became standard currency even for future. After about a century, the invader Timur demanded from the Raja of Jammu a hundred thousand gold *tankahs* (*asharfis*) of Alauddin.[170] In Akbar's reign, when Asaf Khan attacked Gondwana, he lay hold on a hundred large pots full of the *asharfis* of Alauddin. His silver coin has been found in far-off Nepal.[171]

In the Warangal campaign (1310), its Raja Pratap Rudra Deva finding himself helpless consented to the terms of the treaty forced upon him and surrendered all the treasures which had been accumulated during the course of many generations. According to Barani, Pratap Rudra Deva gave 100 elephants (Farishtah has 300 elephants), 7,000 horses and many precious articles and promised to send an equal amount of tribute in future years. Among the precious stones which the Raja surrendered was the famous Koh-i-Nur, which according to many writers, including Khafi Khan, was brought by Malik Kafur from the Deccan.[172] During the Dwarsamudra expedition, Alauddin's general Malik Kafur's gains consisted of 512 elephants (Barani has 612), 5,000 horses of various breeds like Arabi, Yamani and Syrian, and 500 *mans* of jewellery of every description (Barani has 20,000 horses and 96,000 *mans* of gold).[173] In another expedition against the Kakatiya king, Pratap Rudra Deva, promised to give to Khusrau Khan, the commander of

Qutbuddin Mubarak Khalji, a large sum and tribute comprising of 100 elephants, 12,000 horses, gold, jewels and gems beyond compute.[174]

Dowries

Akin to the gains through expeditions, were dowries collected during marriages of relatives of defeated Rajas with the victorious king or his son. Dowry is a word of the English language, *qarardad* is Persian and *jahez* (corrupted as *dahej*) is Arabic. There is perhaps no Hindi or Sanskrit word for dowry. But it was and is an established custom to give good amount of money to a girl at the time of her marriage. Although dowry is not a must in Islam, the marriages of the daughters of the vanquished rulers would have brought lot of wealth into the palaces of the sultans and badshahs who entered into innumerable matrimonial alliances. It would be euphemistic to term the Muslim royalty and nobility in India as polygamous. "Polygamy" does not convey the idea of the large number — one to two thousand, even more — of women which was the norm of a harem in medieval India. The medieval Muslim view was that a large and magnificent harem would inspire awe and respect for the king and enhance his prestige in the minds of the people.[175] In pre-Mughal Hindustan a large harem was the trend of the times and emperor Akbar followed the fashion. "His majesty," writes Abul Fazl, "forms matrimonial alliances with princes of Hindustan and of other countries, and secures by these ties of harmony the peace of the world." Whether peace was actually achieved or bitter memories survived, is beside the point. What is important is that Akbar had 5,000 women in his harem, many of whom were actually married to him. They all brought impressive dowries. For instance, Raja Bihari Mal "made the arrangements for the marriage of his elder daughter to the Mughal emperor Akbar in the most admirable manner and gave substantial dowry."[176]

Each matrimonial contract brought a lot of wealth. Each Rajput princess brought a lot of dowry. The marriage settlement of Man Bai, the daughter of Raja Bhagwan Das, with Prince Salim was fixed at two *krors* of *tankahs*. "The dowry bestowed by Bhagwan Das, included a hundred elephants, several strings of horses, jewels, numerous and diverse golden vessels set with precious stones, utensils of gold and silver, 'and all sorts of stuffs, the quantity of which is beyond computation'. The imperial nobles were presented with Persian, Turkish and Arabian horses, with golden saddles, etc. Along with the bride were given a number of male and female slaves, of Indian, Abyssinian and Circassian origin."[177] A hundred years later , the amount paid by Raja Ajit Singh in the marriage of his daughter with Farrukh Siyar amounted to a *kror* of rupees because when Ajit Singh took her back to Jodhpur after Farrukh Siyar's death, she carried "with her all her jewels and valuables, amounting to a *kror* of rupees in value."[178] Rajput princes vied with one another in providing rich dowries to their relatives married in the Mughal house. Muslim rulers and nobles seeking alliance with Mughal royalty too gave rich and handsome treasures in the form of gifts in gold and jewels and pearls. These marriages thus were a source of economic gain to the emperor and the empire, and wealth of many kingdoms, provinces and individual rulers used to be sucked into the imperial treasury because of the harem system.

Soldiers' loot, tributes and dowries brought in treasures directly and in bulk. In short, India's vastness rendered waging of warfare a perennial phenomenon and in consequence enrichment of Muslim rulers through Khams, and imposed terms of treaties. By the time of Jahangir the coffers of the Mughals were bursting with wealth, precious metals and precious stones so that every other day emperor Jahangir was distributing awards and rewards to his nobles. This information is contained on almost every page of his memoirs. On the other hand, the resources of the Rajputs, who were at the receiving end, had gone on dwindling proportionately. Jahangir himself recounts the straits of the Mewar royal house and other royal houses who were sometimes forced to sell their heirlooms to meet financial stringency. Emperor Jahangir writes that "on the first day he paid his respects he (prince Khurram) laid before me a celebrated ruby of the Rana, which... he had made an offering of to my son, and which the jewellers valued at 60,000 rupees... it was formerly in the possession of Ray Maldeo (Rathore)... his son Chandar Sen, who, in the days of his wretchedness and hopelessness, sold it to Ray Uday Singh. From him it went to Rana Pratap, and afterwards to this Rana Amar Singh. *As they had no more valuable gift in their family*, he presented it on the day that he paid his respects to my fortunate son Baba Khurram, *together with his whole stud of elephants...*"(italics added). Interestingly enough, the rich gifts Jahangir bestowed on Mahabat Khan and the Persian ambassador Mustafa Beg are recorded by him on these very pages.[179]

4.6. TRADE IN SLAVES

In addition to the gains through loot, tribute and dowries obtained during wars, the Muslim state in India found and created many other sources of income like state trading, collection of octrois on sale and purchase of commodities by private traders, transit duties on movements of goods on land and rivers and many other cesses collected centrally or locally. Besides levying taxes on the grains, cloths, articles of food and medicine, slaves, horses and camels and other animals, the royalty and nobility itself traded in these articles.

In the categories of articles in which the regime carried on trade, the sale of slaves may be taken up first. For, the early Muslim invaders and rulers captured slaves in large numbers and sold them in India and abroad and made considerable profit. From the day India became a target of Muslim invaders its people began to be enslaved. Many of them were sold to make a profit. Muslim rulers were no different from Muslim invaders so far as the capturing and selling of slaves was concerned. Slaves was the first commodity Muslims found in India to make profit by sale. The Arab invader of Sindh Muhammad bin Qasim sent to the Khalifa Walid I, his (one-fifth) share of captives of both sexes. The latter sold many of them and distributed the others among his officers.[180] Mahmud Ghaznavi took captive men and women in all his campaigns in India. He took 50,000 slaves in one campaign, 53,000 in another and 200,000 in a third one. He sold them for two to three dirhams (silver coin) each in the slave markets of Ghazni, Khurasan and other places. All the proceeds from such sales were deposited in the Amir's treasury. Under Aibak, Iltutmish, and Balban the captives were sold after every campaign. For example, when Muhammad Ghauri and Qutbuddin Aibak mounted a combined attack on the Salt Range, a large number of captives were taken "so that five Hindu (Khokhar) slaves could be bought for a *dinar*."[181] Many more were also sold in "Khurasan, not long after".[182]

Slavery in Islam was institutionalised from the very beginning. Ibn Ishaq mentions a transaction of the Prophet which set a precedent for Islamic slave trade later on: "Then the apostle sent Sa'd b. Zayd al-Ansari... with some of the captive women of B. Qurayza to Najd and he sold them for horses and weapons."[183] The women had been made captive after their menfolk had been slaughtered en masse in the market place at Medina. Thereafter there was no let up in the policy of slave-taking by the Muslims. Minhaj Siraj writes that "Ulugh Khan Balban's taking of captives, and his capture of the dependents of the great Ranas cannot be recounted". Such was the scale of slave-taking by Muslims in Hindustan that information about it travelled abroad, so that Wassaf writes that in the sack of Somnath in 1299 the Muslim army "took captive a great number of handsome and elegant maidens, amounting to 20,000 and children of both sexes".

Like Wassaf, Shihabuddin Ahmad Abbas also did not visit India but he was informed about the exploits of Muhammad Tughlaq in this field as Wassaf was for Alauddin Khalji. At home Amir Khusrau, the sufi poet, writes in his *Nuh Sipehr* that "the Turks, whenever they please, can seize them, buy them and sell them at will... The Hindu happens to be a (wretched) slave in all respects."[184]

The sale price of slaves in the fourteenth century was like this. The standard price of a working girl was fixed at from 5 to 12 *tankahs*, and that of a good looking girl suitable for concubinage from 20 to 30 and even 40 *tankahs*. The price of a man slave (*ghulam*) usually did not exceed 100 to 200 *tankahs*. The prices of handsome boys were fixed from 20 to 30 *tankahs*; the ill-favoured could be obtained for 7 to 8. The price of a child slave (*ghulam bachchgan naukari*) was fixed at 70 to 80 *tankahs*. The slaves were classified according to their looks and working capacity. In the case of bulk purchases by traders who had ready money and who had the means to carry their flock for sale to other cities,[185] prices were fixed accordingly.

No rules about the sale price could be laid in special cases where the catch was big or a very beautiful slave ("man or woman/boy or girl") of very high price, say, 1,000 to 2,000 *tankahs* was brought for sale in the market. Even then slaves were sometimes purchased for high amounts. The poet Badr Chach claims to have bought a slave named Gul-Chehra (Rose Face) for 900 *tankahs*. The title Hazardinari (of a thousand gold coins) for Malik Kafur shows that a skilled slave could have cost anything. It may therefore be contended that except in the reign of Alauddin when prices were fixed, prices of slaves and concubines were uncertain, varying according to fortunes of war and famine, looks of the person, bargaining talent of the auctioneer, shrewdness of the buyer and fluctuations in the market through influences of demand and supply.

Writing about the days of Sultan Muhammad bin Tughlaq

(1325-51), Shihabuddin al-Umari writes: "The sultan never ceases to show the greatest zeal in making war upon the infidels... Every day thousands of slaves are sold at a very low price, so great is the number of prisoners....(that) the value at Delhi of a young slave girl, for domestic service, does not exceed eight *tankahs*. Those who are deemed fit to fill the parts of domestic and concubine sell for about fifteen *tankahs*. In other cities prices are still lower..." Probably it was so because Ibn Battutah while in Bengal says that a pretty *kaniz* (slave girl) could be had there for one gold dinar (or 10 silver *tankahs*). "I purchased at this price a very beautiful slave girl whose name was Ashura. A friend of mine also bought a young slave named Lulu for two gold coins." It is very difficult to establish a relationship between the prices of Delhi market and those of the provinces. Umari continues, "but still, in spite of low prices of slaves, 20000 *tankahs*, and even more, are paid for young Indian girls. I inquired the reason... and was told that these young girls are remarkable for their beauty, and the grace of their manners."[186] All evidence point to the fact that it was the Muslim ruler who profited from the sale of these slaves. Isami in his *Futuh-us-Salatin* states that when Mahmud of Ghazni defeated Raja Jayapala of the Hindu Shahiya dynasty, he "carried him to the distant part of the kingdom of Ghazni and delivered him to an agent (*dalal*) of the slave market... (and) at the command of the king Mahmud they (the Brokers of the Market, *Muqiman-i-Bazar* in the original) sold Jayapal as a slave for 80 *dinars* and deposited the money realised by the sale in the Treasury." Hodivala adds that "it would be difficult to get better evidence than this of the ruler making the profit."[187]

From the fifteenth century onwards, we have some more information about the sale of slaves at home and abroad. Zahiruddin Muhammad Babur writes in his memoirs that "there are two trade marts on the land route between Hindustan and Khurasan; one is Kabul, the other, Qandhar... from Hindustan, come every year caravans... bringing slaves (*barda*) and other commodities, and sell them at great profit..." The Mughal emperor Akbar disapproved of the custom of enslaving women and children in times of war.[188] He also prohibited enslavement and sale of women and children of the peasants who had defaulted in the payment of revenue. He knew, as Abul Fazl says, that many evil hearted and vicious men used to proceed to villages and *mahals* and sack them. According to W.H. Moreland, "It became a fashion to raid a village or group of villages without any obvious justification and carry off the inhabitants as slaves." In short, there was never an abjuration of the policy of enslavement as mainly it was not the Mughal emperors but the Mughal nobility who must have taken the lion's share of enslavement, deportation and sale by the state. It was not only Jahangir, a comparatively kind-hearted emperor, who used to capture poor people during his hunting expeditions and send them to Kabul in exchange for dogs and horses; all Muslim rulers and governors collected slaves and exploited them in the manner they pleased. In any case, warfare went on as usual even under Akbar and Jahangir and Mughal Generals went on with their usual ways. Abdulla Khan Uzbeg's force destroyed in the Kalpi-Kanauj area alone, all towns, took all their goods, their wives and children as slaves. No wonder he once boasted that "I made prisoners of five lacs of men and women and sold them. They all became Muhammadans. From their progeny there will be crores by the day of the judgement.[189]

Conditions became intolerable by the time of Shahjahan as attested to by Manucci and Manrique. Peasants were compelled to sell their women and children to meet the revenue demand. Manrique writes that "the peasants were carried off... to various markets and fairs (to be sold) with their poor unhappy wives behind them, carrying their small children all crying and lamenting to meet the revenue demand". Bernier too affirms that "the unfortunate peasants who were incapable of discharging the demand of their rapacious lords, were bereft of their children who were carried away as slaves."[190]

In brief, slave trade was mainly carried out by Muslim royalty and nobility throughout the medieval period and it brought them considerable gains.

4.7. TRADE IN GRAIN, CLOTH AND OTHER ARTICLES

As the Muslim government gained in stability, it embarked on trade of many other commodities. The enterprises of the Muslim government today would be called 'public sector undertakings' as against private business. The Muslim state traded in animals, corn and cloth, as it did in slaves. Under Alauddin Khalji the grain market was taken under the control of the government. He ordered that the travelling merchants (caravaneers) should get themselves registered with the Superintendent of the Grain Market. They were required to take up residence with their families in villages bordering on the river Jumna. They were made to sign agreements, collectively and individually, to maintain a regular supply of grain to the market. Similar undertaking was obtained from the magistrates and collectors (*shahnagan* and *mutsarrifan*) in the Doab and regions near the capital to the effect that they would try to obtain as much grain from the cultivators as possible. They were ordered to realize fifty per cent of the produce as land-tax from the agriculturists with the utmost vigour as well as to compel them to sell their surplus stock to the travelling merchants on the fields at rates fixed by the King. Thus all the available grain flowed into the market which remained well-stocked. The Sultan established Government Grain Stores. There was scarcely a *mohalla*, says Barani, where two or three royal stores filled with foodstuffs did not exist. They were godowns where grain was stored in reserve to be released in times of emergency.

Alauddin Khalji advanced money from the treasury to the roving merchants to bring grain into the city; in lieu whereof he gave them commission to support their families. As hinted by Ibn Battutah, Alauddin advanced money to the Sindhi merchants for bringing and selling foodstuffs and other goods in Delhi to have a share in the profits of the trade. His contemporary rulers in some West Asian countries also indulged in such a practice. They introduced market control and took over wholesale trade in grain so that profits accrued to them instead of to private traders.[191] Throughout the medieval period, part of the Kharaj or land-tax was taken in kind. Even when it was calculated in terms of cash, the levy or recovery was often made in the form of grain, partially if not wholly. During the Mughal period jagirs were allotted to Amirs and Mansabdars. They collected their share of the revenue and traded in grain which was surplus with them. Thus the government and nobles earned profit by doing business in foodstuffs. It may be noted that foodgrains were cheap in the medieval period. Medieval chroniclers of the Khalji and Lodi period take pride in mentioning that grains were cheap in their times. In Akbar's camp, Father Monserrate was astounded at the low prices of foodstuffs notwithstanding the immense numbers of men and animals. How much burden of this cheapness was shared between the agriculturists, private traders and royal traders is difficult to determine. But the government did participate in trade in corn and grain and advanced money to *caravaneers* to bring grain for sale and shared in the profit.

This becomes all the more clear in the case of trade in cloth. Sultan Alauddin advanced about two million *tankahs* to Multani or Sindhi merchants to bring merchandise and sell it on behalf of the King. According to Ibn Battutah he advanced money to the merchants and told them: "With this money buy bullock and sheep, and sell them; the price that they will fetch must be paid to the treasury, and you shall receive allowance for selling them." Devagiri silks, horses of foreign breed, swords and many other articles were brought from far off places.

Internal and external trade, royal workshops and private manufactories provided for the requirements of royalty and nobility and their harems. Silk was imported from many foreign countries like China and Persia as well as produced indigenously. Manucci and Bernier talk in general terms, but Abul Fazl gives specific names of cotton, silk and woolen fabrics, Indian as well as those imported from "Turkey, Europe and Portugal".[192] Vincent Smith quoting Monserrate's *Commantarious* says that "Akbar himself was a trader, and did not disdain to earn commercial profits."[193] By the time of Shahjahan more and more foreign stuffs had begun to be imported.[194] Woolen carpets or *qalins* were also imported from Iran and Central Asia.

When the State made purchases advances were offered to the suppliers. Jahangir introduced night-time marketing at his residence. The imperial government traded in articles produced in its karkhanas spread out in many places like Lahore, Agra, Fatehpur, Ahmadabad, Burhanpur and Kashmir. Shahjahan even held the monopoly (*sauda-i-khas*) in cash-earning articles like indigo and saltpetre. "Extensive trading operations were carried on not only by the Emperor and the Princes, governors and imperial nobles, such as Asaf Khan and Mir Jumla, but also by Nur Jahan."[195] The principal trade from India to Europe in the seventeenth century consisted of silk and cotton fabrics, indigo, saltpetre, pepper and spices. "Khafi Khan mentions that the imperial ship, *Ganj-i-Sawai*, which on its way back from pilgrimage was attacked by the English pirates, was bringing fifty-two lacs of rupees in silver and gold, the produce of the sale of Indian goods at Mocha and Jedda."[196]

In brief, internal and external trade by the State provided a good source of income to the exchequer. It is significant that the memoirs of Jahangir as well as his *Tarikh-i-Salim Shahi* repeatedly mention rates of exchange between the Mughal *rupia* and currencies of Iran and Turan.[197] Which would point to continuous Mughal government's trade with these countries. Pietro Della Valle saw a great number of Banians and Indian Gentiles in Isfahan (in Iran), where (they) reside constantly celebrating the festival of Holi with éclat and gaiety.[198] In the pre-Industrial Revolution era, Indian goods and merchants flooded foreign markets and Indian kings made good profit through their trade. The toy trade with Europe was also profitable. It was loaded with curios, presents and bribes to Mughal royalty from the West. However, trade with England had not been established before Akbar's death. From the East China came porcelain in considerable quantities for the use of the Mughal emperor and his nobles. According to Peruschi, Akbar's dinner used to be brought to him in porcelain dishes imported from China. "When he died in 1605, he left in Agra alone more than two million and a half of rupees worth of the most elegant vessels of every kind in porcelain and coloured glass. The glass probably came from Venice."[199] It is not necessary to give a catalogue of imports and exports and an index of balance of trade. Two factors need to be kept in mind in this regard. One, the trade was profitable to the Mughal royalty and nobility; else it would have dried up. Two, traders were strictly forbidden to send out silver. Silver was largely imported; its import benefited the Mughals.

Customs Duties

Where the ruling elite itself was not the trader, it collected imposts on manufactures and customs on sale. Duty on manufacture of high quality products was called *jihat*, and the remainder was known as *sair-jihat*, a term used in the *Ain-i-Akbari* for all kinds of sundry taxes other than land revenue.[200] *Sair-jihat* formed an important source of income of the Mughal state as it included taxes on sale of cloth, oil, grains, articles of food, horses, camels and animal skins. There was a regular staff of police and revenue officials to guard and protect the markets and to collect taxes in them.

So far as the rate of customs duty is concerned, Akbar charged at the rate of 2½ per cent. This rate seems to have continued during the reigns of Jahangir and Shahjahan and also Aurangzeb, but under him for Muslims only. From 1665 Hindu merchants paid 5 per cent and the Muslim 2½ per cent. Thevenot who arrived in 1666 found that the Christians paid 4 per cent and the Hindus (Banians) 5 per cent.[201] In 1667 the Muslim merchants were exempted from the payment of customs duties altogether.

The duty on gold and silver was 2½ per cent, says Thevenot. Any one was free to bring gold, silver or copper to the royal mint and get it converted into coins. The commission earned by the state can be imagined from the statement of Manucci who says that the government derived eleven lakhs of rupees every year from the new coins struck at Surat alone. Mints were owned by the state and merchants were allowed to dig and work out the mines on payment of a fee. Minerals and metals like lead, saltpetre, indigo and even salt were sometimes declared the monopoly of the state.

Merchants in India generally carried their goods by carts and boats. They had to take a 'passport' (*dastak* or *farman*) from the place of their departure and show it at check posts on the journey in order to be allowed to pass without further payments. Manucci says that "if they chance to loose this paper, or it is stolen they are made to pay again either in the same or another province."[202] Tavernier informs us that four rupees were charged on every wagon load of merchandise and one rupee on every chariot, but a different rate was charged for boats. Inland trade was flourishing and the Mughal government made a lot of money through these levies.

Speaking of the income from the ports Manucci says "these seaports also yield him (the Mughal) a large revenue". The port towns were entered in revenue records as *mahals*. The Mughal emperors took sufficient interest in the administration and proper management of their customs offices. "Among them are those of Sind, Broach, Surat and Cambay. Surat alone brings him in usually thirty lakhs, besides the eleven lakhs derived from profit on new coins struck there."[203] At times the income from customs duty of a port was granted as jagir. For example, the customs of Surat was granted by Shahjahan to his daughter Jahanara "to meet her expenditure on betel".[204]

As Abul Fazl rightly remarks: "In every country such demands are troublesome and vexatious to the people. His majesty (Akbar) in his wise statesmanship and benevolence of rule carefully examined the subject and abolished all arbitrary taxation..."[205] But corruption and harassment remained common at least under his successors. The person and goods of the traders in transit were systematically searched. Thevenot says that "men may wait sometimes a month before they can get out their baggage and specially they who have Merchant goods."[206] The evil effects of this system were widely known. Besides abolishing many such taxes in port towns, Jahangir ordered that "Merchants travelling through the country were not to have their bales or packages of any kind opened without their consent."[207] Sometimes religious persecution added to the woes of merchants who closed or threatened to close their business.[208] But royal regulations could not stop extortion. As a modern economic historian points out, "It is mentioned that Mir Jumla once demanded Rs.50,000 from the merchants of Dacca. On refusal they were threatened with death by being trampled by elephants and compromised for Rs.25,000 while the bankers of the city appeased his wrath by paying Rs.30,000 without much ado. Occasionally, however, the mercantile community could protest successfully against the exactions of a governor or high administrative officer by *hartal* or suspension of business."[209] In any case, as mentioned by Jadunath Sarkar, "Foreign trade... occupied a negligible position in the economics of the Mughal empire, on account of its small volume — the total yield of the import duty being probably less than 30 lakhs of Rupees a year, while the land revenue brought to the State one hundred and eleven times that amount."[210] As mentioned earlier, in other Muslim countries customs duties were regularly collected but in Muslim state in India, Muslim traders were granted liberal exemptions. Besides, income from such sources was shared by the king and his officers. And this income was subsidiary or auxiliary. The main sources of income of the Muslim state were the four regular taxes — Khams, Kharaj, Jiziyah and Zakat. It is on these four pillars that the economic structure of the Muslim government rested.

5.8. ESTIMATE OF INCOME OF THE STATE

An estimate of the income of the Muslim state in India has been attempted by a number of scholars. They are aware of the deficiencies in their calculations because contemporary chroniclers give figures of such incomes but rarely. Boundaries of 'empires' were also constantly changing. The currency too was changing — ratios and weights of coins. Even so estimates of the income of the state have been attempted by some indefatigable scholars like Edward Thomas, W.H. Moreland and Jadunath Sarkar, and their findings are being reproduced here.

Edward Thomas has arrived at the following figures of the income during the reigns of monarchs from Firoz Tughlaq to Aurangzeb:

	Silver *tankahs* (or rupees)
"Firoz Shah (Tughlaq), A.D. 1351-1388	6,08,50,000.
Babur, A.D. 1526-1530	2,60,00,000.
Akbar, A.D. 1593	32,00,00,000.
Akbar, *estimated* later returns	33,14,87,772.
Akbar, A.D. 1605	34,90,00,000.
Jahangir, A.D. 1609-1611	50,00,00,000.
Jahangir, A.D. 1628	35,00,00,000.

Shah Jahan, A.D. 1648	44,00,00,000.
Aurangzeb, A.D. 1697	38,71,94,000.

Aurangzeb's total revenue from various sources (was) 77,43,88,000 silver *tankahs* (or rupees)."[211]

Shams Siraj Afif's figure of the income of Sultan Firoz Tughlaq is 67,500,000 *tankahs*.[212] P. Saran writes that Firoz Tughlaq's total income from land revenue, canals, and gardens was nearly 8 crores of *tankahs*. He rightly adds that income from other sources like Zakat, Jiziyah, Khams, octrois, tolls, was also there but it is impossible even to make any rough estimates of the same. He estimates the income of Sher Shah's empire at 16 crores of silver *tankahs* or rupees (about half the income of Akbar's reign).[213]

Jadunath Sarkar makes the following statement on the subject: "Excluding Afghanistan, Mughal empire had a revenue of Rupees 13 *krores* and 21 *lakhs* under Akbar and 33 *krores* and 25 *lakhs* under Aurangzeb. The figure stood for land revenue alone but the amount was never fully realised. It did not include proceeds of taxes like *Zakat* and *Jiziyah*. A rough idea of the state-income can be formed from the figures of Gujarat in Aurangzeb's reign: land revenue Rupees 113 *lakhs*, *Jiziyah* 5 *lakhs*, customs duties of Surat port 12 *lakhs* per annum (the other ports did negligible trade). The amounts of land held as military jagir and Crown lands (*khalsa*) can be judged from the following figures (circa 1690): land revenue assessed on *jagirs* 27.64 *krores* and on *khalsa* 5.81 *krores* of Rupees (for the whole empire)."[214] Stanley Lanepoole, an expert on numismatics and fiscal subjects, also says that the figures of income of the state "represents only the land revenue, including, however, the tribute which took the place of the land-tax in half-subdued States..."[215]

V

Expenditure of the State

The income of the state was expended on various branches of government and administration, on the harems of kings and nobles, and on forts, palaces, mosques and tombs. Large amounts were sent abroad to Muslim holy places like Mecca and Medina and for the Caliphs. At home, men of letters and men of religion were given handsome awards and grants, pensions and lump sum amounts. Salaries and scholarships were given to students and mendicants. Dowries were distributed among the indigent for marriage of their daughters and free kitchens established for distribution of food among the poor. The most important and recurring item of expenditure was on the army and construction of buildings. All this information is provided by medieval chroniclers. What is not mentioned is the actual amount of money spent on them. These, if ever, are given sparingly. We shall, therefore, mention the actual amounts wherever given; about other items of expenditure a sort of probable assessment alone would be surmised. Expenditure was incurred on all the above mentioned items simultaneously. But we can assess the expenditure only item-wise. Architectural activity of the state may be taken up first. It was a major activity of the Muslim government. While the armies, the palaces and the harems have all disappeared with the disappearance of Muslim rule, the one thing that strikes the eye in Delhi and Agra and many other towns and cities is the buildings of the Muslim period called monuments today.

5.1. MONUMENTS

The first thing the Muslim Sultanate of Delhi started on was construction of impressive buildings. The first sultan Qutbuddin Aibak had to establish Muslim power in India and to raise buildings "as quickly as possible, so that no time might be lost in making an impression on their newly-conquered subjects".[1] Architecture was considered as the visual symbol of Muslim political power. It denoted victory with authority. The first two buildings of the early period in Delhi are the Qutb Minar and the congregational mosque named purposefully as the Quwwat-ul-Islam (might of Islam) Masjid. This mosque was commenced by Aibak in 592/1195. It was built with materials and gold obtained by destroying 27 Hindu and Jain temples in Delhi and its neighborhood. A Persian inscription in the mosque testifies to this.[2] The Qutb Minar, planned and commenced by Aibak sometime in or before 1199 and completed by Iltutmish,[3] was also constructed with similar materials, "the sculptured figures on the stones being either defaced or concealed by turning them upside down". A century and a quarter later Ibn Battutah describes the congregational mosque and the Qutb Minar. "About the latter he says that its staircase is so wide that elephants can go up there." About the former his observations are interesting. "Near the eastern gate of the mosque their lie two very big idols of copper connected together by stones. Every one who comes in and goes out of the mosque treads over them. On the site of this mosque was *a bud khana*, that is an idol house. After the conquest of Delhi it was turned into a mosque."[4] The cost of these edifices in terms of money cannot be known. A look at the gigantic Qutb Minar and the strong screen wall of the mosque shows that no amount of money alone could have created such awe-inspiring edifices. They were products of the age of Islamic slavery. People were captured in thousands in war; they were made slaves and drafted on such majestic works.

How many slaves were needed to accomplish the task on these two and the other buildings of Qutbuddin Aibak and Iltutmish such as mosques, *madrasas*, mausoleums, *qasrs* and tanks (e.g. Hauz-i-Shamsi) in and outside Delhi? It is difficult to determine but easy to conjecture their numbers, for these two sultans had embarked on constructional activity on a very large scale.

It is known that Alauddin Khalji, another great builder, had 70,000 slaves working on his buildings, as attested to by the contemporary chronicler Ziyauddin Barani.[5] Alauddin built "masjids, minars, citadels and tanks". But his (incompleted) Qutb Minar alone was an edifice more than equal to all his undertakings. Thus the men working on the buildings of the first two sultans were probably not less than those of Alauddin Khalji; they may have been probably more. These slaves were to dismantle standing temples, very carefully, stone by stone, carry the carved columns, shafts and pillars to the new sites of construction, and raise the new structures. Hasan Nizami says that temples were demolished with the help of elephants and one elephant could haul stones for which 500 men were needed;[6] yet it has to be recognised that not many mechanical devices were available. Most of the work was done by human hands and muscles. Furthermore, Hindu architects, masons and labourers turned slaves under the new dispensation had to do the work in record time. Barani in his enthusiasm says hyperbolically that during Alauddin's reign a palace could be built in 2-3 days and a citadel in two weeks.[7]

In the Sultanate of Delhi, it was considered a matter of pride for a newly crowned king to build a new city of his own to give name and fame to himself and his dynasty. The old city of Iltutmish was abandoned by Balban who built the Qasr-i-Lal or the red palace, and Kaiqubad built the city of Kilughari. Jalaluddin Khalji constructed Shahr-i-Nau, Alauddin Khalji founded the fort-city of Siri, and his successor, Tughlaq Shah, founded Tughlaqabad. "It is their custom," writes Ibn Battutah, "that the king's palace is deserted on his death... and his successor builds a new palace for himself."[8]

The buildings of Alauddin Khalji in Delhi alone would have cost millions of *tankahs*,[9] but no figure of specific buildings have been given by any medieval Muslim chronicler. Constructional enterprises are money consuming. His expeditions in south India and severe revenue regulations had brought him immense wealth. His best architectural works were accomplished after 1311 by which time the Mongol invaders had been completely pushed back and lot of wealth had been brought from the Deccan. It is no mere guess that he spent quite a treasure on his buildings.

Similar is the case with the Tughlaqs. Firoz Tughlaq founded several cities, dug a few canals, constructed forts, palaces, *bands*, mosques, tombs, warehouses, sarais and khanqahs. He built eight large mosques in Delhi each of which could accommodate 10,000 devotees.[10] He repaired the Qutb Minar as well as all the tombs and mausoleum of former sultans and saints. He built khanqahs for travellers who stayed in them as guests of the state for three days. "In 120 khanqahs Muslims (*bandgan-i-khuda*) could thus stay for 360 days (or almost the year round) as a guest of the government." His contemporary chronicler Shams Siraj Afif, says that "in the reign of Firoz Shah, Malik Bukhari was the Shahnah (superintendent) of the Buildings. (In appreciation of his work) the king had bestowed on him a gold baton. (His deputy?) Abdul Haqq, alias Jahir Sondhar, was given a golden mace. Under Firoz Tughlaq expenditure on building was colossal. The Diwan-i-Arz examined the plan of every proposed building and made provision for necessary money from the royal treasury. Such a magnificent Buildings Department, which had been set up during the reign of Firoz Shah, had not been established during the reign of any other king as lakhs (of *tankahs*) were spent on this department. Indeed it would not be an exaggeration to say that countless wealth was spent on it."[11] This of course does not include the free labour of slaves as well as the loss of merchants who were forced to carry free of charge stones on their pack-animals from old Delhi to the site of Kotla Firoz Shah when it was under construction. Firoz was a kind-hearted sultan and so it may be presumed that he paid something to his slave labour also. For, even the shifting of the two Ashokan pillars to Delhi required the services of a few thousand men (*chandin hazar admi*).

Besides the Sultanate, new independent Muslim states sprang up all over the country throughout the fifteenth century. In all of them feverish architectural activity was carried on with the help of local slaves and elephants and money acquired in expeditions. At the centre, Sultan Sikandar Lodi who took keen interest in the welfare of the Musalmans, founded masjids throughout his dominions, and appointed a preacher, a reader and a sweeper to each.[12] Thus he turned masjids almost into government institutions and made foundations of Islam strong.[13]

Similar is the language of Persian historians for Sher Shah's endeavours in this field. Needless to say that all Muslim rulers constructed pious edifices at great cost with great enthusiasm — edifice like mosques, idgahs, dargahs, ziaratgahs (shrines), mazars (tombs), sarais, madrasas and maktabs. From Gaur to the confines of his dominions, Sher Shah built sarais and halting places at every *kos*. At every sarai a masjid, a royal chamber and a well were constructed. To every mosque a muazzin, an imam, and a manager were appointed. There was a road built from Bengal to Avadh, another from Agra to Burhanpur, another from Agra to Jodhpur and Chittor, and another from Bayana to Jaunpur. On the sides of every road were planted fruit trees and gardens. Sher Shah built a total of 1700 sarais. These were maintained by lands and villages allotted at the place for their support.[14] The cost of all these public works was enormous.

The cost of buildings of Sher Shah and Islam Shah

particularly their forts, has not been given by contemporary writers. Figures given by later writers are confusing. According to the *Tarikh-i-Daudi*, Patna fort was ordered to be built by Sher Shah Suri in 1540. It was completed in record time of two years at a cost of five lakh *rupiyas*. The Salimgarh fort built by his son Islam Shah in 1546 cost four lakh *rupiyas*. It was not completed at the time of his death in 1552 and so a lakh or two more would have been spent. But Sher Shah's fort at Rohtas in Punjab cost 35 to 40 lakh rupees, according to Jahangir "4,025,000 rupees, according to the currency of Iran to 120,000 *tuman*, and in the currency of Turan to 1 *arb*, 21 lakhs and 75,000 *khami* (*khami* was equal to one third of a rupee), that is now current". In a footnote Rogers and Beveridge, the translaters of *Tuzuk-i-Jahangiri*, rightly say that "the figures seem wrong, and the MSS differ..." Apparently the correct sum in rupees is 34 lakhs, 25,000.[15] Even this sum is at great variance from the cost of other forts of the Afghans and is about equal to Akbar's magnificent fort built at Agra in fifteen years' time. And the cost of the network of roads of Sher Shah is difficult to estimate. This must have been enormous. However, much of the expense and labour was shared by local people just as the cost of maintaining his sarais was borne by villages in the vicinity.

With the coming of the Mughals more artistic buildings came into being. More information is also available about the expenditure on some of them. Those who built them had unbounded command of both money and slaves. Babur writes that "680 men worked daily on my buildings in Agra... only; while 1491 stone-cutters worked daily on my buildings in Agra, Sikri, Biana, Dulpur (Dholpur), Gwalior and Kuil (Aligarh). In the same way there are numberless artisans and workmen of every sort in Hindustan." Some workers were wage-earners, for says he at another place, "Gifts were made to the stone-cutters, and labourers and the whole body of workmen in the way customary for master-workmen and wage-earners of Agra."[16] Akbar and Jahangir expended large sums in construction work in Agra and Lahore. Akbar's fort at Agra took fifteen years to build and cost 35 lakh rupees.[17] He is credited by Abul Fazl with building in Agra five hundred edifices. Officers and troops used to be stationed in forts built at strategic points from Kashmir to the Deccan. Repair of old and construction of new forts was an ever ongoing activity of the Muslim state. Repair of a fort once cost 20,000 rupees.[18] According to De Laet emperor Akbar had erected many women's apartments at every few miles from Agra, each of which could accommodate sixteen ladies with servants[19] besides the forts of Allahabad and Fatehpur Sikri. "After the death of Akbar, Jahangir tried to rehabilitate towns and *qasbas* which had fallen to ruin." He directed the jagirdars and administrators of the Khalisa estates that towns should be built, mosques erected, sarais constructed and wells dug, of course all at government cost.[20] He also demolished old buildings to be replaced by new ones.[21]

Akbar had begun to build his own mausoleum. Jahangir took much interest in rebuilding from its foundations this mausoleum at Sikandara. He caused fresh designs to be prepared for it and expended large sums on its construction and decoration, "and work went on for three or four years," writes Jahangir in his memoirs. "On the whole they told me the cost of this lofty edifice was 1,500,000 (fifteen lakh) rupees, equivalent to 50,000 current *tumans* of Persia and 4,500,000 *khamis*, according to the currency of Turan."[22] Muhammad Taqi was the Diwan of buildings under Jahangir. Writing on the later years of Jahangir's[23] reign, Francisco Pelsaert mentions that the tomb of Itmad-ud-daula at Agra had cost three and half lakh rupees up to the year 1626, and that ten lakhs more were required for its completion. He speaks also of the numerous sarais and palaces built by the empress Nur Jahan. Jahangir spent large sums in Agra and Lahore, but it was under Shahjahan that the most remarkable developments occurred. "Contemporary writers give figures for the cost of some of his buildings — 10 lakhs for the mosque at Daulatabad, 60 lakhs for the palace at Delhi,

917 lakhs for the Taj Mahal at Agra; and, while these may be inaccurate, they are comparable with the estimate of the Lahore canal, which comes from a similar source." These figures are completely inaccurate. For, while the repair of a mansion sometimes cost one lakh rupees,[24] a canal also cost the same amount. "In 1639 Ali Mardan Khan proposed a canal taking off from the river Ravi, which was sanctioned *at an estimated cost of a lakh of rupees* (emphasis added). Some years later the existing canal from the Jamna to Delhi was reconstructed under his supervision. It was probably comparable in amount with the former and much less than what was being spent on buildings of an ornamental nature."[25]

Despite the discrepancies and inaccuracies in the expenditure on construction of individual edifices from the times of Babur to those of Shahjahan during whose "august reign, when... lovely things reached the zenith of perfection," money in millions and slaves in thousands were employed on erecting the hundreds of huge Mughal buildings still extant.[26] The Taj Mahal is the loveliest of all these building; it also stands as a monument of exploitation of poor labourers. Tavernier says that it was completed in twenty-two years for three crore rupees and 20,000 persons worked on it all the time. Three crores in 22 years comes to 13 lakhs per year and 65 rupees per person per year if he was actually paid the amount. The lower class workmen may have been paid only a rupee or so per month. Another "effect of such undertakings," writes W.H. Moreland, "was inevitably to hinder ordinary commercial activities. Thus all the carts at Agra were impressed for the works in progress at Delhi, and on one occasion goods in transit for the coast had to lie on the way for some months, after they had been by the king's officers cast down in the fields, and the carts taken for his use." But impressment was an ordinary occurrence of the period (Firoz Tughlaq had done it earlier). There appears to be no evidence on what is a matter of much greater interest — the treatment and remuneration of the large number of labourers employed on these buildings.

The example of kings was universally imitated by their principal nobles.[27] The opulent grandees in the provinces esteemed it an honour and obligation to adorn towns and cities of the regions under their control with magnificent buildings. The law of escheat encouraged them to spend lavishly. Pelsaert perhaps has the last word on it. "I have often ventured to ask great lords," says he, "what is their true object in being so eager to amass their treasures, when what they have gathered is of no use to them or to their family (because of escheat)... I have urged they would share it with the poor, who in this country are hundreds of thousands, or indeed innumerable... Their answers have been based on the emptiest worldly vanity..." Buildings they constructed with great zest — gardens, tombs, and palaces — "they build them with so many hundreds of thousands...[28] Once the builder is dead, no one will care for his buildings, but every one tries to erect building of his own, and establish his own reputation alongside that of his ancestors. If all these edifices were attended to and kept in repair, the lands of every city, and even village, would be adorned (covered)[29] with monuments; but as a matter of fact the roads leading to the cities are strewn with fallen columns of stone."[30]

In short, the Turkish and Mughal sultans and nobles were ever busy on a building spree without any thought of preserving the edifices. Preservation may have been uneconomical. Ibn Battutah and Babur affirm that all was destroyed because of moisture. But economy was not a weakness of Muslim royalty and nobility. With them ceaseless construction was a craze.

5.2. THE ARMY

Muslim rule in India was not only established but throughout sustained by its army. In other words, Muslim rule in India was army rule. The state resembled the organisation of an army; its civil functions were meant to support this organisation. Medieval historians and political thinkers like Fakhr-i-Mudabbir, Ziyauddin Barani and Shams Siraj Afif asserted that kingship was the army and the army kingship.[31] On the army was spent the largest chunk of the state income obtained through conquest and loot. Sultan Ghiyasuddin Balban used to say, "I have devoted all the revenue of my kingdom to equip my army." His contemporary chronicler Ziyauddin Barani writing for the early hundred years of Muslim rule (c. 1250-1350) specifically mentions that "all income from Khalisa lands throughout the empire was earmarked to be spent on the soldiers and the Karkhanas (workshops) which manufactured weapons and equipment for the army".[32] So, the agrarian sector, which was the greatest source of revenue of the Sultanate largely paid for the upkeep of the army. We have seen how this sector was fleeced and sponged. It was done to keep the army in good health and shape.

An idea of the expenditure on the army can be had from the computation of salary of soldiers, the pay of officers, maintenance of the various corps like elephant, horse and camel, the cost of building and maintaining forts where army contingents were stationed, and expenditure on the karkhanas (workshops) which turned out weapons and other materials required for war. We shall try to estimate the expenses incurred on these items under the Sultanate and the Mughal empire. This will give an idea of the burden borne by the people mainly agriculturists, for maintaining the Muslim army.

Mercenaries

The army of the Sultanate comprised of the soldiers in the permanent employment of the ruler and special recruits enrolled on the eve of an expedition or for performing a specific task. The Ghaznavid tradition of enrolling mercenaries was continued by the Turkish sultans in India. Writing early in the reign of Iltutmish, Fakhr-i-Muddabir mentions a body of troopers "who have voluntarily joined the forces". Balban employed 3,000 Afghan horse and foot in his campaign against the Mewatis,[33] and appointed thousands of Afghan officers and men in the forts of Gopalgir, Kampil, Patiali, Bhojpur and Jalali to contain the restive elements there.[34] On his way to Lakhnauti Balban enrolled about 2,00,000 horsemen and infantry.[35] So also used to do Sultan Raziyah. Throughout the medieval period, mercenaries (Muslims, says Afif for Sultan Firoz's times) used to be enrolled in the army. Recorded instances imply that such recruitment was an established practice.[36] "It is perhaps safe to guess that such recruitments (with the object of fighting against the infidels) were confined to Muslims only", says Habibullah.[37] Enrolment of fresh levies was a continuous process. It was necessary to replenish the troops, for losses used to be great. In his campaigns against the Mewatis alone Balban is said to have lost one hundred thousand men in the course of one year. Rebels like Tughril Beg of Bengal took two years to subdue only after great losses had been inflicted on the royal troops on two earlier occasions.

The cost of emergency recruitment was high. In the fourteenth century the cost of emergency recruitment and equipping 1000 horsemen in a short time came to three lakh *tankahs*.[38] Prince Alauddin Khalji was the *muqta* of Kara. He was permitted by his uncle Sultan Jalaluddin Khalji to recruit extra troops to lead an expedition into central Hindustan. He enrolled three to four thousand horsemen and two thousand infantry in a short time for leading an expedition to Chanderi en route to Devagiri. The cost of recruiting them can be estimated from the statement of Barani quoted above.

Regular Troops

The soldiers in the permanent employment were paid a regular salary. Since war (Jihad) was a permanent and ever expanding activity of the Muslim regime, most sultans maintained a large standing army on a permanent basis, and did not disband troops after a conquest was accomplished or a foreign invasion repulsed. According to Farishtah Alauddin Khalji's regular army consisted of 4,75,000 horsemen well equipped and accoutred. There were two separate forces. One was meant to repulse Mongol invaders while the other was sent out on the conquest of newer regions.[39] The annual salary paid to a cavalrymen by the Sultan was 234 *tankahs.* In addition 78 *tankahs* were paid to a *do aspa* or to one who possessed an additional horse because maintenance of an extra mount added to the soldier's efficiency.

The salary bill of 4,75,000 horsemen at the rate of 234 *tankahs* alone would have come to 111 million or eleven crore *tankahs* annually. This was high by any standards, more so when it did not include the allowance to *do aspas,* payment to the infantry and expenses on the large staff of officials involved with the upkeep of such a large army. The salary paid to soldiers under the Khaljis was high. Besides there was unrestrained plunder in every campaign. It was probably because of this reason that Alauddin changed the rule regarding Khams. He took away 4/5 of the booty (*ghanimah*) and distributed 1/5 to the participating soldiers. Ghiyasuddin Tughlaq maintained his army on the pattern and regulations of Alauddin Khalji.[40] Muhammad Tughlaq's cavalry is said to have consisted of 900,000 horsemen,[41] double the size of that of Alauddin Khalji. Alauddin had freezed the prices of articles of daily use by soldiers through his Market Control. So, he paid a fixed salary to them. Under Muhammad Tughlaq there was no market control and the salary of troops would probably have gone up. Even at the rates fixed by Alauddin, the salary bill would have come to twenty-two to twenty-five crores annually. Muhammad Tughlaq's empire was vast and revenue from far-off regions of Dwarsamudra to Satgaon and Telingana to Malwa and Gujarat used to be collected without much problem (before the spate of rebellions started). Firoz Tughlaq's army was not that large.[42] Nevertheless as will be seen presently, the expenditure on his army establishment was no less large. There were Arab and Persian contingents in Firoz Tughlaq's army. Sure enough, the size of the army varied from time to time. The Saiyyads were weak and the Lodis not so strong. But even in the newly created Muslim kingdoms of the fifteenth century like Gujarat, Malwa, Jaunpur etc., war remained the most prominent activity and the army consumed most of the revenue.

Salary of the Mughal Soldiers

The salary of soldiers under the Mughals is given in Abul Fazl's *Ain-i-Akbari*. There were several classes of foot soldiers who performed various kinds of duties. The first class infantry man got 500 *dams*; the second, 400 *dams*; the third, 300 *dams*; the fourth, 240 *dams* per month. As a rupia was equal to 40 *dams* the pay of the best foot soldier was about 12 rupia and of the lowest 6 rupia per month. The cavalry was better paid. A cavalryman with an Iraqi horse got 30 rupia per mensem, with a Turki horse 20 rupia, with a Tazi 15 rupia, with a *jangla* (local breed) 12 rupia. Their salary was equal to the (civil) collectors of revenue. "The revenue collectors of domain lands got formerly 25 rupia, but now only 15 rupia."

The pay of Banduqchis or Matchlock bearers, who were (non-commissioned) officers of four grades got 300, 280, 270 and 260 *dams*. The common Banduqchis divided into five classes received 250 to 110 *dams*. The best paid were the Ahadis, "the immediate servants of His Majesty". These "worthy persons whom His Majesty does not appoint to a Mansab, but whom he frees from being under the orders of any one", got as much as 500 rupia per mensem.[43] These are specimens of salaries paid. There were hundreds of types of troops, wrestlers, slaves and *chelas* and hundreds of grades of pay for them and their administrative officers. The remuneration money spent on the troops was, on the whole, not much. This is the conclusion one arrives at by certain statements of Jahangir. "On the day on which the royal troops were ordered to pursue (the rebel prince) Khusrau, 15,000 rupees were given to Mahabat Khan and 20,000 to the Ahadis, and 10,000 more were sent with the army to be given to whom it might be necessary to give it on the way." On another occasion a body of 3,000 (superior kind of) cavalry was despatched under Shah Beg. For the expenses of this force 200,000 rupees were given.[44] These amounts for overall expenses were not much, when to an officer Taj Khan who had been nominated to beat the Afghans of Bangarh, he gave, obviously as a reward, 50,000 rupees.[45]

Pay of Officers

As against the troops and according to all contemporary chroniclers, the army officers were highly paid throughout Muslim rule. Shihabuddin al-Umri says that a Khan received 200,000 *tankahs*, each being worth eight dirhams (silver coin). "This sum belongs to him personally, and he is not expected to disburse any part of it to his soldiers." Every Malik received from 50 to 60 thousand *tankahs* and every Amir 40 to 50 thousand *tankahs*.[46] This amount was paid sometimes in the form of cash salary, at others by the grant of a revenue assignment called *iqta*. There were officers with other ranks as well.

The nobles or Umara were graded as Khans, Maliks, Amirs, Sipehsalars in the Sultanate period and as Mansabdars under the Mughals. According to Barani, a Sarkhail commanded ten horsemen; a Sipehsalar ten Sarkhails; an Amir ten Sipehsalars; a Malik ten Amirs; and a Khan ten Maliks.[47] According to the author of the *Masalik-ul-Absar* a Khan commanded more or less 100,000 troops, an Amir 10,000, a Malik a thousand and so on.[48] The term Amir was normally used in a generic sense to denote a high officer. In Akbar's time and after, all the great men of the Mughal empire were graded and appointed to a Mansab (rank) in the imperial service. From the lowest rank, that of the commander of ten, upto the rank of 400 an officer was known as Mansabdar. From 500 onwards a noble was known as Amir, or Khan, or Khan-i-Azam. They were all generally spoken of as Umara.

The salaries of the Mughal officers and grandees were equally high. W.H. Moreland, the economic historian of the Mughal Empire, computes that a commander of 5000 could count on at least Rs. 18,000 a month under Akbar and his successor. A commander of 1000 could similarly count on receiving Rs. 5000 a month, while a commander of 500 would have received the equivalent of Rs. 500 to 600 "at the present day" (1914). Certainly there was at the time no other career in India which could offer such prospects and prizes. It is therefore no wonder that the most enterprising men from a large portion of Western Asia should have been attracted to the Mughal court.[49] The government both civil and military was conducted by means of officials entered in the army list and graded in successive ranks or Mansabs. According to Jadunath Sarkar, "of these, all those who held any grade from 3 *hazari* upwards were called grandees (*umara-i-azam* or grand commanders), and those below the command of 3000 horse (nominal) were styled simply *mansabdars* or officers". The total number of officials including both Umara and Mansabdars were 1,803 under Akbar (c. 1596), 2,945 under Jahangir (c. 1620), 8,000 under Shahjahan (c. 1647) and 14,449 under Aurangzeb (c. 1690). There was enormous inflation of the army list under Aurangzeb. Under him the annual salary and allowances of the Mansabdars, including the pay of their troops were as follows for the first classes in each grade — 3.5 lakhs of rupees for a 7-*hazari*, 2.5 lakhs for a 5-*hazari*, 50,000 for a *hazari* and 1,000 for a commander of twenty.[50]

Strength of the Mughal Army

V.A. Smith says that Akbar did not maintain a large standing army. According to him the strength of Akbar's army "equipped by the State and paid directly from the Treasury", could not have exceeded 25,000 men. However, on the testimony of Monserrate he himself writes that at the time of his expedition to Kabul (1581), Akbar had 45,000 cavalry, besides 5000 elephants and an unnumbered host on foot.[51] The military character of the Mughal government of Akbar is vouched by all, and yet the estimates of the standing army of the Mughal emperors from Akbar to Aurangzeb have wide variations. Had it been so large as has been made out by some scholars, "we should arrive at so huge an army that it should have been impossible for the country, however heavily taxed, to meet such an expense".[52] The standing army was not large because, according to Abul Fazl, "the zamindars of the country furnish more than four million, four hundred thousand men, as shall be detailed below".[53] These details are given in the Third Book of the *Ain-i-Akbari*. From the detailed Tables provided — a laborious work only a scholar like Abul Fazl could produce — it appears that a quota of troops to be provided to the Mughal emperor on demand by every Raja or Zamindar was fixed in the same manner as was the revenue amount. The Rajput forces were thus completely merged with the Mughal army. Or, it was like the Subsidiary Alliance of the Raj days. Jahangir writes that from "this Subah (of Ajmer) in time of war 86,000 horses and 304,000 Rajput foot are provided".[54] From Malwa, "when needful there are obtained from it about 9,300 horse and 4,70,300, foot-soldiers, with 100 elephants".[55] This system continued under Jahangir and Shahjahan making the Mughal empire the strongest empire in the world till Aurangzeb's bigotry alienated the Rajputs and weakened the Mughal army and the empire.

The actual armed strength of the empire at the close of

Shahjahan's reign (1647) was 2 lakhs of troopers brought to the muster and branding, 8 thousand Mansabdars, 7 thousand Ahadis and Barqandaz, 1,85,000 Tabinan or additional troopers of the princes, Umara and Mansabdars, and 40,000 foot musketeers, gunners, and rocket-men. These numbers underwent a still further increase with Aurangzeb's fresh warfare in the Deccan,[56] for "the total amount of pay claims generated by grant of mansabs pressed directly upon the empire's revenue resources".[57]

Army Corps

The army of the Sultanate comprised both cavalry and infantry. It had an elephant corps also. Elephants were not generally purchased. They were captured from jungles or taken as tribute from defeated rulers. Camels and ponies and other animals were also used for commissariat service. The most important wing of the army was the cavalry. And horses were costly. In India, good horses were found only in some regions like the eastern Punjab and the Salt Range, but they were inferior to the horses of the West Asian breed. This made the importation of war horses from abroad a matter of necessity for the sultans of Delhi. Medieval chronicles speak of Yamani, Shami, Bahri and Qipchaqi horses as being in use by soldiers in India, and there was large-scale importation of horses into India from Arabia, Afghanistan and even the steppe lands of southern Russia known as Tatars. According to Ibn Battutah and Wassaf their cost was high. "The good horses are worth 500 (silver) *dinars* or more." Besides making direct purchases from abroad, the sultans of Delhi replenished their *paigahs* with horses of foreign breed obtained from defeated Indian princes, particularly those with access to the sea as they imported such horses in large numbers. Gujarat and the South provided war horses in particular when, for example, the rulers of Warangal, Dwarsamudra and the Pandya kingdoms surrendered thousands of horses to Malik Kafur in the fourteenth century. The Hindu rulers of the South had imported foreign breed horses through the sea route. Wassaf says that 10,000 horses were imported annually into Mabar, Kambayat and other western Indian ports at the cost of 220 gold *dinars* each. But many times horses obtained in tribute had to be given to Muslim soldiers when their mounts got disabled in battle. Al-Umri mentions that Sultan Muhammad Tughlaq distributed to his army 10,000 Arab horses and countless others. The two great kings of the Sultanate period, Alauddin Khalji and Muhammad Tughlaq, had under their command 475,000 and 900,000 horsemen. Even Firoz Tughlaq who is said to have neglected his army, maintained extensive *paigahs*.[58] The size of the cavalry varied from time to time. The Saiyyads were weak, the Lodis not so strong, but even in the provincial kingdoms of Gujarat, Malwa and Jaunpur the cavalry wing was maintained at high cost. The expenditure on Sher Shah's army too was large. He had 150,000 cavalry and the same numbers were maintained in cantonments. The infantry was 25,000 and 50,000 in garrisoning the forts. He had 5,000 elephants. "It was known that a suitable garrison was maintained in every fort in the country."[59]

Under the Mughals, according to Abul Fazl, "Merchants used to bring to court good horses from Iraq-i-Arab and Iraq-i Ajam, from Turkey, Turkestan, Badakhshan, Shirwan, Qirghis, Thibet, Kashmir and other countries." But unlike the Sultanate period cross-breeding was now freely done in India. In "the breeding of this sensible animal... after a short time Hindustan ranked higher in this respect than Arabia... There are fine horses bred in every part of the country; but horses of Cachh excel, being equal to Arabs", writes Abul Fazl. So, by Akbar's time good quality horses were available in many parts of the country. There were 12,000 horses in Akbar's stables. Their prices were fixed by experts. Khasa horses, meant for the personal use of the king, cost 10 to 20 *mohurs*. Their officers, servants, harness and food all were fixed, and cost not a little. For, Akbar was a man of details and his officers also became so.[60]

The *Ain-i-Akbari* gives a detailed description of the elephant stables under Akbar. The Emperor possessed 5,000 of them. The price of an elephant in his reign varied from one lakh to one hundred rupees. During the reign of Jahangir the price of a well trained war elephant rose much higher. Some elephants were imported from Ceylon (as by Firoz Tughlaq) and some others from Africa (as under Jahangir) and Burma (as by Shahjahan). But they were mostly available in all parts of India. The classification of the imperial elephants, the food allowed to them, the money spent on their harness and their five attendants were all fixed and settled. His Majesty's Khasa (personal) elephants had their personal names. The elephant was a costly corps of the Mughal army.[61] Jahangir gives the unmistakable impression that the Mughals loved their elephants and gave them endearing names. Some of these are Hawai, Ran Bhaga, Bansi Badan, Rup Sundar, Ran Rawat, Panchi Gaj, Fauj Singar, Surat Gaj, Mahipati, Durjansal, Giranbar. One was called Nur Bakht after Jahangir's own name. There are many reasons for this phenomenon. Unlike camels and horses, elephants were bred in India and were found in almost all parts of the country like Agra, Bayana, Narwar, Bastar, modern Madhya Pradesh, Jharkhand, Bengal, Orissa and elsewhere. Abul Fazl says that Panna elephants were the best. Hence the tradition of giving them Hindu names. Moreover, elephant fights provided good entertainment. It was a sagacious animal. The beginning of muster review was with the elephants.[63]

No less important was the camel corps. As in the case of horses, the quality of the camels of the country breed improved with time, and according to Abul Fazl, Indian camels soon surpassed those of Iran and Turan. Camels were numerous in Rajputana, as is the case even today. They were also found in large numbers in Kutch, Gujarat and Bhatinda in Punjab. During the Mughal period their greatest abundance was found in Sindh. Details regarding their food, furniture, servants, expenses have been mentioned in the *Ain-i-Akbari*.[64] The mules were pack animals preferred for transport of men and goods. They were mostly bred in North Punjab and Kashmir.[65]

As in any organisation, there were some good points and some weaknesses in the Muslim army. We cannot go into all these. One point each of the two may receive our attention. On the positive side there was constant vigil and inspection of the forces leading to savings; on the negative side there was corruption which led to loss of revenue. In the Sultanate period there were regular inspections of troops and their horses. There was the system of branding horses and keeping an account of the credentials of soldiers. Sometimes it used to take a fortnight to inspect all the contingents which set out on a campaign. Periodical reviews of the army, whether in headquarters or in camp, kept the soldiers on their toes and their mounts in good shape. The system of *dagh wa chehra* (cauterization and descriptive roll) was introduced by Alauddin Khalji; it was revived by Sikandar Lodi and reintroduced by Sher Shah. It ensured that at the time of review no soldier could send a substitute and no horse could be presented twice, or replaced by an inferior one after the review.[66]

Still better was the position under the Mughals. Akbar was an administrative genius. Most of the important appointments were made and promotions effected by him personally. The muster of men and horses and other animals was often inspected by him. There were regulations about the branding of horses and keeping full complements of the mounts.[67] Even the highest officers' contingents were inspected.

Army Reviews

Emperor Jahangir writes, "On the 25th (March 1617) the contingent of Itimad-ud-daulah passed before me in review on the plain under the *jharokha*. There were 2,000 cavalry well-horsed, most of whom were Moghuls, 500 foot armed with bows and guns, and fourteen elephants. The bakhshis reckoned them up and reported that this force was fully equipped and according to rule."[68] This paragraph in the *Tuzuk* is very important for it brings into prominence three characteristics which made the Mughal army efficient. It shows that even in the reign of the pleasure loving Jahangir, the contingents of the Mansabdars were thoroughly checked by bakhshis and regularly reviewed by the emperor. Secondly, even a high dignitary and close relative of the king like Itimad-ud-daulah was not exempt from equipping and accoutring his troops except "according to rule". Thirdly, the mention of the fact that most of the cavalry was foreign, confirms the observation of Bernier that the Mogul (emperor) is considered a foreigner in India and he ruled with the terror of the foreign army rather than love or respect of the people at large.

At another place he writes that after receiving Prince Khurram on the completion of his Deccan mission, "The bakhshis were ordered to arrange according to their mansabs the Amirs who had come with my son to pay their respects. The first Khan-i-Jahan. After this Abdullah Khan, then Mahabat Khan..."[69] It shows that protocol was maintained and noblemen were positioned in the *darbar* in conformity with their status. This was a positive aspect.

Corruption in the Army

On the negative side, corruption among officers of the army was rampant. From the very beginning of Turkish rule the conquered land used to be distributed by the king among army officers, nobles, government officials and even soldiers as rewards and also in lieu of personal salary, and for paying their soldiers. These grants were not hereditary, and were given as pay for military service. But many a time the landholders continued in possession of their land without rendering any military service. This is what Sultan Balban found about 2,000 of his cavalry officers. Over and above this, corruption was galore in the Diwan-i-Arz. Horses of little value were brought to the Diwan and were passed as serviceable, obviously by greasing the palms of the clerks. This was the situation in the Sultanate period. During Mughal times Abdul Qadir Badaoni writes that "the whole country, with the exception of the *khalisa* lands, was held by the Amirs as *jagir*, and as they were wicked and rebellious, and spent large sums on other stores and workshops, and amassed wealth, they had no leisure to look after the troops or take interest in the people". In case of emergency they came with bedraggled slaves and attendants to the scene of war, "but really useful soldiers there were none".[70] Under Akbar, Shahbaz Khan, the Mir Bakhshi, introduced the custom and rule of *dagh/mahalli* of the times of Alauddin Khalji and Sher Shah, but cheating continued. Akbar divided the Ahadis into *do aspa*, *yak aspa* and even *nim aspa* (having half a share in a horse)", in which latter case two troopers kept one horse together, and shared the stipulated salary, which amounted to six rupees.[71]

The salary of the soldiers and expenditure on their horses usually formed part of the pay of the Umara or Mansabdars who were expected to spend it on them. But this system gave the nobleman an opportunity to retain some money from every man's pay and prepare false returns of the horses he was supposed to provide. "Many of the lords who hold the rank of 5000 horse, do not keep even 1000 in their employ."[72] This practice was universal throughout the medieval period. Niccolao Manucci's comment on the situation is quotable as there was corruption in payment of salaries to the soldiers from the very beginning of Muslim rule in India.[73]

"Throughout the world the vice is rampant of being ambitious for the acquisition of wealth. But in no part of the world is this so much the case as in the Mogul Empire and the rest of India. There our Italian proverb applies: 'The big fish eat the little ones.' Particularly is it true at the court and in the army of the Mogul, where the captains and generals observe no fixed rules in paying their soldiers, conforming neither to the rank they have granted them nor to the men's merit. The rank the soldiers receive is high in name, but as for the pay, it is never more than half what the rank indicates.

"The soldiers accept anything and everything, being forced by necessity; for if they cannot obtain military service they have no means of living. Speaking generally, all these soldiers are badly paid and ill-satisfied, for what should be given them in eight months they do not receive in a year. What is worst of all, they are never paid the exact amount due, but little by little. Then they always have to take in the course of a year's service two months pay in second hand goods. In many cases they are kept two and three years in arrears. This forces the soldiers to borrow money at interest from the traders in the camp; these lend it with the consent of the men's own captains and generals."[74]

To conclude. A brief description of the various wings of the army cannot give an idea of the heavy expenditure incurred on them. For example, many army contingents were stationed in forts spread all over the country. An estimate of the cost of some forts has been given in the section on monuments. The estimates of expenditure on the maintenance of soldiers and artillery stationed there is not possible because of paucity of information available. But it was enormous. In fact Muslim rule in India was military rule so that "the order of the household, the efficiency of the army, and the welfare of the country, are intimately connected with the state of this (Arsenal) department". Akbar took great interest in watching the practice of mechanical arts, and often worked at them, himself. He paid special attention to the founding of new cannon and the manufacture of matchlock guns. He was inventor of good armour, bulletproof breast-plates and other weapons. "His Majesty has made several inventions... He made a gun which, on marches, can easily be taken to pieces, and properly put together again when required. By another invention, His Majesty joins seventeen guns in such a manner as to be able to fire them simultaneously with one match."[75] There were many kinds of swords. As usual there were Khasa swords and guns.[76] All this and much more was manufactured in the royal karkhanas or workshops. Naturally much of the royal revenue, both during the Sultanate and Mughal period, was expended on these karkhanas.

5.3. ROYAL KARKHANAS

During the Sultanate period, royal karkhanas were established to cater to the needs of the king and his army. Their numbers and items of production went on multiplying with time, side by side with the production in private workshops. The domestic needs of the ruling class were vast enough, but the political and military requirements were vaster. Huge standing armies had to be equipped and maintained. Arsenals and store houses of every kind had to be kept full. Artisans worked separately at home or jointly in karkhanas. In the royal karkhanas worked the tent-makers and the saddlers, the upholsters and cloth-makers, the metal workers and armourers and producers of dozens of sundry articles.

Skilful engineers in karkhanas manufactured *minjiniqs* and *arradas* and other engines of war and swords and other arms of every kind for the army. When Balban marched against the rebel Tughril Beg of Bengal, the karkhanas overworked to equip the army till the day of the expedition.[77] When Muhammad Tughlaq was in Gujarat preparing for leading an effective expedition to Sindh, arms and other articles were despatched to the king from Delhi . "Weapons alone cost seven lakh *tankahs*," writes Shams Siraj Afif and adds that "on this basis the cost of other items from other *karkhanas* can be calculated".[78] Ibn Battutah gives a list of the presents which he carried on behalf of Muhammad Tughlaq to Toghan Timur or Shunti, the Mogol emperor of Cathay. These were all stored or manufactured in the karkhanas. Besides men and women slaves, the gifts included 100 pieces of cotton fabric called *bairami* priced at 100 *dinars* per piece, 100 pieces of silk called *juzz* of variegated tints, 104 pieces of *salahiya*, 100 pieces of *shirinbaf*, 100 pieces of *shanbaf*, 500 pieces of *muraz*, a kind of woollen fabric of various colours, 100 pieces of *katan-i-Rumi*, 100 gowns without sleeves, a tent with six pavilions, four golden candlesticks and four embroidered with silver, four gold basins and six silver. There were ten dresses of honour, ten caps one of which was embroidered with jewels, ten quivers one of which was studded with pearls, 10 swords the scabbard of one of which was inlaid with pearls and jewels, 10 gloves embroidered with pearls.[79] All these were prepared in the royal karkhanas. Thus all kinds of civil and military goods were produced in the karkhanas. According to Shahabuddin al-Umri "every year the Sultan (Muhammad Tughlaq) distributes 200,000 complete dresses: 100,000 in spring and 100,000 in autumn (among nobles)... Dresses are also distributed to the monasteries and hermitages (*khanqahs* and *dargahs*). The Sultan keeps in his service 500 manufacturers of golden tissues, who weave the gold brocades worn by the wives of the Sultan, and given away as presents to the amirs and their wives." Shams Siraj Afif writes that there were thirty-six karkhanas in the reign of Firoz Tughlaq and the expenditure on one karkhana was not less than the expense on the city of Multan.[80] The recurring and non-recurring (*rabti wa ghair rabti*) expenditure on one karkhana in a month came to one lakh sixty thousand and six lakh *tankahs* each respectively.[81] Each karkhana was placed under the supervision of an important noble. Khwaja Abul Hasan was the overall administrator and superintendent of all these karkhanas.

There were karkhanas of gold, silver and brass and other metals. There was a manufactory each of wines, perfumes armours. Weapons were all prepared in the karkhanas. There were *paigahs* of horses, camels and dogs. There was pil khana, shukra khana, salah khana and tashdar khana. Some figures of expenditure on karkhanas were like this: alam khana, 80,000 *tankahs* per year, farrash khana 2 lakhs. In jamdar khana six lakh *tankahs* per year were expended on obtaining raw materials per year. 12000 slaves worked in the karkhanas of Firoz Tughlaq and were given a salary of from 100 to 10 *tankahs* according to each one's competence. These workers formed some sort of guilds and produced excellent articles. There was no occupation in which the slaves trained as artisans, handicraftsmen and mechanics did not work. Despite some repetition and confusion in the figures mentioned by Afif, the expenditure on the karkhanas was enormous.

With the passing of time and the expansion of Muslim rule the items produced in the karkhanas and the expenditure incurred on them went on increasing. The karkhanas in the Mughal period produced articles for the king and the ruling class. There were karkhanas set up in the capital cities of Delhi and Agra, and many other provincial and industrial towns like Ahmadabad and Burhanpur. The working conditions and wages in the royal karkhanas were better than those in the private sector.[82] Good and confident artisans, therefore, tried to seek employment in the state workshops where they were sure of getting good remuneration. On the other hand the king also tried to get the best workmen from within the country and abroad to work in the royal karkhanas. So that "the imperial workshops (in) the towns of Lahore, Agra, Fatehpur, Ahmadabad, Gujarat, turn out many masterpieces of workmanship".[83] Often the Mughal emperor Akbar used to personally select and appoint men in the workshops and fix their salaries. These karkhanas set the standard and provided models for the private craftsmen also.

Artisans worked separately at home or jointly in karkhanas. It was a localized industrial system, localized in the sense that the craftsmen were organized differently according to the different social strata they served and also whether they worked individually or in groups in private workshops or in the government karkhanas. But organized they were in "guilds". Guilds regulated various matters of common concern. They served as mutual aid societies, they stood surety for their members, and they entered into collective contracts with local authorities and institutions. This led to diffusion of skill throughout the country, a skill that passed from generation to generation in the caste-oriented, vocation-oriented Indian society. The system ensured employment to all skilled and unskilled workers, in state manufactories or private production units. The Mughal state was the largest manufacturer, or rather the only manufacturer on a large scale in respect of several commodities.[85] But it catered only for the elite and not for the commoners.

The karkhanas produced articles for civil and military use; they also served as warehouses. "All articles which have been bought," writes Abul Fazl, "or woven to order or received as tribute or presents, are carefully preserved."[86] Two major items of manufacture were arms and clothes. "His Majesty also ordered that people of certain ranks should wear certain articles; and this was done in order to regulate the demand."

Francois Bernier who witnessed the working of the karkhanas in the capital observes that there were "karkhanas in large halls seen in many places. In one hall embroiderers are busily employed, superintended by a master. In another you see goldsmiths; in the third painters; in the fourth, varnishers with lacquer-work; in a fifth joiners, turners, tailors, and shoe makers; in a sixth manufacturers of silk, brocade and those fine muslins of which are made turbans, girdles with golden flowers and drawers beautifully embroidered with needle work. The artisans repair every morning to their respective workshops, where they remain employed the whole day; and in the evening return to their homes."[87]

Of men's wear produced in the karkhanas, mention may be made of robes of honour or khilats distributed by the emperor on festive occasions, such as the coronation anniversary, the two Ids, the Lunar and Solar weighments etc. Such items were needed in thousands right from the fourteenth century as detailed earlier. Al-Umri gives details of men's khilats but in the Mughal period we get description of the items of luxury-wear also. "His Majesty (Akbar)," writes Abul Fazl, "pays much attention to various stuffs; hence Irani, European, and Mongol articles of wear are in abundance. Skilful masters and workmen have settled in this country to teach people an improved system of manufacture... His Majesty himself acquired in a short time a theoretical and practical knowledge of the whole trade; and on account of the care bestowed upon them the intelligent workmen of this country soon improved. All kinds of hair-weaving and silk-spinning were brought to perfection; and the imperial workshops furnish all those stuffs which are made in other countries." The list of cloths, shawls, clothes, khilats given by Abul Fazl shows that millions and millions of rupees would have been spent in the karkhanas on the manufacture and import of these items.[88]

As always, the expenditure on women's wardrobe was much more than that on men's. Harem ladies dressed in the best and costliest clothes, whether of cotton, silk or wool. Every day they changed their clothes several times. "Ordinarily," writes Manucci, "they wear two or even three garments, each weighing not more than one ounce, and worth from forty to fifty rupees each. This is without counting the (gold) lace they are in the habit of adding."[89] Some drawers worn by them were so delicately fine as to wear out in one night. They covered their heads with a sheet of cloth of gold spangled with stars of different makes or wore turbans with an aigrette with ostrich feathers and a ruby plum which too would have been very costly.[90] Manucci and Bernier talk in general terms, but Abul Fazl gives specific names of cotton, silk and woollen fabrics, Indian as well as those imported from "Turkey, Europe and Portugal".[91] The well known fabrics were Satin, Atlas, Kimkhab, Katan, Tafta, Ambari, Tasser, Pashmina etc. Plain and brocaded velvet (*makhmal*) was imported from Europe, Sashan, Yazd, Mashad, Herat and many other places. By the time of Shahjahan more and more foreign stuffs had begun to be imported.[92] Internal and external trade, royal workshops and private manufactories, provided the requirements of the *haramsara*. Silk was imported from many foreign countries like China and Persia as well as produced indigenously. Bernier says that the consumption of fine cloths of gold, brocades, silks, embroideries, pearls, musk, amber and sweet essences in the seraglio "is greater than can be conceived". All their clothes were perfumed with essence of rose and other flowers. Abul Fazl's catalogue of perfumes and the method of their preparation shows how much Mughal ladies and lords loved perfumes and how costly they were.[93] Even their shoes used to be splendid, some with gold and silver spangles, some indeed were studded with precious stones.

Clothes, embroideries, carpets, shoes, vanity boxes, items of furniture and scores of other nick-nack were prepared in the royal karkhanas or imported from abroad. Quilts and coverlets, bedsheets and pillows, were made at home. Silk quilts of Satgaon were famous. These were also prepared at Patna, Qasim Bazar, Murshidabad and Orissa.[94] Banaras silks and embroidered silk fabrics were rightly renowned. Terry says that the country, "yields good store of silk which they weave curiously, sometimes mingled with silver or gold. They make velvets and satin taffetos...".[95] Fine cotton cloth was manufactured at Delhi, Lahore, Agra, Patna, Banaras, Burhanpur, Dacca and many other places.[96] "Dacca produced prodigious quantity of fine white cloth and silken stuffs (*malmal*)."[97]

European ambassadors, traders and visitors were happy to provide large and small looking glasses, gold and silver laces, fine scarlet and green broad cloths and several articles of Chinese and Japanese workmanship. The Royal manufactories or karkhanas were spread all over the country from Kashmir, Lahore and Agra to Ahmedabad, Fatehpur and Burhanpur. The workmanship of Kashmir was renowned. Its *palkis*, bedsheets, trunks, inkstands, boxes, and spoons, were used all over India. But its shawls were superb. "Great pains have been taken to manufacture similar shawls in Patna, Agra, and Lahore, but notwithstanding every possible care, they never have the delicate texture and softness of the Kashmir shawls." Kashmir, Fatehpur and Jaunpur carpets were also famous. Woollen carpets or *qalins* were imported from Iran and Central Asia. Thick carpets were called *pari* while *shatranji* carpets were both woollen and cotton.[98]

Jewellery and ornaments were the costliest items. These were worn by harem ladies in profusion. Ornaments the harem inmates wore from early childhood, and they remained "the very joy of their hearts" throughout their lives. Abul Fazl gives a list of the then popular ornaments. Manucci describes them: "They (the princesses) wore on their arms, above the elbow, rich armlets two inches wide, enriched on the surface with stones, and having small bunches of pearls depending from them. At their wrists are very rich bracelets, or bands of pearls, which usually go round nine or twelve times. On their fingers are rich rings, and on the right thumb there is always a ring, where in place of stones, there is mounted a little round mirror, having pearls around it. This mirror (*arsi*) they use to look at themselves, an act of which they are very fond at any and every moment. In addition, they are girded with great stones; at the end of the strings which tie up their drawers there are bunches of pearls made up of fifteen strings, five fingers in length. Round the bottom of their legs are valuable metal rings or strings of costly pearls... There hangs from the middle of their head in the centre of their forehead a bunch of pearls or precious ornaments in the shape of star, sun or moon or flower beset with glittering jewels." He continues, "All these princesses own six to eight sets of jewels", besides other sets. No wonder "goldsmiths (both Indian and European) are almost continuously busy making ornaments. The best and the most costly of their productions are for the king's person, the queens and the princesses...".[99] The karkhanas were located in many important towns and cities of the empire. They were thus spread all over the country. They manufactured everything the Mughals needed. From delicate stuffs worn inside the palace to arms, armours and ammunition used by soldiers and nobles on the battlefield, the karkhanas manufactured and stored all royal requirements. There was no item of delicate craftsmanship or heavy construction which was not the responsibility of the karkhanas to produce. So that the karkhanas, in one way or the other, were concerned with the manufacturing of, say, not only palace furniture but also associated with constructing palaces, mosques, roads, canals, and forts. The expenditure incurred on some items finds a stray reference here and there in the chronicles, but the overall expenditure on karkhanas cannot be calculated. All that can be said is that it was colossal.

5.4. ROYAL BENEVOLENCE

Royal largesses knew no bounds after a victory, on coronation, during festivals (like Id, and Nauroz) and on the days of weighments of kings and princes (under the Mughals). The beneficiaries of the king's bounty were Muslims of all classes from rich nobles to poor artisans and labourers and many more. Muslim state in India was meant to serve the cause of Islam. Therefore, Muslims were provided with all kinds of facilities like land grants, pensions and rewards. Foreign Muslim scholars and sufis, adventurers and nobles were invited in large numbers from abroad and liberally provided for. Muslims at home were given similar benefits.

In the medieval Muslim state, the enrichment of the courtiers was the first duty of the ruler, and the Muslim *darbar* specialized in rewarding its partners in conquest and governance. The nobles on their part were determined to milk the system. But in all this the generosity of the king played a significant role. Sultan Shamsuddin Iltutmish appreciated talent and rewarded it well. Minhaj Siraj says that people from Persia (and adjoining countries) came to India in "various capacities".[100] A great scholar of Iltutmish's reign was Amir Ruhani; he had come from Bukhara to Delhi during Chingiz's upheaval. Qazi Hamid-ud-din Nagori had also come from abroad.[101] Fakhr-ul-Mulk Isami, who had been Wazir at Baghdad for thirty years but then had suffered some disappointment, arrived in India and was appointed Wazir by Iltutmish. Sultan Iltutmish gave to Khwaja Taj-ud-din Bukhari and his brother two villages and one lakh *tankahs* in cash for writing a book titled the *Adab-us-Salatin* or rules for the rulers.[102] Nuruddin Muhammad Ufi, the author of *Jama-ul-Hikayat,* had also come to Delhi during Iltutmish's reign. They all held important positions in India. Because of the Mongol upheaval, in the court of Iltutmish there arrived twenty-five princes with their retinues from Iraq, Khurasan and Mawaraun Nahr. During the reign of Sultan Balban fifteen more refugee princes arrived from Turkistan, Mawaraun Nahr, Khurasan, Iraq, Azarbaijan, Persia, Rum and Sham. It appears that each one came with a large number of followers because Balban allotted for their residence a locality (*mohalla*) each.[103] Their followers comprised masters of pen and of sword, scholars and *mashaikh*.

On his accession Jalaludin Khalji gave ministries and assignments to his nobles with a free hand. So did Alauddin Khalji. For deserting the cause of Jalaluddin and siding with Alauddin many nobles had received 20,30, and even 50 *man* of gold from the latter. Their soldiers also got 100 *tankahs* each. During the twenty years of his reign, Muhammad Tughlaq had squandered his wealth on his nobles so that the treasury was in a bad shape when Firoz Tughlaq ascended the throne. Under Muhammad Tughlaq, the Chief Qazi enjoyed a salary of 60,000 *tankahs* a year. The Qazi of the Capital was subordinate to him. Ibn Battutah was appointed on this post on a salary of 12,000 *tankahs* a year. A Mir Dad was appointed by the king on 50,000 *tankahs.*[104] After Firoz Tughlaq came to the throne, during the forty years of his reign he devoted himself to generosity and "the benefit of the Musalmans", by distributing villages and lands among his followers. He made all posts and all allotments hereditary. "If an officer of the army died, he was to be succeeded by his son; if he had no son, by his son-in-law; if he had no son-in law, by his slave (*ghulam*); if he had no slave, by his nearest relation; and if he had no relation, by his wives."[105] Qiwan-ul-Mulk was a high dignitary in the reign of Muhammad Tughlaq. His mansion was 'golden' in some parts. He was appointed the Chief Wazir (Wazir-i-Kul) by Firoz on his arrival in Delhi from Thatta. Khan-i-Jahan Maqbul attained to high dignity. He had a great number of children. When a son was born to him Sultan Firoz gave 11,000 *tankahs* for his maintenance. To a daughter was given 15,000 *tankahs* at the time of marriage.[106] Firoz Tughlaq gave to many nobles and scholars, reciters of the Quran and Saiyyads *wazifas* of ten, five and two thousand *tankahs* each.[107]

During Muslim rule in India, foreign and Indian Muslims were freely bestowed jobs and gifts. Foreign Muslims were most welcome here. They came in large numbers and were well provided for. Muhammad Tughlaq was specially kind to them, as averred by Ibn Battutah. He writes that "the countries contiguous to India like Yemen, Khurasan and Fars are filled with anecdotes about... his generosity to the foreigners in so far as he prefers them to the Indians, honours them, confers on them great favours and makes them rich presents and appoints them to high offices and awards them great benefits". He calls them *aziz* or dear ones and has instructed his courtiers not to address them as foreigners. 'The sultan ordered for me," writes Ibn Battutah, "a sum of six thousand *tankahs*, and ordered a sum of ten thousand for Ibn Qazi Misr. Similarly, he ordered sums to be given to all foreigners (*a'izza*) who were to stay at Delhi, but nothing was given to the metropolitans."[108] He gave robes of honour to all, including Ibn Battutah and Shihabuddin, a merchant of Kazarun, a town in Iran. When Shihabuddin fell ill, Muhammad Tughlaq sent him one lakh of gold *tankahs*, "so that his heart be cheered up". Shihabuddin later sailed to Hormuz, but he was deprived of all his possessions in the "civil war that broke out between the ruler of Hormuz and his two nephews...". Shihabuddin was not the only victim of violence in the Islamic lands of turbulence. Ziyauddin Barani, like Ibn Battutah, knew that the fear of robbers in Muslim lands had restricted Muhammad Tughlaq's generosity to the foreigners.

There are scores of instances of Muhammad Tughlaq's generosity to foreigners. The sultan had sent a present to Caliph Abul Abbas in Egypt soliciting a letter of investiture. The Caliph sent the desired letter through Ruknuddin, the grand Shaikh of Egypt. The envoy was sent back to his country with many rich gifts, including horseshoes made of gold. Ruknuddin lost the gifts in a conflict and Sultan Muhammad replaced them. Similarly, Nasiruddin, the preacher of Egypt, came to wait on the sultan and remained with him for one year enjoying his favours. The sultan granted Nasiruddin a gilded robe of honour embellished with precious stones, a tent enclosure made entirely of silk of different colours, some gold utensils, several pitchers, a flask, a jug, a four-legged table and a stand for books — all made of gold. On his arrival the sultan had given Nasiruddin money amounting to a hundred thousand *tankahs* with two hundred slaves, some of whom he manumitted while others he took away. Abdul Aziz was a jurist, well versed in Hadis.

He had studied at Damascus and came on a visit to India. One day he incidentally related to the sultan a few of the Prophet's sayings. The sultan was so impressed by the recital that he kissed the jurist's feet and ordered a gold tray to be brought containing two thousand *tankahs.* He poured the tray with his own hands over the jurist saying, "This as well as the tray is for you." To the jurist and poet Shamsuddin Andkani of Khurasan, who had presented an ode containing twenty-seven verses praising the sultan, Muhammad Tughlaq awarded a sum of one thousand dinars for each verse. To many other accomplished Muslims like Azuddin the jurist, Qazi Majduddin a man of great parts, and Burhanuddin the renowned preacher, handsome amounts of money were sent in their home towns — they did not visit India.

The story of Haji Kaun may be mentioned as the last case. Haji Kaun was a cousin of Sultan Abu Said, the king of Iraq. His brother Musa was also a ruler in some parts of Iraq. Haji Kaun waited on Muhammad Tughlaq and was honoured with rich gifts. One day the Wazir Khwaja Jahan sent to the sultan a present including three trays — the first filled with rubies, the second with emeralds, and the third with pearls. Haji Kaun being present the sultan gave him a considerable portion out of these. Later he again gave him enormous wealth. Haji Kaun left for Iraq. His brother had died and he reclaimed the throne. But he behaved cruelly towards his nobles and was killed by them, and all the wealth he had carried from India was lost.[109] Muhammad Tughlaq's generous gifts to Ghiyasuddin, a scion of the Caliph, would be listed later on. The point to note here is that under Sultan Muhammad so much wealth was awarded to so many deserving and undeserving foreign Muslims that at the close of his reign the Delhi treasury had become bankrupt. There was also the loss of popularity because "the people of India hate the foreigners (Persians, Turks, Khurasanis) because of the favour the sultan shows them,"[110] and they hated the sultan for the same reason.

The Saiyyad rulers, because of their unpopularity as Timur's nominees in India, needed outside help for sustaining their position and power. During their rule therefore many Afghans arrived in India at their invitation. Afghans had earlier been employed by Mahmud of Ghazni, Iltutmish and Balban to fight Hindu Rajas and Zamindars. From the time of Khizr Khan they came in large groups. They were assigned important *iqtas*. Afghan colonization was a costly affair. The Afghan nobility, devoid of discipline and greedy of gathering wealth, added to the expenditure of the Sultanate. To add to the expenditure many nobles, who had lost their positions during the invasion of Timur, were re-allotted their old offices, parganas and *iqtas*.[111] The ascendancy of the Afghans during the Saiyyad rule paved the way for their ascension to the throne of Delhi. During the Lodi regime (1451-1526), Afghan tribal leaders became a still more privileged class in the polity of the Sultanate. All the best lands were distributed among them. Similarly, in the Sharqi kingdom, the court of Sultan Ibrahim, according to Farishtah, rivalled that of Iran, and the capital Jaunpur came to be known as second Shiraz.[112] In other Muslim kingdoms, like Gujarat and Malwa also, the kings spent equally lavishly on rewarding their nobles, scholars, and men of religion. According to the *Akhbar-ul-Akhiyar*, Sikandar Lodi invited learned men from Arabia, Iran and Central Asia and many of them adopted Hindustan as their home. For example, Shaikh Husain Tahir, who lived during the reigns of Bahlul and Sikandar, was known as a walking encyclopaedia.[113] It is said that Sultan Sikandar bestowed lands and gifts upon the learned and the religious to the extent that had never been done in former reigns.[114]

The Sur Afghans were no different from their Lodi compatriots. "Sher Shah gave to many of his kindred who came from Roh money and property far exceeding their expectations." This statement of Abbas Sarwani is repeated and elaborated still later on. He says: "To every pious Afghan who came into his presence from Afghanistan, Sher Shah used to give money to an amount exceeding his expectations, and he would say, 'This is your share of the kingdom of Hind, which has fallen into my hands, this is assigned to you, come every year to receive it.'" And to his own tribe and family of Sur, who dwelt in the land of Roh, he sent an annual stipend of money, in proportion to the members of his family and retainers; and during the period of his dominion no Afghan, whether in Hind or Roh was in want, but all became men of substance. It was the custom of the Afghans during the time of sultans Bahlul and Sikandar, and as long as the dominions of the Afghans lasted, that if any Afghan received a sum of money or a dress of honour, "that sum of money or dress of honour was regularly apportioned to him, and he received it every year". Sher Shah Suri too said, "It is incumbent upon kings to give grants to *imams*; for the prosperity and populousment of the cities of Hind are dependent on the *imams* and holy men... whoever wishes that God Almighty should make him great, should cherish *Ulama* and pious persons, that he may obtain honour in this world and felicity in the next."[115]

Zahiruddin Muhammad Babur, after his victory over Ibrahim Lodi liberally distributed gold and gifts among his people. "To some Begs 10 lakhs were given, 8, 7 or 6 to others. Erksine estimated these sums as very large sums for the age. Suitable money gifts were bestowed from the Treasury on the whole army, to every tribe there was, Afghan, Hazara, Arab, Biluch *etc.* to each according to its position. Every trader and student, indeed every man who had come with the army, took ample portion and share of bounteous gift and largess. Many gifts went to the begs and soldiery on that side (Tramontana)", i.e. homeland. Largesses were also distributed on festivals like Id.[116] The awards to officers who had done good work in the battle against Rana Sanga were generous. The government of Mewat with its chief town Tijara was bestowed on Chin Timur "together with an allowance of 50 *lakhs* for his support". Alwar and an allowance of 15 *lakhs* was bestowed on Tardi *yakka*. The contents of the Alwar treasury were bestowed on Humayun.[117]

If this could be given to the nobles and army officers, princes and ladies of the royalty of course were most lavishly rewarded. The first Mughal emperor Babur's bounty in this regard earned him the sobriquet of *qalandar*, that is, he gave away with both hands and was left with nothing for himself. Babur distributed the wealth on 11th or 12th of May, 1526. This is what we find noted in his memoirs about the distribution of treasure in Agra: "To Humayun were given 70 lakhs from the treasury, and, over and above this, a treasure house was bestowed on him just as it was... 17 lakhs were given to Kamran, 15 lakhs to Muhammad Zaman Mirza, while to Askari and Hindal and other relations and younger children went masses of gold and silver, of 'plenishing jewels and slaves'."

"Valuable gifts (*saughat*) were sent for the various relations in Samarkand, Khurasan, Kashgar and Iraq." Details about these are given by Babur's daughter Gulbadan Begum. Khwaja Kilan Beg carried them to Kabul to be distributed among the Begums and other relatives as per the conqueror's instructions. "To each Begum is to be delivered as follows: one special dancing girl of the dancing girls of sultan Ibrahim, with one gold plate full of jewels — ruby and pearl, cornelian and diamond, emerald and turquoise, topaz and cat's-eye — and two small mother-of-pearl trays full of *asharfis*, and two other trays of *shahrukhis*." Similar gifts were to be given to other inmates of the harems and kinsmen (of officers serving in India under Babur) and Aghas or guardians of the harems. An *asharfi* weighing fifteen *sirs* of Hind, the only one of its kind, was sent for the Asas or the night-guard. When all the begums and khanums arrived in India, ninety-six persons in all, they all received houses and lands and gifts to their hearts' desire.[118]

Let us continue with the distribution of gifts to royal ladies into the later Mughal times. Nur Jahan Begum received from her royal husband Jahangir, grants of land, gifts of gold and jewels, and countless treasures. She also got gifts and presents from Indian Rajas and foreign merchants. The jagirs she held spread all over the country, and "would have conferred on her the title of a commander of 30,000". Her large jagir of Ramsar was situated about 30 kilometres south-east of Ajmer. In 1617, on the happy occasion of Shahjahan's victory in the Deccan, Nur Jahan was given the pargana of Toda as jagir. It lay 80 kilometres south-east of Ajmer on the medieval trade route from Surat to Agra and brought her an annual income of two lakhs of rupees.[119] Besides she had received the right of collecting octroi duty at Sikandarabad[120] on the merchandise coming from Purab or the eastern country of Allahabad, Bihar and Orissa as well as Bengal and Bhutan.[121] Obviously Nur Jahan Begum's income from cesses and octroi duties was substantial. To this may be added her income from trade and commerce in which she was keenly interested. Indian ships carried from India textiles, spices, ginger, pepper, dyes, opium and various other drugs to West Asian countries like Arabia, Persia, North Africa, and brought back wines, perfumes, brocades, China goods, gold, silver, ivory, amber, pearls, horses etc. Nur Jahan maintained a number of ships and carried on foreign trade mainly in indigo and embroidered cloth.[122] Her commercial enterprises brought her immense profits.[123] She had to compromise with the fact that the Emperor, his mother and many other members of the royal family were also trading on their own account, and Nur Jahan could not monopolize any item of trade. Many European trading companies like the Portuguese, Dutch and English were at this time busy in commercial activity in India. Nur Jahan's relations with the English were good. She sent her goods in English ships, preferring them to those of the Portuguese with whom the Mughal relations were not good.

The English profited by her favours. She managed *farmans* for them conferring concessions.[124] In these transactions Nur Jahan's brother Asaf Khan was the chief agent and intermediary. Gifts and presents were exchanged between the English and the royal family. She also received valuable and costly curios, gifts, *nazars* and bribes from foreigners and Indians.[125]

Similarly, Jahan Ara Begum possessed enormous wealth. On his accession Shahjahan had given her one hundred thousand *asharfis* and four hundred thousand rupees and fixed her an allowance at six hundred thousand rupees.[126] In the case of royal ladies whose allowances were large, usually one half of the amount was paid to them in cash and the other half was given in the form of assignments of land or customs revenue. Jahan Ara received many such assignments. The jagirs assigned to her included, among others, Achhbal and Vernag in Kashmir, Doraha[127] and Panipat in Punjab, Bachhpur or Machalpur in Central India and Shafipur in U.P. The revenue of the sarkar of Doraha was given to her for the upkeep of her gardens and that of the flourishing port city of Surat for her expenditure on betel.[128] That is how the poor of the country were fleeced to keep the princes and princesses rich. In 1648-49, on the inaugural of the twenty-third year of his reign, Shahjahan granted her the pargana of Panipat, the annual revenue of which was one crore *dams*. "She had in addition many precious stones and jewels that had been given to her by her father." It was customary in the harem to reciprocate such gestures and she also gave presents to her father and brothers. Once on the occasion of the weighing ceremony of Shahjahan, she gave him a pearl of great value and distributed gold and silver in *nisar*. On the accession of Aurangzeb she presented precious jewels to the new emperor and again sent presents to him on the occasion of his weighing ceremony. On another occasion when Shahjahan recovered from illness the princess along with some other ladies distributed fifty thousand rupees to the poor.

"This princess," writes Bernier, "accumulated great riches by means of her large allowances and of the costly presents which flowed in from all quarters, in consideration of numberless negotiations intrusted to her sole management." As in the case of Nur Jahan, these came from both Indian and foreign channels. The Dutch sought her favours to resolve their problems. She also received presents from the English consisting of perfumed oils, broad cloth, embroidered cloth, mirrors and cabinets. Tavernier, who came to India in 1641, presented rich gifts to her. In 1654 Raja Prithvichand of Srinagar in Garhwal sought the pardon of emperor Shahjahan through Jahan Ara Begum to whom he naturally presented with gifts. In the same year Qutb Shah of Golkunda, who had been troubled by Aurangzeb, appealed to Jahan Ara and she secured his pardon against payment of indemnity. There are many more such instances when her intercession brought her gifts and gold. Jahan Ara Begum's finances were also augmented by her commercial enterprise. She owned a number of ships and used to carry on trade on her own account. She contracted friendly commercial relations with the Dutch and the English and with their co-operation carried on extensive commercial activities and made enormous profits. According to Manucci, her income was thirty lakhs of rupees a year besides precious stones and jewels.[129]

Nur Jahan and Jahan Ara are big names. All princes and princesses were given allowances and gifts of cash and jewels. Jahangir describes the gifts he bestowed on Shahzada Khurram on many occasions and on Prince Parwez at the time of his marriage. On one occasion when Roshan Ara Begum was given seven lakh fifty thousand rupees by Aurangzeb, Zaib-un-nisa Begum got four lakhs, Zinat-un-nisa two lakhs, Badr-un-nisa one lakh seventy thousand, and Zabt-un-nisa one lakh fifty thousand.[130] High and mighty begums maintained their own establishments but others lived in the harem and their expenses were borne by the state exchequer. When it is recollected that Akbar's harem had

5,000 women and Prince Shah Alam's 2,000, the expenditure on the harem can well be visualized. Since the harem ladies had little work to do — work was considered a degrading activity among the Mughal elite — they spent their time in make-up and gossip. All their hobbies and necessities were expensive but provided for.

Like nobles, princes and princesses men of learning and religion too were awarded presents and granted pensions liberally. Nor were the poor ignored. Muslim state in India was a welfare state for the Muslims,[131] as desired by the Islamic religion and its scriptures. From the very beginning of Muslim rule lands and gardens, orchards and villages and cash awards were granted as scholarships and pensions to Ulama, Mutalaqin, Sufis, Hafiz, Saadat, Mashaikah, Arbab-i-Masjid, Khanqah-dwellers, Astanadars, Qalandars, Faqirs, the deprived, the widows, the old, orphaned, blind, deformed, spastic, physically handicapped, teachers, Muftis, Khatibs, students, poets etc., etc.[132] For example, Firoz Tughlaq sanctioned thirty-six lakh *tankahs* for ulema and *mashaikh* and one crore *tankahs* yearly for the needy and the helpless (*faqir wa miskin*), besides allotting *qasbas* for Saadats.[133] 34,200 persons received these monthly allowances. All Muslim kings were exceedingly benevolent to men of religion — including the secular Akbar and Jahangir. Jahangir writes: "During the reign of my father, the ministers of religion and students of law and literature, to the number of two and three thousand, in the principal cities of the empire, were already allowed pensions from the state; and to these, in conformity with the regulations established by my father, I directed Miran Sadr Jahan (spelling normalised) one of the noblest among the Seyeds of Herat, to allot a subsistence corresponding with their situation; and this is not only to the subjects of my own realms, but to foreigners — to natives of Persia, Roum, Bokhara, and Azerbaijan, with strict charge that this class of men should not be permitted either want or inconvenience of any type."[134] Jahangir also directed Miran

Sadr "that he should every day produce before me deserving people (worthy of charity)."[135]

But let us begin with the beginning. From Minhaj Siraj to Farishtah, all Muslim chroniclers bestow lavish praise upon Muhammad Ghauri for his munificence and patronage of the learned. Qutbuddin Aibak's generosity is praised by all writers who style him as *lakhbakhsh* or giver of lakhs. Balban used to visit the houses of the men of religion and learning and bestow gifts on them. So also were treated the poor and the weak. Scattering of coins among the poor was a common practice. Sometimes ingenuous methods were devised to reward people to make them happy. During his march from Kara to Delhi to occupy the throne Alauddin Khalji used a *manjaniq* or catapult engine to hurl at every halt five *man* of gold coins among the people and thereby gained their goodwill. Emperor Jahangir used to scatter rupees, half-rupees and quarter rupees to faqirs and indigent persons on both sides of the road during excursions.[136] On Alauddin's accession liberal gifts were bestowed upon the people at large, and for some time wine and beauty and music became the order of the day. Pavilions were erected in the bazars and wine, soft drinks and *pan* were distributed free. The army was given six months salary as a reward, the shaikhs and ulema were awarded gratuities, and all high and low partook of the royal bounty.[137] Similarly, when Firoz Tughlaq arrived in Delhi after his coronation, "pavilions (*kaba*) were raised and decorated *according to the times of former kings*". There were six such pavilions. One lakh *tankahs* was expended on each pavilion in food and sherbet for twenty-one days and no one was excluded.

Diwan-i-Khairat

The *Tarikh-i-Firoz* Shahi of Shams Siraj Afif contains a fairly good account of the social life of the Sultanate period. While Ziyauddin Barani's *Tarikh* and most other chronicles are primarily political histories, Afif's work has a social bias. It gives in detail the measures Firoz Tughlaq took for the benefit of the poor, but it was a continuation of a tradition, and things were done "according to the times of former kings". In brief, measures such as his were taken throughout the medieval period. Sultan Firoz founded an establishment by the name of Diwan-i-Khairat. It was meant to help promotion of marriages of daughters of needy Musalmans. Those who could not provide a marriage portion for their daughters were given fifty *tankahs*, thirty *tankahs* and twenty-five *tankahs* as per their social standing.[138]

Similarly, according to Motamid Khan, Nur Jahan Begum in the seventeenth century, "if ever she learnt that any orphan girl was destitute, she would bring about her marriage, and give her a wedding portion". She was an asylum for all sufferers, and helpless girls were married at the expense of her private purse. She must have portioned about 500 girls and thousands were grateful for her generosity.[139] Muslim rulers and nobles throughout the medieval period tried to earn merit by doing this work of *sawab*.

Sultan Firoz established a government hospital for he relief of the sick. Able physicians and doctors were appointed to treat the patients and provision was made for the supply of medicines. The sultan settled some rich villages to provide for the expenses of this hospital, so that medicines, food, drinks and other expenses of the patients were borne by the state treasury. Al-Umari speaks of many private hospitals in the reign of Muhammad Tughlaq. But Firoz's was a government hospital. Jahangir also takes credit for doing the same. He gave orders that the jagirdars "should found hospitals in the great cities, and appoint physicians for the healing of the sick; whatever the expenditure might be, should be given from the *khalisa* establishment".[140] After recovery the patient was discharged after being provided with a "sufficient sum of money for his exigencies".[141]

Sultan Firoz Tughlaq also saw to it that no workman

remained unemployed. Sometimes respectable people, out of shame, would not make their necessities known. But once they were brought before the Sultan, he provided them with some employment. Men of pen and intelligent men of business were sent to government karkhanas, others to other suitable jobs. Slaves were also assigned to nobles or absorbed in the king's establishment . He himself had about 2 lakhs of them.

Like Firoz Shah Tughlaq, Sultan Sikandar Lodi was specially kind towards his co-religionists. Every six months he got prepared a list of the indigent and the meritorious and fixed suitable allowances for each one of them. Every winter he distributed clothes and covering to the needy. Cooked and uncooked food was distributed free at various places every day. On certain days like Id, Barawafat, the anniversary of the Prophet's death, and in the month of Ramzan, charities were freely distributed. Following upon the example of the king, the nobles also vied with one another in giving charities.[142] What has been said about Firoz Tughlaq or Sikandar Lodi stands true for all Muslim kings and references of such benevolences lie scattered in most Persian histories. Government expenditure on helping the poor was high.

Sikandar Lodi encouraged learning among his clansmen. Education was mostly imparted in schools attached to mosques. Schools and colleges at Agra, Sambhal, Mathura, Narwar and many other places flourished under the royal patronage, and Muslim learning "spread in the countryside".[143] Its cost was borne by the Muslim state. It need hardly be added that "these Madrasas were strongholds of orthodoxy and were subsidised by the state."[144]

Sikandar Lodi was an orthodox ruler while Sher Shah is considered to be a secular king. But so far as looking after the interests and welfare of the Muslims is concerned, all sultans and badshahs were alike. Religious considerations prompted their actions. Sher Shah often said, "It behoves kings to inscribe the pages of their history with the characters of religion. It behoves kings not to disobey the commands of God."[145] Two institutions, says Rizqullah, "were kept up during his reign without any interruption: one, the religious establishments (*imarat khana*) and the other the houses for the poor... He himself used to take his meals with the learned and the *Shaikhs*.[146] His private kitchen was very extensive, for several thousand people fed there every day. There was a general order, that if any soldier or religious personage, or any cultivator, should be in need of food, he should feed at the kings's kitchen..." The daily cost of these meals, and of these places for the distribution of food, was 500 gold pieces (*asharfis*) or rupees 2,37,25,000 per year.[147] "Destitute people, who were unable to provide for their own subsistence, like the blind, the old, the weak in body, widows, and the sick, etc., to such he gave stipends from the treasury of the town in which they were resident..." All Muslim rulers as a rule, and without exception, provided free food to the poor. Even the stingy Aurangzeb was keen on setting up free kitchens. Distribution of free meals benefited the destitute but such generosity would also have encouraged laziness and beggary among the Muslims. As Jadunath Sarkar writes, "The vast sums spent by the State in maintaining pauper houses and in scattering alms during Ramzan and other holy days and joyous ceremonies, were a direct premium on laziness. Thus a lazy and pampered class was created in the empire, who was the first to suffer when its prosperity was arrested."[148] Sher Shah noted that distribution of stipends to the sick and old through religious officials encouraged the imams to embezzle money. In medieval times wherever there was money there was corruption. And free kitchens involved lot of money. Sher Shah took steps to curb imams' dishonesty.

Charities were distributed among the poor and the needy on occasions both happy and sad. Money was spent like water at the birth of a prince, his marriage, accession of the king, or at the time of sickness or of death in the royal family.

Happy occasions were many. And Jahangir's memoirs are full of accounts of these. For example, when early in his reign, Jahangir was at Kabul, he ordered that so long as he was there, 12,000 rupees were to be distributed every Thursday among the poor. Or, he gave 9,000 rupees to be distributed in alms to faqirs and other poor people on the occasion of Prince Parwez's marriage. When princess Jahanara was badly burnt Shahjahan distributed 5000 rupees daily in alms totalling seven lakhs. On her recovery he gave 5 lakhs more in charity. The slave Arif who had prepared the ointment which healed her burns was weighed against gold and given 7,000 coins in cash. On Shahjahan's death Jahanara distributed two thousand gold coins among the poor.

One practice of the Mughals, namely *tuladan*, which was borrowed from the Hindus provided many occasions in the course of the year for distributing charity among the poor. It was started by Akbar and it continued till the twelfth year of Aurangzeb's reign. Even after that many princes continued celebrating their birthday by *tuladan*.[149] Kings and princes were weighed on both solar and lunar birthdays and money equal to their weight was distributed among the faqirs. For instance, on the solar weighing of Prince Parwez, the whole proceedings were given to the poor. On the fortieth *wazan-i-qamari* of Jahangir (weighing according to lunar year), he gave 10,000 rupees of the money of the weighing to be distributed among the deserving and the needy. Prince Khurram was weighed in his sixteenth lunar year against gold, silver and other materials which were given away to the faqirs. But the most interesting was the double celebration of lunar and solar weighments of the late emperor Akbar by his son. Jahangir writes that "I determined that the value of all the articles which he (Akbar) used to order for his own weighing in the solar and lunar years should be estimated, and that what this came to should be sent to the large cities for the repose of the soul of that enlightened one, and be divided amongst the necessitous and the faqirs. The total came to 100,000 rupees, equal to 300 Iraq *tumans*, and 300,000 of the currency of the people of Mawaraun-nahr."[150] In this way many millions of rupees must have gone in charity in the course of a hundred years.

Artists, poets, scholars and musicians, were of course given liberal grants, stipends and rewards. Their lists are found in almost all Muslim chronicles. One example should suffice. In the third volume of W. Haig's translation of Abdul Qadir Badaoni's *Muntakhab-ut-Tawarikh*, there are accounts of 38 shaikhs, 69 scholars, 15 philosophers and physicians and about 167 poets of the time of Akbar. It is said that there were 300 painters in Akbar's court alone. It is not necessary to give many more lists.

5.5. GIFTS TO CALIPHS, MECCA AND MEDINA

The generosity of Muslim rulers was not confined to Musalmans in India alone. It extended to Muslims anywhere and everywhere. In the case of sending presents and wealth to the Caliphs and the holy cities of Mecca and Medina their liberality was unrestricted.

Lot of wealth was sent to the Caliph by the sultans of Hindustan. The first four Caliphs were directly related to the Prophet. Muawiyah, the founder of the Ummayad Caliphate, was a cousin and Abbas (the ancestor of the Abbasid Caliphate) an uncle of Prophet Muhammad. There was therefore very great reverence for the Caliphs in the world of Islam. The Abbasids had built up a large empire with capital at Baghdad.[151] Its provinces were administered by the Turkish slave governors and Turkish mercenary troops. These Turkish governors became independent in course of time but officially they were only slaves. So they thought it politic to pay tribute to the Khalifa and in return seek from him recognition of their 'sovereignty'. The Arab invader Muhammad bin Qasim as well as the later governors of Sindh used to read the *khutbah* in the name of the

Ummayad Caliph and used to send him the legal one-fifth part of the booty (Khams).[152] For example, when Muhammad bin Qasim attacked Debal, "700 beautiful females, who were under the protection of Budh (that is, had taken shelter in the temple) were all captured with their valuable ornaments..." Muhammad despatched seventy-five damsels as Khams to Hajjaj. Thereafter, whichever places he sacked he slew the men and captured the women and children, and batches of them were despatched to the Caliph at regular intervals. On one occasion alone 20,000 slaves of both sexes were sent to the Caliph.[153] The amount of cash and valuables sent to Caliph counted to 120 million dirhams (120 thousand dirhams according to Al-Kufi).

Mahmud Ghaznavi's campaigns in India had Caliphal blessings. In return, Mahmud was always careful to inscribe the Caliph's name on his coins, and send to Baghdad presents from the plunder of his campaigns.[154] These consisted of large amounts of all kinds of wealth including indigo, the valuable dyestuff which was collected as tribute from India.[155] The accession of Mahmud's successor Masud was not peaceful and, therefore, soon after coming to the throne he applied to the Khalifa for recognition of his title to succession. "He sent an envoy to Qadir Billah, and promising to send him every year a sum of 2,00,000 *dinars*, 10,000 pieces of cloth, besides other presents, requested him to recognise his claim. The Khalifa was pleased to send him a formal investiture..."[156] His successor continued with the tradition. By such remittances the sultans obtained recognition and moral support of the Caliph while the latter gained in financial resources and remained supreme in the Islamic world.

Like the Ghaznavids the Ghaurids were also alive to the importance of obtaining the confirmation of their sovereignty from the Caliphs of Baghdad. Ghiyasuddin, the elder brother of Muizzuddin or Muhammad Ghauri, obtained sanctions from the Abbasid Caliph of Baghdad. The earliest Muslim rulers of Hindustan were originally slaves, and it was recognised in all quarters that their position as rulers would be buttressed if they could receive caliphal recognition. Tajuddin Yilduz, the ruler of Ghazni, obtained the Caliph's sanction for his authority. After Yilduz and Qubacha had been destroyed by Iltutmish, the latter received the investiture from the Abbasid Caliph al-Mustansir Billah as a legal sanction of his monarchy.[157] The formal patent of investiture was called *manshur* and the robe of honour, turban, swords, ensigns and other gifts were called *karamat*. It is not known if Iltutmish had requested the Khalifa for it, or how much wealth and presents he sent in return, but he must have sent lot of wealth as that was but customary.

Muhammad bin Tughlaq probably crossed all limits of generosity in sending the Caliph enormous wealth. Surely the Sultan must have sent a substantial amount, because when Ghiyasuddin, who was only a descendent of the extinct caliphal house of Baghdad, visited India, Muhammad's bounty knew no bounds. Writing on the basis of Muslim histories, Wolseley Haig says that "the vessels in his (Ghiyasuddin's) palace were of gold and silver, the bath being of gold and on the first occasion of his using it a gift of 400,000 *tangas* was sent to him; he was supplied with male and female servants, and slaves. He was allowed a daily sum of 300 *tangas*, though much of the food consumed by him and his household came from the royal kitchen; he received in fee the whole of Alauddin's city of Siri, one of the four cities (Delhi, Siri, Tughlaqabad, and Jahanpanah) which composed the capital, with all its buildings, and adjacent gardens and lands and a hundred villages; he was appointed governor of the eastern district of the province of Delhi; he received thirty mules with trappings of gold; and whenever he visited the court he was entitled too receive the carpet on which the king sat." And all this wealth was bestowed on a "mean and miserly" wretch who could not bear to see others eating good food and who did not return a loan he owed to

Ibn Battutah.[158] If this treasure was given to a scion of a house which had become defunct, how much more was sent to the living Caliph at Cairo, is difficult to sumrise. No wonder it elicited a comment from the contemporary chronicler Ziyauddin Barani: "So great was the faith of the Sultan in the Abbasid Khalifas," says he, "that he would have sent all his treasures in Delhi to Egypt, had it not been for the fear of robbers."[159] That is how the wealth of India, milked from the labours of the poor, was squandered on foreign Muslims. No wonder that because of the generosity of the Sultan in his time the Caliphal investitures were received more than once. Muhammad Tughlaq included the names of Abbasid al-Mustakfi and his successors al-Wathiq I and al-Hakim in his *khutbah* and inscribed on his coins their names to the exclusion of his own.[160] Such an attitude of subservience combined with munificence encouraged the Caliph to send to Muhammad's successor Firoz Tughlaq, a patent of investiture entrusting to him the territories of Hind.

With the fall of the Tughlaq dynasty the name of the Caliph was dropped from Delhi coins. But the outflow of wealth did not cease. To the Saiyyad rulers, Timur and his successors played the role of the Caliphs. It is they who provided moral and material support to Saiyyad sultans. More than once, role of honour came from Shah Rukh to Delhi for Khizr Khan and Mubarak Khan. In return annual tribute was sent to Shah Rukh.[161] Sultan Muhammad Saiyyad also remained loyal to him.[162] It was not only the sultans of Delhi, but also of Jaunpur and Bengal who called themselves vice-regents of the Abbasid Caliphs.[163] The Caliph al-Mustanjid Billah sent to Sultan Mahmud Khalji of Malwa robes of honour and a letter patent. Mahmud accepted the gifts of the Khalifa with due honour and gave in return to the envoy *tashrifat*, and a large amount of gold and silver. Even some rebels of the Delhi Sultanate received the caliphal investiture[164] in return for gifts of money and gold and slaves. Needless to add that money, gifts and presents were sent to Caliphs; not only to Caliphs but also to Mecca and Medina and to Muslim brethren in their homelands.

Mecca and Medina

This is borne out by some figures available for the Mughal period.

In war and peace, gifts were regularly sent to Mecca (Makka) and Medina (Madinah). The Prophet had ensured prosperity of Arabia permanently through income from Hajj pilgrimage and presents from pious Muslims to these holy centres of Islam. If the sultans sent treasures to Caliphs, the Mughals excelled in forwarding gifts and charities, gold and silver, to the Muslim holy cities of Mecca and Medina. "He made Hajj i.e., pilgrimage to the Kaaba, an old pre-Islamic Arab rite, a basic tenet of his religion to impress upon foreign Muslims the sanctity of Arabia, and create an ever lasting source of income for the Arabs." This "income counted as the mainstay of the Arabs before they discovered their oil wealth".[165]

Some interesting information is available from the west coast, where Muslim traders had settled, regarding numbers of gifts being sent to the Muslim holy cities from earliest times. A lengthy bilingual inscription from Somnath Patan in Arabic and Sanskrit dated 662 H/1264 CE mentions about Nakhuda Nuruddin Firoz, the ship master. He built a mosque on land which was either purchased or gifted by Briha Raja Chhada. Provision was made by Nuruddin for *muallims* and *muazzins*. "Any surplus which remained was to be sent to Mecca and Medina." The lengthy Sanskrit text has a shorter Arabic counterpart. Missing in the Sanskrit is the significant invocation: "... in the city of Somnath, may God make it one of the cities of Islam and (banish) infidelity and idols." Another inscription from Junagarh mentions an Arab ship master who was "the prop of the pilgrims to the holy cities of Mecca and Medina".[166]

With the arrival of Babur information about such gifts abounds. Babur sent to holy men belonging to Samarqand and Khurasan offerings vowed to God (*nuzur*); so too to Mecca and Medina. "We gave one *shahrukhi* for every soul in the country of Kabul and the vale-side of Varsak, man and woman, bond and free, of age or non-age."[167]

Akbar regularly sent money and gifts to Mecca and Medina. "Though debarred from leaving Hindustan himself, he helped many others to fulfill this primary duty of their faith, and opened wide his purse for their expenses. Each year he named a leader of the caravan and provided him with gifts and ample funds for the two cities. When Gulbadan Begum, his paternal aunt, went for Hajj, Sultan Khwaja, Gulbadan's cicerone, took among other presents, 12,000 dresses of honour."[168] As mentioned earlier both Akbar and Jahangir sent to the religious men of Persia, Rum and Azarbaijan subsistence allowance on the principle: "Wealth is from God... and these are his servants", be they in Hindustan or any other Muslim country.[169] "Shahjahan despatched to Mecca an amber candlestick covered with a network of gold and inlaid with gems and diamonds by his own artisans. It was a most gorgeous piece of work turned out by the craftsmen, worth two and a half lacs of rupees."[170]

These are just a few specimens. Kings and nobles and rich Hajis regularly sent out wealth from India to Mecca and Medina.

5.6. KINGS AND NOBLES

Life of Muslim kings and nobles in India can be termed as fully lived. It was characterised by the absence of any sense of economy. Those who could liberally distribute money among the rich and the poor alike — umara, ulema, saiyyads, sufis, artists, poets and faqirs —, those who sent abroad millions of rupees to their Muslim brothers and religious leaders, could not by themselves live a life of austerity. They did not conquer countries and rule over kingdoms to live parsimoniously. They lived a full-fledged life full of physical comfort. There was no difference between the income of the state and the private purse of the king. Technically, all wealth of the state was spent on and on the command of the emperor. It is significant that the *Ain-i-Akbari* of Abul Fazl covering various items of the state's income and expenditure begins with the chapter on Household, the imperial household and imperial treasuries. For everything in a Muslim state was directed towards the person of the king and the order of his household. His household was his harem. We have already written about the life of the Mughal harem in a full-size monograph.[171] Therein one can get details about the expenses incurred on the harems of Muslim royalty and nobility. We shall therefore be very brief here on the subject of the expenditure of the Muslim ruling class in India.

The government of the early Turks revolved round the sultan's household establishment. The public revenue could be spent or squandered in the pursuit of his pleasure. Sultan Ruknuddin Firoz, son of Iltutmish, emptied the treasury on the providers of pleasure. Sultan Kaiqubad, the grandson of Balban, is said to have spent all the surplus revenues, so assiduously collected by his minister Nizamuddin, on his dancing girls.[172] Dancing girls were the chief means of diversion. Some selected girls were trained from young age in the art of dancing, music and coquetry for the pleasure of the king.[173] As time went on, these entertainments became, from private amusement, a conventional court practice. Wine was as indispensable as music. Right through the medieval period the elite drank with enthusiasm. Even the adolescent drank, and all princess drank in secret.[174] The king was imitated by his ministers and nobles who were also his partners through thick and thin. They all combined to make the court life notoriously licentious and corrupt, and men of all ranks gave themselves up to the pursuit of pleasure. This is an old story known to all serious students of medieval history. But the point to note is that much of the revenue of the state was spent on the pleasure-seeking activities of kings and nobles.

To have an idea of the wealth spent by the king and his nobles let us give some examples, or rather samples, for the range of the study covers a period of a thousand years, even more. A bejewelled crown of Muhammad Tughlaq cost one lakh *tankahs*, while another 80,000.[175] A shoe of the time of Firoz Tughlaq again cost 80,000 *tankahs*.[176] Múhammad Tughlaq spent so generously during his reign of twenty-seven years that he exhausted the Delhi treasury.[177] And the luxurious life of the nobles in the time of Firoz Tughlaq is thus described by the contemporary chronicler Shams Siraj Afif. "In the store house of every noble there were good carpets. A group of pretty and sonorous-voiced dancing girls and concubines were there to remove all traces of anxiety and sadness. Wherever the Amir halted in the course of a journey all kinds of food and pleasure were made available to him including intimate companionship (*lataif-i-wasl*)."[178] Sultan Firoz gave to some of his nobles eight lakh *tankahs*, to others six lakh and four lakh, each according to his position and status. The Wazir Khan-i-Jahan Maqbul received thirteen lakh *tankahs* as personal pay. It is reported that he had two thousand women including many of Rum and Chin, in his harem. He had numerous sons and sons-in-law. The Sultan made a provision that every son born to him should from his birth receive an allowance of 11,000 *tankahs* for his maintenance and every daughter on her marriage 15,000 *tankahs*. His munificence reached to such a pitch, that the Sultan was often heard to say that Khan-i-Jahan was the grand and magnificent king of Delhi.[179]

This was the position in the Sultanate period. The Mughal emperors lived still more luxuriously. They maintained a magnificent court and a splendid harem. Their personal living was of a very high standard. Their army was large, their nobility prosperous. All this entailed a heavy expenditure.

To meet this expenditure the Mughal emperors taxed the people to the limit that could be borne by them. The Mughal king wore jewels all over. Akbar wore gold ornaments, pearls and jewellery. Jahangir wore more precious stones than his father. So did Shahjahan. For these three emperors, it was gold and jewels from head to foot. The crowns were of gold and jewels and pearls. Precious stones served as buttons of garments. Shoes, made of leather or velvet, were embroidered in gold and studded with pearls. They wore costly perfumes. Their personal weapons (*qur*) were also studded with precious stones and stored in the *Qur khana*. Even the orthodox Aurangzeb could not completely discard wearing jewels. Needless to add that they were always soaked in costliest perfumes.

We have referred to weighments of Akbar, his successors and many of the royal princes on their lunar and solar birthdays. Sir Thomas Roe describes one such weighment of emperor Jahangir thus: "The king's birthday and the solemnity of his weighing to which I went... was carried into a very large and beautiful garden... where was prepared the scale, being hung in large trestles, and a cross-beam... the seals of massy gold, the borders set with small stones... the chains of gold large and massy... Here attended the nobility, all sitting about on carpets (and the ladies watched from behind the curtains). The king... appeared clothed, or rather laden with diamonds, rubies, pearls and other precious vanities, so great, so glorious; he was weighed with gold and jewels... Then against cloth of gold, silk, stuffs, linen, spices... Lastly, against meal, butter, corn... and all the rest of the stuff..."[180] The ladies celebrated the occasion with great enthusiasm and often received gifts from the king.

When kings dressed like this and wore so much jewellery, the queens and nobles' ladies could only excel them. This has been mentioned before. Some instances of such happy occasions and the exchange of gifts may be mentioned. Emperor Jahangir writes that when "Prince

Khurram had hastened to the capture of the Deccan he had obtained the title of Shah, and now, in reward for his distinguished service, I gave him a mansab of 30,000 personal and 20,000 horse and bestowed on him the title of Shah Jahan... A special dress of honour with a gold-embroidered *charqab*, with collar, the end of the sleeves and the skirt decorated with pearls, worth 50,000 rupees, a jewelled sword with a jewelled *pardala* (belt), and a jewelled dagger were bestowed upon him. I myself... poured over his head a small tray of jewels and a tray of gold (coins)."[181] What Shahjahan presented to emperor Jahangir is noted by the royal parent thus: "If the private offerings of my son and those of the rulers of the Deccan were to be written down in detail, it would be too long a business. What I accepted of his presents was worth 2,000,000 rupees. In addition to this he gave his (step-)mother, Nur Jahan Begum, offerings worth 200,000 rupees, or 75,000 tumans of the currency of Iran or 6,780,000 current Turan-khanis. Such offerings had never been made during this dynasty."[182] And "Nur Jahan Begum prepared a feast of victory for my son Shah Jahan and conferred on him dresses of honour of great price, with a *nadiri* with embroidered flowers, adorned with rare pearls, a *sarpech* (turban ornament) decorated with rare gems, a turban with a fringe of pearls, a waistbelt studded with pearls, a sword with jewelled *pardala* (belt), a *phul katara* (dagger) a *sada* (?) of pearls, with two horses one of which had a jewelled saddle, and a special elephant with two females. In the same way she gave his children and his ladies dresses of honour, *tuquz* (nine pieces) of cloth with all sorts of gold ornaments, and to his chief servants as presents a horse, a dress of honour, and jewelled dagger. The cost of this entertainment was about 300,000 rupees."[183] On another occasion "I held a meeting in one of the houses of the palace of Nur Jahan Begum, which was situated in the midst of large tanks, and summoning the Amirs and courtiers to the feast which had been prepared by the

Begum, I ordered them to give the people cups and all kinds of intoxicating drinks... All sorts of roast meats, and fruits by way of relish, were ordered to be placed before everyone. It was a wonderful assembly... they lighted lanterns and lamps all round the tanks and buildings. A grand entertainment took place, and the drinkers of cups took more cups than they could carry."[184]

In a sultan's dinner wine was not an essential part, as for example, in the banquets of Muhammed bin Tughlaq as described by Ibn Battutah. But the rich fare speaks for the cost. Al-Umari was informed that in the royal kitchen of the Sultan thousands of oxen and sheep, fatted horses and birds of all kinds were slaughtered daily to prepare the meals. The imperial kitchen, both during the Sultanate and Mughal times, was a full-fledged state department with branches like *matbakhi* (kitchen), *abdar khana* which catered for drinking water and wine, and *mewa khana* for fruits. Each branch was manned by a hierarchy of officials. Ganga water was brought for the emperor from long distances. It was carried to as far away as Daulatabad when Sultan Muhammad Tughlaq encamped there. Akbar drank only Ganga water. Provision of this water in the palace would have cost a lot. In matters of food only Akbar was abstemious. Most other rulers ate to satiation as did members of the royal household and the nobles. There were two types of dinner. One was *khasa* or the special dinner which was attended by the Sultan, and the other was general. There was an elaborate ritual observed while taking the meal. At the *khasa* dinner about twenty guests were present, at others many more. In the middle of the *dastarkhwan* there sat the qazi, khatib, faqih, sharif (saiyyad) and shaikh (sufi), and then the relatives of the Sultan and the chief Amirs. The meal started with sherbet of rose and sugar candy. It was served in bowls of silver, gold and glass. The meal served consisted of *chapatis*, roasted meat, sweet *samosas*, salt *samosas* and rice and chicken. Before everyone present were placed *roomali rotis*, one-fourth or one-sixth piece of a whole roasted sheep. Then *puries* were served with *halwa sabuni* stuffed inside it (it is still sold in large quantities in Aligarh). Next was served in China plates meat cooked in ghee, onion, and green ginger. Four or five *samosas*, stuffed with mince meat, almonds, walnuts, pistachios and various other condiments and fried in ghee were served before each. Rice cooked in ghee garnished with a roasted fowl placed over it was the next dish. All this was rounded off with two items of sweet dish, called *hashimi* and *qahiria*. At the end there was a drink of barley water to push so much stuff down the system. The dinner was over after powdered *pan-masala* and fifteen rolled packets of pan tied with red silken thread were presented to each guest. The royal dinner was held twice in the day.[185] It appears that all items could not be eaten to the full even by a glutton, but these were served because a royal dinner was a royal dinner. Still, a variety of pickles (*achars*) were added to the menu to whip up the action of the stomach. *Aijaz-i-Khusravi* of Amir Khusrau and *Kitab-ur-Rehla* of Ibn Battutah are full of references to these delicacies without which medieval Indian royal meals were not complete. Details of a banquet during the Mughal period may also be given. It was arranged by Asaf Khan, Jahangir's brother-in-law in honour of Sir Thomas Roe, the ambassador of James I to the court of emperor Jahangir (1615-18), and has been described by his chaplain Edward Terry. "The Asaph Chan (Asaf Khan) entertained my Lord Ambassador in a very spacious and very beautiful tent... That tent was kept full of very pleasant perfume; in which scents the King and grandees there take very much delight. The floor of the tent was first covered all over with very rich and large carpets, which were covered again in the places where our dinner stood with other good carpets made of stitched leather... and these were covered again with pure white and fine calico cloths; and all those covered with very many dishes of silver... The Ambassador had more dishes by ten, and I less by ten, than our entertainer had; yet for my part I had fifty dishes. They were all set before us at once... I tasted of all set before me... Now of the provision itself... our larger dishes were filled with rice... some of it white... some of it made yellow with saffron, some of it was made green, and some of it put into a purple colour... several of our dishes were furnished with flesh of several kinds, and with hens and other sorts of fowl cut in pieces... To these we had jellies and culices (meat jellies), rice ground to flour, then boiled, and sweetened with sugar-candy and rose-water, to be eaten cold... The flour of rice mingled with sweet almonds... Many other dishes we had, (were) made up of cakes of several forms, of the finest of the wheat flour, mingled with almonds and sugar-candy... To these potatoes excellently well dressed; and to them diverse salads of the curious fruits of that country... and for our drink, some of it was brew'd... At this entertainment we sat long... our feast in that place was better than Apicius, that famous Epicure of Rome, with all his witty gluttony..."[186] Manrique describes an equally elaborate banquet given by Asaf Khan to his imperial son-in-law Shahjahan. It lasted for four hours.[187] Royal dinners and the dinners of the elites were of course costly, but how much money was spent on them is difficult to say because food grains were very cheap and other items of food not very dear throughout the medieval period. Still, with meals taken many times during the course of the day, and with the garnishing of endless dishes, the dinners of royalty and nobility must have been a major item of expenditure of the Mughal society.

Dinners were accompanied by and ended with 'brew'd' drinks. Most sultans, Mughal badshahs and their nobles were heavy drinkers. Emperors from Babur to Jahangir drank freely. When Muslims were promised liberal allowances of wine in Paradise,[188] they could not be debarred from drinking in this world. With wine the Mughals took opium and other drugs. Strong constitution saved some princes from the debilitating effects of *araq*. However all princes and some princesses also drank. Detailed description of this activity is provided by Muslim chroniclers and European visitors. There were regular breweries in palaces of kings and mansions of nobles.

The remains of their palaces show the grandeur of their times and the wealth spent on their decoration and illumination. Their gardens and reservoirs consumed a lot of money and labour. Money on their tents in camp was as freely spent as on building permanent edifices. Even some carpets cost 60,000 rupees and more. Mahals of ladies swarmed with servants. Mistresses and servants consumed lot of wealth on decor, dresses and ornaments. Feasts and festivals, Khushroz and Mina Bazar were celebrated with great éclat. All the resources available in India were fully exploited to provide comforts and luxuries to the Muslim ruling and religious classes. Muslim chronicles vouch for this fact. They also vouch for the fact that the enjoyment of the Muslim elite was provided mainly by the poorest peasants through a crushing tax system.

NOTES

1. INTRODUCTION

1. The Indian Press, Allahabad, 1936.

2. K.M. Munshi, 'End of Ancient India' in Bharatiya Vidya Bhavan's *Journal*, vol. IV, no. II, December 29, 1959, pp. 8, 14.

3. Cited in Ram Swarup, *Hindu View of Christianity and Islam*, Voice of India, New Delhi, 1992, pp. 48-49.

4. P.K. Hitti, *The Arabs*, London, 1948, p. 31.

5. Ram Swarup, *Understanding Islam through Hadis*, New Delhi reprint, 1983, pp. vii, xi.

6. Trs. by A. Guillaume under the title *The Life of Muhammad,* Oxford University Press, 1958.

7. Hitti, *op. cit.*, p. 29.

8. *Ibid.*, p. 78.

9. Trs. by Charles Hamilton, 4 vols. London, 1791.

10. Hughes, T.P., *Dictionary of Islam*, p. 174; D.S. Margoliouth, *Mohammed and the Rise of Islam*, pp. xix-xx..

11. It was translated into English by Charles Hamilton of the East India Company and published in England in 1791. It is easily available in a recent reprint.

12. A. Khuda Bakhsh, *Essays, Indian and Islamic,* London, 1927, p. 51.

13. In the *Lagacy of Islam*, Ed. Sir Thomas Arnold and Alfred Guillaume, Oxford University Press, London, 1931, p. 42.

14. T.W. Arnold, *The Preaching of Islam*, London, 1913, pp. 45-101.

15. P.K. Hitti, *The Arabs*, p. 44.

16. Anwar Shaikh, *Islam, The Arab National Movement*, 1995. It may be pertinent to mention here that Anwar Shaikh (born 1928) is living in Britain since 1956 under a *fatwa* of death (April 1994) because he has candidly written much that is unpalatable to Muslims. He is safe because he is settled in England and also because the assassins feel that killing him would draw attention to his ideas and writings more pointedly. However, a campaign against him is on, For example, Arshad Ali Khan in *Daily Jang*, London, April 30, 1995, calls on Muslim scholars of *all sects of Islam* to rebut Anwar Shaikh's views *to save Islam.*

17. *Ibid.*, Preface; also *Hagarism; The Making of Islamic World* by Patricia Crone and Michael Cook, Cambridge, 1977, p. 78.

18. Quran Majid, Rampur, Preface by Muhammad Farukh Khan, p. 11.

19. *Islam, The Arab National Movement*, pp. 24, 25, 28, 32, 38.

20. *Sunan ibn Majah*, vol. II, p. 259, *ahadis* 893-94; pp. 261-62, *hadis* 902.

21. *Ibid.*, p. 197, *ahadis* 663-64.
22. *Ibid.*, p. 199, *hadis* 673, p. 201, *ahadis* 681-682, p. 203, *hadis* 687-88, p. 224, *hadis* 771.
23. The income to Saudi Arabia from Hajj every year is considerable. See also Hajj pilgrimage in Part II — Politics.
24. Ruben Levy, *The Social Structure of Islam*, p. 161.
25. Anwar Shaikh, *Islam*, p. 54.
26. Ibn Warraq, *Why I Am Not A Muslim*, Amhest, N.Y., U.S.A., 1995, p. 202.
27. K.A. Nizami, *Religion and Politics*, p. 1.
28. Ibn Warraq, p. 115.
29. S.K. Malik, *The Quranic Concept of War*, p. 74.
30. Colin Clarke, *Population Growth and Land Use*, p. 64.
31. Andre Wink, *Al-Hind*, vol. I, p. 151.
32. For a detailed discussion on this phenomenon, see K.S. Lal, *Growth of Scheduled Tribes and Castes in Medieval India*, pp. 25-27, 88-94.
33. Manucci, vol. III, pp. 112, 141, 151 and footnotes, 244-45.
34. *Siyasat Nama* (ed. Shefer), pp. 77-80, 138-156.
35. Aziz Ahmad, *Studies in Islamic Culture in the Indian Environment*, Oxford, 1964, p. 79.
36. *Alberuni's India*, vol. I, p. 22.
37. Quoted by Charis Waddy in *The Muslim Mind*, Longmans, 1976 and reproduced in Devendra Swarup (ed.), *Politics of Conversion*, Deendayal Research Institute, New Delhi, 1986. p. 179 note.
38. Aziz Ahmad, *Studies in Islamic Culture*, pp. 81-84; M. Mujeeb, *Indian Muslims*, p. 22.

II — THE STATE

1. *History of Aurangzib*, vol. III, pp. 269-97.
2. *Some Aspects of Muslim Administration*, p. 2.
3. *Life and Conditions of the People of Hindustan*, pp. 138-42.
4. *Dictionary of Islam*, p. 711.
5. Luzac & Co., London, 1913-34, vol. I, p. 259.
6. Tripathi, *op. cit.*, p. 2.
7. *The Administration of the Sultanate of Delhi*, p. 41.
8. Cf. Peter Hardy in Philips, *Historians of India, Pakistan and Ceylon*, p. 302.
9. Introduction to the English trs. of Ziyauddin Barani's *Fatawa-i-Jahandari*, p. vi.
10. Concise Oxford Dictionary and Chambers Twentieth Century Dictionary.
11. P.K. Hitti, *History of the Arabs*, (London, 1951), p. 117.

12. Nizami, *Religion and Politics*, p. 15.
13. Arnold and Guillume (ed.), *The Legacy of Islam*, p. 286.
14. Qureshi, *op. cit.*, p. 41.
15. Ibn Hasan, *The Central Structure of the Mughal Empire*, pp. 255-56.
16. *Ibid.*, p. 258.
17. Quran VIII, 39-40; English trs. by George Sale, p. 172; Jadunath Sarkar, *Aurangzib*, vol. III, p. 249.
18. Quran IX, 5, 6; Sale, p. 179.
19. P.K. Hitti, *History of the Arabs*, pp. 177, 179.
20. This aspect has been discussed by me in some detail in my *Growth of Muslim Population in Medieval India*, pp. 187-190.
21. Farishtah, trs. Briggs, vol. II, pp. 230-32.
22. *Journal of the Bombay Branch of the Royal Asiatic Society*, vol. XXII, p. 28.
23. *Babur Nama*, vol. II, p. 484.
24. *The Book of Duarte Barbosa*, vol. I, p. 202.
25. *Ain.*, Jarret, vol. III, p. 8 and note by J. Sarkar.
26. Badaoni, vol. II, p. 246.
27. Barani, pp. 262-64; 295-96.
28. Barani, *Fatawa-i-Jahandari*, pp. 39, 64.
29. *Akbar Nama*, vol. II, p. 316.
30. Du Jarric, p. 75.
31. Sri Ram Sharma, *Religious policy of the Mughal Emperors*, pp. 19-20.
32. Ibn Majah, II, p. 101, *ahadis*. 307-8.
33. Badaoni, vol. II, p. 391; Sharma, p. 21.
34. Badaoni, vol. II, p. 317.
35. Badaoni, vol. II, p. 273. Also E.D. vol. IV, p. 547 note.
36. Badaoni, vol. II, p. 307.
37. *Ibid.*, p. 211. This paragraph has been reproduced from my essay "Akbar's Din-i-Ilahi" published in Lal, *Studies in Medieval Indian History*, p. 236.
38. Badaoni, Persian text, Calcutta, 1865, vol. II, p. 257.
39. *Ibid.*, p. 258.
40. *Ibid.*, pp. 261-62, 303.
41. *Tuzuk*, vol. I, pp. 244-45.
42. Eg. Ashoka's Twelfth Rock-Edict advocates respect for all creeds. "King Devanampriya Priyadarshin is honouring all sects... promotion of essentials of all sects should take place... neither praising one's own sect nor blaming other sects should take place... Concord is alone meritorious."

Emperor Ashoka's Eighth Pillar Edict also says, "Persuasion be still Ashoka's ways... I value inward inspiration."

Quoted in Om Prakash, *Religion and Society in Ancient India*, p. 10.

43. Ibn Warraq, p. 119.

44. A.J. Toynbee, *One World and India*, p. 19.

45. For details Lal, *Twilight*, pp. 190-94.

46. *Babur Nama*, vol. II, pp. 554-55.

47. *Ibid.*, p. 340, Also Archaeological Survey Report, XII, pp. 26-27. Sri Ram Sharma. *The Religious policy of the Mughal Emperors*, p. 9.

48. The alleged Will was brought to the notice of scholars by the Government of Bhopal (Central India) at one of the meetings of the Indian Historical Records Commission, vide *Indian Review* 1923 and *The Twentieth Century*, Allahabad, January, 1936. The controversy about its genuineness would require a pamphlet to be written. The latest information comes from the Librarian of the Sultania Library, Bhopal, who says that 'no such document was available', vide R. Nath, 'The Lost Testament', *The Times of India*, Review, New Delhi, 5 December, 1993.

Dr. Gopi Chand Varma, writing in the *Rajasthan Patrika*, Jaipur, dated 27 April 1997, on the controversy of Babur's *Wasiatnama* or Will has raised some new points and made some fresh suggestions. He writes that Babur's Will (*Wasiatnama*) is supposed to have been written on Jamad-ul-Avval 935 H (11 January 1529). From then on up to 1857, for 328 years, it does not find a mention in any Persian history; Babur too has not referred to it in his own *Tuzuk-i-Baburi*. Varma asks: Why did he not say so in his memoirs? Babur wrote his memoirs in Turki, why is this *Wasiatnama* written in Persian? He asks many more such questions.

According to him, "The *Wasiatnama* was not written by Babur, but by a group of Muslims during the Khilafat movement. They had realised that if the Khilafat movement was to succeed, it was possible only through the cooperation and participation of Hindus. Therefore, in December 1919 the Muslim League passed a resolution putting a ban on the slaughter of cows." Babur's supposed exhortation not to destroy shrines of peoples of other faiths, says Varma, also coincides with the attempt by the League at Hindu-Muslim cooperation during the Khilafat agitation. "This belief becomes amply clear from its motives — that the Will was written by interested Muslims in 1919 and not by Babur in 1529. It was placed in Sultania State Library of Bhopal where its secrecy and security could be ensured. But when the Khalifa in Turkey was removed and there the institution of Khilafat was abolished [on 3 March 1924], there was no sense in preserving the document any more. That is why this forged and supposed (*jali aur farzi*) *Wasiatnama* was removed from the Bhopal library as secretly as it was placed there."

A point has been made by Gopi Chand Varma. What value should be attached to it is an open question.

49. Abbas Sarwani, E.D. vol. IV, pp. 410-424. Also Rizqullah, p. 549.

50. Sharma, *op. cit.*, pp. 10-11.

51. *Ain.*, vol. I, p. 164.

52. All the above facts have been mentioned by S.R. Sharma in his *The Religious Policy of the Mughal Emperors*, pp. 7-19, quoting original Persian sources.

53. *Ibid.*, p. 39.

54. *Tuzuk*, vol. I, p. 254.

55. Pelsaert, p. 75.

56. *Ain.*, vol. I, pp. 398-99 and note; *Tuzuk*, vol. I, pp. 224-225 note.

57. *Tuzuk*, *ibid.*, p. 320.

58. V.A. Smith, *Akbar the Great Mogul*, p. 233.
Smith writes on the authority of Du Jarric, vol. III, p. 133. Also Sharma, *op. cit.*, p. 61 quoting Mulla Ahmad, pp. 1, 2, 46.

59. Tripathi, *op. cit.*, p. 56.

60. Afif, p. 29.

61. Sharafuddin Yazdi, *Zafar Nama*, II, p. 15.

62. Badaoni, p. 306.

63. Qureshi, *op. cit.*, p. 41.

64. Kingsley Davis, *The Population of India and Pakistan*, p. 191.

65. P.K. Hitti, *The Arabs*, p. 53, 83, 89.

66. But as the Muslim empire expanded, Muawiyah founded the line of Umayyad Caliphs at Damascus (661 CE). The Abbasids who succeeded them, became Caliphs at Baghdad (750 CE) and Samarra (836 CE). Another line of Umayyad Caliphs ruled at Cordova or Qurtuba (756 CE). The Fatamid Caliphs were rulers in Cairo upto 1751 and the Ayyubids up to 1836.

67. Ruben Levy, *The Social Structure of Islam*, p. 284.

68. M. Habib, Introduction to Elliot and Dowson's *History of India as told by its own Historians*, Aligarh reprint, 1952, vol. II, p. 6.

69. Barani, p. 153.

70. *Sunan Abu Daud*, vol. II, pp. 458-59, *hadis* 1158.

71. *Fatawa-i-Jahandari*, p. 10; *Adab-ul-Harb*, British Museum Ms. fol. 52(a).

72. Lal, *History of the Khaljis*, p. 157.

73. For qualities of Ariz, see *Fatawa-i-Jahandari*, p. 24.

74. Steingass, *Persian English Dictionary*, p. 574.

75. For its important officers see my *Legacy of Muslim Rule*, p. 140.

76. *Ain*, I, pp. 5-6.

77. Tripathi, R.P., *Some Aspects of Muslim Administration*, pp. 105-124.

78. Arnold, *The Caliphate*, p. 202

79. *Mishkat-ul Sharif*, vol. II, p. 5.

80. *Ibid.*, pp. 5, 7, 9.

81. *Mishkat*, vol. II, p. 56.

82. *Sunan ibn Majah*, vol. I, p. 32, *hadis* 3.

83. *Ibid.*, vol. I, p. 43, vol. II, pp. 190-93, *ahadis* 637-39, 641, 649; *Mishkat-ul-Sharif*, vol. II, pp. 5, 15-16 quoting *ahadis* from Muslim and Bukhari.

84. *Mishkat*, vol. II, p. 6.

85. K.A. Nizami, *Religion and Politics*, pp. 95-96 and n. 4.

86. Fazl bin Ruzbahan al-Isfani's *Suluk-ul-Muluk*, Barani's *Fatawa-i-Jahandari* and Khusrau's *Nuh Sipiher* as summarised by I.H. Qureshi, *Administration of the Sultanate of Delhi*, p. 47. Also Nizami, p. 110 n.

87. Cited in Bosworth, *The Ghaznavids*, p. 49.

88. Alberuni, vol. II, p. 161. Also Barani, *Fatawa-i-Jahandari*.

89. Fakhr-i-Mudabbir, *Tarikh-i-Fakhruddin Mubarak Shah*, p. 13.

90. *Ain*, vol. I, p. 2.

91. Sarkar, *A Short History of Aurangzib*, p. 464.

92. *Ain*, vol. I, pp. 2-3, 6.

93. Barani, pp. 293-294.

94. Barani, p. 64.

95. Barani, *Fatawa-i-Jahandari*, p. 73.

96. Fakhr-i-Mudabbir, *Adab-ul-Harb*, fols. 132b-133a.

97. Barani, *Fatawa-i-Jahandari*, Advice II, pp. 2-3.

98. Babur cites the example of Bengal, which of course was applicable to all Muslim rulers. "The royal office is permanent and there are permanent offices of amirs, wazirs (etc.)... Any person who (even) kills the ruler and seats himself on the throne, becomes ruler himself; amirs, wazirs, soldiers and peasants submit to him, at once. (They) say 'we are faithful to the throne; we loyally obey whoever occupies it'." *Babur Nama*, pp. 482-83.

99. *Sunan ibn Majah*, vol. I, pp. 88-89, 94; *ahadis* 205, 208, 224.

100. *Ibid.*, vol. II, 468-69, 477; *ahadis* 1733, 1736-37, 1557.

101. *Ibid.*, vol. I, pp. 53, 59-60; *ahadis* 73-75, 92, 97.

102. Abu Daud, vol. II, pp. 440-41, 450-51, *hadis* 1135.

103. Ibn Warraq, p. 182.

104. *Ibid.*, p. 239.

105. Abu Daud, vol. II, pp. 327, 373, 375, *ahadis* 944, 948-49.

106. Hasan Nizami, *Tajul Maasir*, trs. by S.H. Askari, Patna University Journal (Arts), vol. 18, no. 3 (1963), p. 58. Also Ruben Levy, *Social Structure of Islam*, Cambridge, 1962, p. 252.

107. Barani, p. 72. See also *Fatawa-i-Jahandari*, p. 40.

III — OBLIGATIONS OF THE STATE

1. Ruben Levy, *op. cit.*, p. 293.
2. Malik, *The Quranic Concept of War*, p. 44.
3. *Ibid.*, p. 43 quoting from Quran, Nisaa: 95.
4. *Ibid.*, p. 20.

5. Anfal: 12.
6. Al-Imran: 151.
7. Ahzab: 26-27.
8. Malik *op. cit.*, pp. 59-60. The Quranic quotations are given by Malik.
9. *Ibid.*, pp. 27-28 quoting from the Quran, Baqara:193; Anfal:39. Consequently "each country has its own account of horrors (of forced conversions and persecutions). In the eighth century we had massacres in Sindh. In the ninth century there were the massacres of Spanish Christians in and around Seville. In the tenth, the persecutions of non-Muslims under the Caliph al-Hakim are well known. In the eleventh, the Jews of Granada and Fez met their fate... Mahmud destroyed the Hindus and their temples during the same period. In the twelfth, the Almohads of North Africa spread terror wherever they went. In the thirteenth, the Christians of Damascus were killed or sold into slavery and their churches burned to the ground..." The blood-soaked story goes on and on. Ibn Warraq, pp. 233-237.
10. Anwar Shaikh, *Islam*, pp. 42, 49, 51.
11. T.P. Hughes, p. 243.
12. "The Holy Quran issued instructions to the Muslims about the selection of their objectives, 'Smite ye above their necks', it said, 'and smite all their finger tips off them' (Anfal: 12). The most sensitive parts lie above the neck. An effective strike against these parts can finish off the opponent completely. At Badr, however, most of the Koraish warriors were wearing armour. The Holy Quran counselled the Muslims to smite the finger tips off such opponents... our effort should be to choose those targets which when struck, will deprive him of his ability to use his weapons..." S.K. Malik, *The Quranic Concept of War*, pp. 64-65.
13. Ibn Majah, vol. II, pp. 188-89, *hadis* 636.
14. *Sahih Muslim, hadis* 4311. This definition of war is found in all Hadis collections, e.g., *Mishkat*, vol. II, p. 61.
15. Ibn Majah, vol. II, p. 429, *hadis* 1605.
16. Arun Shourie, *The World of Fatwas*, p. 576, quoting *Sahih-ul-Bukhari*, vol. IV, p. 41 and *Sunan Abu Daud*, vol. II, pp. 756-58. But this *hadis* is found in all collections, e.g. ibn Majah, vol. II, p. 171, *hadis* 562; p. 183, *ahadis* 613-615.
17. *Sahih Muslim, hadis* 4636.
18. *Ibid., hadis* 4314.
19. Quran, cited in Muir, *Life of Mahomet*, pp. 74-75; Hughes, *Dictionary of Islam*, p. 449.
20. Ibn Majah, vol. II, p. 602 *hadis* 2142 has it that a Mujahid will get 72 women, seventy of whom belonging to Kafirs in Hell will be transferred for the Muslims in Paradise. Which means that "all *ahl-i-jannat* will be masters of the women of Kafirs". This in part explains the determination of Muslims to fight and kill Kafirs — to possess their women.

21. Ibn Majah, vol. II, p. 169, *hadis* 556; pp. 174-75, *ahadis* 576-78; Quran 61:10-13.

22. *Sahih-ul-Bukhari*, vol. IV, p. 36.

23. Ibn Majah, vol. II, pp. 161-62, *hadis* 529; p. 175, *ahadis* 577-78. *Mishkat*, vol. II, p. 32.

24. Ibn Majah, vol. II, pp. 596-602, *ahadis* 2126-2142.

25. *Dictionary of Islam*, pp. 243-248, esp. p. 243.

26. *The Indian Muslims*, p. 68, also p. 71.

27. For Jihad also see K.S. Lal, *The Legacy of Muslim Rule in India*, pp. 85-86; Arun Shourie, *The World of Fatwas*, pp. 573-82; Suhas Majumdar, *Jihad*, New Delhi, 1994, pp. 12, 16, 63.

28. *Fatawa-i-Alamgiri*, Matba al-Kubra, Egypt, 1310 H., vol. V, pp. 346-48, quoted in Mujeeb, *The Indian Muslims*, p. 71.

29. S.R. Chowdhry, *Al Hajjaj ibn Yusuf*, Delhi University Press, 1976, p. 35.

30. *Ibid.*, p. 145.

31. Ruben Levy, *The Baghdad Chronicle*, Cambridge, 1929, p. 14.

32. K.S. Lal, *Early Muslims in India*, pp. 16-22, 30-33; and *Growth of Muslim Population in Medieval India*, pp. 212-17.

33. Utbi, *Tarikh-i-Yamini*, E.D. vol. II, pp. 40-41, 49-50.

34. "Tamerlane systematically destroyed the Christians, and as a result the Nestorians and Jocobites of Mesopotamia have never recovered. At Sivas, 4,000 Christians were buried alive; at Tus there were 10,000 victims. Historians estimate the number of dead at Saray to be 100,000; at Baghdad 90,000; at Isfahan 70,000." Ibn Warraq, p. 235.

35. E.D. vol. IV, p. 547 n.

36. Farishtah, vol. I, p. 295; Robert Sewell, *A Forgotten Empire*, pp. 30-31, 38.

37. Amir Khusrau, *Miftah-ul-Futuh*, Aligarh text, 1954, p. 22; Lal, *Khaljis*, p. 250 and footnote.

38. Amir Khusrau, *Khazain-ul-Futuh*, trs., in E.D. vol. III, p. 77.

39. Amir Khusrau, *Ashiqa*, Aligarh, 1917, p. 46.

40. Barani, pp. 216-17, also pp. 41-42, 44, 72-75.

41. Barani, *Fatawa-i-Jahandari*, pp. 46-48, also Introduction, p. v.

42. *Encyclopaedia of Islam*, I, p. 958.

Abu Yusuf, *Kitab-ul-Kharaj*, cited in Tripathi, *Some Aspects of Muslim Administration*, p. 340.

43. Lal, *Khaljis*, p. 113.

44. *Ibid.*, pp. 252-53.

45. Mahdi Husain, *Tughluq Dynasty*, Calcutta, 1963, pp. 195-257.

46. Robert Sewell, *A Forgotten Empire*, pp. 30-31.

47. Farishtah, I, p. 295. Also Sewell, p. 38.

48. *Babur Nama*, pp. 474-75 and n. Ahmad Yadgar, *Tarikh-i-Salatin-i-*

Afghana, pp. 98ff. and trs. in E.D. vol. V, p. 30; K.S. Lal, *Twilight*, pp. 224-225.

49. *Babur Nama*, pp. 554-55.

50. *Ibid.*, pp. 550-573. These pages in particular are full of quotations from the Quran.

51. *Ibid.*, pp. 574, 576.

52. *Ibid.*, pp. 483-84, 596.

53. Badaoni, *Muntakhab-ut-Tawarikh*, vol. II, p. 383; Smith, *Akbar the Great Mogul*, p. 108.

54. *Tarikh-i-Salim Shahi*, trs. Price, pp. 225-226.

55. *Sunan ibn Majah*, vol. II, p. 185, *hadis* 624; p. 585, *ahadis* 2092-2095. Also *Sunan Abu Daud*, vol. II, p. 364.

56. Hughes, *Dictionary of Islam*, p. 248; Hitti, *The Arabs*, pp. 23-26.

57. I am obliged to my friend Dr. S.P. Bhatnagar, A-98 Ashok Vihar, Phase II, Delhi, for lending me a typed copy of the pamphlet.

58. *Jama-i-Tirmizi*, vol. I, p. 497.

59. Barani, *Fatawa-i-Jahandari*, p. 16.

60. Jadunath Sarkar, *The Mughal Administration*, p. 106.

61. Quran, 24:2-5; *Sunan ibn Majah*, vol. II, pp. 322-23, 337.

62. Quran, 5:38-39; *Sunan ibn Majah*, vol. II, p. 117, also p. 104.

63. Ram Swarup, *op. cit.*, p. 87, 93, 96. Quran 2:282.

64. *Sunan ibn Majah*, vol. II, p. 101.

65. *Sahih Muslim*, *ahadis* 4130, 4132; Ram Swarup, *op. cit.*, p. 89.

66. *Sunan Abu Daud*, vol. I, p. 576 and note.

67. Manucci, vol. IV, p. 422.

68. Barani, p. 318.

69. Sale's Quran, p. 152.

70. Barani, pp. 289, 382.

71. Yahiya, *Tarikh-i-Mubarak Shahi*, reproduced in Badaoni, Ranking, vol. I, pp. 318-19.

72. Ibn Battutah, Def. and Sang., vol. III, p. 440, cited in Ishwari Prasad, *Quraunah Turks*, p. 273. Also trs. by Mahdi Husain, pp. 57, 85, 103-104.

73. *Fatuhat-i-Firoz Shahi*, E.D. vol. III, p. 385.

74. For references see Ishwari Prasad, *Qaraunah Turks*, pp. 270-74, esp. p. 273. Also Afif, p. 121.

75. *Ain.*, vol. I, p. 164.

76. *Tarikh-i-Salim Shahi*, trans. Price, p. 12.

77. *Tuzuk*, vol. I, p. 9.

78. For details about *Fatawa-i-Alamgiri* see K.S. Lal, *Muslim Slave System in Medieval India*, pp. 139-42, 149. Also Ali Muhammad Khan, *Mirat-i-Ahmadi*, English trs. M.F. Lokhandwala, Gaekwad Oriental Series, Baroda, 1965, pp. 248-52. Also Jadunath Sarkar, *Mughal Administration*, pp. 109-115.

79. *Travels of Pietro Della Valle in India*, vol. I, pp. 66, 70.

80. *Ain.*, vol. III, pp. 132-33 and note.

81. It is related by his own brother. A medical person with ten other Franks "sent for a large bowl and knife... actually severed head from the body, both the head and his blood being received in the bowl. When the bleeding had ceased they took away the bowl of blood, which they immediately poured into a pot of boiling oil brought for the purpose, stirring the whole together with a ladle until both blood and oil became completely amalgamated. Will it be believed, that after this they took the head and again fixing it exactly to the body, they continued to rub the adjoining parts with the mixture of blood and oil until the whole had been applied... At the expiry of three days from this," they sent for his brother who to his surprise "beheld my brother restored to perfect health... the instant he perceived me he drew his sword, and made a furious cut at me... The Portuguese physician was ordered to send for me, and applying some styptic to the wound it quickly healed." Jahangir thought that this could be effected by alchemy "known to be extensively practised among the Franks... (and) jugglers from Bengal". *Tarikh-i-Salim Shahi*, trs. David Price as *Memoirs of the Emperor Jahangueir*, pp. 182-190.

82. *Tarikh-i-Salim Shahi*, pp. 166-96.

83. *Tuzuk*, vol. I, pp. 123-24.

84. *Ibid.*, p. 174 and note.

85. Nasai records a case in the days of the Prophet. Hazrat Arfaja bin Sa'd lost his nose in the battle of Kalab. He began to wear a nose of sliver. It started emitting bad odour. The Prophet ordered him to get a nose of gold. In this probably no surgery was involved. *Sunan Nasai Sharif*, vol. III, pp. 456-57, *hadis* 5166.

86. "The surgeons belonging to the country cut the skin of the forehead above the eyebrows, and made it fall down over the wounds on the nose. Then, giving it a twist so that the live flesh might meet the other live surface, by healing applications they fashioned for them other imperfect noses. There is left above, between the eyebrows, a small hole, caused by the twist given to the skin to bring the two live surfaces together. In a short time the wounds heal up, some obstacle being placed beneath to allow of respiration. I saw many persons with such noses, and they were not so disfigured as they would have been without any nose at all, but they bore between their eyebrows the mark of the incision." Manucci, vol. II, p. 301. Such restorations were done in Kangra also.

87. Barani, pp. 289, 382.

88. Lal, *Khaljis*, pp. 164, 176, 188.

89. Ibn Hasan, *The Central Structure of the Mughal Empire*, p. 336.

90. *Tarikh-i-Salim Shahi*, p. 17.

91. *Tuzuk-i-Jahangiri*, vol. I, p. 345; vol. II, pp. 59-60.

92. Nasai, vol. III, pp. 606-626, *ahadis* 5676ff. Also *Sahih Muslim*, vol. I, Part I, pp. 99.
93. *Sahih Bukhari*, vol. II, p. 67, *hadis* 80.
94. Tirmizi, vol. I, p. 545.
95. Ishwari Prasad, *Medieval India*, p. 293; *Tarikh-i-Daudi*, p. 37, trs. in E.D. vol. IV, p. 446.
96. Manucci, vol. II, p. 393.
97. Barani, p. 299.
98. *Ibid.*, pp. 251-52.
99. For example Bernier, *Travels*, pp. 235-36; Finch in Purchas, vol. IV, pp. 72-73.
100. Jadunath Sarkar, *Mughal Administration*, p. 98.
101. Terry, in Purchas, vol. IX, p. 47.
102. Ibn Hasan, *op. cit.*, p. 339.
103. Jafar Sharif, *Qanun-i-Islam*, trs. Herklots, p. 111.
104. William Muir, *The Life of Mahomet*, p. 188.
105. *Sunan ibn Majah*, vol. I, pp. 220-21; *Sunan Abu Daud*, vol. I, pp. 212-13, and 397-424; Tirmizi, vol. I, p. 209; *The Quran*, Sale, p. 450n; Hughes, p. 131.
106. Margoliouth, *Mohammed*, p. 248. Also *Sunan ibn Majah*, vol. II, p. 313, *hadis* 1131.
107. *Ibid.*, p. 222; *Sunan Abu Daud*, vol. I, pp. 212-13; *Sunan ibn Majah*, vol. II, p. 225, *hadis* 772. Also vol. I, p. 213.
108. *Sunan ibn Majah*, vol. I, p. 243, *hadis* 837, 81; *Sunan Abu Daud*, vol. I, p. 234; Tirmizi, vol. I, p. 123.
109. *Sunan ibn Majah*, vol. I, p. 243, *hadis* 838.
110. *Ibid.*, p. 242, *ahadis* 832-35.
111. *Sunan Abu Daud*, vol. I, pp. 404-405.
112. *Sunan ibn Majah*, vol. II, p. 295, *hadis* 1040; p. 304, *ahadis* 1075-76.
113. *Ibid.*, vol. II, p. 205, *hadis* 772.
114. *Ibid.*, vol. II, pp. 468-69, *ahadis* 1733-37. Also *Sunan Abu Daud*, vol. II, pp. 526-27, *hadis* 1296.
115. S.K. Malik, *The Quranic Concept of War*, p. 70 quoting Fath:29.
116. *Sunan ibn Majah*, vol. I, p. 313, *hadis* 1135; *Sunan Abn Daud*, vol. I, pp. 161-65; Tirmizi, vol. I, p. 212.
117. Hughes, p. 465.
118. *Sunan ibn Majah*, vol. I, p. 323, *ahadis* 1174-75; Tirmizi, vol. I, p. 213.
119. *Sunan Abu Daud*, vol. I, p. 211; Tirmizi, vol. I, p. 184.
120. *Ibid.*, pp. 462-63. All portions of the prayer are translated and accompanying exercises sketched in Hughes, *Dictionary of Islam*, pp. 465-69.
121. *Sunan ibn Majah*, vol. I, p. 311, *ahadis*, 1126-1128.

122. Ram Swarup, Introduction to the Reprint of William Muir's *The Life of Mahomet*, p. 9.
123. *Sunan Abu Daud*, vol. I, p. 278.
124. Tirmizi, vol. I, p. 125.
125. *Ibid.*, vol. I, p. 126.
126. *Ibid.*, pp. 277-78, 281-82; *Sunan ibn Majah*, vol. II, p. 282, *hadis* 1002.

Similar cases of 'pollution' of namaz are mentioned on pp. 281-286 of *Sunan Abu Daud*, vol. I, p. 284.

127. Jafar Sharif, *Qanun-i-Islam*, trs. Herklots, p. 205, note quoting *Encyclopaedia of Religion and Ethics*, vol. VIII, p. 875. Also Margoliouth, p. 103.
128. Gillaume, *The Life of Muhammad*, being a translation of Ibn Ishaq's *Sirat Rasul Allah*, OUP, Eighth Impression, Karachi, 1987, p. 628.
129. Abu Daud, vol. I, pp. 198-200; Ibn Majah, vol. I, p. 230, *hadis* 789.
130. Sita Ram Goel, *Hindu Temples: What happened to them*, 1991, vol. II, p. 416, citing the *Rauzat-us-Safa*.
131. *ibid.*, p. 412.
132. Ibn Majah, vol. II, pp. 465-67, *ahadis* 1724-26.
133. *Ibid.*, pp. 229-30, *hadis* 787.
134. *Taj-ul-Maasir*, E.D. vol. II, p. 231; Farishtah, vol. I, p. 62.
135. *Epigraphia Indo-Moslemica*, 1938, pp. 59-61.
136. *Epigraphia Indica — Arabic and Persian Supplement*, 1959-60, p. 73.
137. Lal, *Khaljis*, Appendix B, pp. 350-53, also pp. 332-333.
138. Mahdi Husain, *The Tughlaq Dynasty*, p. 617.
139. Barani, pp. 69-79; Bughra Khan to son, pp. 154-55; *Wasaya* also trs. in Nizami, *op. cit.*, pp. 98-103.
140. *Chachnama*, E.D. vol. I, p. 207.
141. Ibn Battutah, p. 83.
142. *Ibid.*, p. 56.
143. Afif, pp. 254-60.
144. *Ibid.*, pp. 367-69.
145. *Ibid.*, p. 135.
146. *Tabqat-i-Akbari*, vol. I, p. 336; *Makhzan-i-Afghani*, fol. 76a. For detailed references see Lal, *Twilight*, pp. 232-33.
147. *Archaeological Survey Report*, No. XVII, p. 105.
148. *Epigraphia Indica — Arabic and Persian Supplement*, 1969, p. 69 and footnote 2.
149. P.M. Currie, *The Shrine and Cult of Muin-al-din Chishti*, p. 105.
150. *Maasir-i-Alamgiri*, English translation by Jadunath Sarkar, Calcutta, 1947, pp. 51-52, 55, 60. Also J. Sarkar, *History of Aurangzib*, vol. III, Calcutta, 1972, pp. 194-95.

151. *Journal of the Asiatic Society of Bengal*, 1843, p. 73.

See Lal, *Khaljis*, for copious footnotes and references on the history and many other aspects of the life at Somnath.

152. *Babur Nama*, p. 656 and footnote.

153. Manucci, vol. III, pp. 244-45.

154. Since the events leading to the destruction of the Babri structure are recent, a number of articles and books have lately appeared and are still appearing on the subject. One of the best books on this topic is Koenraad Elst's *Ram Janmabhoomi vs. Babri Masjid*, Voice of India, New Delhi, 1990.

155. Gauri Shankar Ojha, *Udaipur ka Itihasa*, vol. I, p. 35.

156. Sita Ram Goel has given a list of Mosques, Idgahs, Dargahs and Mazars built by Muslims on the sites of Hindu shrines and with the materials obtained from them in his two books titled *Hindu Temples: What happened to them*, vol. I, 1990, pp. 88-191 and vol. II, pp. 104-290.

157. Sharma, *op. cit.*, p. 34.

158. *Growth of Muslim Population in Medieval India*, published by Research Publications in Social Sciences, Delhi and Jaipur, 1973.

159. *Indian Muslims: Who are they*, New Delhi, 1990, reprint 1993.

160. Murray Titus, *Islam in India and Pakistan*, Calcutta, 1959, p. 8.

IV — INCOME OF THE STATE

1. *Sunan Abu Daud*, vol. II, pp. 473-4.
2. *Ibid.*, pp. 384-85.
3. Margoliouth, *Mohammed*, pp. 245-46.
4. Quran, 8:42. Hughes, *Dictionary of Islam*, pp. 375-76.
5. *Mishkat*, II, pp. 78-87.
6. Muir, *The Life of Mahomet*, p. 229.
7. For a fuller account of the Civil List (*Diwan*), one can refer to the *Tarikh-i-Tabari*, Part I, Khilafat Rashida, Urdu, vol. II, Nafis Academy, Karachi, n.d. pp. 476-479.
8. Ram Swarup in his introduction to Sir William Muir's *The Life of Mahomet*, New Delhi reprint, 1992, pp. 11-12.
9. It may be mentioned here that besides gains in war, Khams was also levied on mines and treasure troves. "The products of mines and the finds of treasure troves were regarded as spoils of war because it was believed that they formerly belonged to the infidels and became Muslim property on conquest." U.N. Day, *The Government of the Sultanate*, Kumar Brothers, New Delhi, 1972, p. 107; *Sunan ibn Majah*, vol. II, p. 94, *hadis* 281.

As regards mines and treasure troves, however, the jurists greatly differ about the share of the state. The Hanafi school makes it one-fifth, the

Shafite nil and the Maliki holds that Zakat or one-fortieth be paid on it. Loot of Muslim property was against the law and was prohibited. Any treasure trove of unknown ownership discovered in the house of a Musalman was permitted to be retained by him. Eg. Rizqullah, *Waqiat-i-Mushtaqi*, fol. 21a; Ahmad Yadgar, *Tarikh-i-Salatin-i-Afghana*, p. 36.

10. Hamilton, *Hedaya*, vol. II, p. 178.

11. Hughes, *Dictionary of Islam*, p. 378.

12. S.R. Chowdhry, *Al-Hajjaj ibn Yusuf*, Delhi, 1972, p. 118 on the authority of al-Biladuri's *Futuh-ul-Buldan*.

13. C.H.I. III, p. 3; *Chachnama*, E.D. vol. I, pp. 174-75.

14. *Chachnama*, E.D. vol. I, pp. 174-75.

15. *Ibid.*, p. 183, also p. 160.

16. *Ibid.*, p. 185, also p. 182.

17. *Ibid.*, p. 186.

18. Utbi, Reynolds, p. 282.

19. The house was quite large, covering an area of about a thousand square feet. Hodivala also says that the canopy must have been what the old annalists of Gujarat call a *Mandapika*. It was a folding pavilion for being used in royal journeys, and not a throne. Hodivala, *Studies in Indo-Muslim History*, p. 143.

20. On return to Ghazni, Mahmud ordered this impressive treasure to be displayed in the courtyard of his palace. "Ambassadors from foreign countries including the envoy from Taghan Khan, king of Turkistan, assembled to see the wealth... which had never been accumulated by kings of Persia or of Rum" (Utbi, Reynolds, pp. 342-43; E.D. vol. II, p. 35).

21. Utbi, E.D. vol. II, p. 45; Reynolds, pp. 455-57. I have elsewhere calculated that 70 *misqals* were equal to one seer of 24 tolas in the Sultanate period. See my *History of the Khaljis* 2nd ed., Bombay, 1967, pp. 199-200. On the basis of the above calculation the weight of five gold idols comes to 10.5 maunds, each idol being of about 2 maunds.

22. Bosworth, *op. cit.*, p. 78.

23. *Ibid.*, pp. 76, 120, 126; Hodivala, *op. cit.*, pp. 139-40, 176; Fakhr-i-Mudabbir, *Adab-ul-Harb*, trs. in Rizvi, *Adi Turk Kalin Bharat*, Aligarh, 1965, p. 258; Utbi, *op. cit.*, p. 33; *Taj-ul-Maasir*, E.D. vol. II, p. 227.

24. *Mishkat*, vol. II, p. 87.

25. There are many *ahadis* on this policy, e.g., *Mishkat*, vol. II, pp. 65-67.

26. Fakhr-i-Mudabbir, *Tarikh Fakhruddin Mubarak Shah*, p. 20.

27. Hitti, *The Arabs*, p. 76.

28. *Chachnama*, Kalichbeg, p. 163; E.D. vol. I, p. 181.

29. Farishtah, vol. I, pp. 59-60.

30. *Sunan ibn Majah*, vol. I, pp. 521-22.

31. *Sunan Abu Daud*, vol. II, pp. 160-61.

32. For some facts and figures of humans, especially women, captured in Muslim wars in India, see my *Muslim Slave System in Medieval*

India, pp. 17-24, 41-59, 70-73. Also my *The Mughal Harem*, pp. 29, 32, 37, 167-68.

33. Shah Nawaz Khan, *Maasir-ul-Umara*, vol. I, p. 105.
34. *Sunan ibn Majah*, vol. II, pp. 602-604.
35. *Fatuhat-i-Firoz Shahi*, Aligarh, 1954, p. 6.
36. Abbas Sarwani, *Tarikh-i-Sher Shahi*, E.D. vol. IV, p. 314.
37. E.G. Abu Daud, vol. II, p. 369; Tirmizi, vol. I, p. 529.
38. *Mutla'us Sadain*, E.D. vol. IV, p. 109, also pp. 106-107.
39. Farishtah, vol. I, p. 120.
40. Wassaf, *Tazjiyat-ul-Amsar*, text, vol. IV, p. 447. trs. in E.D. vol. III, p. 43.
41. Lal, *Khaljis*, pp. 67-73.
42. Barani, p. 253.
43. Tirmizi, vol. I, p. 584.
44. Isami, *Futuh-us-Salatin*, p. 243.
45. Tirmizi, vol. I, p. 586.
46. *Waqiat-i-Mushtaqi*, E.D. vol. IV, p. 547.
47. Smith, *Akbar the Great Mogul*, pp. 51-52.
48. Alberuni's *India*, p. 22.
49. Wassaf, *op. cit.*, E.D. vol. III, p. 43.
50. Suresh Mishra, *Garha ke Gond Raj ka Utthan aur Patan* (Hindi), pp. 59-61.
51. Bernier, pp. 226-227.
52. Regarding the glories of pre-Buddhist Aryan rule in West Asia, see Jamna Das Akhtar's article in the *Organiser* dated 16 November 1997.
53. Alberuni, Preface by Sachau, p. xiv.
54. *Ain*, Jarret, vol. III, p. 224.
55. *Tuzuk*, vol. I, p. 92.
56. Quran, Al Taubah: 29.
57. Harsh Narain, *Jizyah and the spread of Islam*, New Delhi, 1990, pp. 10-12.
58. *Encyclopaedia of Islam*, vol. I, pp. 958-59.
59. *Dictionary of Islam*, p. 711.
60. Aghnides, *Muhammadan Theories of Finance*, pp. 399, 406-7, 528, 530.
61. *Mishkat*, vol. II, pp. 38-45; Abu Daud, vol. II, p. 290.
62. Tirmizi, vol. I, pp. 594-599.
63. Abu Daud, vol. II, pp. 511-13, 518, *ahadis* 1263-64, 1279.
64. *Ibid.*, p. 513, *ahadis* 1268-69.
65. Tirmizi, vol. I, pp. 604-05.
66. Barani, pp. 216-217, 290-91. Also his *Fatawa-i-Jahandari*, pp. 46-48.
67. Quoted in S.R. Sharma, *Religious Policy of the Mughal Emperors*, p. 19, quotation cited in note 47, p. 50.
68. S.A.A. Rizvi, *Muslim Revivalist Movements*, pp. 247-49.

S.A.A. Rizvi, *Shah Waliullah and his Times*, Canberra, 1980, pp. 218, 285-86.

Aziz Ahmad, *Studies in Islamic Culture in the Indian Environment*, p. 204.

Many more references are found in Sita Ram Goel, *Muslim Separatism*, Voice of India, New Delhi, Revised ed., 1995, pp. 33-56.

69. *Chachnama*, trs. Kalichbeg, p. 165.

70. Habibullah, *The Foundation of Muslim Rule in India*, p. 281 and notes 8, 9 and 10 on p. 292.

71. Barani, p. 574.

72. *Ibid.*, p. 218.

73. Afif, pp. 382-84.

74. *Akbar Nama*, trs. Beveridge, vol. II, pp. 316-17.

75. *Hedaya*, trs. Hamilton, vol. II, p. 211.

76. Tripathi, *Some Aspects of Muslim Administration*, pp. 340-41.

77. Afif. pp. 382-84.

78. Saqi Mustaad Khan, *Maasir-i-Alamgiri*, trs Sarkar, pp. 78, 94, 95; Lal, *Legacy of Muslim Rule*, pp. 221-223 for detailed references.

79. Khafi Khan, Text, pp. 278-79, 339.

80. Barani, p. 291.

81. Trs. in Jadunath Sarkar, *Aurangzib*, vol. III, pp. 325-27.

82. S.R. Sharma, *op. cit.*, p. 154, also pp. 152-58.

83. *Maasir-i-Alamgiri*, p. 174; *Mirat-i-Ahmadi*, vol. I, pp. 296-98.

84. Manucci, vol. III, pp. 288-91.

85. *Ibid.*, p. 288. Also Athar Ali, *The Mughal Nobility under Aurangzeb*, p. 99.

86. Trs in E.D. vol. III, p. 386.

87. Afif., p. 383.

88. Sarkar, *Short History of Aurangzib*, p. 157.

89. *Ibid.*, pp. 157-58.

90. This was according to both Hindu and Buddhist ideas. U.N. Ghoshal, *A History of the Hindu Political Theories*, Oxford, 1923, pp. 65-209.

91. *Ibid.*, pp. 237-238.

92. P.V. Kane, *History of Dharmashastra*, vol. II, Part II, pp. 865-69; *Arthashastra*, English trs. by R. Shama Shastry, Mysore, 1923, p. 140; *Proceedings of the Indian History Congress*, 1944, pp. 43-51.

93. *Shukraniti*, trs., B.K. Sarkar, Allahabad, 1914, pp. 147-148.

94. Cited in A.S. Altekar, *Rashtrakutas and their Times*, Oriental Book Agency, Poona, 1934, p. 217.

95. Alberuni, vol. II, p. 149. Also Hiuen Tsang, I, p. 176.

96. *Si-yu-ki*, vol. I, pp. 87-88 cited in B.K. Sarkar, *The Political Institutions and Theories of the Hindus*, Leipzig, 1922, p. 111.

97. Altekar, *Rashtrakutas*, p. 223.

98. Altekar, *Village Communities in Western India*, Humphrey Milford, Madras, 1927, p. 70.

99. Idrisi, *Nazhat-ul-Mushtaq*, E.D. vol. I, pp. 85-86.

100. K.S. Aiyangar, *Ancient India*, Madras, 1911, pp. 181-182.

101. Barani, pp. 61-63.

102. *Ibid.*, pp. 50-51.

103. *Ibid.*, p. 100.

104. Habibullah, *op. cit.*, p. 316.

105. Ibn Majah, vol. I, p. 514, *hadis* 1897.

106. Aghnides, *Muhammadan Theories of Finance*, p. 378.

107. Fakhr-i-Mudabbir, *Tarikh-i-Fakhruddin Mubarak Shah*, pp. 31-32.

108. Barani, pp. 216-17 and *Fatawa-i-Jahandari*, pp. 46-48.

109. Barani, p. 287; Lal, *Khaljis*, pp. 182-183.

110. Aghnides, *Muhammadan Theories of Finance*, pp. 251-54.

111. Afif, p. 98.

112. *Sunan Abu Daud*, vol. II, pp. 463-64, *hadis* 1171.

113. Barani, pp. 291, 297-98.

114. Isami, *Futuh-us-Salatin*, Agra text, pp. 569-70; *Tarikh-i-Wassaf*, Bombay text, Book V, pp. 646, 647.

115. Barani, p. 288.

116. *Ibid.*, pp. 288, 305, 307.

117. R.P. Tripathi, *Some Aspects of Muslim Administration* p. 262.

118. Barani, pp. 288-89, 292.

119. For Alauddin Khalji's Market Control see Lal, *Khaljis*, pp. 197-225.

120. Barani, p. 107.

121. *Ibid.*, pp. 46, 287-89.

122. *Ibid.*, pp. 262, 304.

123. Lal, *Khaljis*, pp. 93, 97.

124. Actual spitting in the mouth of the non-Muslims was not uncommon. Ganga Devi wife of Kumar Kampana (died 1374 CE) of Vijayanagar writes as follows in her *Madhuravijayam* regarding the state of things in the Madura region when it was under Muslim rule: "The temples in the land have fallen into neglect, as worship in them has been stopped... The sweet odour of the sacrificial smoke and chant of the Vedas have deserted the villages which are now filled with the foul smell of roasted flesh and the fierce noise of the ruffianly Turushkas... The wicked *mlechchas* pollute the religion of the Hindus every day."

Chaitanya-magala, a biography of the great Vaishnava saint of medieval India, presents the plight of the Hindus in Navadvipa on the eve of the saint's birth in 1484 CE. The author Jayananda writes "...The king plunders the houses of those who wear sacred threads on the shoulder and put sacred marks on the forehead, and then binds them. He breaks the temples and uproots *tulsi* plants... The bathing in Ganga is prohibited..."

Vijaya Gupta wrote a poem in praise of Husain Shah of Bengal (1493-1519 CE) The two Qazi brothers, Hasan and Husain, are typical Islamic characters in this poem. "The peons employed by the Qazis tore away the sacred threads of the Brahmans *and spat saliva in their mouths* (italics ours)." Isana Nagara describes the condition of the Hindus under Husain Shah as follows: "The wicked *mlecchhas* urinate like dogs on the *tulsi* plant and deliberately pass faeces in the Hindu temples. They throw water from their mouths on the Hindus engaged in worship, and harass the Hindu saints..."

This was the state of things in those parts of the country which were ruled by Muslim monarchs ever since Qutbuddin Aibak set up his first Islamic state in Delhi in 1206 CE. "Hindu records of what the 'law' of Islam meant to the Hindus are few and far between. But whenever they are available, they confirm the medieval Muslim historians." Sita Ram Goel, *The Story of Islamic Imperialism in India*, New Delhi, 1994 ed., pp. 97-99.

The Delhi Sultanate, Bharatiya Vidya Bhavan, 1960, pp. 631-33.

125. *Hidaya*, vol. II, p. 204; Hughes, p. 269.
126. Margoliouth, pp. 358-59.
127. For references see Lal, *Khaljis*, p. 181.
128. Barani, p. 340.
129. *Ibid.*, p. 430.
130. Hajiuddabir, *Zafar-ul-Wali*; Barani, pp. 479-80. For a detailed discussion on the Sultan's measures see Ishwari Prasad, *A History of the Quraunah Turks in India*, pp. 67-74.
131. Barani, pp. 468-473, 482-83, 486-87.
132. Lal, *Twilight of the Sultanate*, pp. 114-131.
133. W.H. Moreland, *From Akbar to Aurangzeb*, pp. 253-55.
134. Moreland in *Journal of Indian History*, IV, pp. 78-79 and XIV, p. 64.
135. Abul Fazl, *Akbar Nama*, Beveridge, vol. II, 159-60.
136. *Ain*, Jarret, vol. II, p. 73.
137. Manucci, vol. II, p. 451.
138. *Ibid.*, vol. III, pp. 48-49.
139. Manrique II, p. 272.
140. *Ibid.*, vol. III, pp. 290-91
141. Mucucci, vol. III, p. 232.
142. Bernier, p. 205.
143. *Babur Nama*, p. 470 and n.
144. *Tarikh-i-Salim Shahi*, p. 12.
145. *Tuzuk-i-Jahangiri*, I, pp. 8-9.
146. E.D., vol. VI, Appendix, pp. 493-512, esp. p. 493 n.
147. In an article on Zakat in *Arab Times*, Kuwait, February 19, 1996,

Ramadan 30, 1416 A.H. As the date shows the article appeared in the holy month of Ramzan.

Also Abu Daud, vol. I, p. 576. After the Prophet's death Abu Bəkr said that he would fight those who say namaz but do not pay Zakat.

Ibn Majah, vol. I, pp. 499-500, *hadis* 1849; pp. 507-09, *ahadis* 1867-78.

148. Aghnides, *Muhammadan Theories of Finance*, pp. 207, 297, 318.

Also Tripathi, *Some Aspects of Muslim Administration*, p. 345; Lal, *Khaljis*, pp. 185-86.

149. Aghinides, p. 213.

150. Tripathi, p. 345.

151. *Ibid.*, 346; Aghnides, p. 526.

152. Aghnides, pp. 530-33. See such a case of evasion in *Ain.*, Blochmann, vol. I, 181.

Lal, *Khaljis*, pp. 185-86.

U.N. Day, *Government of the Sultunate*, pp. 106-07.

153. Such cunning was not uncommon, E.G. Makhdum-ul Mulk's "tricks with the *Shari'at* in evading the payment of *Zakat* by transferring his property towards the end of the year to his wife and then getting it transferred to himself, completely shattered his position at (Akbar's) court."

Azra Alavi, *Socio-Relgious outlook of Abul Fazl*, p. 25, quoting Badaoni, II, p. 204, trs. Lowe, II, p. 206.

154. Aghnides, p. 525.

155. *Hedaya*, trs. Hamilton, vol. I, pp. 33-34.

156. Afif, p. 379, also p. 375; Rizvi, *Tughlaq Kalin Bharat*, vol. II, 1959, pp. 328-29; *Fatuhat-i-Firoz Shahi*, Aligarh, 1954, p. 5; Barani, p. 287; Farishtah, vol. I, p. 109; Aghnides, pp. 251-52, 253-54.

157. *Ain.*, Jarret, vol. II, pp. 72-73.

158. *Tuzuk*, vol. I, p. 7.

159. A. Athar Ali, *The Mughal Nobility under Aurangzeb*, p. 159.

160. *Tarikhi, Salim Shahi*, p. 8

161. *Babur Nama*, p. 555.

162. *Tuzuk*, vol. I, p. 47

163. *Ibid.*, pp. 167-108.

164. *Ibid.*, p. 417.

165. Smith, *Akbar the Great Mogul*, p. 298.

166. Farishtah, vol. I, p. 95; Kincaid and Parasanis, *A History of the Maratha People*, vol. I, pp. 36-37.

167. Yule, *Ser Marco Polo*, vol. II, p. 357.

168. *Mutla-us-Sadain*, E.D. vol. IV, pp. 106-07.

169. Farishtah, vol. I, 96; Barani, p. 223, 258.

170. Sharafuddin Yazdi, *Zafar Nama*, vol. II, pp. 164ff; *Mulfuzat-i-*

Timuri, E.D. vol. III, p. 470; Farishatah, vol. II, p. 340; *Rauzat-us-Safa*, vol. VI, p. 116.

171. Lal, *Khaljis*, Appendix, pp. 347-49.

172. Barani, p. 330; Taverier's *Travels*, vol. II, App. 1; *Khazain-ul-Futuh*, Habib trs., p. 77.

173. *Khazain*, Habib trs., pp. 105-107.

174. Barani 398.

175. *Ibid.*, p. 294.

176. Jagdish Singh Gehlot, *Rajputana ka Itihas*, Jodhpur, 1966, vol. III, p. 63; *Akbar Nama*, vol. II, p. 243; Lal, *The Mughal Harem*, pp. 25-29.

177. *Akbar Nama*, vol. III, p. 677-68; Beni Prasad, p. 24.

178. Khalji Khan, vol. VII, p. 883.

179. *Tuzuk*, vol. I, pp. 284-85.

180. *Chachnama*, Kalichbeg, pp. 154, 163.

181. Hasan Nizami, *Taj-ul-Maasir*, E.D. vol. II, p. 235; Minhaj, *Tabqat-i-Nasiri*, Raverty, p. 484 note.

182. Minhaj, p. 487 note.

183. *The Life of Muhammad*: A translation of Ibn Ishaq's *Sirat Rasul Allah* by A. Gillaume, OUP, Karachi, 1955, Eighth Impression, 1987, p. 466; Hughes, *Dictionary of Islam*, p. 600.

184. Amir Khusrau, *Nuh Sipehr*, Wahid Mirza ed., Calcutta, 1998, Sipehr II, pp. 89, 130-131.

185. Barani, pp. 314-15.

186. *Masalik-ul-Absar*, E.D. vol. III, pp. 580-81.

187. Hodivala, *Studies in Indo-Muslim History*, pp. 192-193.

188. *Akbar Nama*, vol. II, p. 246; Du Jarric, *Akbar and the Jesuits*, pp. 152-59, also pp. 28, 30, 70, 92.

189. Shah Nawaz Khan, *Maasir-ul-Umara*, vol. I, p. 105. For detailed references about the sale of slaves, see my *Muslim Slave System in Medieval India*.

190. Manucci, vol. II, p. 451; Manrique, vol. II, p. 272; Bernier, p. 205. For details see Lal, *Legacy*. pp. 249-55.

191. Ira Marvin Lapidus, *Muslim Cities in the Later Middle Ages*, Cambridge, Mass., 1967, pp. 54ff; Lal, *Khaljis*, pp. 201-203, 207-208, 218-219.

192. *Ain.*, vol., I, pp. 93-102.

193. *Akbar the Great Mogul*. p. 298.

194. Manucci, vol. II, p. 340; Lal, *Mughal Harem*, pp. 123-24.

195. R.K. Mukerjee, *The Economic History of India*, pp, 88-89-91.

196. *Ibid.*, p. 99

197. *Tuzuk*, vol. I, pp. 12, 298, 401; *Tarikh-i-Salim Shahi*, p. 8.

198. *Travels in India*, vol. I, p. 122.

199. Smith, *op. cit.*, pp. 298-99, quoting De Laet and Manrique in 'The Treasure of Akbar', J.R.A.S., 1915, p. 242.

200. *Ain.*, Jarret, vol. II, p. 63.
201. Thevenot, *Travels*, pp. 3-4; Manucci, vol. II, p. 389.
202. Manucci, vol. II, p. 389.
203. *Ibid.*, p. 392.
204. *Ibid.*, vol. I, p. 63.
205. *Ain.*, Jarret, vol. I, p. 63.
206. Thevenot, p. 4.
207. *Tarikh-i-Salim Shahi*, p. 9
208. Lal, *Legacy of Muslim Rule*, pp. 225-27.
209. Mukerjee, *Economic History*, p. 73.
210. *Short History of Aurangzib*, p. 479.
211. Edward Thomas, *The Chronicles of the Pathan Kings of Delhi*, p. 445, for details see pp. 435-445.
212. Afif, p. 94, has "*shash karor wa haftad wa panj lak tankah*". Moreland, *The Agrarian System of the Moslem India*, p. 57, has 5 krores through mistaken reading or printing error because he quotes the same page number 94.
213. "Annual Income and Expenditure of Sher Shah" in his *Studies in Medieval Indian History*, pp. 90-103.
214. Sarkar, *op. cit.*, pp. 476-77.
215. S. Lanepoole, *Aurangzeb*, Ruler of India Series, Oxford, MCMVIII, p. 122, detail on pp. 121-125.

V — EXPENDITURE OF THE STATE

1. Gordon Sanderson, 'Archaeology at the Qutb', Archaeological Survey of India Report, 1912-13, pp. 120, 131.
2. It is reproduced in Thomas, *Chronicles of the Pathan Kings of Delhi*, pp. 22-23.
3. Sir John Marshall in C.H.I.III, p. 578 n. 1.
4. Ibn Battutah, p. 27; Rizvi *Tughlaq Kalin Bharat,* vol. I, p. 175.
5. Barani, p. 341.
6. *Taj-ul-Maasir*, E.D. vol. II, p. 222.
7. Barani, p. 341.
8. Ibn Battutah, p. 77.
9. Lal, *Khaljis*, pp. 325-333.
10. Afif, p. 135.
11. *Ibid.*, pp. 330-333.
12. Nizam-ud-din Ahmad, vol. I, p. 336; Niamatullah, fol. 67(a).
13. *List of Muhammadan and Hindu Monuments*, vol. III, p. 189.
14. Abbas Sarwani, *Tarikh-i-Shar Shahi*, pp. 417-18 and Rizqullah *Waqiat-i-Mushtaqi*, p. 550, trs. in E.D. vol. IV.
15. *Tuzuk*, vol. I, p. 96 and footnotes 1 and 2.
16. *Babur Nama*, vol. II, pp. 520, 634.

17. *Tuzuk*, vol. I, p. 3; Wolseley Haig, C.H.I.IV, p. 89.
18. *Ibid.*, p. 105.
19. De Laet, *The Empire of the Great Mogal*, p. 44. Also Finch in Foster, *Early Travels in India* (1583-1610), p. 149.
20. *Tuzuk*, vol. I, pp. 7-8; *Tarikhi-Salim Shahi*, pp. 8-9.
21. *Ibid.*, vol. I, p. 118.
22. *Ibid.*, I, p. 152.
23. *Ibid.*, p. 258.
24. *Ibid.*, p. 12.
25. Moreland, *India from Akbar to Aurangzeb*, pp. 196-97.
26. *Badshah Nama*, vol. I, p. 221. Also C.H.I.IV, p. 554.
27. For mansions of nobles see my *The Mughal Harem*, pp. 45-47.
28. W.H. Moreland is the translator of Pelsaert's *Jahangir's India* and the author of *India from Akbar to Aurangzeb*. He says that this paragraph of Pelsaert has some problems of translation, Pelsaert, 56n., and hundreds of thousands may be taken as referring to either money or labourers.
29. 'Adorned' in Pelsaert, p. 56, 'covered' in *Akbar to Aurangzeb*, p. 197. The two words convey very different impressions.
30. Pelsaert, pp. 55-56; Moreland, *Akbar to Aurangzeb*, 197.
31. Barani, p. 102; *Fatawa-i-Jahandari*, p. 22; Afif, p. 283.
32. Barani, pp. 50-51, 60, 141, 303, 323-24.
33. Minhaj, Text, p. 315.
34. Barani, pp. 57-58.
35. Fakhr-i-Mudabbir, *Adab-ul-Harb wa Shujaat*, Hindi trs. by S.A.A. Rizvi in *Adi Turk Kalin Bharat* from B.M. Ms fol. 109b; Minhaj, text, p. 317; Barani, p. 80; Afif, p. 289.
36. Minhaj, text, pp. 195, 310.
37. Habibullah, *op. cit.*, p. 265.
38. Barani, p., 508.
39. *Ibid.*, p. 326.
Lal, *Khaljis*, pp. 193-96.
40. Barani, pp. 438-39.
41. Al-Umri, *Masalik-ul-Absar*, E.D. vol. III, p. 576.
Al-Qalqashindi, *Subh-ul-Asha*, p. 66.
42. Afif, pp. 221-222.
43. *Ain.*, I, pp. 123, 259-61.
44. *Tuzuk*, vol. I, p. 66, 82, also p. 71.
45. *Ibid.*, p. 111.
46. *Masalik*, E.D. vol. III, p. 577; Afif, pp. 296-97 and 437-38; Alqalqashindi, p. 71; Ibn Battutah, p. 129.
47. Barani, p. 145.
48. Al-Umri, *Masalik*, E.D. vol. III, p. 577. Also Hajiuddabir, *Zafar-ul-Walih*, p. 782.

49. Moreland, *India at the Death of Akbar*, pp. 68-69.
50. Jadunath Sarkar, *A Short History of Aurangzib*, p. 477.
51. Smith, *Akbar the Great Mogul*, pp. 261-62.
52. Irvine, *The Army of the Indian Moghuls*, pp. 58, 61-62.
53. *Ain.*, vol. I, p. 241, also Tables in *Ain.*, Vol. III.
54. *Tuzuk*, vol. I, p. 341 and n. *Ain.*, Jarraet, II, p. 277.
55. *Tuzuk*, vol. I, p. 349. Jarret, *Ain.*, vol. II, p. 198 has 29, 668, which appears to be correct.
56. Athar Ali, *The Apparatus of Empire*, Introduction and also pp. 36, 90, 345.
57. *Ibid.*, p. 478.
58. Afif, pp. 339-340.
59. *Waqiat-i-Mushtaqi*, E.D. vol. IV, p. 551; P. Saran, *Studies in Medieval Indian History*, p. 101.
60. *Ain.*, vol. I, Blochmann, pp. 140-150.
61. *Ibid.*, pp. 131-139.
62. *Ibid.*
63. *Ain.*, vol. I, pp. 129-30, 223; Smith, p. 38; *Tuzuk*, vol. I, pp. 237, 261, 287-89, 323, 400, 418,432.
64. *Ibid.*, pp. 150-156.
65. *Ibid.*, pp. 160-61.
66. Barani, pp. 145, 319; Ibn Battutah, p. 14.
67. *Ain.*, Blochmann, vol. I, pp. 147-49 169-70.
68. *Tuzuk*, I, pp. 374-75.
69. *Ibid.*, pp. 394-95.
70. Badaoni, II, p. 190 as cited in *Ain.*, I, p. 252.
71. *Ain.*, Blochmann, p. 253.
72. Pelsaert, p. 54.
73. Habibullah, p. 238.
74. Manucci, vol. IV, pp. 409ff.
75. *Ain.*, vol. I, p. 119.
76. *Ibid.*, pp. 115-123.
77. Barani, pp. 60, 141.
78. Afif, pp. 222-223.
79. Ibn Battutah, pp. 150-51. Also listed in Ishwari Prasad, *Qaraunah Turks*, pp. 138-39.
80. Afif, p. 339.
81. *Ibid.*, pp. 337-38, 370.
82. Bernier, pp. 255-56.
83. *Ain.*, vol. I, pp. 93-94.
84. *Ibid.*, p. 170.
85. Jadunath Sarkar, *Mughal Administration*, Calcutta, 1952, p. 9.
86. *Ain.*, vol. I, p. 94.

87. Bernier, p. 258-59.
88. *Ain.*, vol. I, pp. 93-94, 95-102.
89. Manucci, vol. II, p. 341. Also Bernier, p. 258.
90. Abdul Aziz, *Arms and Jewellery of the Indian Mughals*, pp. 212-13.
91. *Ain..*, vol. I, pp. 93-102.
92. *Ain.*, vol. I, pp. 98-100; Lahori, vol. II, Pt I, pp. 363-64; Manucci, vol. II, p. 340.
93. *Ain.*, I, pp. 83-93; *Tuzuk*, vol. I, p. 271.
94. R.K. Mukerjee, *Economic History of India*, pp. 117-19.
95. Terry in Foster's, *Early Travels*, p. 302.
96. Manrique, vol. I, p. 56, vol. II pp. 147, 180, 424.
97. Manucci, vol. II, p. 430.
98. Bernier, pp. 128, 292, 258-59, 402-403.
99. *Tuzuk*, vol. II, pp. 80-82; Manucci, vol. II, p. 339.
100. Minhaj, pp. 157-60.
101. Ferishtah, vol. I, p. 66, 67.
102. Barani, p. 145.
103. Ferishtah, vol. I, pp. 73, 75.
104. *Masalik*, cited by Qureshi, *Administration*, pp. 160-61.
105. Afif, pp. 95, 97. Incidentally, it indicates the lowly position of wives in the medieval Muslim household.
106. *Ibid.*, p. 400.
107. *Ibid.*, p. 94.
108. Ibn Battutah, trs. Mahdi Husain, p. 140.
109. *Ibid.*, pp. 67-72.
110. *Ibid.*, p. 105-107.
111. Minhaj, p. 315; Niamatullah, N.B. Roy trs., pp. 12, 13; Yahiya, p. 183; Farishtah, vol. I, p. 163; Nizamuddin, vol. I, p. 266.
112. Farishtah, vol. II, pp. 305-306.
113. Abdul Haqq, *Akhbar-ul-Akhiyar*, pp. 195-96; Abdullah, *Tarikh-i-Daudi*, pp. 60-63.
114. Ahmad Yadgar, *Tarikh-i-Salatin-i-Afghana*, p. 46. Also Badaoni, Ranking, vol. I, p. 427.
115. Abbas Sarwani, *Tarikh-i-Sher Shahi*, trs. E.D. vol. IV, pp. 390, 424.
116. *Babur Nama*, p. 522, 527.
117. *Ibid.*, pp. 578-79.
118. Gulbadan Begum, *Humayun Nama*, pp. 94-97; *Babur Nama*, p. 522. Erskine puts the *shahrukhi* at about one shilling; Steingass the *ashrafi* equal to 16 rupias. p. 95 n. 3.
119. *Tuzuk*, vol. I. p. 380.
120. To be distinguished from Sikandara, the place where Akbar's tomb stands and which lies some distance west of the river, Pelsaert, p. 4n.
121. De Laet, p. 41; Pelsaert, pp. 4-5.

122. D. Pant, *Commercial Policy of the Mughal Emperors*, pp. 106-079, 164.
123. *English Factory Records* (1642-45), p. 148.
124. Thomas Roe and John Fryer, *Travels in India in the Seventeenth Century*, p. 144.
125. Lal, *Mughal Harem*, p. 74.
126. Saksena, *Shahjahan*, pp. 63-64.
127. Lahori, vol. I, Pt. II, p. 51; also vol. II, Pt. I, p. 207.
128. Manucci, vol. I, pp. 67, 216.
129. *Ibid.*, p. 216. For further references see my *Mughal Harem*, pp. 94-95, 107.
130. *Tuzuk*, vol. I, p. 10, 79; *Alamgir Nama* I, p. 368.
131. For repeated references to this fact in one book alone see Barani, pp. 103, 117, 433-35, 440-42, 538-44.
132. Afif, pp. 80, 132-33, 349ff. Also Barani, pp. 145, 203, 291, 360, 426, 558-61, 597.
133. Afif, pp. 179ff., 196.
134. *Tarikh-i-Salim Shahi*, p. 16.
135. *Tuzuk*, vol. I, p. 10.
136. Barani, p. 243; *Tuzuk*, vol. I, p. 105.
137. Lal, *Khaljis*, p. 62.
138. Afif, p. 349.
139. For detailed references see Lal, *The Mughal Harem*, pp. 78, 87-88.
140. Afif, pp. 349ff; *Tuzuk*, vol. I, p. 9.
141. *Tarikh-i-Salim Shahi*, p. 13.
142. Niamatullah, *Makhzan-i-Afghani*, fols. 66(b), 68(a); Dorn, vol. I, p. 66; Rizqullah, *Waqiat-i-Mushtaqi*, fols. 7 a, b.
143. Nizamuddhin Ahmad, *Tabqat-i-Akbari*, vol. I, p. 336.
144. Yusuf Husain Khan, *Glimpses of Medieval Indian Culture*, pp. 69, 74.
145. Abbas Sarwani, E.D. vol. IV, pp. 410, 424.
146. *Waqiat-i-Mushtaqi*, E.D. vol. IV, p. 549.
147. P. Saran, *op. cit.*, p. 101.
148. Abbas Sarwani, p. 423; Sarkar, *A Short History of Aurangzib*, p. 154.
149. Sharma, *Religious Policy of the Mughal Emperors*, p. 107.
150. *Tuzuk*, vol. I, pp. 81, 107, 111, 115, pp. 127-28.
151. Mu'awiyah founded the line of Umayyad Caliphs at Damascus (CE 661), the Abbasids became Caliphs at Baghdad (CE 750) and Samarra (CE 836), and another line of Ummayad Caliphs ruled at Cordova or Qurtuba (CE 756). The Fatimid Caliphs were rulers in Cairo up to CE 1751 and the Ayyubids up to 1836.

Ruben Levy, *The Baghdad Chronicle*, p. 13.

J.H. Kramer in Sir Thomas Arnold, *The Legacy of Islam*, pp. 79-80.

Ruben Levy, *The Social Structure of Islam* p. 282.

152. Murray Titus, *Islam in India and Pakistan*, p. 55; Al-Biladuri, E.D.

vol. I, p. 201. Also E.D. vol. I, Appendix, p. 462.
Khuda Baksh, *Orient Under the Caliphs*, p. 218.
Istakhri, E.D. vol. I, p. 28.

153. Al-Kufi, *Chachnama*, trs. Kalichbeg, pp. 154, 163; E.D. vol. I, pp. 172-173, 181.
154. Al-Biladuri, E.D. vol. I., p. 123. See also Elliot's Appendix, vol. I, p. 470 and n.
155. C.E. Bosworth, *The Ghaznavids*, p. 53-54.
Aziz Ahmad, *Studies in Islamic Culture in the Indian Environment*, p. 5.
Hodivala, *Studies in Indo-Muslim History*, p. 176.
156. Baihaqi as cited in R.P. Tripathi, *op. cit.*, pp. 10-11.
157. Minhaj Siraj, *Tabqat-i-Nasiri*, Raverty, I, p. 61 and n. 4.
158. C.H.I. III, p. 159. Also Ibn Battutah, p. 73.
159. Barani, p. 493.
160. Thomas, *Chronicles*, pp. 207-16, 249-53, 259-60.
161. Yahiya, *Tarikh-i-Mubarak Shahi*, Persian text, p. 218; Lal, *Twilight*, p. 93 n. 50.
162. Muhammad Bihamad Khani, *Tarikh-i-Muhammadi*, trs. M. Zaki, p. 95.
163. Thomas, *Chronicles*, pp. 194, 197, 321-22.
164. Aziz Ahmad, *Studies in Islamic Culture*, p. 10; C.H.I.III, p. 358.
165. Anwar Shaikh, *Islam, The Arab National Movement*, p. 24, also p. 42.
166. Z.A. Desai, "*Arabic Inscriptions of the Rajput period from Gujarat*", *Epigraphia Indica — Arabic and Persian Supplement*, 1961, pp. 1-24. Also S.C. Misra, *Muslim Communities in Gujarat*, Asia Publishing House, Bombay, 1964, pp. 5-7.
167. *Babur Nama*, pp. 522-23.
168. Gulbadan Begum,. *Humayun Nama*, p. 69.
169. *Tarikh-i-Salim Shahi*, pp. 16-17.
170. Mukerjee, *Economic History of India*, p. 92.
171. K.S. Lal, *The Mughal Harem*, Aditya Prakashan, New Delhi, 1988.
172. Barani, p. 164.
173. *Ibid.*, p. 157.
174. Manucci, vol. II, p. 397.
175. Afif, pp. 40, 116.
176. *Ibid.*, p. 401.
177. *Ibid.*, p. 43.
178. *Ibid.*, pp. 288-89.
179. *Ibid.*, pp. 399-400.
180. *The Embassy of Sir Thomas Roe*, pp. 411-13.
181. *Tuzuk*, vol. I, p. 395.
182. *Ibid.*, p. 401.
183. *Ibid.*, p. 397.

184. *Ibid.*, p. 385.
185. Ibn Battutah, pp. 15-16, 65-66, trs. Rizvi, *Tughlaq Kalin Bharat*, vol. I, pp. 166-67, 190-91; Al-Umari, *Masalik*, p. 579; Alqalqashinidi, *Subh-ul-Asha*, p. 50; Ashraf, *Life and Conditions of the People of Hindustan*, pp. 282-83; Lal, *Twilight*, pp. 274-75.
186. Edward Terry, *A Voyage to East India*, pp. 195-98 cited in Smith, *Akbar the Great Mogul*, pp. 293-94.
187. Manrique, *Travels*, vol. II, pp. 113, 120.
188. Quran, Surah 52, ayats 17-24; Surah 55, ayats 12-36.

Part II

POLITICS

VI

Muslim State in India Today

The invasions of Muhammad bin Qasim, Mahmud of Ghazni and Amir Timur seem to have happened yesterday. The Qutb Minar in Delhi reminds one of Aibak and Iltutmish. One who visits the Taj Mahal of Agra, remembers Shahjahan. Akbar and Aurangzeb are still the talk of the town. Truly has Bernard Croce said that all history is contemporary. Our living present is the extension of the past which in many ways is still with us. No wonder then that Muslim state in India has not ceased to exist. It is not known as Nizam-i-Mustafa, as, in the Indian secular democracy, it cannot be known by that nomenclature. But it has been internalised in the Muslim psyche and is expressed in a number of euphemistic phrases like Muslim Identity, Muslim Personal Law, (Muslim) Minorities Commission, Muslim Waqf Board, Muslim (Madrasa) Education, and so on. All in all, Muslims by their personal law and separate identity represent a separate system within the secular Indian state, if not a separate state within the Indian state.

6.1. SEPARATE IDENTITY

The idea of Muslim exclusiveness and preservation of a separate identity is nothing new. In Islam all human beings are not treated as equals. It makes a distinction between

Muslims and non-Muslims. This distinction has been repeated in passages after passages both in the Quran and the Hadis and observed by Muslims the world over. A non-Muslim is a Kafir, an inferior being. Non-Muslims do not enjoy any human rights in this world; they cannot enter Paradise after death. Let us repeat some of the "revelations" about non-Muslims to drive home the point. "The unbelievers among the people of the Book (Jews and Christians) and the pagans shall burn forever in the fire of Hell. They are the vilest of creatures." "When you meet the unbelievers in the battlefield, strike off their heads." "Do not yield to the unbelievers but fight them strenuously." "Muhammad is Allah's apostle. Those who follow him are ruthless to the unbelievers but merciful to one another." "Make war on them (the idolaters)." "Allah will chastise them through you and humble them." "Allah has promised the hypocrites, both men and women, and the unbelievers the fire of Hell. They shall abide in it forever — the curse of Allah is upon them. Theirs shall be a lasting torment." "With chains and shackles round their necks they shall be dragged through boiling water and burnt in the fire of Hell." "Scalding water shall be poured upon their heads, melting their skins... They shall be lashed with the rods of iron ." "Whenever in their anguish, they try to escape from Hell, the angels will drag them back, saying: 'Taste the torment of Hell-fire'."[1] On the other hand, Muslims will repose in Paradise as portrayed in the Quran. "They shall recline on coaches lined with thick brocade... They shall dwell with bashful virgins — virgins as fair as corals and rubies." "They shall recline on jewelled coaches face to face, and there shall wait on them immortal youths with bowls and ewers and cups of purest wine." "The righteous (i.e. believers) shall dwell in bliss... their Lord will shield them from the scourge of Hell. He will say: Eat and drink in joy. This is the reward of your labours."[2]

All this and much more has already been cited before. The need to repeat it is to emphasise the Islamic injunction that Muslims and non-Muslims are distinct entities and the two cannot meet on terms of equality. This separate identity was crystallized in the twenty conditions laid down by Caliph Umar for the governance of the Zimmis. The Zimmis (originally Christians and Jews and later Hindus) were those subjects whose life was spared and who were a protected people (although no punishment was awarded to a Muslim who attacked a Zimmi). The conditions are like this. The Muslims are to be respected. The Zimmis are not to dress like Muslims. They must wear a humble dress so that they may be distinguished from Muslims. They are not to give each other Muslim names. They are not to ride on horses with saddle and bridle. They are not to possess swords and arrows. They are not to wear signet rings and seals on their fingers. They are not to rebuild any old buildings which have been destroyed. Muslim travellers are not to be prevented from staying in their temples. They are not to mourn their dead loudly. They are not to buy Muslim slaves. They are not to propagate the customs and usages of polytheists among Muslims. If any of their people show any inclination towards Islam, they are not to be prevented from doing so.[3]

One of the important condition was that the Zimmis were not to build their homes in the neighbourhood of those of Muslims. There are clear injunctions in the Quran for Muslims not to befriend infidels. "Believers, do not choose the infidels... for your friends." The danger in the living together with unbelievers is clearly spelled out in the Quran. "Believers, take neither Jews nor Christians for your friends... whoever of you seeks their friendship shall become one of their number... if you yield to the infidels, they will drag you back to unbelief and you will return headlong to perdition..."[4] The Prophet ordained: "Momins do not marry infidel women until they accept Islam. A Momin slave girl is better than a *mushrik* woman however pleasing she may look to you. (Similarly) do not give a Muslim woman in marriage to an infidel until he becomes Muslaman.

Because however good a *mushrik* may look to you, a Muslim slave is better than an infidel."[5] This is one very important reason for treating the non-Muslims as aliens, even enemies. Their contact could contaminate. The life promised by Islam in this world and the next is full of material comforts — women, wine and rich food. A Muslim whose soul hankers after spiritual elevation may be attracted to move over to 'infidel' cultures and become one with them. Hence there is persistent command to keep away from them. The *tablighis* in India are ever face to face with this problem.

The name given to the unbeliever or infidel in Islam is Kafir. It was freely used for non-Muslims by Muslim historians, rulers, elites, soldiers and common men in medieval India. The non-Muslims were treated as inferior beings in the theocratic Muslim state. In today's Indian republic the Hindus are in a vast majority. They cannot be openly addressed with contempt like this. But among Muslims, they are. Mr. Ram Nayak of Bombay has brought out a booklet wherein he asks how come there is no law to prevent 87 per cent Hindus from being abused as Kafirs whereas there is a law known as the civil protection act to prosecute anyone abusing Dalits.[6] The problem is whether Muslims should have the Kafirs treat them as they treat the Kafirs. Anwar Shaikh's important work, 338-page *Eternity,* rejects the division of humanity into believers and infidels or heathens. He lives abroad under fatwa of death. Dr. Abid Raza Bedar, liberal Indian Muslim also advocates that the word Kafir should exclude the Hindus from its purview. There are not many Muslims who support him because the Quran contains clear cut injunctions regarding Kafirs. It is free from any vagueness about the treatment to be meted out to the non-Muslims; it believes in their complete subservience or total annihilation. Muslim scriptures lay down that the faithful must live separately and exclusively and not form part of the mainstream of the social and political life of a non-Muslim majority country like India. Their exclusiveness is so acute that nationalist Hindus constantly exhort the 'minorities' (read Muslims) to join the national mainstream by laying emphasis on the tolerant principle of *sarvadharma samabhava* while Muslims insist on their separate identity. Islam lacks any doctrine of co-existence, and the Shariat stifles free discussion. Muslim madrasas cannot shed their Kafir complex. That is why the majority of Muslims keep quiet on such issues as raised by Abid Raza Bedar. The present adjustment for co-existence is a temporary expediency in India. In Kashmir, in Assam, and in regions where Muslims are in a majority or are growing in numbers, the plan is to claim a separate state for Muslims. In Muslim countries, even in Pakistan and Bangladesh, the non-Muslims are by and large accorded the status of only Kafirs.[7] Dr. Zafar-ul-Islam Aslahi of the Department of Islamic Studies, Aligarh Muslim University, says that in the light of the Shariat, imposition of Jiziyah on non-Muslims is justified.[8]

To conclude. There is a keen desire on the part of the Muslims, bordering on determination, to maintain their separate identity. They talk of composite Indian culture only to emphasise that it is Muslim culture. Harsh Narain therefore rightly argues that there is no composite culture in India.[9] The ghetto mentality of poor Muslims living in Mominpuras of all large and small cities, is shared by the highest elites in Muslim society. The situation is best described by Ram Swarup in his inimitable style. "In his book *My Eleven Years with Fakhruddin Ahmad*, Mr. Fazle Ahmed Rehmany quotes an incident which throws interesting light on the psychology of secularism and its need to keep Muslims in isolation and in a sort of protective custody. During the Emergency period some followers of the Jamaat-e-Islami found themselves in the same jail as the members of the RSS; here they began to discover that the latter were no monsters as described by the 'nationalist' and secularist propaganda. Therefore they began to think better of the Hindus. This alarmed the secularists and the interested Maulvis. Some Maulvis belonging to the Jamiat-ul-Ulema-i-Hind met President Fakhruddin Ahmad, and reported to him about the growing rapport between the members of the two communities. This 'stunned' the President and he said that this boded an 'ominous' future for Congress Muslim leaders and he promised that he would speak to Indiraji about this dangerous development and ensure that Muslims remain Muslims."

For Muslims to remain Muslims it is necessary that they are not governed by any laws except their own Shariat. It is the teaching of Islam to shun contact with non-Muslims except with a view to converting them. This should clear the doubt in the minds of those who wonder how a converted people can claim to form a separate nation. Muslim separatism expresses itself in multitudinous ways. One is Muslim Personal law.

6.2. MUSLIM PERSONAL LAW

Muslims constantly harp on their personal law. India is a land of many religions and followers of all these religions have their own religious or personal conventions or rules relating to marriage, divorce, adoption, inheritance, wills etc. Therefore it is realised that there should be some sort of uniformity in the civil laws of the land so that no community is discriminated against or favoured by the state in the eyes of the law. Moreover, for the progress of the Indian society as a whole, it is necessary to have a common civil code for all citizens. For example, as per the Indian Penal Code a Hindu or Parsi or Christian husband can be convicted for bigamy. But Muslims are excluded from this law because polygamy is recognised as a valid institution amongst their community. Thus while bigamy is a penal offence, Muslims enjoy exclusion from it. Apart from polygamy, another core issue is the divorce system (triple *talaq* or otherwise) among the

Muslims. Hindus and Christians cannot secure divorce so easily. It has been constantly said that there was no reason why the Muslim community was not given the benefit of social reforms regarding bigamy and divorce. Two of the more important features of a uniform civil law of course would be a ban on polygamy and instant *talaq*. This will not only give greater security to Muslim women, but also prevent irresponsible Hindu males from embracing Islam just to be able to marry more than one woman. Polygamy and instant *talaq* are both sanctioned by the Shariat law. Both are loaded in favour of Muslim men. Muslim women are sufferers.

Woman in Islam

"Men have preeminence above women because God has made them superior to the latter. Also men spend their money... Good wives are obedient to men... Those who disobey you, first advise them politely to behave themselves. If they do not improve, stop sleeping with them. If even then they do not improve, beat them up...," says the Quran.[10] The Quran also imposes elaborate veil on women. Momins are instructed to tell their wives and daughters to cover themselves with veil when going out.[11] "Enjoin believing women to keep their eyes low, to preserve their chastity, to cover their adornments, to draw their veils over their bosoms and not to reveal their finery."[12] Women were primarily meant to procreate, to produce Muslims. "Your wives are as a tilth unto you. So approach your tilth when and how you will" — by ploughing, sowing and raising crops, says the Quran. Or, "Your women are your field — go unto them as you will."[13] Woman in Islam is not regarded as a person but as a field. Her husband cultivates it and reaps the harvest, for the harvest belongs to the proprietor. She is nothing but her husband's domain. Women could be beaten up for disloyalty and sexual non-comformity.[14]

No wonder, with such freedom on the part of men and such restrictions on the part of women, believers took to marrying freely from the very beginning of Islam. It is common knowledge that in Islam a man can marry four wives and possess numberless concubines. According to a tradition of Abu Abbas, the Prophet had said: "In my Ummah, he is the best who has the largest number of wives." Umar, the second Caliph (581-644 CE) had already married four times before the Hijra; in Medina he married five more times, the last when he was sixty. Umar said: "Prevent women from learning to write; say no to their capricious ways... Adopt positions opposite those of women. There is great merit in such opposition." At 57 Umar married Umm Kulsum, daughter of Ali and Fatima. Ali (600-661) was the Prophet's cousin and the fourth Caliph. He said: "The entire woman is an evil and what is worse is that it is a necessary evil... You should never ask a woman her advice because her advice is worthless. Hide them so that they cannot see other men." Islam was the first to impose the elaborate veil on women. Other *ahadis* advised likewise. In many of these women are depicted as *fitna* (evil). The Prophet said that "After me I will not leave any greater *fitna* for men than women". Women are *naqis-ul-aql* and *naqis-ul-din.* They are found in hell in large numbers. Men will be destroyed on account of women.[15]

In short, there was a spate of marriages, flood of divorces, lot of restrictions and damaging diatribes against women among the faithful. Ali's son, al-Hasan, the brother of al-Husain of the Karbala fame, had won a highly individual title for himself: "the great divorcer." He died at the age of forty-five and he had by that time succeeded in making and unmaking no less than one hundred marriages. Al-Hasan had twenty children, fifteen sons and five daughters, from whom are descended one section of the great Saiyyads.[16] It is well known that polygamy and Jihad helped Muslim expansion and colonization. "No wonder that in the annals of history, Muslim imperialism probably endured the longest."[17]

This was a great achievement of Islam. But it also resulted in damnation of half of the Muslim population, that of Muslim women, droves of whom had been obtained in Jihad. They were declared to be inferior to men in every way. They were to be freely beaten. "Wife-beating was perhaps already there, but Islam brought to it a heavenly sanction."[18] Testimony of two women was considered equal to that of one man. In matters of sex man's desire was all that mattered. Captured women were like slaves or concubines or "what your right hand possesses". They were meant for amusement of Muslim men. Women could be married at will and divorced at will. No explanation was needed for divorcing a woman. "Islam has always considered women as creatures inferior in every way: physically, intellectually, and morally. This negative vision is divinely sanctioned in the Koran, corroborated by the hadiths and perpetuated by the commentaries of the theologians, the custodians of Muslim dogma and ignorance."[19] In short, polygamy is a crucial point of Muslim Personal law.

Stir for Muslim Women's Liberation

It is noteworthy that a debate is going on among the Muslims themselves about having a second look at the Shariat laws regarding women and divorce, alimony and maintenance. But it is a low key controversy. For, the Prophet's revelations are final. The laws have been issued. Other societies adopt new laws as the need arises, as traditions change. This is not possible in Islam. "Islamic laws on marriage and divorce are not just social legislations... They are revealed truths, Allah's commands. To seek to change them is... rebellion against God." All that a Muslim can do is to 'reinterpret' the Prophet's decrees — by itself not an easy task. For example, Zafar Jung's article "Islamic law needs to be revised", ends by saying that the change should be in the spirit of the pristine purity of Islam. Abdul

Moghni (Patna) reacting to Zafar Jung's article says: "It can be improved upon only by authentic Islamic scholars and accredited institutions rather than by the so-called secularists who are ignorant of Islam and its laws."[20] "Consequently and as usual, all debate ends where it begins — everything is to be thought and done within the permissible limits of Islam."

The debate has not remained confined to men alone. Farida Rahman, an active feminist, jurist and a member of parliament of the Bangladesh Nationalist Party, demanding women's share in property said: "I do not advocate that the holy Koran should be rewritten but I do demand that there be equal rights for men and women and that is why I would circumvent the laws laid down in the Koran in this particular case." For this remark Bangladesh fundamentalist leader Maulana Fazlul Huq Amini demanded her death — "Farida Rahman being a Muslim must be hanged for speaking against the holy Koran."[21] A fatwa has been issued against her for demanding equality between men and women. Farida Rahman is safe(?) outside Islamic Bangladesh as she has sought refuge in Sweden. Riffat Hassan is also safe outside Pakistan. Born and brought up in Lahore, Riffat presently is a professor of religious studies in the United States. According to her the activities of Muslim fundamentalist groups throughout the world and especially in Afghanistan, Iran, Egypt, Sudan and Bangladesh have strengthened the view that Islam cannot coexist with liberal attitudes. Riffat Hasan is out to demolish the stereotype of a partriarchal Islam. Her struggle is against fundamentalists especially in Muslim majority states who are "working overtime to make Muslim women faceless and nameless".[22]

The demand that "Farida Rahman being a Muslim must be hanged for speaking against the holy Koran", is in keeping with the Islamic tradition. But Farida Rahman rightly raises her voice against the attempt to humiliate and ridicule Muslim women and make them helpless and faceless. Two examples of this attitude may be cited. A news item from Dhaka says that "A radical Muslim priest has offered love and marriage to Bangladesh's most controversial feminist writer, Taslima Nasreen, in order to bring her to the faith". "She will be my third wife," said Mr. Rahim Baksh, an Islamic cleric in Cox's Bazar town in southeastern Bangladesh.[23] Another: "One of the most pathetic stories told during a recent video magazine programme on the triple *talaq* controversy was that of a middle aged Muslim woman who recounted how a group of mullahs laughed at her when she took her complaint about her marriage to them. She felt so helpless, she said, in a room full of bearded clerics — all men, of course — laughing at her plight and making it abundantly clear that she was living in a man's world where her grievances against her husband would bring no relief."[24] It is clear that the iron law of the fundamentalists still has the community in its grip, preventing the articulation of any views or the adoption of any behaviour which carry a hint of nonconformism. Since all Muslims, including the liberals, seem resigned to let the bigots rule the roost, it only helps their opponents to buttress the case against their closer assimilation in Indian society. Any possibility of a successful rebellion against the medieval concepts is out of the question in the Islamic countries, but not totally unfeasible in an open polity like India's. But the initiative has to come from within the Muslim community, declare secularist political parties.

In a free country like India, Muslim women sometimes speak out. A few days ago a group of Muslim women took out a procession in Mumbai. They were protesting against polygamy and triple *talaq* as practised by Muslim men. Their delegation also met the Chief Minister Mr. Manohar Joshi. Working women stated that sometimes when they returned home late from workplace, their husbands pronounced *talaq* and in a moment they were rendered homeless and helpless.

For a woman's right of inheritance is illusory. The concept of alimony is unknown is Islam, and the Quran sanctions maintenance for the customary period of *iddat.*[25] Manohar Joshi promised to look into their problems sympathetically. What followed was published as a news item in *The Times of India,* Mumbai, dated 30 April 1997. "The Samajwadi Party has protested against chief minister Manohar Joshi's assertion that his government would introduce a uniform civil code in Maharashtra... Samajwadi Party spokesman Nasir Jamal said here on Tuesday that Mr. Joshi's statement had 'created a feeling of insecurity among the Muslim masses'. 'Several Muslim organisations are planning to come together and jointly oppose any move to impose a uniform code,' he added. Mr. Jamal appealed to the Shiv Sena-Bharatiya Janata Party government not to 'tamper with Muslim religious laws'."[26] So even a talk of reform creates a feeling of insecurity among the Muslims. A similar attempt of Kerala *talaq* victims to fight against polygamy through their newly formed forum 'Nisha' (Nisa in Arabic means women) and the movement called 'Makkal Samaram' (stir by children for share in fathers' property) are also facing rough weather from the orthodox section of the Muslim community.[27]

The remedy for most of such problems lies in having a common civil code for all citizens. This was realised by the framers of the Constitution of India. Article 44 of the Constitution says: "The state shall endeavour to secure for the citizens a uniform civil code throughout the territory of India." Many a time aggrieved parties (like divorced Muslim women) have approached the courts for redressal and many a time the Supreme Court has asked the government to explain the steps it has taken for securing uniformity in the personal laws, particularly those of the Muslims, leading to the enactment of a common civil code for all Indians.

Many Muslims in India, both liberal and orthodox, are engaged in a debate on the merits of prohibition of polygamy and triple *talaq* and many other matters like adoption and inheritance and the desirability of having a common civil code. But since the demand for a uniform civil code comes from the Hindu forums also, it is resisted by Muslims in general and mullahs in particular. Muslims are generally allergic to the advocacy by Hindus of a common civil code. They consider it an interference of non-Muslims in the personal laws of Islam. That is why Nasir Jamal appealed particularly to "Shiv Sena-Bharatiya Janata Party government not to tamper with Muslim religious laws". Any innovation or change is taboo in Islam because it is believed that the best code of laws for "all humanity and for all time" has already been sent by God fourteen hundred years ago and any suggestion for change is not only irrelevant but also "creates a feeling of insecurity among Muslims". Some Hindus in anger say: "Let them go to hell; let them stew in their own juice." But Indian society cannot progress if the condition of only some women (Hindu) improves through reform while the Muslim women are left out. If the society has to progress it has to progress as whole; there has to be a uniform civil code for all. The Bharatiya Janata Party wants enactment of a common civil code. The Congress Party opposes it. This is party politics, a basic of democracy. That is how Nasir Jamal's contention in Mumbai gets support from the Congress. Mr. Gurudas Kamat, a member of the interim committee overseeing the affairs of the Mumbai unit of the Congress, said that "the Congress would vehemently oppose any move to bring in the code. According to him the Sena was trying to create fear in the minds of the minorities in the state." It is well known that the Hindu secularists help Muslim fundamentalists in keeping the banner of instant *talaq* and polygamy flying. "Union government has already expressed its helplessness in enacting a common Uniform Civil Code (UCC), applicable to all the religious communities. It feels that such a legislation would be against its policy not to interfere with the personal laws of minority communities... The government maintains that until the initiative for change comes from the community, it cannot interfere with its personal laws."[28] The problem of enactment of a uniform civil code has become a grinding stone placed round the neck of the country. The political parties, the Parliament and state legislatures, the Judiciary — from lower courts to the Supreme Court —, the intelligentsia, the media, the ulema have all got involved with it in one way or the other, but there seems to be no way out. It is true that a few Muslim women seek relief from law courts,[29] but naturally not all the aggrieved parties can take their problems to the courts all the time. The courts themselves are handicapped because of variance of religious laws of so many faiths and ask the government what steps are being taken to implement the provision of the Constitution "to secure for the citizens uniform civil code throughout the territory of India".

It is necessary to admit that social reforms are not easy to effect. The more things change the more they remain the same. There is inevitability of gradualness in the field of social reform. In the West the Christians have moved a little faster, or so it appears. They have both the will to change and the determination to move forward. Hindus possess the will but change but little. They are aware of the evils in their society and pass laws to remove them. Laws have been enacted against untouchability, against child marriage, against demanding dowry, against begging, against child labour, against employment of children in hazardous industries, and in a dozen other areas. This shows the zeal of the Hindus in establishing a better social order. But in actual fact little change in these fields has come about, if things have not actually deteriorated. Some "progressive" Muslims sometimes talk of change with regard to rules of polygamy, divorce, adoption, inheritance etc. But other equally "progressive" Muslims oppose any such move. (The indoctrinated, poor and uneducated Muslims of course have no opinion to offer.) So they do the next best thing — defend everything Islamic. In place of improving the lot of their women, they assert that the status of women in Islam is the best, that their divorce rules are the best, and that their education in madrasas is correct and complete. They claim that their social rules enacted fourteen hundred years ago in the desert land of Arabia in the camel age are good in all countries for all times. If there is any suggestion from outside, they consider it an interference in their Personal Law.

As has been discussed in detail earlier, Islam has little to do with democracy. It does not concede equal status to Muslims and non-Muslims. In a Muslim state non-Muslims do not enjoy human rights as defined in modern times. Muslim religious and political leaders repeatedly claims that the Shariat laws and fatwas of Muftis have greater sanctity for Muslims than provisions of the Indian Constitution.

Although this attitude in many ways comes in the way of Muslims joining India's national mainstream, it does not debar them from enjoying the advantages flowing from Indian democracy. The Constitution of India provides for special consideration to the minorities and Muslims take full advantage of this situation. Besides, democracy is based on elections. Muslim voters take advantage of such a situation and minorityism flourishes in India through the assistance of some 'secularist' politicians and betrayal by some intellectuals. All political parties in India run after Muslim votes. This turns Indian democracy into politics of minorityism and vote banks, and helps the Muslims to remain a state within the state — with their own personal laws — and the absence of a uniform civil code keeps the torch of Muslim separatism burning. Still the condition of Muslim women in India is better than that in many Islamic countries for reasons more than one. For one, there is lot of Hindu influence on Muslim culture. *Purdah*-less Muslim women are a common sight. For another, Indian judiciary comes to the rescue of oppressed Muslim women in matters of maintenance and alimony.

In many parts of the Middle East women have been

increasingly abused for not covering their hair, for going to beaches or for travelling in public transport simply because there was no provision in them for segregating the men from the women. Women working in the public sector were also threatened with death if they did not give up their jobs.

According to the findings of the Amnesty International recorded in their latest report, "Women in the Middle East: Human rights under attack", in several Middle East countries women face imprisonment, cruel punishments and even death under the law which is discriminatory and heavily loaded against women. Consequently, from being prosecuted for the clothes they wear or do not wear, women can be locked up for driving a car even.

In Saudi Arabia, driving by women has been banned through legislation. The Iranian law, in turn, states that a women should be buried upto her chest for sexual offences while specifying the type of stones that should be used. According to article 104 of the Penal Code which refers to adultery, "In the punishment of stoning to death, the stones should not be too large so that the person dies on being hit by one or two of them; they should not be too small either so that they could not be defined as stones."[30]

While in Iran, both men and women face sentences of flogging and stoning to death for sexual offences for *hudud* offences such as adultery, according to the Amnesty report a large number of women have been executed by being stoned to death. Such executions are of common occurrence. Three men and women were stoned to death in October 1997.[31] However, men who kill for the sake of honour are let free. In Iran women also risk arrest and flogging if they fail to obey the dress code. The law provides for 74 lashes for violating the "dress law". Women of course do not observe *purdah* with women. In women's clubs (Hijab clubs), they can play games, swim, and practice athletics under women coaches, but all Islamic laws are applicable to them. They cannot, according to the Constitution, become presidents, judges or religious leaders. Men can divorce at will. "Women cannot travel without *the written permission* (emphasis added) of their husbands or fathers, and a woman's testimony in court carries just half the weight of man's."[32]

In Sudan women have been flogged for dressing in the ways that infringe the military Government's law on public morality. The Amnesty International has recorded that a woman living in Omdurman was fined and sentenced to 35 lashes because she was wearing trousers. Another woman a student at Khartoum University who was wearing a blouse and skirt was lashed 25 times for the offence.

As Muzaffar Hussain writes, "In Algeria the fanatics are out to brutally subjugate women who have some experience of women's liberty since the French connection. If a Muslim woman is seen without *purdah* or uncovered hair she is shot dead. If a Muslim woman continues in her old attire of the French colonial days of skirt and blouse, her bare legs are exposed to a fusillade of stones and before long she falls a cripple. In 1993-94 according to the official reports about 300 women were killed for various reasons." On March 6, when the rest of the world was celebrating Women's Day, in the very capital city of Algeria 16 women were mowed down for having seen a dramatic performance in a theatre. According to the information available with the UN there are fifty-five million refugees in the world; about forty million of them are Muslims. When a person has to leave his home and hearth and take to an unending road the most severe hardships come to the lot of women. In the world 17,500,00 Muslim women with their 75,00,000 children are roaming in search of shelter. The petro-dollar rich Arab and other countries that swear by their Islamic faith have no time to think about them.[33] Algeria, Morocco and Tunisia are considered progressive nations of North Africa. The position of women in other Islamic countries is not better if not worse. Fatima Mernissi, Professor of Sociology, Mohammad V University in Rabat, Morocco, in her book *Islam and*

Democracy — Fear of the Modern World, dates "the powerlessness of women to the advent of Islam."[34] Still, and as usual, it is claimed that "by comparison, women in Islam were in a much better and more protected position".[35] This is true of India but not Islamic countries.

Indian 'secularist' politicians join the "minorities" in opposing a common civil code with a view to please the Muslims to garner their votes. They find many other ways for the same reason. One such gesture is the government's granting subsidy on Hajj pilgrimage.

6.3. HAJJ PILGRIMAGE

Pilgrimage to Mecca and Medina is a religious obligation on every Muslim. Consequently Hajj pilgrims converge on these holy cities once every year from all over the world. This year (1997) the estimated number of Hajj pilgrims from India totals to about 82,000. Of these about 32,000 went on their own while more than 50,000 persons were government sponsored: in other words their journey to Saudi Arabia was subsidised by the Government of India. There are many Indian Muslims who sell their houses and personal belongings to go to Mecca for Hajj. But we are here concerned with Indian 'secular' government's subsidy of crores of rupees annually *on this pilgrimage.* The Indian Parliament was informed by the External Affairs Minister Mr. Inder Kumar Gujral on 17 March 1997 that "a total of Rs.84.66 crores was spent on subsidising travel of over 1.06 lakh Haj pilgrims from 1994 till 1996."[36] The First Report of the Standing Committee on External Affairs (1993-94) approved by the Tenth Lok Sabha, was laid on the table of the House on 19 April 1993. It stated:

"An amount of Rs.21 crores is estimated to be spent in 1993-94 for payment to SBI (State Bank of India) on account of foreign exchange released to Haj Pilgrims at official rate of exchange. It has been decided in January, 1993 that the pilgrims will be given foreign exchange at the official rate and the difference between the official and market rate of exchange would be borne through the Ministry of External Affairs' budgetary provision. The difference in the rates of exchange comes to Rs.21 crores.

"This year (1993) arrangements have been finalised with Aeroflot carrying pilgrims to Jeddah and back against a sum of Rs.18,000 per pilgrim. A pilgrim would however pay Rs.11,000. For 20,000 pilgrims travelling by air, a sum of Rs.14 crores will have to be set aside as subsidy at the rate of Rs.7,000. Besides a sum of Rs.8.80 [37] crores approximately will be required to be earmarked for subsidy on 4,700 pilgrims' journey by sea. Facilities extended by the Government of India for the Haj Pilgrims include subsidised fares by sea/air. Haj pilgrims are also exempted from payment of International Airport Tax of Rs.300, a courtesy which costs the Government Rs.6 lakhs.

"Government of India also sends a 45 members team of medical/paramedical personnel for the duration of Haj every year. 6 Assistant Haj Officers and 8 Haj Assistants are being sent for the assistance of pilgrims during the Haj. Medicines worth Rs.7.17 lakhs have also been sent for the Hajis. All these and the additional staff recruited locally by the CGI Jeddah for the assistance of the pilgrims during the Haj season and the regular Haj establishment in Indian consulate cost Government of India Rs.1.02 crores every year.

"The Committee desire that while maintaining the services for the welfare of the Indian Haj pilgrims while in Saudi Arabia at an adequate level, the Government should progressively reduce and eventually eliminate the element of subsidy on their transportation to and from India. The Committee, however, do not see any justification for the newly instituted subsidy on the purchase of foreign exchange by the pilgrims."[38]

But in the place of progressively reducing the subsidy, the government is spending more and more on Hajj pilgrims.

The number of Hajj pilgrims over the years has been on the increase. Earlier only 18 to 22 thousand pilgrims used to go from India. Last year, it was 50 thousand which swelled to 82 thousand this year. This year, 1997, the government's expenditure on Hajj has been reported to Parliament as being Rs.93 crore. A fire in the pilgrim's camp has killed more than 200 Indian pilgrims and injured an unspecified number, some critically. Doctors, medicines and goodwill missions have been rushed to the site. The government has promised to pay rupees one lakh each to the kin of the dead and the disabled. All this would come to a hundred crores. A country which has millions of people under poverty line to feed can ill afford such generosity. Giving of so much subsidy by the "Secular Government" for a religious minority puts a question mark on its credibility. For, it was the secularist Jawaharlal Nehru who introduced the Haj Bill in Parliament in 1959 to facilitate and subsidise Muslim pilgrims visiting Mecca. But, as seen above, it has now grown into a monster costing the Government 93 crores in 1997 alone. In addition to the Central Government, many State Governments and large cities like Mumbai, Bangalore and Delhi run Hajj Centres at taxpayers' expense.

There is also loss of revenue to Air India, the official government owned airlines. The dislocation in its normal services due to Hajj adversely affects its finance and reputation. Scores of flights are specially arranged to fly from Mumbai, Delhi, Chennai, Hyderabad and Thiruanantapuram to carry the pilgrims to Jeddah. And the Air Carriers have to return empty, obviously. On the reverse journey, Carriers fly empty to Jeddah to bring back the pilgrims from there. Newspapers are full of details of losses incurred by the government airlines every year. One report by Srinivas Laxman in *The Times of India News Service*, 24 March 1997, on the problem would suffice:

"Mumbai: Air-India's international flight schedules have been badly hit following diversion of several aircraft for Haj. Sources in A-I admitted that the diversion of aircraft had affected its flight schedules. This has tarnished the airline's image... He expressed helplessness saying the decision to divert aircraft was taken at the political level. A-I would now operate 142 special Haj flights for transporting 55,000 pilgrims. The Haj season is expected to end on May 21 and the special flights have forced A-I to drastically curtail its services, even to some of the lucrative destinations... The disruption in A-I services has been severely criticised by travellers and foreign tour operators. A foreign tour operator, who requested anonymity, said: The credibility of the airline has taken a severe drubbing again because of the suspension of services."

Dhananjayan K. Machingal, president of a German travel agency, was stated to have described the flight suspensions as a "political ploy" aimed at a vote bank in India. He is further quoted as saying that A-I was the "number one obstacle" to be surmounted for promoting India as an international tourist destination.

So revenue from Air India is lost, its flight-credibility suffers and Indian tourism gets a beating besides the Government losing crores of rupees on subsidising Hajj pilgrimage. This is not the end of the story. A few ships ply between the mainland and Andamans and numerous other small islands carrying essential supplies to those living on the islands. During the Hajj season some of these ships are diverted to carry pilgrims to Saudi Arabia. This results in acute shortage of necessities of life for island people including servicemen. So even the country's security is made subservient to vote bank politics.

On the other hand, the income to Saudi Arabia from Hajj every year is considerable, and this pilgrimage will keep it rich always, even if its oil reserves dry up. Because of this the Saudis have an old feud with Iran and Libya, with regard to the Muslim holy cities. Iranian police and pilgrims fought with Arab police in the main mosque in 1987. Libya wants Mecca and Medina to be declared as international townships, with the status of 'Vatican', arguing that they are common property of all Muslims.

6.4. IMAMS AS GOVERNMENT SERVANTS

Concessions to Muslims do not stop at Hajj subsidy. In the medieval period the Muslim state in India maintained the staff of the mosques at the expense of the royal exchequer. We have already said that Muslim state in India has not ceased to exist, so that the union government has taken the first step fixing regular pay scales for 1.15 lakh imams leading prayers in the various mosques across the country. The beneficiaries are 26,000 'alims' 46,000 'hafiz' and 43,000 'nazrah'. For implementation of this decision the government would have to bear an estimated expenditure of Rs.243 crores. Besides for coming three years an additional Rs.405 crores would be paid to the three categories of imams. Under the scheme, *imam alim's* pay scale will be Rs.1,000-1,600, *imam hafiz's* Rs.950-1,550, *imam nazrah's* Rs.850-1,400 and *muazin's* Rs. 800-1,400. In addition, Rs.30 per month will also be paid to the imams as medical allowance. Although these scales have been finalised, it has specifically been stated that the Wakf Board in charge of a state can pay higher scales. At least 1.15 lakh *imam alim, imam hafiz, imam nazrah* and *muazin* would get about rupees one lakh each towards back-wages and arrears since the court accepted the All India Imam Organisation (AIIO)'s plea for fixing their salaries. The governments' decision to frame a salary scheme for imams has been made despite the attorney-general's strong dissent that the state can neither promote a religion nor have one to nurture it. The governments' decision is being seen as a move to woo the imams for the elections which are round the corner.[39] During Muslim rule masjids of course were government institutions, and preachers and readers were paid from the state treasury.[40] Plan of making payment of salaries to imams today would also make them government servants.

But there is always a slip between the cup and the lip. The ruling party's plan to garner Muslim votes by paying salaries to imams of masjids alerted other political parties also. They also offered a deal and a better one at that. Muslim leaders also felt shy of the community's religious heads accepting such open inducement. They protested against the imams serving as government agents by accepting a salary from it. The Congress Party which had made the original offer also lost elections and went out of office. The case of making the imams salaried servants was shelved (for the time being?). But the project of payment speaks for itself. It tells (a) how a political party calling itself secular craves for Muslim communal votes, and (b) how the Muslims try to derive the best advantage from India's secular democracy.

Modern democracy is based on elections. Come elections (and they come so often), and Muslim leaders, religious and secular, are approached for support by individuals and political parties. Various Muslim outfits by themselves descend in the election arena to advocate the cause of the 'minority' community. The Shahi Imam of Jama Masjid, Delhi, has been a keen participant in election politics and shown the way to Muslim clergy, maulanas, imams and overseers of *dargahs* to participate in electoral politics. Muslim votes account for a good percentage of the electorate, ranging from 10 to 35 or even 40 percent in some constituencies. Like any other community, they are divided on political issues. "The only point of agreement among the minority voters is their antipathy to the BJP..."[41] The Congress and now the United Front is ever ready to exploit this mullah reserve for their anti-BJP party politics. Incidentally, by giving prestige to the mullahs and maulvis and by giving them a platform of anti-BJPism, 'secular' parties rekindled amongst them the Jihadist mentality which was never dormant and had witnessed the holocausts of Calcutta and Noakhali. The terrorist activities of Jihadist outfits from Kashmir to Kerala via Coimbatore are a direct result of this secularist syndrome. Secularist politicians and intelligentsia find it easy to enjoy power and influence by not criticising infiltrators, smugglers and other anti-national elements. They find it profitable to attack Hindus only and call them communalists.

6.5. FRIDAY CONGREGATIONAL SERVICE

Curiously enough in the Indian state as in any Muslim state the mosque is a place of religious prayer *and* political activity. Friday sermon is the imam's 'Order of the Day'. It is so today in the Jama Masjid of Delhi as well as all other important masjids in the country. In the Delhi Jama Masjid Prime Minister V.P. Singh of the 'Social Justice' fame paid a visit to the Shahi Imam, Syed Abdulla Bukhari. His son Syed Ahmad Bukhari, the Naib Imam, has delivered venomous Friday sermons especially in the wake of the destruction of the disputed Babri structure at Ayodhya in December 1992. A fiery speech was made in early January 1993. The police naturally charged him with sedition and inflaming communal passions by his anti-national diatribe. The police filed the charge-sheet without arresting the Naib Imam on the ground that it would cause a law and order problem. Pampered by the Prime Ministers, these imams have developed a clout. The court issued summons and later on non-bailable warrants against the accused, but Ahmad Bukhari obtained a stay on the proceedings from the High Court.

Even while Ahmad Bukhari's plea is pending in the High Court, the secular Government headed by H.D. Deve Gowda instructed the Delhi Lieutenant Governor to move the court for the withdrawal of the case against the Naib Imam on the plea that dropping of sedition charge against him would help create a peaceful atmosphere in society. This step so alarmed the Hindus living in the Jama Masjid area that one Shyam Lal resident of Sita Ram Bazar and four others in his vicinity, moved an application in the court of the Metropolitan Magistrate opposing the withdrawal of the case. Shyam Lal pleaded that the people living in the area were terribly scared following the speech of Ahmad Bukhari and therefore the case should not be dropped against the Naib imam.

While it is rumoured that the decision to withdraw the case on the part of the United Front Government was due to a deal seeking Bukhari's support in Uttar Pradesh elections, the terror inspired by this centre of religio-political activity is due to many more reasons. Thousands of Muslims assemble in one place and collection of such a crowd generates a feeling of fright. The roads in front of the mosque are blocked on Friday afternoon. The *namazis* who assemble for prayer overflow into the adjoining streets, hindering movement of people and flow of traffic. This problem is acute in Mumbai. Then there are microphones. They screech loudly to call the Muslims to prayer. This problem is a headache for the government in Calcutta. One has only to see on any Friday the deployment of police force in the environs of the main mosques to realise that the Jama Masjid is a symbol of Muslim state within the Indian state. On collective prayers days like Idul-zuha and Idul-fitr, or on any Friday afternoon the whole atmosphere inspires awe into the hearts of the peaceful people of the vicinity. But this is no problem with 'secular' parties. Their problem is winning elections.

6.6. EXTRA-TERRITORIAL LOYALTY

Islam is an exotic religion in India. It was born outside and was imposed upon India by waves of conquering armies which periodically inundated the country. Throughout the history of Muslim rule in India, distinguished soldiers, scholars, administrators, merchants and sufis came from abroad and remained loyal to their homelands. Muslims of foreign extraction and even of indigenous birth looked to foreign Islamic lands for guidance and support. Muslim scriptures teach a Muslim that he belongs to the world of Islam. Love of a non-Muslim country, even if it be the country of his birth, is not incumbent upon him. Islamdom (*umma*) is more important for him than nationalism. We have written about the psychology developed by this philosophy in the preceding pages. Therefore, for modern times, only one or two examples may suffice of their extra-territorialism.

The Times of India, Bombay edition of 29 August 1925, published the following report which speaks for itself. "The Muslims of Bombay, including every sect, observed Friday as Yowmud-Dua by a general hartal by suspending all business in the city and offering special prayers after the usual Jumma prayers for the liberation of Medina from the horrors of the Wahabis. Prayers were offered in every mosque during the afternoon. The spiritual feeling with which they have been drawn to the Holy Places, especially the tomb of the Prophet at Medina, was demonstrated by the fact that they went in procession to the Jumma Masjid in Shaikh Memon Street and the Hamidia Masjid at Pydownie. The Muslim quarters of the city presented a gloomy appearance as a result of the suspension of business." Such sorrow is not always gloomy. It takes an angry and aggressive form with dire consequences for the victims. A few years ago the al-Aqsa mosque was damaged during Arab-Israel tension. The event had nothing to do with India or Indians. But Indian Muslims without any provocation at home indulged in lot of rioting and destroyed Hindu temples in many places.

The love of Arabia by Muslims everywhere resulted in developing a feeling of contempt among them for their own country and culture. "*As a result, the foreign Muslims have no loyalty to their own motherland...* The Muslims of India, Pakistan and Bangladesh... are refugees in their own countries for having no real love and respect for their own motherlands... By destroying the national spirit of non-Arab Muslims, Islam has demolished the Asian centres of civilization such as Egypt, Iran and India." Muslims of India, Pakistan and Bangladesh "feel proud of bullying and bruising and bashing the honour of their Hindu ancestors and they pretend to be the progeny of the Arabs, the Turks and the Mughals, who were nothing but their oppressors."

In the medieval times Khilafat had an importance which Muslims everywhere recognised. We have seen how Indian sultans paid obeisance to Caliphs living outside India. They held him in reverence and transmitted treasures to him. Ibn Battutah gives an instance of the servility of Indian sultans to the Caliph. Once the son of the Abbasid Caliph of Baghdad, Ibn-ul-Khalifa Ghiyasuddin, during his visit to Delhi got annoyed with Muhammad bin Tughlaq. The Sultan instantly rode to his residence and apologised to him. "Ghiyasuddin accepted his apology, yet the sultan said, 'By God I shall not believe that you are pleased with me, until you place your foot on my neck'... then he placed his head on the ground, and the great Malik Qabula lifting Ibn-ul-Khalifa's foot with his hand placed it on the sultan's neck. This done, the sultan stood up and said, 'Now I know you are pleased with me, and my heart is at rest.'"[42]

In modern times the issue of Khilafat formed a part of the Indian struggle for freedom as late as 1920s. Even when Khilafat was abolished in Turkey, Indian Muslims remained attached to it. The revival of a universal Khalifa is preferable for many Muslims to a national secular state even today. In a front-page article entitled *Khilafat or Jihalat* (Khilafat or Mental Backwardness), the mass-circulating Urdu weekly *Nai Duniya* (Delhi, February 11-18), analyses the Muslim community's "psychological compulsion" for Pan-Islamic unity and revival of a glorious past, under a single Khalifa or supreme head (*Amir-ul-mominin*) in keeping with the Prophet's injunctions. The real question, it says, as posed by the founder of the movement Maulana Asri Falahi, is which one to choose, "Khilafat or Nationalism". The paper explains that the conception of Khilafat or the installation of one religious-cum-temporal head for all the Muslim countries of the world "holds a great attraction for Muslims of the world in general and Indian Muslims in particular" as it is based on the concept of the brotherhood of the *Kalima* — that is unity of all Muslims owing allegiance to the *Kalima* proclaiming faith in one and the same God.

As a result, a new movement for the revival of Khilafat has been started in India recently. It has been spearheaded by the youthful Student Islamic Movement of India (SIMI). It was launched with a call for a Muslim awakening from November 29 to December 8, 1996 on a national scale. Its avowed aim is to acquaint the Muslims with the "harmful consequences of nationalism". The core of its ideology is based on the premise that Pan-Islamic community is an ideological as well as a divine entity, and that it is its God-ordained duty to establish one religious-cum-temporal head "to strengthen Islamic foundations, to instill fearlessness among Muslims so as to perform the holy mission of freeing the whole humanity from slavery".

This is a goal with which no Muslim organisation, including the Jamiat-ul-Ulama disagrees. However, there is woeful lack of infrastructure for such a worldwide institution of Khilafat. To cap it all, the Muslim countries themselves are caught in mutually destructive controversies. Urdu weekly *Nasheman* of Bangalore (December 1, 1996) is greatly worried about the lack of unity and cohesive action among the Muslim countries of the world, which, it says, is hindering the fulfilment of the supreme Islamic mission of establishing the Islamic system and Islamic order all over the world. For, according to the paper, "only Allah's system can work on this Allah-given earth". By which of course is taken to mean the Quranic and the Shariat system of governance and jurisprudence.[43]

The idea of revival of the universal Khilafat is not as innocent as asking for quota for jobs or promotion of Urdu. Even in embryo, it is an attempt to reestablish a Muslim state, of Allah's system, of weaning away Muslims from the 'harmful consequences' of nationalism. In short, it is an attempt to revive Nizam-i-Mustafa in India, an independent

Muslim state, if not entirely independent, at least a Muslim state within the Indian secular and nationalistic state. There are already pockets of such independent states as for example in Deoband (Saharanpur), Nadwa (Lucknow), Bareilly, Rae Bareli, Ahmedabad, Mumbai and so many other places. The literature produced there is a mirror of their psyche. The autonomy enjoyed by them is a security risk for the country — as the 1994 incident at Nadwa shows.

The Nadwa Incident

In 1947 India was partitioned on the basis of the notorious two-nation theory. The theory stipulated that in India Muslims were a nation different and separate from the Hindus and that they needed a separate homeland. After Partition Pakistan was established as an Islamic state. There, in 1991, was also enacted a Law of Ideology. It punishes anyone who writes against the two-nation ideology of Pakistan. The penalty is 10 years rigorous imprisonment.[44] On the other hand a secular democratic republic was set up in India. Here there is no 'law' of ideology. But the researcher is expected to remain secular. His secular writings cover so much but cover up still more. What is covered up is Indian Muslims' seeking help and inspiration from Pakistan. Indian Muslims have their problems like any other section of society. But they look to Pakistan and other Muslim states for their solution. Of course there are loyal and patriotic Muslims in India. But most Muslims still think India as their battle-ground and Pakistan as their saviour. In India they are constantly harping on job reservations, minority rights, preservation of personal law and Urdu; they look to Pakistan for help in achieving their goals. Their attitude is best reflected and symbolised in what Ali Mian said in Karachi in July 1978 at the First Islamic Asian Conference. Addressing the delegates of the Conference he said: "The Musalmans of Hindustan (and) Musalmans of the whole world were looking to Pakistan with hope and longing eyes for guidance and help. Indian Muslims were also affected by whatever was happening in Pakistan or any other Muslim country. Indian Muslims were greatly pained at the defeat of Pakistan in 1971." Ali Mian (full name Maulana Syed Abul Hasan Ali Nadwi) is the Nazim (Rector) of Nadwat-ul-Ulum, a renowned academy of Islamic learning at Lucknow. Born into a Hanafi Muslim family of Rae Bareli in 1914, he is known as a leading scholar of Islam. He has produced 75 books. His word has a weight in Islamic countries. Known as a rather liberal Muslim he, living in India, openly declared that he was not happy at (non-Muslim) India's victory and (Muslim) Pakistan's defeat in 1971.

Most Muslims living in India think and behave like Ali Mian. Their sympathetic attitude towards Muslim Pakistan encourages the latter to send terrorists in Muslim majority Kashmir and those other parts of India which have substantial Muslim population for destabilising the country. It is by now well-known that Pakistan is waging a proxy war against India. Its terrorists and agents provocateurs are trained in Pakistani camps and are sent to India with the help of ISI (Pakistani Inter Services Intelligence). They have built their pockets in the Tarai region — Pilibhit, Bareilly, Rampur and Moradabad. In forty out of 65 districts of Uttar Pradesh alone they have about 400 active and about 10,000 sleeping agents. In five districts of U.P. — Ghaziabad, Aligarh, Meerut, Saharanpur and Moradabad — there are many places which have become centres of Pakistan spies and terrorists.[45] Here highways are no longer safe. On 6 December 1993 bombs were simultaneously exploded in some superfast Rajdhani express trains in India. Rape, murder and mayhem is perpetrated by them in Kashmir every day. Some American and British tourists were abducted by Afghan terrorists of Hizb-ul-Mujahidin and Harkat-ul-Ansar cadres and brought over to village Masuri in Ghaziabad which they had made their centre of activity. The Indian intelligence and police traced the terrorists, who had perpetrated these crimes, to Nadwat-ul-Ulum in Lucknow. Abu Baqar, a Guyanese national responsible for blasts in Rajdhani expresses on 6 December 1993, was a student of Nadwa for eight years. Many terrorists were living in Nadwa hostels as regular students. The Intelligence Bureau, after careful planning, raided the Nadwa college in search of the Kashmiri militants. Seven young men were arrested. Abu Baqar, who was responsible for bomb explosions in Rajdhani expresses, was one of them. The Delhi Police and IB was in search of a man called Khursheed Ahmad. He was in Nadwa but having got an inkling of the raid, fled the scene. IB sleuths arrested an ISI agent hiding in Dar-ul-Ulum Deoband College of Islamic Studies in Saharanpur.

Ali Mian was all rage. He of course denied sheltering of terrorists in the hostels of Nadwa. He demanded an apology from the Central and U.P. State governments for the raid on such a venerated institution of Islamic learning. He called a meeting of the Personal Law Board of which he is the chairman. He said in a statement that any attempt to malign the Nadwa college amounted to insulting the entire Muslim community in India. He wrote to seven or eight heads of member states of the Organisation of Islamic Countries (OIC). He insisted on OIC to raise the issue of police raid on Nadwa at its international fora. *The Arab News* published from Saudi Arabia, *Akbar-ul-Mujtama* published from Kuwait, as well as *Khalij Times*, *Gulf Times* and some other newspapers published in Gulf countries printed the news prominently. Some wrote editorials on the event, says Maulana Ishaq Husaini of Nadwa. A minister of U.P., Azam Khan, wrote to the President of India protesting against the Intelligence Bureau's taking photographs of those arrested and requested for the return of the photographs and their negatives.

How could Ali Mian behave as he did? Because in U.P. there was the government of the Samajwadi Party headed by Mr. Mulayam Singh Yadav and at the Centre there was the government of the Indian National Congress headed by Mr. P.V. Narasimha Rao. The party politics in democracy helped Mulayam Singh to blame Rao for the raid on Nadwa. The Bharatiya Janata Party (BJP) utilized this opportunity to repeat its warning against anti-national elements residing in India. Meanwhile there were strikes and *hartals* in Muslim dominated areas of Lucknow and Kanpur.[46] Communal tension prevailed in many other towns. Frenzied mobs crowded the streets shouting slogans like 'Long live Mulayam Singh, down with Narasimha Rao'. Effigies of Prime Minister Narasimha Rao and officers of Lucknow district administration were burnt. Rao sent Railway Minister Jaffer Sharif to meet Ali Mian and assuage his ruffled feelings. "Mr. CK Jaffer Sharif, abandoned his election campaign in Karnataka and flew to Lucknow to offer apologies on behalf of the Prime Minister." Mulayam Singh Yadav also apologised for raid on an educational institution. The Chief Minister said he was not informed about the raid in advance. Many police and intelligence officials were warned and transferred.

Why did the Prime Minister and Chief Minister of U.P. and other politicians behave as they did? U.P. has a substantial Muslim population. Muslim votes influence elections both to Parliament and State Assembly. There was a time when the Congress was the most prominent and powerful party in U.P. Now new political parties have come up. All the old and new parties are keen to preserve and increase the number of their Muslim voters. Even the BJP is keen to garner their votes. It debunks the propaganda that it is anti-Muslim. It says it is only against anti-national elements. Hence the Prime Minister, the U.P. Chief Minister — the political parties like the Congress, the SP, BJP, BSP — all try to befriend the Muslim vote bank. Hence parties and politicians in power ignore the aberrations of anti-national and anti-social elements. Hence they are specially considerate to Muslim leaders and their restive followers. If Muslims behave like bullies, they concede them their status. They overlook minor militant attacks. They even look the other way when Muslim infiltrators from neigbouring countries sneak into India. It is even said that they encourage such clandestine immigration because it increases their vote bank.

Clandestine Immigration

Undoubtedly, Muslim voters are ever increasing. The Lok Sabha was informed on Tuesday, 6 May 1997, that 11,000 Pakistani nationals were found overstaying in India till 1996. Replying to a query by a BJP member, the Home Minister said that the centre had asked the state governments to launch special drive to detect and deport foreigners residing in the country illegally. The Border Security Force intercepted a total of 57,391 infiltrators from Bangladesh during the last three years ending 1996, while pushing back 42,246 illegal migrants from across the eastern border, he said. Union Home Minister Indrajit Gupta told the Lok Sabha that it was difficult to detect illegal aliens from neighbouring Pakistan and Bangladesh as, racially, they were all of the same stock as Indians. The Bharatiya Janata Party MPs who had raised the issue were quite flummoxed when Mr. Gupta candidly admitted that the number of such aliens was close to 10 million.[47]

Many of these infiltrators and overstayers are Pakistani agents. They find shelter from Bahraich to Bangalore, Hyderabad to Chennai. Details of their activities cannot be publicly known but they are under surveillance of police and intelligence agencies. Reports about them lie concealed in secret files of government and police. At times the politicians and police form a nexus and keep inconvenient information a secret. At others intelligence officers work under unfavourable conditions, as for example with regard to Nadwa raid. "How can we carry on investigations against the people to whom our political masters have been offering unconditional apologies," said a senior official on condition of anonymity. Even the CBI sleuths are reluctant to continue with the investigations. The central intelligence agencies express helplessness in view of blatant political patronage to the people figuring in their list of suspects. "When the State Government can accuse us of keeping it in dark about the raid, although we had informed (concerned officers), it is not difficult to guess the state of our morale," he said.[48] When such situations arise and some politicians in power in government are found to trifle with the country's security for their vote bank, other politicians in the "Opposition" expose them in and outside Parliament and compel them keep on the right path. This is the advantage of having democracy; it compels the government to be transparent.

The people in general come to know about anti-national activities through the newspapers mainly. Their correspondents are ever busy in hunting for stories and interviewing persons who know. For instance news items and reports of the Nadwa episode were brought to light by all leading local and national dailies like *Jansatta*, *Sahara Samachar*, *Nav Bharat Times*, *Amar Ujala*, *Nadeem*, the *Indian Express*, *The Times of India* etc. etc. These have been collected and published by Lok Abhiyan Samiti, Lucknow, in the form of a booklet of 108 pages under the title of *Nadwa ka Sacch* (Truth about Nadwa).[49] This is the benefit of having a free press in a free country. Newspapers carry reports of anti-national and anti-social elements in town and country. Every day newspapers carry reports of raids on terrorist hideouts and arrest of them and Pakistani agents. Large hauls of arms and ammunitions are also reported every now and then. For example, when the Gujarat police recovered arms and explosives worth more than 12 lakhs of rupees from as far away a place as Bijnor in U.P., the details were published in *The Times of India*.[50] Thus the "Opposition", the media and the Intelligence (not intelligentsia) keep the people informed and help the government in performing its duty of safeguarding the country's security. That is how the country is kept safe from the extra-territorial loyalty of anti-national people.

6.7. PROSELYTIZATION

The main object of Islam was, and still is, to spread Muslim religion throughout the world. The Quran, the Hadis, the *Hidayah* and the Sunnah all direct the faithful to fulfill this 'pious' task. In Islamic scripture there are found commands, directions and exhortations; there is no mention of discussion or consensus on this issue. However, as the *Dictionary of Islam* says, Muslim writers are "unanimous in asserting that in the time of the Prophet... the only choice given to the idolaters of Arabia was death or reception of Islam". Obviously, force was the medium of spreading Islam in early stages. So also it was in India. Early medieval Indian Muslim chronicles mention the sword as the greatest harvester of converts. Islam was made to spread, as the old saying goes, with Quran in one hand and sword in the other. Sword was freely used in forcing people to become Musalmans. There was a pride felt in converting people forcibly as exhibited by aggressors like al-Hajjaj or Mahmud of Ghazni. In the Islamic march for proselytization in medieval times there should be no temptation to discover any peaceful missionary movement because there was none. "The spread of Islam was military." Every Muslim is taught that this *din* will be established for ever. "A group of Muslims will always fight for its cause till the day of Judgement."[51]

Hiding the face of Islam

These days a group of Muslim writers is busy making an all out effort to present Islam with a benign face. A long series of defeats at the hands of Christian Europe and persistent resistance of Hindus in India, has resulted in inculcating in the Muslim masses a hatred of the West and the Hindus. At the same time it has also prompted some Muslim scholars to present Islam as religion of peace, to put it on par with, say, Hinduism, Jainism or Buddhism. One such writes is Asghar Ali Engineer. He is a prolific writer and does not make a secret of his aim when he says that "Islam needs an ecumenical movement".[52] At one place he says: "Islam is all too often portrayed as a fanatical, violent religion which encourages its followers to wipe out *kufr*, unbelief. It is also believed that Islam incites its followers to spread the Prophet's message by the sword, and that it executes all believers who renounce that message. The fight in defence of Allah's way, is termed *jihad* by the Koran. Thus *jihad* is essentially a war for justice, not for aggression or lust for power... The real *jihad* lies in striving to control our own negative tendencies... The Sufis, in particular, have never approved of wars of aggression... The Sufis could practise absolute non-violence because they had withdrawn from the empirical world and confined themselves to the spiritual life... Islam is as non-violent a religion as any religion could be: the Koran repeatedly describes Allah as 'the Merciful, the Compassionate, the Forgiving'."[53]

The truth is farthest from all this. The bluff of Islam as a religion of compassion has been called by its history, tradition and fatwas.

Islam cannot be non-violent with Jihad as its major duty and inspiration. In all Hadis collections, scores of pages have been devoted to the waging of real Jihad. In the Quran itself Jihad is described in many *Surahs* and *ayats.* A few ayats are given here as specimens.

"Kill those who join other gods with God wherever you may find them. When the sacred months are over slay the idol-worshippers wherever you find them. Arrest them, besiege them, and lie in ambush everywhere for them (9:5-6).

"O ye who believe! murder those of the unbelievers... and let them find harshness in you (9:123).

"I shall cast terror into the hearts of the infidels. Strike off their heads, maim them in every limb (8:12).

It is a great sin for a Muslim to shirk the Jihad against the unbelievers — those who do will roast in hell. It is abundantly clear from the many of the above verses that the Quran is not talking of metaphorical battles or talking of controlling of "our own negative tendencies". It is talking of the battlefield and advocating bloodthirsty injunctions against Kafirs. The Quran does not read like a religious book but a war manual. It does not preach non-violence.

Nor could the sufis "practise absolute non-violence because they had withdrawn from the empirical world and confined themselves to the spiritual life". The sufis belonged to a number of orders. Four of those orders — Chishti, Suhrawardi, Qadiri and Naqshabandi — became prominent in India. The first two became popular, for the latter two were extremely orthodox and fanatical. Very few sufis shunned material wealth; most of them received land and wealth from rulers and nobles and some lived in a lavish style. They did not withdraw from the world to confine themselves to spiritual life, but often instigated their patrons to wage wars against non-Muslims, and themselves participated in battles. Even Shaikh Muinuddin Chishti's "picture of tolerance is replaced by a portrait of him as a warrior of Islam."[54] There is a whole array of sufi warriors from the days of Muinuddin to those of Shah Waliullah. They took active part in religion, politics and war. Shah Waliullah, a renowned sufi scholar, greatly venerated among Muslims, wrote to the Afghan king Ahmad Shah Abdali to invade India to help Muslim brethren against the infidels.

Like Asghar Ali Engineer, Maulana Wahiduddin Khan of the Islamic Centre, New Delhi, writes that "Some extremist Muslims indulging in violence in our times have led people to the conclusion that Islam is an intolerant religion. But this is certainly not true. Islam is as tolerant a religion as any other."[56] He also says that the propagation of Islam in India was through peaceful means. Writing about the present-day *tablighi* proselytizers, he says, "After the prayer, the despatching of missionary groups from Bangla Wali Masjid near the tomb of Nizamuddin Auliya (a mosque which had been a centre of *tablighi* conversion movements for decades) was attended to. The names of those who were undertaking the journey were called out one by one, and each in turn came out to the chief to shake hands with him and receive his blessings before he departed. Such a poignant scene evoked memories of the Prophet sitting in the Masjid-i-Nabwi, exhorting people and sending them in groups to propagate the message to those who were ignorant."[57] Or, as he writes elsewhere, "Islam aims not so much at conversion as at making people aware of its message... so far as forced conversion is concerned, it is totally unlawful in Islam."[58] According to him, "The Quran is a collection of revelations which the Prophet received over 23 years. If the Prophet received negative responses from some, and was persecuted by others, he strictly avoided confrontation, and followed the path of forbearance."[59]

Both these statements are not correct. Prophet Muhammad did not send any groups to spread Islam through peaceful means. What he sent were military expeditions inviting one Arab tribe after another to embrace Islam at the point of the sword. Out of the nineteen *ghazwahs* ('holy' expeditions) carried out in his time, he personally participated in seventeen.[60] The Prophet never avoided confrontation or followed the path of forbearance.

He fought wars and struck terror into the hearts of his opponents. The Hadis collections mention scores of cases in which his pet order about any defaulter was "kill him".[61] His victims were sceptics or those who dared to oppose him. Similarly, and in actual fact, forced conversions were accomplished first; the converted Muslims were made aware of the message of Islam later on through the apparatus of *tabligh*. Hence the need for *tablighi* movement even today for Islamizing those Muslims whose ancestors were converted centuries ago.

Asghar Ali Engineer, Maulana Wahiduddin and Zafar Jung are not historians. They belong to institutions whose aim is to give a face-lift to Islam and present it as a religion of peace. Such institutions receive liberal funds from Gulf states for this and similar purposes. Zafar Jung, President of the Muslim Mainstream Movement, New Delhi, declares that "the word Islam means peace. The Quran and Hadith foster communal harmony."[62] Howsoever untrue, Zafar Jung is doing his duty to his Movement. But historians should not suppress or twist facts to hide the true face of Islam. This is what Muhammad Mujeeb tries to do. Regarding conversion of Hindus to Islam he misinterprets well-known facts in cleverly carved language. Says he: "The vast majority of the Indian Muslims are converts. Force was used on occasions, but the existing historical evidence does not enable us to estimate either the scale or effectiveness of such conversions. Also, the risks involved in a policy of conversion by force should not be understated. Islam was adopted by families or groups of families who were regarded as outcasts in Hindu society... Service in the army was an attraction, specially for tribal groups with war-like traditions, and this service would inevitably make them outcasts... The main agency for conversion were the mystics, and most of the largescale conversions seem to have taken place in the fifteenth and sixteenth centuries. But legend and fact have become so mixed up that hardly any such event can be precisely dated."[63]

I knew Muhammad Mujeeb personally. He was Head of the Department of History and Shaikh-ul-Jamia or Vice-Chancellor of the Jamia Millia Islamia University, New Delhi. I used to visit Jamia in connection with sundry academic work in the History Department. In 1972, however, there was a mild 'confrontation' between him and me.

Sometime that year there was a Selection Committee

meeting for the post of Professor of History in Delhi University. I was then a Reader and candidate for the post of Professor. Mujeeb was an 'expert'. About this time my *Growth of Muslim Population in Medieval India* was in the press. Mujeeb asked me a question: "Why did the Hindu convert to Islam?" It was a loaded question carrying the suggestion that the initiative for conversion came from the Hindu. In all probability Mujeeb expected me to say that the Hindus suffered from the injustices of the caste system, that Islam was spiritually so great and its message of social equality so attractive that the Hindus queued up for conversion the moment they came in contact with Islamic invaders. A tactful candidate (not a truthful one) would have said what Mujeeb desired, but my answer was different. I said that Hindus did not (voluntarily) convert to Islam; they were converted, often forcibly, as told by Muslim chroniclers. Muslim invaders and rulers felt proud of their achievements in the fields of loot and destruction, enslavement and proselytization. Their chroniclers, writing at their command or independently, speak about their achievements in these spheres in glowing terms. They repeatedly write about the choice offered to the Hindus — "Islam or death". Mujeeb expected a different answer. I was not selected.

A few months after this confrontation, the University of Jodhpur sent me an offer of Professorship. There is a proviso in University advertisements for the post of *Professor* that the University is free to offer the post to even one who may not have applied. I had not applied but the Selection Committee in Jodhpur recommended my name for the post on the basis of my academic work. I joined Jodhpur University on 1 January 1973. Later on, while at Jodhpur, I was offered the post of Professor in the Department of Islamic History and Culture, University of Calcutta, and still later by the newly established Central University at Hyderabad. I joined at Hyderabad in October 1979 and finally retired from there in June 1983.

It is more than twenty-five years since I met Professor

Muhammad Mujeeb at the memorable Selection Committee meeting in Delhi. It is now an old story recollected with contradictory feelings of resentment and all-that-happens-happens-for-good. In retrospect, however, I realise that even today I cannot answer Mujeeb's question to his satisfaction. To my mind such a question can be answered by Muslims who have converted from Hindus, say, a Hashmat Ali can tell why he became a Hashmat Ali from Brij Mohan — or some such person. But evidence of this nature is hard to come by. It is amazing that while there are millions and millions of converted Muslims in India, not one, to my knowledge, has written why or how he or his father or grandfather converted to Islam. I have done some research in this sphere in my *Growth of Muslim Population in Medieval India* and *Indian Muslims: Who are they*. But if a Muslim wrote it, it would have the stamp of personal experience inherited in the family or families of relatives. As per human nature, had they been happy or proud at their conversion, a few at least would have narrated the event with great enthusiasm. In the absence of such records, the only sources of information available are medieval chronicles. These are replete with details of war, capture of captives and choice of 'Islam or death' offered to them. But such evidence is not palatable to 'secular' Muslims like Mujeeb whose mission it is to project Islam as a religion of peace.

The scale and effectiveness of conversions by force are clearly detailed in al-Kufi's *Chachnama* (for Muhammad Qasim in Sindh), Utbi's *Tarikh-i-Yamini* (for Mahmud of Ghazni) Hasan Nizami's *Taj-ul-Maasir* (for Muhammad Ghauri, Qutbuddin Aibak etc.) and Minhaj Siraj's. *Tabqat-i-Nasiri* (for the early years of the Sultanate period). All Muslim chronicles from the thirteenth to the eighteenth century write with pride about forcible conversions by rulers and nobles. Mujeeb must have seen these chronicles and still he declares the existing historical evidence as inadequate for estimating the scale and effectiveness of conversions by force.[64] He has also not elaborated on the risks involved in conversion by force. There were no risks involved because force backed by powerful armies eliminated all risks. Indeed Muslim invaders themselves together with their chroniclers and poets, sing in praise of their achievements in proselytization by force.

The stereotyped theory that low caste or outcast people willingly embraced Islam also stands exploded. It is now well known that low caste people were more determined to preserve their caste and strove to preserve it at all costs, even at the cost of fleeing into the forests and living a miserable life of tribals rather than accepting Islam.[65] Service in the army for tribal groups did not make them outcasts. 'Scheduled' tribes and castes joined the Kshatriyas in continually fighting Muslims rulers' atrocities.[66] The myth that "the main agency for conversion were the mystics" also stands exploded.[67] It is true that largescale conversions took place in the fifteenth and sixteenth centuries (as was also the case in earlier centuries), for the Delhi Sultanate had split into a number of Muslim kingdoms where more effective proselytizing endeavour became concentrated as it became in small areas. Legend and fact have not got mixed up to create confusion. There were of courses some conversions accomplished through peaceful means. Some Hindus opted for Islam to escape from financial burden as in the time of Firoz Tughlaq or to save their lands as during the reign of Aurangzeb. Firoz Tughlaq writes that when he rescinded the Jiziyah to attract people to Islam, groups of Hindus, "day by day from every quarter" came flocking to become Muslamans.[68] These groups generally belonged to the poor sections which included low castes who found it hard to pay Jiziyah. But low caste people as such were not attracted by Islam. In fact they put up tough resistance against conversion.

The facts mentioned by chroniclers about largescale forcible conversions are dated and detailed. Despite the way the apologists would like to depict it, Islam was spread by the sword and maintained by terror throughout its history. As Jan Knappert aptly states, "Islamic propaganda, funded by the unlimited means of the Gulf states, is responsible for a plethora of untrue ideas of Islam. Firstly, that it is a religion of peace. It is not and never was, witness the endless expansive wars fought by Muslim rulers and raiders. Even now the majority of conflicts of the world have Islam at their roots: Bosnia, about which we are particularly misinformed, the Sudan and Chechenia, Afghanistan, Sin Kiang, Kashmir, Timor, Azerbaijan and the Philippines. Muslims will not rest before they rule the state."[69]

There is no need to feel apologetic if most conversions were forcible. Force and violence have a special place in Islamic history throughout the world. The heroes of Islam in India are men like Muhammad bin Qasim, Mahmud of Ghazni, Timur and Aurangzeb. They, their chroniclers and their poets, all become lyrical when they describe their achievements in the service of Allah which included conversions by force. There is no justification for M. Mujeeb to unseat these old Muslim heroes from their ferocious pedestals and turn them into pacifists like Hindus and Buddhists. Rizwan Salim briefly but effectively spells out what the Muslims really did in India.[70]

True face of Islam

If writers like Engineer, Wahiduddin Khan, Rafiq Zakaria and Mujeeb do not suffer from "the struggling pangs of conscious truth to hide", there are some brave and conscientious Muslims who write about Islam's true nature with courage and conviction. These Muslim writers fall into two categories — one who denounce and the other who defend extremism of Islam — but the "essentialist" core of Islam in both is the same. Those who denounce the fierce nature of Islam are few but they are there in all Muslim countries including Iran, Egypt and Turkey. Of those who trace their 'origins' from the Indian subcontinent, some prominent names are Anwar Shaikh, Ibn Warraq, Salman Rushdie and Taslima Nasreen. Ibn Warraq is in all probability a pseudonym which points to the fear (of fatwa) of death which stalks them. They have all settled in Europe or America for the same reason. Residence in their homeland is not safe for them since they bring out the true nature of Islam. The generality of Muslims may dislike their daring, but those in authority in Islam would not tolerate such 'renegade' Muslims although their account of Islam confirms the true nature of Islam as spelled out by Anwar Shaikh and Warraq. These scholars, and interpreters of Islam, certainly wield greater authority than Muslims like Engineer and Mujeeb. Only one such authority may be mentioned — Ayatollah Ruhollah Khomeini.

Ten years before the fatwa of death against Salman Rushdie was issued, there appeared, in 1980, a book entitled *Sayings of Ayatollah Khomeini.*[71] Its contents show that the fatwa was not issued by him in any excitement or hurry. It was based on the great divine's study of the teachings of Islam. In the book he says: "Moslems have no alternative, if they wish to correct the political balance of society and those in power to conform to the laws and principles of Islam, to an armed holy war against profane Governments... *Holy war means the conquest of all non-Moslem territories.* Such a war may well be declared after the formation of an Islamic Government worthy of that name, at the direction of the Islamic Imam or under his orders. It will then be the duty of every able-bodied adult male to volunteer for this war of conquest, the final aim of which is to put Koranic law in power from one end of the earth to the other... that is not only our duty in Iran, but it is also the duty of all Moslems in the world, in all Moslem countries, to carry the Islamic political revolution to its final victory." That is why French monks in Algeria, Greek and German tourists in Egypt, foreign and mother country tourists in Kashmir, as non-Muslims are considered a fair game for Muslim "warriors". That is how the fatwa of death against Salman Rushdie is irrevocable and this fact is reiterated again and again by those in authority in Iran.[72] Incidentally, it may be mentioned that the very ones who say that verses in the Quran and references to *ahadis* in Islamic scriptural collections are dated, that these pertained only to the contexts in which they were revealed, are the very ones who, when it is convenient, say that the provisions of the Quran and Hadis are eternal and cannot be disregarded or altered or confined to any particular context, without destroying Islam itself.

Hatred of non-Muslims is a cardinal principle of Islamic theology. But many Muslims like Anwar Shaikh and Ibn Warraq hate the idea of hating non-Muslims and challenge these repulsive characteristics that are written into the Quran. Ibn Warraq's support for Rushdie has to be seen as a part of a larger war against this fundamentalist Islam. He cites in his support the war that is taking place in Algeria, the Sudan, Iran, Saudi Arabia and Pakistan, "a war whose principal victims are Muslims, Muslim women, Muslim intellectuals, writers, ordinary decent people..." "The best thing we can do for Muslims is to free them from Islam." Similarly, Anwar Shaikh wants the world to be saved from Muslims. In India both Hindus and Muslims need to be saved from Islam. Taslima Nasreen advocates a revision of the Hadis.

Although wherever there is secessionism, terrorism, bomb blasts and planned killings, Islam is somehow associated with them. The Christian West is too strong to be browbeaten by Islam. Israel too can look after itself against the Jihad of Hamas. In India the Islamic cult of knife may not return because of Hindu resurgence. But the historian can certainly pity the Muslim victims of Islam. For the throats that are being slit in Algeria are Muslim throats. The Sunnis who are shooting down Shias and Shias who are killing Sunnis in Pakistan are all Muslims. So also is the case with the

Ahmadiyas, the Mohajirs and the Zikris. In Afghanistan the victims of the Taliban fundamentalists, who revel in public executions of men and flogging of women, are Muslims. Men and women who are flogged or stoned to death in Islamic countries are Muslims only.

In the modern world some Muslims react to this scenario with a feeling of revulsion, others with helplessness, but still some others, to be on the safe side, lament: "Mine is the voice of those who are born Muslims but wish to recant in adulthood, yet are not permitted on pain of death. Someone who does not live in an Islamic society cannot imagine the sanctions, both self-imposed and external, that militate against expressing religious disbelief... So we hold our tongues, those of us who doubt."[73] Another Muslim from Pakistan, Professor Mubarak Ali, mourns that "in the present times of grave crisis we need dissident intellectuals who can challenge the establishment... Pakistan did not develop any tradition of dissident intellectual activity."[74] Dissidence is precisely what Islam does not permit. All Hadis point to the fact that only one Will prevails. This Will derives its strength from being the command of Allah.[75] Hence dissidence is ruled out, not only in Pakistan but in all Islamic countries. So that Ibn Warraq's scholarly work must be written under a pseudonym for fear of death at the hands of fundamentalists. Islamic fundamentalism holds unchangeability as the strength of Islam. All believing Muslims being fundamentalists, they threaten with death the Muslims who try to dissent. Muslims live in fear. "There is fear of the foreign West, fear of the Imam, fear of Democracy, fear of Freedom of thought, fear of Individualism, fear of the Past, fear of the Present."[77]

The Islamic principles of denigrating the non-Muslims, of aggression and violence against them, principles that perpetually incite to riot and rapine, have boomeranged. Howsoever brave face the fundamentalists may try to put up, the victims of Islam today are by and large Muslims themselves. The Prophet must have known that violence begets violence and repeatedly exhorted Muslims not to kill one another after his death.[78] He also had premonition that violence of Islam against non-Muslims will be met with a backlash. There is a *hadis* in *Sahih Muslim* which says that once the Rasul opined that Islam which began in poverty in Medina would one day return to Medina in poverty. "Just as a snake crawls back and coils itself into its small hole, so will Islam be hunted out from everywhere and return to be confined to Mecca and Medina."[79] The increasing power of the non-Muslim West and the disenchantment of Muslim dissidents like Anwar Shaikh, Ibn Warraq, Fatima Mernissi and a host of others in many Islamic countries point towards that possibility, howsoever remote.

To resume. There is a uniqueness about Islam. Non-Muslims are to be converted to Islam freely. But once a Kafir becomes a Musalman, he has to remain so for ever thereafter. He is not permitted to renounce Islam or revert to his original faith. Punishment for such apostasy (*irtidad*) is death. "So here is a psyche for which logic and conscience have no meaning, which converts others by force and which prevents apostasy by force." Such nature of Muslim dogma ill-prepared the Muslims for defeat. The long series of defeats at the hands of Christian Europe and resistance of Hindu India at last stayed their hand from making forcible conversions. Forcible conversions are not possible in India today. Therefore recourse is taken to other means. What is significant is that conversions to Islam still go on as if India is still a Muslim state. The only difference is that now sword is not used to make converts. On the other hand conversions are often effected in a hush-hush manner. Pamphlets are secretly distributed among Muslims providing them with guidelines for proselytization work. Influential Muslims and politicians (M.L.As, M.Ps) visit villages of Dalit Hindus, mostly at night, and promise all kinds of inducements for becoming Musalman. Petro-dollars are received from Muslim countries like Saudi Arabia and Gulf emirates for proselytization work. Lucrative jobs are promised to Indian youth in Muslim countries. Only Muslims can be appointed to these, thus prompting many to change their religion to earn good remuneration abroad. There are many other methods of converting non-Muslims to Islam.

Of the many pamphlets and brochures in Urdu instructing Muslims in the ways of converting Hindus,[80] only one may be examined to give an idea of the stuff contained in such literature. It is the *Daiye Islam* (Propagation of Islam) by Khwaja Hasan Nizami (1878-1957). Hasan Nizami was a sufi divine connected with the *dargah* of Nizamuddin Awliya of Delhi. The pamphlet teaches the Muslims the quickest and comprehensive way of converting Kafirs to Islam. The Khwaja exhorted Muslims of all categories from the highest to the lowest, to serve the cause of Islam by helping in the conversion of non-Muslims to Islam. In this missionary endeavour Zamindars and Nawabs, doctors and prostitutes, *ekka* players and bangle sellers were all invited to make their contribution. Muslim lawyers and doctors were to influence their Hindu clients to convert. Nawabs and Zamindars were to pressurize Hindu tenants under them to become Musalman. The prostitute was required to exert her influence on her Hindu visitors and admirers into becoming Muslims. The bangle seller was to seduce young Hindu girls and the *ekka* driver was to seduce away Hindu ladies and children. Such a recipe was neither spiritual nor edifying but it fitted with the Muslim mentality. The pamphlet recorded wide sale among Muslims. The Nizam of Hyderabad fixed an allowance for the Khwaja and other Muslims Chiefs and Zamindars followed suit. Muslim magistrates, police and excise inspectors and other influential officials were found working according to the plan laid out by this sufi devotee of Islam.

We have already dwelt on the *tablighi* endeavours of many mullahs in North India,[81] and therefore, will refrain from repeating the same here. In the South local M.L.As and M.Ps belonging to the Muslim League are equally busy in bullying and inducing Hindu Harijans to become Musalmans. Their field of activity is mainly Kerala and Tamil Nadu, their target, poor villagers.

Meenakshipuram

The story of the conversion of almost the whole village of Meenakshipuram is in general the story of the proselytization of low caste Hindus to Islam in modern times. Meenakshipuram is a small hamlet near Pampohzi village in Tenkasi, Tirunelveli District. On Thursday 19 February 1981, a function was arranged here with great pomp and éclat. About 4,000 Muslims from neighbouring Tenkasi, Kadayanallur, Vadakari, Vavanagram and other places participated in the conversion ceremony. The village, which had hardly ever been visited by any outsider, witnessed a sudden rush of visitors — mostly Muslim V.I.Ps. Prominent among them were Mr. Sahul Hameed, the Muslim League M.L.A., Mr. A.K. Rifai, a former M.P., and Mr. Abul Hasan Sahad Ali, the Jamat-ul-Ulema chief of that area. The Jamat chief explained how Islam treated all its followers as equal. Then he chanted the *Kalima*. Repeating after him the villagers knelt down facing west for their first prayers to Allah. In less than an hour, Sunderraj had become Sardar Mohammad, Madaswamy had become Mohammad Soaib, Jabamoni had become Jabarulla Khan, Murugesan had become Muhammad Islami. Then, some of the visiting women went to bring the Harijan women who were still in their houses. With their heads now covered, they were escorted to the *maidan* where a maulvi (borrowed from the Panpoli mosque) married the wives again to their respective husbands, according to Islamic rites. Unmarried women too got new names and a new religion. The conversion was now complete; more than three-fourths of the Harijans of the village had abandoned their faith of generations. A village which had no Muslim ever before had around 1,000 of them now. Meenakshipuram was renamed Rahmatnagar. The mass conversion ceremony sent a wave of resentment and, for Muslims, excitement. The Parliament committee on the welfare of SC & ST visited Meenakshipuram on 11th August 1981. It said that the "the Muslims of the area and certain Muslims who had come from outside had arranged a feast and invited the Harijans for feast (*bara khana*). Those Harijans who did not want to go were dragged to that feast. The conversions followed the feast... Prior to that a local M.L.A. belonging to Muslim League and a Member of Parliament belonging to the same party were seen visiting the village. They generally came after 10 P.M... It was alleged that many well-to-do Muslims were putting pressure on them (the Harijans) to get converted." In a subsequent note it stated that "conversion of scheduled castes to Islam was being done in an organised way". Replying to a discussion in Parliament, Home Minister Zail Singh said that it was a matter concerning one and all. "Because this kind of conversion is politically motivated, and this is not a good method of changing religion."[82] In fact this mass conversion jamboree was timed to coincide with the Sixth All-India Conference of the Jamaat-i-Islami Hind, held in Hyderabad. "The tenor of Hyderabad conference was set by Maulana Muhammad Yusuf, Ameer-e-Jamaat-e-Islami Hind, in his presidential address, when he outlined the duties and responsibilities of Indian Muslims. The Maulana harped on Muslims being a distinct, separate entity, with more things in common with their co-religionists in foreign lands than their compatriots."[83] About this we have already referred to in the extra-territorial loyalty syndrome of the Muslims. A year after the mass conversion of Harijans to Islam at Meenakshipuram the stage was set for a new wave of conversions.[84] Home Minister Zail Singh in reply to a question, informed the Lok Sabha on 19 August 1981 that "about 2000 Harijans in Tamilnadu have embraced Islam since February 1981. Some isolated cases of conversion of Harijans to Islam have also been reported from some other parts of the country," like Malappuram in Kerala.

Sword of Islam Liberally Lubricated

In fact it was reported that there is a move, "funded by the Gulf countries, to convert at least one million Harijan families into Islam every year. The London based Islamic Cultural Centre recently circulated a report which said that 50 Harijan families had been converted to Islam simply by a grant of Rs.400,000 for an agricultural project. The expectation was that the sword of Islam, liberally lubricated with oil from the Gulf, would cut a deep swathe across the lower strata of the Hindu society, raising the Muslim population from 80 million to 200 million at the end of the decade."[85]

In Hyderabad, for example, a few hundred *maulvis* fan out of the city every year and scout around villages for people willing to embrace Islam. From a meagre 50 such cases before independence, the number of conversions has now gone up to 500 a year.[86] Money, of course, played its due role in the politics of conversion without conviction. "Subramanium, who returned to the Hindu fold last week after having embraced Islam under the name of Ashraf Ali early this year, told a UNI correspondent that he had received Rs. 500 on February 21, the day mass conversion took place, and had been promised more assistance. A Police official added that wealthy Muslims from Madurai and Tiruchirapalli handed gifts including cash to the converts. A strong-willed Harijan youth, Ayyapan by name, spurned the offer of 500 in cash to induce him to renounce his faith at Meenakshipuram."[87] Ishaath-ul-Islam Sabha which claims to have arranged 17,000 conversions in Tamil Nadu since its inception 37 years ago, reported that "Thousands of non-Muslims are waiting to join the holy faith of Islam but they are kept in the waiting list for want of funds". Similarly, about 1,000 people at Sivakasi in Ramnathpuram were ready for conversion. But it was being delayed due to lack of funds for clothes, food and circumcision.[88] It is reported, however, that the Islam Sabha has stepped up its proselytizing activities in recent times and has been raising funds abroad. It is stated that a donation of Rs. 20,000 was promised by a religious preacher from Saudi Arabia for building a mosque for which he laid the foundation stone. He also assured that he would soon arrange to take five converted boys to Arabian countries for the study of Islamic culture. Three converted boys had already been sent by Jamaith to study Arabic. The RSS (Rashtriya Swayamsevak Sangh) study team throws further light on the scenario. It says that "the conversion in Attiyuttu village and surrounding villages in Tirunelveli are being organised and executed by the Keelakarai money. Keelakarai is a notorious place in the South for smuggling operations... The Keelakarai Muslims have intimate relations in and with the Gulf countries. Illegal remittances of money from Gulf countries are arranged through Ceylon and Singapore. There has been a sudden increase in grants and remittances from Gulf countries to individuals and institutions (like Jamaat-i-Islami and Dar-ul-Ulum) in the sensitive districts. For instance, *Satguna Vaidyasalai* has received Rs.1.25 crores from Libya, allegedly for running a technical school. The Government is well aware of such sudden increase in remittances from Gulf countries. However, inflow of illegal foreign money goes on unchecked."[89]

If people could be made to change their ancestral faith just for a pittance of Rs.500, it speaks for their extreme poverty and deprivation rather than any merit for the creed for which they opt. A well-to-do Hindu, well-versed in his own faith and that of Islam, will not renounce his religion. But backwardness, hunger, poverty, caste inequality, all kinds of oppression, make the Harijans turn to a new God, the Bread, which Christianity or Islam (temporarily) provide. Both the creeds have been competing to convert the Dalit Hindus. The Dalits hardly understand anything about these religions, but

Rs. 500 provide them food, for some time at least. In the race between Christianity and Islam, however, the latter has an upper hand because of permission of polygamy. "Those in quest of dowry seem to have found a new way out. The latest is bigamy by changing one's religion. There is little the law of the land can do if a man changes his religion from Hinduism to Islam and takes on a new wife."[90] Details of many such marriages are interesting to read,[91] many more take place all over India every now and then, making still more exciting reading.

Hindu Response to Muslim Proselytization

The mass conversion of Hindus at Meenakshipuram, and ongoing individual conversions at many other places, have made Indians sit up. The Government, the political parties, the politicians for whom social justice is a game of numbers have all been shaken. But the most shaken are the Hindus in general. The Hindus would have taken these conversions like they bore the brunt in medieval times, but the proclamation by many Muslim leaders that through conversions they seek political power and one day would convert secular India into an Islamic state has alerted the Hindus.[92] The motive for conversion may be petty — temptation for some cash and gifts, lure for employment in Gulf countries, lust for a second "wife" — but the potential for mischief is self-evident. A news item 'from the states' datelined Guwahati says, "The proportion of Hindus in Assam has declined by five percent since 1971, according to the 1991 census released here on Friday."[93] Hence Hindu individuals and organisations have geared up to meet the challenge.

Of the individual "rebels", we have already referred to the case of Subramanium. He was given the name of Ashraf Ali but he returned to his original religion. Paramasivam, 45, a Harijan, whose name was also changed to Ashraf Ali (common name given to converted men is Ashraf Ali, to women Aisha), said he was forcibly converted. On the day of conversion he came to Meenakshipuram and his name was also included. Some one placed a cap on his head and gave him the new name. Before he could come out of the daze, everything was over. He went home only to be scolded by his family and was ostracised.[94] We have seen how the sufi divine Khwaja Hasan Nizami in his *Daiye Islam* had instructed the Muslims on the ways to convert Hindus to Islam. His over-enthusiasm cautioned the Hindus. The instructions did not remain a secret, the book was translated and the Hindus found out how and why secret kidnappings, abductions and seductions of Hindu girls by Muslims in almost every town and city of northern India had become the order of the day. Hindus, individually and through their organisations, began to exercise vigilance. They began to undo such dirty attempts by rescuing Hindu girls, widows and orphans and bringing the offenders to book. This same Nizami also announced that an important Hindu Raja was soon going to embrace Islam. It was people's guess that the reference was to Maharaja Hari Singh of Jammu and Kashmir. The result was that the Maharaja came under the influence of the Arya Samaj. He appointed Justice Meher Chand Mahajan, who was known for his Samajist leanings, as the Prime Minister of J&K in September 1947.[95]

The blatant *tablighi* endeavours, even after the partition of the country in 1947, prompted the Hindus also to reconvert people to Hinduism. Hinduism is not a proselytizing religion. But conversions cannot remain a one way traffic for ever. Hindu religious leaders raised their voice against untouchability which is one of the causes of conversion. Heads of various Hindu religious orders (*mathadhipatis*) declared at the Visva Hindu Conference at Udupi in 1969 that untouchability has no scriptural sanction. They ordained that all Hindus should behave with one another as equals, that untouchability is *adharma*. In September 1981, the leading *mathadhipatis* in Karnataka came forward to give *mantra deeksha* (initiation), which was till then reserved for their own followers, to all Hindus, including Harijans. They also declared their *maths* open to all Hindus, including Harijans. Scores of *mathadhipatis* and sannyasis are now mixing with the Harijans in their *mohallas*, visiting their houses, worshiping in their temples and partaking of the *prasad*. Mass awakening movements like Jana Jagaran Abhiyan, Hindu Seva Sangh, Hindu Seva Pratisthan (Bangalore), Hindu Munani (Kanya Kumari) began to meet the challenge of conversion to non-Hindu creeds. The Arya Samaj, the Hindu Mahasabha, the Vishva Hindu Parishad, in one way or the other, were already persuading those who had converted to Islam to return to the Hindu fold. They have succeeded in some group conversions (of Hindu Christians) in some tribal areas and (of Hindu Muslims) in Mewat and Rajasthan regions. Individuals and political and social organisations keep a watch on the inflow of foreign money. They inform and pressurize the Government to stop such clandestine remittances. They expose those parties and groups which treat Muslim immigration and conversion as addition to their vote bank. "Some commentators, especially those close to Vishva Hindu Parishad seem to be satisfied that the tide of conversions has been contained..."[96] This may or may not be true. But the Hindus have also learnt from Muslims to proselytize and demolish shrines of other religions even if their attempts are only token and symbolic.

6.8. ICONOCLASM

Like proselytization, desecrating and demolishing the temples of non-Muslims is also central to Islam. Iconoclasm derives its justification from the Quranic revelations and the Prophet's Sunnah or practice. Muhammad had himself destroyed temples in Arabia and so had set an example for his followers. In return the *mujahid*, or fighter of Jihad, is promised handsome rewards in this world as well as in the world to come. Because of early successes at home, Islam developed a full-fledged theory of iconoclasm.[97] India too suffered terribly as thousands of Hindu temples and sacred edifices disappeared in northern India by the time of Sikandar Lodi and Babur. Will Durant rightly laments in the *Story of Civilization* that "We can never know from looking at India today, what grandeur and beauty it once possessed". In Delhi, after the demolition of twenty-seven Hindu and Jain temples, the materials of which were utilized to construct the Quwwat-ul-Islam masjid, it was after 700 years that the Birla Mandir could be constructed in 1930s.

Sita Ram Goel has brought out two excellent volumes on *Hindu Temples: What happened to them.*[98] These informative volumes give a list of Hindu shrines and their history of destruction in the medieval period on the basis of Muslim evidence itself. This of course does not cover all the shrines razed. Muslims broke temples recklessly. Those held in special veneration by Hindus like the ones at Somnath, Ayodhya, Kashi and Mathura, were special targets of Muslims, and whenever the Hindus could manage to rebuild their shrines at these places, they were again destroyed by Muslim rulers. From the time of Mahmud of Ghazni who destroyed the temples at Somnath and Mathura to Babur who struck at Ayodhya to Aurangzeb who razed the temples at Kashi Mathura and Somnath, the story is repeated again and again.

Hindu Retaliation

Sometimes the Hindus have also retaliated. Just as the Hindus do not believe in converting people of other faiths to Hinduism, yet, when Muslim proselytization continued unabated, Hindus also retaliated, although in a token way, by reconverting and taking back into Hinduism those who had fallen a prey to Muslim spree of conversion. In the same way Hindus do not desecrate or break the shrines of peoples of other faiths. But when Muslim vandalism got beyond Hindu patience, they also reconverted some Hindu temples which had been turned into mosques by Muslim invaders and rulers. But while the Muslims convert Hindus openly, punishment for renouncing Islam is death. Similarly, while the shrines of non-Muslims are regularly destroyed, non-Muslims cannot reclaim their desecrated temples. This is the law of Islam. Hindus are not bound by it. Muslims razed the temple of Somnath repeatedly; the Hindus rebuilt it again and again, so that the present majestic temple built after Independence is the seventh in the series. Similar is the attachment of Hindus to the temples of Ayodhya, Mathura and Kashi. The Babri structure at Ayodhya was built by Babur with the debris of a Hindu temple dedicated to Lord Ram. The Hindus destroyed the Muslim structure on 6 December 1992 and reclaimed the site of the temple. The interesting part of the story is that not a day passes without some remark made about the demolition of the Ayodhya structure in 1992, particularly by Muslim secularists and Hindu Marxists and "intelligentsia". But Ayodhya is not the first act of people's reaction against the desecration of their shrines. Muslim armies of Delhi attacked Gujarat in 1299, and again sacked the temple of Somnath. They looted the opulent city of Anhilvara and sacked a number of monasteries, palaces and temples in Asavalli, Vanmanthali, Surat, Dholka and Khambayat. The Gujaratis could not forget or forgive this vandalism. 40,000 brave Dalit Barwaris from Gujarat arrived in Delhi over the years and sacked the main mosque in Siri in Delhi in 1320 under the rule of Sultan Nasiruddin Khusrau, a half-convert. Idol worship was started inside the palace and mosque. Copies of the Quran were torn to pieces and used as seats for idols which were placed in the *mehrabs* (niches) of the mosques, and the slaughter of cows was forbidden.[99] The Barwaris had known Muslim invader and rulers breaking temples, burning their religious books, and enslaving their women and children. The Barwaris paid them back in their own coin. They say "revenge is a kind of wild justice". And there are many more such examples of which only a few may be mentioned here. When Sher Shah conquered and occupied Jodhpur, the temple in the fort was converted into a mosque. There was retaliation and when the mosque was taken back by Hindus, they prevented the reading of Friday prayers there.[100] Temples were freely destroyed under Firoz Tughlaq and Sikandar Lodi. In return Rana Kumbha also claims to have broken a mosque.[101] Medini Rai in Malwa turned some Muslim women into slave girls,[102] a practice freely indulged in by Muslims in regard to Hindu women.

Those who cannot forget 6 December 1992, should also remember another date, 9 April 1669. On this day Aurangzeb issued a general order "to demolish all schools and temples of the infidels and to put down their religious teaching and practice". Much vandalism had preceded this order and reckless destruction of shrines followed.

During Aurangzeb's reign temples were desecrated and destroyed everywhere; 235 temples were destroyed in Rajasthan alone. This enraged Bhim, the younger son of the Rana of Udaipur, who retaliated by attacking Ahmadnagar and demolishing many mosques there.[103] Temples in Mathura and Kashi were destroyed by orders of Aurangzeb and mosques built in their stead. The Satnamis, the Jats, Marathas and Sikhs struck back against this fanaticism by destroying mosques at many places when they gathered strength.

Recent events about Ayodhya are well-known. Long before the structure was pulled down, Muslims in Bangladesh had destroyed more than 200 temples in November 1989 (reacting against the *Shilanyas* at Ayodhya). In November 1990 another 50 temples were razed or burnt, not to mention about the women raped and men killed. So also was done in Pakistan. The Kashmir Samiti has produced a report titled *Riots in Kashmir*, listing 85 temples destroyed, and claiming that 550 people had been killed in the Islamic purification campaign in 1990.[104] And still many Muslims and some Hindu "intellectuals" make a hell of a noise about Ayodhya. Hindu religion and scriptures do not permit, much less 'advocate' desecration of the religious places of other peoples. But there is a limit to forbearance. Destruction of the shrines of other faiths cannot for ever remain a one way traffic.

But Hindu fear of Muslim iconoclasm still remains. A thousand years of aggression and terror cannot be easily erased. While many Hindus are happy at the achievements of *Karsevaks* in eliminating centuries old humiliation at Ayodhya, they do not exhibit any bravado about it. Contrast it with the assertion of Taliban in Afghanistan. They openly declared recently that they would destroy the statues of the Buddha at Bamiyan. On the other hand in India many Hindu leaders plead that the destruction of the Babri structure was unfortunate, that they do not know who did it. In this context they mention the letter of Mr. Arjun Singh dated 1 December 1992 addressed to Mr. S. Rajgopal, Cabinet Secretary, which says: "There is indication that some agent provocateurs from Pakistan have been able to infiltrate into Ayodhya and would try to damage the Babri masjid if the VHP *Karsevaks* fail in their mission to do the same. The resulting civil strife as consequence of this event is what Pakistan would very much like to happen."[105] The credit due to *Karsevaks* is thus tried to be snatched away by the fear in the Hindu intelligentsia generated by centuries of iconoclastic oppression of Islam. Those who approved of the destruction of Babri structure and reclamation of their holy Ram Lala temple, should be obliged to Pakistan if it repeated Ayodhya in Mathura and Kashi also and helped them in not soiling their hands by repeating such "unfortunate" acts in Mathura and Varanasi also. Such disordered thinking cannot be sustained. As has been repeatedly said, all history is contemporary. It is not possible to forget 9 April 1669 because it is 'remote past' and continue to be apologetic about 6 December 1992 because it is 'immediate past'. Nothing is past. These two dates are just two points on the eternity of Time in which action and reaction go on and on in the course of our history.

NOTES

II — POLITICS

1. Quran, Surah 98, ayat 6; 25:52; 9:14; 68:40, 69-74; 22:19-22
2. Quran, Surah 55, ayats 47-77; 12:36; 52:17-24.
3. These conditions are reproduced in many books, e.g., *Zakhirat-ul-Mulk* by Shaikh Hamdani quoted in *Sources of Indian Tradition*, Columbia University Press, New York, 1958, pp. 489-90; *The Delhi Sultanate*, R.C. Majumdar (ed.), Bharatiya Vidya Bhavan, Bombay, 1960, pp. 618-20.
4. Quran, Surah 4, ayat 144; 5:51.
5. Quran, Surah 2, ayat 221.
6. "Focus on Muslim appeasement", *Times of India*, 24 January 1994.
7. "Harassed minorities in Bangladesh", by Saradindu Mukherjee, *The Times of India*, New Delhi, 15 November 1994.
8. *Mashriqi Awaz*, New Delhi, 2 March 1995. Also *Myths of Composite Culture*, New Delhi, 1991.
9. "Indian Secularism X-rayed", *Indian Express*, 2 January 1991.
10. Surah 4, ayat 34.
11. 33:59
12. 24:30-31, also 33:35.
13. Surah 24, ayat 223; *Sunan Ibn Daud*, vol. II, pp. 155-63; *Sahih Muslim*, vol. II, part 3, p. 55.
14. Ibn Majah, vol. I, pp. 552-53, *ahadis* 2053-56; Tirmizi, vol. I, pp. 428-31.
15. E.g. Ibn Majah, vol. II, pp. 489-91, *ahadis* 1796-1801.
16. Hitti, *The Arabs*, p. 59; Hughes, *Dictionary of Islam*, p. 168
17. Ram Swarup, *Woman in Islam*, pp. 3-4, 20, 21.
18. *Ibid*, p. 3.
19. Ibn Warraq, *op. cit.*, p. 293.
20. *Times of India*, New Delhi, 20 October and 1 November, 1994.
21. *Ibid.*, New Delhi, 30 March, 1995.
22. *Ibid.*, Saturday Interview, New Delhi, 30 November 1996.
23. *Ibid.*, Briefs, New Delhi, 22.11.93.
24. Amulya Ganguli, "Bigotry in Islam: The silent majority's surrender", *Ibid.*, New Delhi, 3 January 1994.
25. Surah 2, ayat 228.
26. *Times of India*, 'Saturday Interview', New Delhi, 30 November 1996
27. *Ibid.*, New Delhi, 23 June 1997.
28. Rakesh Bhatnagar, "Legal View", *The Times of India*, New Delhi, 4 March 1997.

29. The Shah Bano case is known to all. "Talat Parveen is an educated, fairly westernised medical practitioner living in Delhi. Attractive and successful at the age of 22, she is already a divorcee. The reason: her former husband pronounced the three deadly words which Muslim women have come to dread: *Talaq, talaq, talaq*; without weighing the spin-off, her husband had annulled the marriage without any ceremony. Unfortunately for the woman her cause did not have many backers. The Ulema sided with the husband interpreting the holy book in their own way. That left the woman no option but to sound the court. It was here that a young Delhi High Court lawyer M. Aytab Siddiqui came to her rescue, and after a short legal battle, he ensured that Parveen's maintenance, at least until the birth of her child, would be the responsibility of her husband. This is one of the cases that the Indian courts are tackling, and it remains at best the tip of the iceberg. The real problem is far below. In this particular case, the woman was aware enough and had some support from her immediate family. In a majority of cases, divorced women have nowhere to go." A *fatwa* issued by the Jamat-i-Ahl-i-Hadis which includes members from the Muslim Law Board and All India Milli Council, has challenged the traditional preserve of the mullah, and proclaimed that pronouncement of *talaq* thrice in a row would be considered only a single *talaq*.

30. Kumkum Chadha's article entitled "War of Veils in Middle East" in *The Hindustan Times*, New Delhi, 7 October 1995.

31. "Around the world" column in *The Times of India*, New Delhi, 28 October' 97.

32. "Veiled, yet free to let their hair down", *The Times of India*, New Delhi, 5 November 1997.

33. Muzaffar Hussain in "Islamic atrocities on Women". *Organiser,* New Delhi, 16 July 1995.

34. Addison-Wesley Publishing Company, New York, cited in "Crime or Punishment ?" (in Pakistan), by Anwar Azeem, *The Hindustan Times,* New Delhi, 8 February, 1988. Also Review by Seema Alavi in the *Indian Express,* 28 May 1995.

35. Zafar Jung, "Women in Islam", *The Times of India,* New Delhi, 25 August 1994.

36. As reported in *The Times of India,* New Delhi, 18 March 1997.

37. MEA (Ministry of External Affairs) has informed in a note dated 27.4.1993 (received on 28.4.1993) that the amount is Rs.5.33 crores as intimated to them by the Department of Shipping.

38. Lok Sabha Secretariat, New Delhi, April 1993, pp. 4, 8-9.

39. The above piece has been summarised from Rakesh Bhatnagar's reports in *The Times of India,* New Delhi, 18 December 1995 and 15 January 1996.

40. See my *Twilight of the Sultanate,* p. 187.

41. *The Hindustan Times,* New Delhi, 24 September 1996.

42. Ibn Battuta, p. 75.

43. Summarized from *Organiser,* 9 March 1997, p. 12.

44. "Heresy and History", interview with Pakistani historian Mubarak Ali, *Indian Express,* Sunday Magazine, 6 February 1994.

45. *Sahara Samachar,* Lucknow, 7 November 1994. Also the *Indian Express.*

46. *Jansatta,* Lucknow, 23 November, 1994.

47. *The Times of India,* New Delhi, 7 May 1997.

48. *Nadwa ka Sacch,* pp. 13-14.

49. *Nadwa ka Sacch,* Ali Mian's phone calls to foreign countries p. 35, Bomb blasts in Delhi p. 43, Nadwa raid pp. 57-59, Muslims active in U.P. p. 77, Foreign reaction on Nadwa, pp. 90-92, 100.

50. *The Times of India,* Ahmedabad, 2 December 1994.

51. Abu Daud, vol. II, p. 281; *Mishkat,* vol. II, pp. 34-35.

52. *The Times of India,* New Delhi, 20 August 1997.

53. "The holy war within the self" by Asghar Ali Engineer in *The Times of India,* New Delhi, 1 October 1997. This is restated in another article by Engineer entitled "The multiple paths of faith", *The Times of India,* New Delhi, 16 February 1998.

54. P.M. Currie, *The Shrine and Cult of Muin-al-din Chishti of Ajmer,* Oxford, Delhi, 1989, pp. 1-19, 66-96.

55. Richard Maxwell Eaton, *Sufis of Bijapur,* Princeton, 1978, particularly the chapter titled "Sufi Warriors".

56. *The Hindustan Times,* New Delhi, under "Meditations", 17 November 1997.

57. Wahiduddin Khan, *Tabligh Movement,* Al Risala Books, The Islamic Centre, New Delhi, second reprint, 1994, p. 55, cited in *Time For Stock Taking,* Voice of India, New Delhi, 1997, p. 430.

58. *The Hindustan Times,* 17 November 1997.

59. "Discourses on Religion and Philosophy" in *The Times of India,* New Delhi, 4 September, 1997.

60. *Sahih Bukhari,* vol. II, p. 495, *hadis* 1127 and p. 706, *hadis* 1588. Bukhari gives the details of all expeditions in *Kitab-ul-Maghazi,* vol. II, pp. 495-706; *Sahih Muslim,* vol. III, part 5, p. 105.

61. Eg. Ibn Majah, vol. II, p. 109, *hadis* 337; *Sahih Muslim,* vol. III, part 5, p.72.

62. In "Distorted facts", in a letter to the Editor, *The Hindustan Times,* New Delhi, 14 November 1997. Zafar Jung's articles and letters themselves are full of distorted facts.

63. M. Mujeeb, *The Indian Muslims,* pp. 21-22.

64. This has been done by me for some centuries — as samples. See my *Indian Muslims: Who are they.* pp. 8-14.

65. See my *Growth of Scheduled Tribes and Castes in Medieval India.*

66. *Ibid.*, pp. 72-99.

67. By M. Titus, S.A.A. Rizvi, Mohammad Habib and others. For details see my *Indian Muslims: Who are they*, pp. 92-95.

68. Bribe was given for making converts from the very beginning of Islam. For example, Nasai, vol. II, pp. 176-77, *hadis* 2582.

69. Jan Knappert, cited in *Time For Stock Taking*, pp. 339-40.

70. *The Hindustan Times*, New Delhi, 28 December 1997.

71. Bantam Books, Canada and USA, 1980. It was translated from Persian into French in 1979 and from French into English in 1980 and carries an introduction by Clive Irving.

72. Nine years have passed since the fatwa (religious ruling) was issued by Iran's late spiritual leader Ayatollah Ruholla Khomeini months before his death. The fatwa condemned Salman Rushdie to death for alleged blasphemy against Islam in his novel *The Satanic Verses.* It said that any Muslim in a position to kill the author had a duty to do so. After this many rewards were announced for the killing. On its ninth anniversary the British Foreign Secretary wrote to the Government of Iran for revocation of the fatwa. Iranian foreign ministry spokesman Mahmoud Mohammadi said a fatwa issued by a supreme religious jurisprudent is irrevocable and will remain so throughout history, *The Times of India*, New Delhi, 16 February 1998.

73. This anonymous letter from Pakistan was published in London's *Observer* newspaper and has been quoted by Professor Daniel Pipes of Harvard University in his review of Ibn Warraq's book *Why I Am Not A Muslim* published in *The Weekly Standard* of New York dated 22 January 1996. See in *Time For Stock Taking*, p. 311.

74. In an interview published in *The Times of India*, New Delhi, 29 October 1997.

75. *Sahih Muslim*, vol. I, pp. 106, 125, 135.

76. *Sahih Muslim*, vol. II, part 4, pp. 299-30, 307. Bukhari, vol. I, p. 567, *hadis* 1406, also p. 636, *hadis* 1623; Nasai, vol. II, p. 193, *hadis* 263.

77. Fatima Merrissi, *op. cit.*

78. Bukhari, vol. I, pp. 103-4, 145, 511, *hadis* 1257.

79. *Sahih Muslim*, vol. I, part I, *Kitab-ul-Iman*, pp. 244-45. Also Bukhari, vol. I, p. 677, *hadis* 1749.

80. Manzur-ul-Haqq Siddiqi, *Massir-ul-Jadad*, published by al-Maktaba al-Saifia, Shish Mahal Road, Lahore, 1964, pp. 94-115, esp. pp. 98, 106. Muhammad Abul Shakur, *Aslah-i-Mewat,* Sadar Bazar, Delhi, 1925, pp. 2-3, 35-40. Also see K.C. Yadav, "Urdu Sahityakaron ki Haryanvi ko den", in *Harigandha*, September-October, 1989, pp. 26-28, for similar literature.

81. See my *Legacy of Muslim Rule in India*, pp. 315-18.

82. Devendra Swarup (ed.), *Politics of Conversion*, pp. 10, 28, 29

83. *The Statesman*, New Delhi, 22 July 1981.

84. *Indian Express*, New Delhi, 15 February 1982.

85. *India Today*, New Delhi, 16-31 July 1981; *The Times of India*, 21 March 1981.

86. *Politics of Conversion*, p. 31.

87. *Indian Express*, New Delhi, 26 June 1981.

88. *Indian Express*, New Delhi 15 February 1982.

89. *Politics of Conversion*, pp. 29, 32.

90. *The Hindustan Times*, New Delhi, 23 July 1981.

91. *Politics of Conversion*, pp. 24-25.

92. "Muslim Reaction to Mass Conversions" by Brij Bhushan Bhatnagar in *Politics of Conversion*, pp. 224-230, esp. p. 228.

93. *The Times of India*, New Delhi, Saturday, 7 June 1997.

94. *Indian Express*, New Delhi, 13 April 1981.

95. V.P. Bhatia, "The Ever Green Mulla Power", in *Organiser*, 27 October 1996 citing references from B.R. Ambedkar, *Pakistan and Partition of India*; Indra Prakash, *The History of Hindu Mahasabha*; and Shaikh Abdullah, *Aatish-e-Chinar*.

96. Dev Dutt, "Conversions: a Viewpoint" in *Politics of Conversion*, p. 36.

97. D.S. Margoliouth, *Mohammed and the Rise of Islam*, pp. 24, 377-409; P.K. Hitti, *The Arabs*, p. 28; Edward Gibbon, *Decline and Fall of the Roman Empire*, vol. II, pp. 649-660.

98. Volume I, 1990; vol. II, 1991, revised ed. 1993, Voice of India, New Delhi.

99. Yahiya, *Tarikh-i-Mubarak Shahi*, p. 87; Ibn Batuttah, p. 47; Barani, p. 411. Also Lal, *Khaljis*, pp. 69-70, 314-15.

100. Sri Ram Sharma, *The Religious Policy of the Mughal Emperors*, p. 11. Sher Shah's mosque is still there.

Also Qureshi, *The Administration of the Sultanate of Delhi*, p. 221.

101. *The Delhi Sultanate*, Bharatiya Vidya Bhavan, p. 639, n. 17.

102. Nizamuddin Ahmad, *Tabqat-i-Akbari*, vol. III, p. 597.

103. Sharma, *op. cit.*, pp. 134-136.

104. Koenraad Elst, *Ayodhya and After*, New Delhi, 1991, pp. 59, 61, 296.

105. K.R. Malkani, "Subverting Nationalism", *The Times of India*, New Delhi, 22 July 1996.

Part III

REPOSTE ON REVIEWS

VII
A Riposte on Reviews

In the preliminary pages, the list of books "by the same author" shows that during the past fifty years I have written a dozen books on medieval Indian history beginning from 1950 onwards. As usual these have been reviewed in journals in India and abroad, bestowing both praise and blame as per the custom of the reviewers. However, during the last fifteen years or so, some of my books have received special attention of a *certain brand of scholars* for adverse criticism. Although this gives me publicity and raises demand for my books because such reviews arouse curiosity of readers, it also provides me with an opportunity to defend myself from my detractors determined to denigrate my work. It is not customary to answer the reviewers — they have their right of judgement — but when a systematic smear campaign is launched criticising everything that I say, without a single word of appreciation for anything, a rebuttal is called for, more so when a connection and not mere coincidence is discernible between the uncharitable review of one of my books in a British journal and some other harsh reviews by a group of Aligarh historians in Indian historical journals. In some Western universities, Aligarh is known to be the only centre of research on medieval Indian history.

7.1. *The Legacy of Muslim Rule in India*

Peter Jackson has reviewed my book *The Legacy of Muslim Rule in India* (Aditya Prakashan, New Delhi) 1992, in the

Journal of the Royal Asiatic Society of Great Britain, Third Series, Vol. 4, Part 3, November 1994, pp. 421-23. He writes: "Those who have read Professor Lal's *History of the Khaljis* and *Twilight of the Sultanate*, both still standard works, may well approach this book with pleasurable anticipation. They will be disappointed." And then follows a list of harsh observations on selective basis. These may be taken up one after another.

1. In the words of the reviewer "what disturbs me is the way in which a markedly selective and one-sided account of India's Muslim past is pressed into service in support of his (author's) position".

2. According to the author, "Appeasement of Indian Muslims by the Congress might have been understandable prior to Partition, as a means of maximising support against the Raj; as a policy deliberately espoused by successive governments of India since 1947, it is pitifully inappropriate — and dangerous. In particular Lal deplores the government sponsored attempts to rewrite Indian history in the interests of 'minorityism' by suppressing unpalatable truths about the character of Muslim rule."

3. According to the author, "a strict watch was kept on their (the Hindus) thought and expression" and that "they could not worship their gods in public." "Some limited degree of repression may have been possible in Delhi, or in the sultan's itinerant court," writes Jackson, "it was surely impractical in provincial centres, still more so in the countryside."

4. "If Muslim rule was so iconoclastic and oppressive, how are we to account for the fierce loyalty shown to successive Delhi Sultans by their Hindu *Paik* guards... And what of the thousands of Hindu troops who are found serving in the armies of Hindu potentates from Mahmud of Ghazna... onwards?"

5. "The implication is that toleration of Hindu practices was always opposed by the 'Ulama'... It is clear that the '*ulama*'

are going to be damned whatever they did or did not do... A similar fate awaits the Sufi *mashaikh* (pp. 193ff)."

6. "One final example of the methods employed in this book deserves mention, namely, the failure to distinguish the conduct of Muslim rulers within India from that of their co-religionists who appeared in the subcontinent only temporarily. Of the Muslim armies in peacetime... we still await the evidence of his statement on rowdyism."

7. "Use of archaic and misleading term 'Muhammadan' is of a piece with Lal's reliance on dated secondary authorities like Sir Elliot's introduction to *The History of India as told by its own Historians.*"

8. According to the author of the book, "Muslims still live, as they have always lived, in the Middle Ages. Islam is inherently a religion of violence; its followers... are not concerned about equality with the devotees of other faiths."

9. "One thinks of the works of Peter Hardy, of Yohannan Friedmann, and of the Aligarh school now headed by Irfan Habib. It might be inferred that these scholars are to be numbered among the 'Marxists, pseudo-secularists, progressives etc.' whom Lal denounces (p. 348). But their writings were irrelevant to his purpose. His is not a work of scholarship but an exercise in propaganda, and rather crude propaganda at that."

1. With all humility I would like to say that most history is selective. Selective study is common everywhere, in Aligarh, in Jackson's review itself. Jackson himself gives a rare instance mentioned in *Epigraphia Indica* 1957-8 of Hindus benefiting "from the Muslim governor's active assistance in the construction of their temple which had been destroyed in a (Muslim) insurrection against Muhammad bin Tughluq". How selective! Would it mean that it was common with Muslim governors to help build temples? Just the contrary was the tradition. The fact is that such exceptions only prove the rule. A markedly selective and one-sided claim is that

Aurangzeb donated so many *bighas* of land to so and so temple without mentioning the case of hundreds of others he desecrated and razed. Am I more selective than the historians who indulge in such selectivity day in and day out? In all fairness the reviewer should concede to me also the freedom of "selective choices" he allows to himself and others, particularly in Aligarh.

2. The reviewer has put words in my book which are not there at all, like "maximising support against the Raj" or "a policy espoused by successive governments". What I said in the *Legacy* (p. 336) is this:

> The policy of the Indian National Congress before Partition was alright. It appeased the Muslims to somehow save the country from division. But after the country was partitioned on Hindu-Muslim basis, continuance of the old policy of appeasement showed bankruptcy of political acumen and a betrayal of the implicit trust reposed by the people in the Congress — in particular Jawaharlal Nehru. With all his knowledge of history he could not understand Islam and its fundamentalism.

This paragraph needs neither reiteration nor elaboration. "Religious harmony is a desirable thing. But it takes two to play the game. Unfortunately such a sentiment holds a low position in Islamic theology," rightly writes Ram Swarup. Muslim attitude before 1947 was that the 'Muslim nation' could not live with the Hindus; they must have a separate state. Efforts at unity and 'living together' was a one-sided endeavour of the Congress. It failed before 1947 because Muslim theology does not believe in living together with non-Muslims on equal terms. That is also why the Congress effort seems to be failing after 1947. Threat of secession is heard every day (as in Kashmir) or of further division of the country (if a uniform civil law is enacted for all Indians).

Should it be a matter of criticism if I deplore "government-sponsored attempts to rewrite Indian history in the interest of minorityism by suppressing unpalatable truths about the character of Muslim rule"? I have quoted from government circulars addressed to authors of school and college textbooks. Here some instructions/suggestions are reproduced. These appear on p. 70 of the *Legacy*. "Muslim rule should not attract any criticism... Destruction of temples by Muslim invaders and rulers should not be mentioned... Ignore and delete mention of forcible conversions to Islam" etc., etc. Curiously enough the instructions themselves admit of destruction of temples and forcible conversions. Why are there no instructions about writing the history of the ancient (Hindu) period or the British period? Does it mean that the record of Muslim rule in India alone is unmentionable? Or, does it mean that only the destruction of temples by Muslim rulers and invaders should not be mentioned (for the appeasement of one minority), while destruction by Portuguese invaders and rulers should be freely mentioned? Evils of Hindu society may be discussed but the evils of Muslim society should not. Warren Hastings, Wellesley and Dalhousie may be impeached relentlessly but no Muslim governor or ruler. These are double angles of approach, double standards of judgement recommended for writing Indian history. But this is actually being done by historians engaged by the establishment for writing school and college textbooks. Koenraad Elst has written a book on this subject entitled *Negationism in India: Concealing the Record of Islam* (New Delhi, 1992).

Negationism is practised in many countries, but their laws in this regard are different. As an example, let me quote from a report carried by *The Times of India*, datelined New Delhi, 7 May 1992. "HISTORIAN FINED FOR A 'HOAX'. Munich: A district court here fined a British historian 10,000 marks ($ 6,000) on Tuesday for publicly insisting that the Nazi gas chambers at Auschwitz were a hoax, AP reports. Judge Thomas Stelzne ruled that David Irving, a right-wing historian was guilty of slandering and disparaging the memory of the dead, a crime in Germany. Irving, 54, has claimed that gas chambers in Auschwitz death camp were a post-war hoax to draw tourists to the area in Poland. Irving once insisted that Nazi dictator Adolf Hitler knew nothing about the Holocaust, which claimed the lives of 6 million Jews." On the other hand, in India, when a 'historian' spreads the canard that the temple at Banaras was razed by Aurangzeb because a Rani was molested in its premises (of course, without producing any historical evidence), he is rewarded with cash and high offices and hailed as a great Gandhian and a champion of secularism and national integration.[1]

In these circumstances, it is no wonder that the Bharatiya Shikshan Mandal, "a National Voluntary Oraganisation working in the field of Education with the active involvement of Intellectuals, Educationists, Thinkers, Policy makers and teachers at all levels, has undertaken... to request the Central and State Governments to put an end to the distortion in the textbooks of History and other subjects at all levels (and) to insist upon the teaching of complete and impartial History of Indian Freedom Struggle against foreign invaders covering the last 2500 years."

3. It is re-asserted that a strict watch was kept on Hindu thought and expression. Hindu learning in general was suppressed since Hindu and Buddhist schools were attached to temples and monasteries. These were regularly destroyed from the very beginning and with them schools of learning. Qutbuddin Aibak razed the Sanskrit College of Vishaldeva at Ajmer and in its place built a mosque called *Arhai din ka Jhonpra*. In the east Ikhtiyauddin Bakhtiyar Khalji sacked the Buddhist university centres in Bihar like Odantapuri, Nalanda and Vikramshila between 1197-1202. There, according to the contemporary chronicler Minhaj Siraj, "the greater number of the inhabitants of the place were Brahmans, and the whole of those Brahmans had their heads shaven (probably Buddhist monks mistaken for Brahmans) and they were all slain. There were a great number of books there; and the Musalmans...

summoned a number of Hindus that they might give them information respecting the import of these books; but the whole of the Hindus had been killed." All that the invader could learn was that "the whole of the fortress was a college and in the Hindi tongue, they call a college (madrasa) Bihar."[2] During this period there were large numbers of centres of learning spread all over India. B.P. Mazumdar has listed some of these centres in the eleventh and twelfth centuries as existing in Northern India. In Bihar they were Nalanda, Vikramshila, Odantapuri and Phullahari near Monghyr. In North and Eastern Bengal they were Jagaddala, Somapura and Devikota in North Bengal, Vikrampuri in Dacca, Pattikeraka in Comilla, and Panditavihara in Chittagong. Minor *viharas* were in existence at Gaya and Valabhi and Bundelkhand.

Hieun Tsang, in the seventh century, had noted that monasteries existed in all parts of the country. Many of these continued to flourish in the eleventh-twelfth centuries. Hiuen Tsang's list included "Nagarkot, Udyana, Jalandhar, Sthanesvara, Srughna Matipura, Brahmapura, Govisana, Ahichchatra, Samkasya, Kanauj, Navadevakula, Ayodhya, Hayamuka, Prayag, Visoka, Kapilvastu, Banaras, Ramagrama, Ghazipur, Tilosika, Gunamati, Silabhadra near Gaya, Kajangala, Pundravardhana, Kamarupa, Samatata, Orissa, Berar, Malwa, Valabhi, Anandapura, Surat, Ujjayini and Chitor." The adventurer Ikhtiayaruddin Bakhtiyar Khalji sacked Bihar during sultan Aibak's reign, and centres of learning were specially sacked. So thorough was the massacre by the Khalji warrior in Bihar and later on by others in other places that those who could read ancient inscriptions became rare if not extinct. So that when Sultan Firoz Shah Tughlaq (fourteenth century) shifted two Ashokan pillars from Khizrabad and Meerut to Delhi and installed them there, he called some learned Brahmans to read the inscriptions engraved in Ashokan Brahmi script on the pillars; they failed to read the script. Some of them tried to please the Sultan with funny stories by saying that it was recorded in the inscriptions that no one would be able to remove the monoliths till the advent of Firoz.[3]

Demolition of schools and temples was continued by most Muslim rulers right up to the time of Aurangzeb, both at the centre and in the provinces. Aurangzeb was one of the enthusiastic sort in this respect, although he was no exception.

The *Maasir-i-Alamgiri* records that in April 1669, "It reached the ears of his Majesty, the protector of the faith, that in the province of Thatta, Multan, and Banaras, but especially in the latter, *foolish Brahmans were in the habit of expounding frivolous books in their schools*, and that students and learners, Muslims as well as Hindus went there, even from long distances, led by the desire to become acquainted with the *wicked sciences they taught.* The Director of the Faith, consequently issued orders *to all governors of provinces to destroy with a willing hand the schools and temples* of the infidels. In obedience of this order the temple of Bishnath at Banaras was destroyed."[4] With such evidences on hand, Jackson is forced to concede that "some limited degree of repression may have been feasible in Delhi or in the vicinity of the sultan's itinerant court; it was surely impractical in the provincial centres, still more so in the countryside". I have resided in Delhi, Bhopal and Hyderabad (Deccan) for many years. In all these places I could hardly locate any temples left of the medieval period. Hindu learning was dependent on schools and Brahman teachers, and both were attached to temples mostly in urban areas. And all the three — schools, teachers and temples — were systematically destroyed. Muslim rulers in general and Firoz Tuglaq and Sikandar Lodi in particular considered the Brahmans as "the very keys of chambers of idolatry" and treated them with great severity.[5] The level of education in the countryside is not known. But the credit for whatever could be saved of Hindu education goes to the freedom fighters of medieval India and not to the indulgence of the Muslim government.

4. Fierce loyalty of "Hindu *Paik* guards" may not be a correct description. Paik is a Hindi word, but all paiks were not Hindu. They can be called urban infantry comprising of both Hindus and Muslims. Once captured or enrolled in the sultan's service, most Hindu troops were converted to Islam. That is why the paiks who saved Alauddin Khalji on his expedition to Ranthambhor have been called retainers because Barani calls them "foot-soldiers", "foot-slaves".[6] One of them was Manik. The name is Hindu and probably he was a Hindu. During mass conversions sometimes old names were not given up and Manik may as well have been Musalman with Hindu name. The paiks who killed Malik Kafur, to save Alauddin's son Qutbuddin Mubarak Khalji, were all Muslims — Mubshir, Bashir, Saleh and Munir as noted by Isami and Farishtah.[7] Of the thousands of Hindu troops serving under Muslim rulers from Mahmud Ghazni onwards, some were enrolled troops, others were loyal soldiers under loyal Rajas.

Once a man gave up the plough and adopted the profession of arms, he became a professional soldier available for service with any employer, Hindu or Muslim. It is not only defeated Hindu Rajas or professional Hindu soldiers who served under Muslim rulers, vice versa was also the case. Mahmud Ghaznavi and Hindu Shahiya kings both had Afghan troops under them. Vijayanagar employed thousands of Muslims in both civil and military establishments. An entire contingent of Rana Sanga was Muslim. In Shivaji's army a substantial section was adherent of Islam. Churaman jat enrolled Meos and Afghans against Mughal government. Ibrahim Khan Gardi with 9,000 sepoys fought under Marathas against Ahmad Shah Abdali in the Third Battle of Panipat.

Loyalty to salt was a special feature of the medieval period. It did not, as it could not, hinder the Muslim rule from being iconoclastic and oppressive to non-Muslims as its character was determined by the dictates of the Shariat.

5. I have said nothing objectionable about the life of the ulema and *mashaikh* in medieval India and their role in the contemporary politics (pp. 189-207). This is what I have said about the ulema, "Their presence was indispensable to a ruler who was generally uneducated (in the Law). They kept the rulers and the ruling class on the path of Islam and virtue by informing them correctly about their duty towards the non-Muslims. Some modern secularist historians blame the Ulama for making Muslim rulers intolerant through their orthodox advice... I have not come across any instance where the Ulama deliberately gave a distorted version of their scriptures in this context... They were as much interested in seeing the Muslim state being run according to the Shariat as the Sultan." No sober scholar would say that I have damned the ulema and also insinuate that "The 'Ulama' are going to be damned (by me) whatever they did or did not do".

Similar is the case about the sufi saints. In nine pages (193-201) I have written about the various orders and their contribution to Muslim rule. In three pages (204-206) I have given a brief resume of their life and political activities. So I have been attacked for what is not there in the book. The insinuation and comments of Jackson on my statements on the ulema and the *mashaikh* suggest that he is determined to condemn my book without proper reading.

6. There is criticism of "the methods employed ... namely, the (author's) failure to distinguish the conduct of Muslim rulers within India from that of their co-religionists who appeared in the subcontinent only temporarily".

There is no failure on my part to distinguish between the conduct of the two; there is hardly any difference, because both followed the same ideology, the same Quranic laws and rules in dealing with the Hindus. Let us compare the achievements and activities of Sultan Firoz Tuglaq, a ruler within India, with those of a foreign invader Timur. Firoz

Shah used to shed tears when he was forced to fight against Muslims; for "Muslim men would be killed and their women widowed". But he felt satisfied when called upon to fight non-Muslims. After his sack of Orissa, Firoz Shah attacked an island on the sea-coast where "nearly 100,000 men of Jajnagar had taken refuge with their women, children, kinsmen and relations". His soldiers turned "the island into a basin of blood by the massacre of the unbelievers". When the pious Sultan attacked Nagarkot (Kangra) and sacked the shrine of Jwalamukhi, Farihstah records that "the Sultan broke idols of the temple, mixed their fragments with the flesh of cows and hung them in nosebags round the necks of Brahmans. He sent the principal idol as trophy to Medina." Firoz Tuglaq was resident Sultan of Hindustan and was known for his piety among contemporary Muslims. Ten years after his death appeared the foreign invader Timur in the subcontinent, temporarily. But the ideas and actions of the two were similar. Timur starts by quoting from the Quran in his *Tuzuk-i-Timuri*: "O Prophet, make war upon the infidels and unbelievers, and treat them severely." He continues: "My great object in invading Hindustan has been to wage a religious war against the infidel Hindus." Similar was the object of Firoz Tughlaq and other sultans "within India". Timur laid siege of Bhatnir and even after the garrison had surrendered, "in a short space of time all the people in the fort were put to the sword, and in the course of one hour the heads of 10,000 infidels were cut off. The sword of Islam was washed in the blood of the infidels and all the goods and effects... became the spoil of my soldiers." At Sarsuti "all the infidel Hindus were slain, their wives and children were made prisoners and their property and goods became the spoil of victors". In Haryana, Timur directed his soldiers to "plunder and destroy and kill every one whom they met". Killing of men and capturing of women and children went on wherever he went.

Firoz Tughlaq was one of the distinguished rulers within

India. He had reigned for more than thirty-five years after Muslim rule had been established for 150 years. His dynasty itself ruled for seventy-five years. Timur was his co-religionist who appeared in India only temporarily. But there is nothing to distinguish between the actions and ideas of the Muslim sultan within India and a temporary foreign Muslim invader. Both are praised by contemporary chroniclers for their pious acts against the infidels. Is it enough to settle down in India in order to become an Indian even if the settler continues to despise everything Indian and admire everything Arabic and Persian and Turkish, even if the settler continues to massacre in cold blood thousands of Indians and convert many more by force, sell women and children as slaves in Muslim lands, destroy great creations of art and science and literature? From Mahmud of Ghazni, the invader, to Aurangzeb, 'the Great Mughal' within India, the story is the same. In truth, Aurangzeb spent his long life towards one end — in fulfilling the task initiated by Mahmud. If those who appeared temporarily were hated, the sultans within India too are no heroes of Indians.

Rowdyism of Muslim armies is well-known. There are dozens of examples available of loot and extortion by Muslim soldiers in peacetime. The reforms of Sher Shah and his strict orders about troops not to damage peasants' fields while on move bear testimony to it. Both Shams Siraj Afif and Ziyauddin Barani refer to such behaviour.[8] But a paragraph from Emperor Jahangir's own pen depicts the scenario clearly. "After carrying out these matters I left the city for the purpose of hunting... As the Rabi Fasl (Spring season) had arrived, for fear any damage should happen to the cultivation of the ryots from the passage of the army, and not withstanding that I had appointed *qurisawul* (provost marshal) with the band of ahadis for the purpose of guarding the fields, I ordered certain men to see what damage had been done to the crops from stage to stage and pay compensation to the ryots."[9] A little later he again writes that

"In order that the grain and cultivation should not be trodden down by men I ordered that all should remain in the city but the men who were actually wanted and my personal servants" only should accompany him on his hunting expedition.[10] In the countryside only grain or crops could be looted or destroyed. In the villages, there was hardly any gold or silver with the peasants on which the soldiers could lay hands on. There are references of such loot in the cities. Rowdyism, extortion and abduction by soldiers in peace time was not uncommon.

7. No, it is neither old fashioned nor archaic to use the term Muhammadanism. Islam is understood more correctly when it is called Muhammadanism. Muhammad is the central figure in Islam. He controls the hearts and minds of all Muslims everywhere. Had their been no Muhammad there would have been no Islam. The word Muhammadanism is therefore not misleading. Its use is very apt and correct.

Elliot's *History of India as told by its own Historians* is no secondary authority. It contains English translation of passages of contemporary Persian chronicles. Sir Henry Elliot's Introduction just as Professor Mohammad Habib's 102-page Introduction to the second volume of Elliot's work published from Aligarh, contains the views of the two. As per Jackson, should both be termed as "dated secondary authorities?"

8. According to the author of the book (a) "Muslims still live, as they have always lived, in the Middle Ages; (b) Islam is inherently a religion of violence; and (c) its followers are not concerned about equality with the devotees of other faiths."

(a) It is true that most Muslims still live in the Middle Ages. The few who dare to be 'modern', face unsurmountable difficulties. The reason is that as a religion and social system, Islam is changeless. It is based on the Quran and the Sunnah which are changeless. This has not been said by me but by most Muslims including the historian Ishtiaq Husain Qureshi whose assertion has been quoted by me on pp. 116 and 320 of my book under review. I.H. Qureshi says: "The Quran is believed by every Muslim to be the word of God revealed to his Prophet Muhammad." This word of God cannot be amended, cannot be changed because "not even the Prophet could change the revelation". Equally important is the Sunnah. Muslim Law is built on the Quran and the Hadis. "There are no local variations of the Muslim Law." Muhammad himself did not want any change in the religion he had initiated. In the closing year of his life, 632 CE, he performed what is known as the Valedictory Pilgrimage. At Mina he preached and urged the pilgrims "not to depart from the exact observances of the religion which he had appointed".[11]

Muslim Shariat law was enacted in the Middle Ages. Muslim pattern of life was set in the Middle Ages. Any pleas for change are dubbed as "innovations" and are denounced with fatwas. Muslims in India can only indulge in unlimited praise of Islam, or, discreetly keep quiet. There is no third choice. Those who raise even a faint voice of criticism have ultimately to seek refuge in foreign lands (Taslima Nasreen, Anwar Shaikh). Polygamy is still practised and amputation of limbs and flogging, especially of women, practised (Bangladesh). The medieval Muhtasib is still at work. What Shaikh Ghaznavi recommended to Iltutmish about Jihad and treatment of Kafirs in the thirteenth century or Qazi Mughisuddin told Alauddin Khalji in the fourteenth or Shah Waliullah in the eighteenth is still the norm of thought. Two years ago a meeting of the Personal Law Board was held at Jaipur. It recommended censorship on any progressive views. Such views are considered "innovations" in Islam. Besides other resolutions, there was one on setting up media-watch committees throughout the country to monitor media reports about "attack on Islam" (that is, anything analytical or critical regarding Islam), and establishment of Shariat courts (as reported in *The Times of India*, New Delhi, Oct. 17, 1993). Muslims live, as they have always lived, in the Middle

Ages. Else, there was no need for Salamat Masih to seek asylum outside Pakistan and Taslima Nasreen to flee from Bangladesh. No poet, scholar or writer even in modern times is impregnable from the argus eye of the Muhtasib. A few instances will suffice to drive home the point.

An Urdu poet Mohammad Alvi based in Ahmedabad recited a *ghazal* at a *mushaira*. The *ghazal* was repeated from Alvi's famous collection, *Chautha Aasman*, which won the Sahitya Akademi award. But on April 4, 1995, Mufti Shabbir Siddiqui of the Dar-ul-Uloom Shah-i-Alam, a small religious school in Ahmedabad, issued a fatwa terming Mohammed Alvi, a Kafir and apostate, ordered him to tender a public apology, renew his faith in Islam and remarry his wife, failing which the Mufti called upon the Muslims to excommunicate Alvi and break all social contact with him.

The couplets, which led to the issuance of the fatwa 17 years after they were written, reflected the poet's concern at the happenings around him. Considering that evil, violence and injustice have made this world God-forsaken and suggesting that God has become indifferent, in sheer pain and agony he prays to Allah:

"Agar tujhko fursat nahin, to na aa
magar ek acchha Nabi bhej de,
Bahot nek bande hain ab bhi tire
kisi pe tu ya Rab Vahi bhej de,
Qayamat ka din kho na jaye kahin,
ye achchi ghadi hai abhi bhej de."

(O Allah, if you do not have time, do not come, but at least send a good guide; there are numerous pious people in this world, bestow a divine message upon someone. This is the right time, lest we miss the doomsday.) What provoked the Mufti to issue the fatwa was a letter written to him by the Nazim-i-Ala of Dar-ul-Uloom Shah-i-Alam, Usman Khatri. When asked whether Alvi was invited to appear before him and defend his case, the principal of Dar-ul-Uloom, Maulana Moinuddin Razvi, said there was no need to call Alvi. If a thing was wrong in the Shariat, prima facie the Mufti had the right to issue the fatwa.

Asked whether the Mufti was authorised to issue such a fatwa, the principal said: "We do not have to seek anybody's authority."

Mohammed Alvi, however, said he did not have the slightest inclination to disbelieve in the finality of the Prophet, which is an Islamic injunction, nor had he tried to malign Allah. It was a simple poetic imagination where he called upon Allah to send a messenger or a guide (and not Prophet) with a divine message. There was nothing blasphemous in the three couplets, he maintained. On receiving an unconditional apology from Alvi, Mufti Shabbir Siddiqi pardoned the Kafir! "Now he is back in our fraternity", said he in Urdu on telephone.[12]

The fatwa against the lawyer in Beed in South India is another example of the gag on the freedom of expression by Muslims. "The maulvis of Beed town today (July 23, 95) excommunicated a lawyer, Shaikh Altaf Ahmed, from the community for writing an article expressing his opinion on the uniform civil code. Mr. Ahmed is reported to have opposed polygamy and *talaq* in an article in the district newspaper *Zunjar Neta* on July 11. This infuriated some religious leaders who expressed their displeasure over the article. Fundamentalists, too, started threatening Mr. Ahmed with dire consequences and some of them pelted stones on his residence on July 19. It is alleged that they even made an attempt on his life. The *fatwa* to expel the advocate was issued during the Friday *namaz* in his absence. He was asked to leave Beed at once. Mr. Ahmed apologised publicly clarifying that his intention was not to hurt religious sentiments but only to point out certain misconceptions. However, the Muslim clerics were not satisfied and declared that the decision to expel him would stand. The apology was not expressed as per Islamic rules, they added."[13]

Islam superintends every action of Muslims, and there are

fatwas directing them to do this and do not do that. According to newspaper reports, the Milli Parliament recently issued a fatwa directing Muslims to refrain from exercising their franchise in the on-going elections (India's 1996 General Elections). "It is completely unlawful for Muslims," the Milli Parliament is reported to have pronounced, "to give authority to any non-Muslim political party or group to rule over Muslims, for in the Quran we are told that Allah does not allow disbelievers to have any authority over the believers." Professor Imtiaz Ahmad protested against this fatwa on the ground that "One of the explicit requirements of Islam is that a *fatwa* can be issued only by someone who is learned in the scripture, the traditions and Islamic jurisprudence. The Milli Parliament's credentials on this count are seriously questionable. Even otherwise, the Milli Parliament's pronouncement is wholly misguided. For one thing, even though Muslims constitute a minority, they are co-sharers of political power within the framework of the Constitution. Wilfred Cantwell Smith had drawn pointed attention to the uniqueness of this situation in the Muslim world in *Islam in History*. Under the circumstances, for the Milli Parliament to invoke the distinction between believers and disbelievers amounts to sticking to outmoded ways of thinking and repudiating the emerging realities of Islam."[14] The fact is that invoking the distinction between believers and disbelievers, does not amount to outmoded ways of thinking; it forms the very basic principle of Islamic ideology. Whether it is competent or not, the Milli Parliament has issued a fatwa. And it stands. Imtiaz Ahmad talks about India's democratic set up. There is no democracy in Islam. There is even no word for democracy in Islam. The "progressive" Imtiaz Ahmad can hardly make a dent in the think-tank of the Milli Parliament.

However, after challenging the fatwa, Imtiaz Ahmad, like any discreet Muslim thought it necessary to add the following: "There is a verse in the Quran to the effect that Allah does not change the situation of a people who are unwilling to change their character (*ausaf*). For over fifty years a particular brand of Muslim religio-political leaders in the country have indulged in ways of thinking and acting which are the source of their community's predicament in contemporary India. It is time that this brand of leaders, of which the Milli Parliament is the latest example, drew guidance from this Quranic verse and corrected its obsolete ways of thinking and action so as to be able to act as real leaders of the community." Appeal to a Quranic verse protects Imtiaz from any adverse reaction of the clerics or the community even if the obsolete thinking is not changed even a whit. The fatwas are not confined to Muslims alone, the issuers have the audacity of admonishing and threatening people of other faiths also. The Express News Service reports from London how a "Fatwa forces editor into hiding":

"In the normal course of things, Mr. Namassiwayam Ramalingam, the editor-in-chief of the weekly *L'Independent*, would have been back in Port Louis, Mauritius, planning his next issue. But for the past two months or so, Mr. Ramalingam has been holed up in a small hotel in Croydon, on the outskirts of London, waiting for an elusive phone call that will inform him that it is safe to return home and resume publication.

"The wait is likely to be prolonged. The government of Sir Aneerudh Juggnauth is in a serious dilemma about what to do with an editor who is now threatened with a fate similar to that of Salman Rushdie and Tasleema Nasreen.

"The facts are somewhat bizarre. In March this year, on the occasion of the beginning of Ramzan, Mr. Ramalingam *reprinted* an article on the life and times of the Prophet Muhammad from the well-known French weekly *Le Point*. Matters would have ended there had not one Maulana Haroon read sinister meaning and blasphemy in the article.

"Within days of the publication, Maulana Haroon convened a public meeting in the Muslim-dominated Plaine Verte locality of Port Louis and, after arousing religious passions, issue a fatwa of death against Mr. Ramalingam.

"Muslims constitute 18 per cent of the population of Mauritius. The Hindu community is in a majority with 52 per cent.

"Two days later, the press of *L'Independent* was fire-bombed, and although the March 17 issue of the weekly hit the stands, it was the last. On March 24, Mr. Ramalingam boarded a flight to London, leaving his family in Mauritius, hoping that a small period of absence would allow passions to cool.

"Mr. Ramalingam, on the advice of Prime Minister Juggnauth, also tendered an apology for any unintended offence to the Muslim community."[15]

When we turn our attention to countries beyond the Indian subcontinent, especially the Islamic countries, we realize how the Muslims still live in the Middle Ages. There are no churches in Saudi Arabia and of course no Hindu temples. It is stated that no Hindu can take any idol into Saudi Arabia. And about this situation Indian Muslims are not only satisfied but also encourage the Arabs not to give equal treatment to non-Muslims. Such an one is Maulana Abul Hasan Ali Nadvi, the Rector of the Nadwat-ul-Ulama, popularly known as Ali Mian, whom we have met before. He is opposed to the construction of houses of worship of non-Muslims in the Arabian peninsula. He wrote a letter to this effect to the Emir of Kuwait first in 1963. That letter has been re-published in one of his books. Ali Mian's letter said: "You know that the Prophet of Allah made the Arabian peninsula exclusive to Islam. The Caliph Umar has reported that he heard the Prophet say: 'I shall throw the Christians out of the Arabian peninsula and will not allow anyone but the Muslims to live there.' Near the time of his death the Prophet said: 'There will never be two religions in the Arab land.'" Referring to (newly-built) non-Muslim houses of worship in Kuwait, Ali Mian said they were a threat to that country's integrity. He warned that it was necessary to be vigilant concerning the presence of alien minorities in Kuwait which could lead "to the creation of a nation within a nation". (Here he is conscious of the role of Muslims in India.) *Communalism Combat* (February, 1995) published the letter under the heading: "Is This Ali Mian's Islam?" The letter-writer C.M. Naim, ended by saying: "Ali Mian has been to the United States and Europe several times. One hopes that visiting the numerous mosques there has produced in him some reciprocal sentiment of acceptance of the ways of worship of God by others." Obviously, not.

This is what Muzaffar Hussain has to say about the situation in Iran and other Islamic countries:

"Iran's criminal law is reverting to the mediaeval system of punishment. A woman accused of adultery is condemned to be buried chest-deep and killed by hitting her with rocks and stones... under Section 104 of the Iranian Criminal Code... Today when everywhere there is the din of slogans for protection of human rights and women's liberty groups are going from strength to strength, in the last decade of the 20th century, there is no one to protest against the cruel law that instructs people to kill women suspected of adultery by crushing them under a shower of stones... In Pakistan the *Hadud law* under the rule of General Zia was meted out to women, and today it is being practised in Iran. Today, progressive governments and enlightened societies do not stomach the outdated practices like *purdah*... if any government resists *purdah*, they will kill twenty women who have already discarded it. Retaliate one veiled with 20 veilless! It is reminiscent of the fanatics' slogan of *Hum panch, hamare pachis* in retaliation of the Indian government's legend for family planning, *Hum do, hamare do.* This is the description of the state of affairs in the Muslim countries especially in Saudi Arabia and Iran. *The Muslim intellectuals do not speak for fear of death* (emphasis ours), and when the non-Muslim world comments on such incidents, attempts are made to fool the world opinion by branding these comments as misinformation conspiracy by the Christians and the Israelis...

"The Human Rights Commission contains a news item that women were imprisoned for driving cars or defying the supposedly Islamic tradition of dress. In Saudi Arabia, some educated women gathered together and decided to drive cars simultaneously to defy the reactionary law prohibiting female car-driving. Thus 22 women came on the roads and began driving their cars. The Saudi Government... not only seized their cars but shut up the women drivers in jails.

"In the matter of restriction on women's attires, Iran is followed by Sudan. In Sudan, if a woman defies the rules regarding women's clothes she invites the punishment of 74 lashes of flogging. A girl student of Khartoum was subjected to 35 lashes for daring to flaunt a skirt-and-blouse ensemble. In the town of Oumdarman a woman received 37 lashes for committing the 'immodesty' of wearing a pyjama. The Human Rights Commission report is a collection of such blood-curdling tales. *When these dark-age societies will be liberated from the repressive system of the fanatics who perpetrate these crimes in the fair name of Islam, only the savior Allah knows*!" (emphasis ours).[16]

And of course the, fatwa on Rushdie will be implemented. A news item from Tehran says: "Iran's chief judge, Ayatollah Mohammad Yazdi said on Sunday the *fatwa* threatening the life of Indian born British author Salman Rushdie will eventually be implemented. The implementation of the decree is upto Muslims of the entire world and not only Iran. So Iran will not make any effort nor will pay money to kill Mr. Rushdie." (DPA)[17]

The problems faced by Governments in countries like Egypt, Turkey and Algeria against pure Islamists are well known. About their difficulties in dealing with the fundamentalists, the less said the better. The crux of the problem is the fact that "true" Muslims still live, as they have always lived in the Middle Ages when their unchanging and changeless religion was revealed to them — in all countries by force.

(b) Islam is inherently a religion of aggression, violence, and dominance. Jihad is still proclaimed and practised. Allah-o-Akbar is as much a battle cry heard during communal riots, as it is heard during the call for prayer. Islam divides humanity between followers of the faith and infidels. Infidels are proclaimed as the enemies of Allah (think of it, God has enemies in poor humans), and are to be killed if they do not accept Islam. Words like Jihad, Zimmi, Kafir, Munkir, Mushrik hurled at unoffending people belonging to other faiths do not denote non-violence or peaceful co-existence. Jihad is advocated by Shariat and not a single Muslim will dare to say publicly that Shariat is unacceptable. Muslims are so much accustomed to violence that if there are no non-Muslim Kafirs available to fight with, one section of Muslims calls another Kafir and continues with the killing spree. There was a time when Afghanistan was Hindu and Buddhist. There was peace. Now it is torn by unceasing conflict. Let it revert to its ancient faith and, I challenge, who knows peace will automatically return.

In many areas in the world today, wherever there is violence, terrorism and conflict, there is involvement of Islam. Muslims have been practising terrorism in many non-Muslim as well as Muslim countries on trumped up grievances, for Islam is inherently a religion of violence.

(c) India is not a Muslim country. It is a secular state; Parsis, Jews, Christians, Hindus and Muslims live here on terms of equality. There is no problem with Parsis and Christians. But Muslims are not concerned with the problems of adherents of other faiths. They are only concerned about themselves and their 'Separate Identity'. For example, India wants to improve the condition of women. Women suffer from many disabilities. Muslim women in particular are at a disadvantage in matters of divorce, inheritance, polygamy and unequal status in Islamic society. For improving their lot and prohibiting polygamy among all religious groups a common civil code is needed. But Muslims oppose its enactment. Changeless Islam, founded in the Middle Ages, stands in the way of any reform. An Anti-Common Civil Code Convention was held by Muslims at the Talkatora Indoor Stadium in New Delhi on July 4, 1995. The Convention demanded that the Muslims should be exempted from the purview of Article 44 of the Constitution which envisages such a code. Asad Madani, the chief of the Jamiat, called the demand for a common civil code a conspiracy to finish off the Muslims in India. He advised all Muslims to have four wives to increase the Muslim population and to enhance their influence with the Government. Zafaryab Jilani described the move for a common civil code as anti-Islamic and aimed at finishing Islam in India. Mufti Abdul Razzaq of Bhopal wanted Muslims to wage Jihad against the Government and to kill those who opposed Muslim Personal Law. Many more separatist statements were made. If the Muslims were concerned about equality with devotees of other faiths, they would not oppose a common civil code meant *for and applicable to all Indians.* Instead of opposing it they should grab this opportunity to get into the proposed code all the good things in the Shariat concerning the "high status of women in Islam" about which Muslims are so vociferous. But they shun to live on terms of equality with the people of other faiths, they do not like to join the mainstream of Indian social and cultural life. They insist on asserting their separate identity not only in India but wherever they happen to be in a minority, United Kingdom and France included. This aspect has already been discussed in the *Legacy* (pp. 345-48) and need not be restated here.

9. In his hurried determination to belittle my book, Jackson failed to notice that I am well aware of the work of Peter Hardy and have quoted him at two places in the *Legacy* on pages 63-64 and 115. I have, however, not seen any book written by Yohannon Friedmann or Peter Jackson. I know that

Irfan Habib headed the school of historical studies at Aligarh, but he has retired. There were newspaper reports that his continuance was resented by mány members of the History Department who counted him, like me, among the "Marxists, pseudo-secularists, progressives etc." Like them, I am not bound to accept his views. The last-minute refusal of the Aligarh Muslim University authorities to grant permission to the Association for the Study of History and Archaeology (ASHA) to hold its second annual conference in their university stirred a controversy. The timing of the AMU authorities' refusal coincided with the removal of Prof. Habib from the post of coordinator, Centre of Advanced Study of History, AMU.

Fifteen years ago, Irfan Habib reviewed my book *Growth of Muslim Population in Medieval India* (A.D. 1000-1800), brought out by Research Publications in Social Sciences, Delhi, in 1973. The similarity of spirit of criticism between the reviews of Peter Jackson and Irfan Habib is significant.

7.2. *Growth of Muslim Population in Medieval India*

At the 39th Annual Session of the Indian History Congress held at Hyderabad in December, 1978, Professor Irfan Habib presented a forty-page cyclostyled paper entitled "Economic History of the Delhi Sultanate — An Essay in Interpretation".

One half of the paper deals with the topic, the other consists of charges against me, Professor K.A. Nizami, and Professor Lallanji Gopal. However, the main thrust of his paper is an adverse criticism of my book. I presented a rejoinder to his paper at the 1979 session of the Indian History Culture Society, New Delhi. It was published in the Proceedings of the Society. The volume was entitled *Bias in Indian Historiography* and was edited by the late Dr. Devahuti. My rejoinder to Habib's criticism of my book as published in the Proceedings volume is being reproduced here with slight changes here and there.

Professor Irfan Habib starts with: "Professor Lallanji Gopal ... has discovered that poverty in India began with the coming of the Muslims", and "...Professor K.S. Lal has made the equally startling discovery that the sultans reduced the population of the country by over a third". This is followed by a stereotyped attack on Elliot for writing about "the murders and massacres" perpetrated by the "Mohamedans" (pp. 2, 29-40 of his cyclostyled paper).

Professor Habib betrays a rather unscholarly strain by encompassing in the one sentence quoted above the entire impact of 130 pages of my study (pp. 26 to 156) *Growth of Muslim Population in Medieval India.* As I have said in the Preface of the book: "Any study of the population of the pre-census times can be based only on estimates, and estimates by their very nature tend to be tentative" (p. vi). I claim no finality about my assessments of demographic quantification nor, I beg to submit, can Professor Habib. But he does not make any assessment at all; he merely challenges and criticises my conclusions — a very easy task! In my computation, however, sufficient historical evidence has been set forth for any demographic behaviour and on that basis I have arrived at the conclusion that the population of India in A.D. 1000 was about 200 million and in the year 1500 it was 170 million. However, Irfan Habib gives a twist to my observation on the decline of population by saying that "the sultans reduced the population of the country by over a third" (p. 2) which would mean that I have stated that the sultans deliberately killed people to reduce the population of India. I have shown in my book under reference that the population of India in the ancient period was large and prosperous, citing the authority of Greek writers, Chinese travellers and Arab geographers together with the conclusions arrived at by many modern writers (pp. 25-32). What happened to this huge population? It was decimated by Muslim invaders and invaders like Muhammad bin Qasim, Mahmud Ghaznavi, Muhammad Ghauri and Qutbuddin Aibak, some of whom took pride in claiming that they had killed people by lakhs (hundreds of thousands). Their chroniclers have also credited them with tremendous achievements in this regard.[18]

Irfan Habib is all praise for Professor Mohammad Habib who was "so conscious of the negative aspects of the medieval Islamic civilization or so sensitive to the devastation that the wars and compaigns of the sultans wrought on the inhabitants" (page 3) while he attacks Professor Nizami for writing "without that critical view of Islamic society and the destruction accompanying the invasions" (p. 5). On the other hand, when I refer to this devastation and destruction resulting in the decline of Indian population, Irfan Habib finds it unpalatable. I should have thought that a dispute was out of the question as Habib has used the same sources in computing the number of slaves captured in some campaigns of the sultans as I have for the assessment of demographic decline. This is what Irfan Habib has to say about the acquisition of slaves by the sultans: "The evidence for such enslavement is there for all to see. So economically important was it that the success of military campaigns was often judged by the number of captives (*burdas*) obtained for enslavement. Qutbuddin Aibak's campaign in Gujarat in 1195 netted him 20,000 slaves, seven years later a campaign against Kalinjar yielded 50,000. In 1253 Balban obtained countless 'horses and slaves' from an expedition in Kalinjar. In the instructions that Alauddin Khalji is said to have issued to Malik Kafur before his campaigns in the Deccan it is assumed that 'horses and slaves' would form a large part of the booty. As the Sultanate began to be consolidated, the suppression of *mawas* or rebellious villages within its limits yielded a continuously rich harvest of slaves. Balban's successful expedition in the Doab made slaves cheap in the capital. How people of the village could be made slaves for non-payment of revenue is described in the 14th century sources; and women so enslaved are mentioned in different contexts in two others" (pp. 16-17). This statement of Irfan reflects the imperialist style, in total disregard of the feeling of the slaves taken. When I write from the view of the victims, Jackson regards it as "propaganda, and rather crude propaganda at that". But of this a little more later on.

Does not the netting of captives presuppose desperate struggle? Surely people did not come rushing to the invading armies to be made slaves. They were captured and enslaved during invasions only after bitter fighting in which many more were killed. As I have shown in my book, the extent of the loss of population through killings in wars was enormous. The loss of Indian population during Mahmud of Ghaznavi's invasions was about 2 million as studied in some detail in Appendix A of the *Growth of Muslim Population in Medieval India* (pp. 211-17). Thereafter, with the establishment of Turkish rule, India suffered badly so far as its population was concerned. But Habib not only overlooks this fact, he also challenges it.

Habib gives some figures of slaves made during the time of Qutbuddin Aibak to Alauddin Khalji. Here are some figures of the loss of lives during the same period. Qutbuddin Aibak's conquests (c. 1200-10) included Gwalior, parts of Bundelkhand, Ajmer, Ranthambhor, Anhilwara as well as parts of U.P. and Malwa. In Naharwala alone 50,000 persons were killed during Aibak's campaign. No wonder that besides earning the honorific of *lakhbakhsh* (giver of Lakhs) he also earned the nickname of *killer of lakhs*. Bakhtiyar Khalji marched through Bihar into Bengal and massacred people in both the regions. During his expedition to Gwalior, Iltutmish (1210-36) massacred 7000 persons besides those killed in the battle on both sides. His attacks on Malwa (Vidisha and Ujjain) were met with stiff resistance and were accompanied by great loss of life. He is also credited with killing 12,000 Khokhars (Ghakkars) during Aibak's reign. The successors of Iltutmish (Raziyah, Bahram etc.) too fought and killed zealously. During the reign of Nasiruddin and Balban (1246-86) warfare for consolidation and expansion of

Turkish dominions went on apace. Trailokyavarman, who ruled over Southern U.P., Bundelkhand and Baghelkhand, and is called Dalaki va Malaki by Persian chroniclers, was defeated after great slaughter (1248). In 1251, Gwalior, Chanderi, Narwar and Malwa were attacked. The Raja of Malwa had 5,000 cavalry and 200,000 infantry and would have been defeated only after great slaughter. The inhabitants of Kaithal were given such severe punishment (1254) that "they might not forget the lesson for the rest of their lives". In 1256 Ulugh Khan Balban carried on devastating warfare in Saimur, and "so many of the rebellious Hindus were killed that numbers cannot be computed or described". Ranthambhor was attacked in 1259 and many of its valiant fighting men were killed. In the punitive expedition to Mewat (1260) "numberless Hindus perished. In the same year 12,000 men, women and children were put to the sword in Hariyana." When Balban became the sultan "large sections of the male population were massacred in Katehar and, according to Barani, in villages and jungles heaps of human corpses were left rotting". During the expedition to Bengal, "on either side of the principal bazar (of Lakhnauti), in a street two miles in length, a row of stakes was set up and the adherents of Tughril were impaled upon them".

"Alauddin Khalji and Muhammad bin Tughlaq (c. 1296-1350) were great warriors and killers. Alauddin's conquest of Gujarat (1299) and the massacres by his generals in Anhilwara, Cambay, Asvalli, Vanmanthali etc. earned him, according to the *Rasmala*, the nickname of *khuni*. His contemporary chronicler proclaims that Alauddin shed more blood than the Pharaos did. He captured Ranthambhor after very heavy casualties. Chittor's capture was followed by a massacre of 30,000 people, after Jauhar had been performed and the Rajputs had died fighting in large numbers. When Malwa was attacked (1305) its Raja is said to have possessed 40,000 horse and 100,000 foot. After the battle, "so far as human eye could see, the ground was muddy with blood". Many cities of Malwa like Mandu, Ujjain, Dharanagri and Chanderi were captured after great resistance. The capitulation of Sevana and Jalor (1308, 1311) were accompanied by massacres after years of prolonged warfare. In Alauddin's wars in the South, similar killings took place, especially in Karnataka and Tamil Nadu. In the latter campaign Malik Kafur went from place to place, and to some places many times over, and in his rage at not finding the fleeing prince Vira Pandya, he killed the people mercilessly. His successor Mubarak Khalji once again sacked Gujarat and Devagiri.

In short, the Turkish rulers were ruthless in war and merciless towards rebels with the result that their killings were heavy. Hence the extirpating campaigns of Balban and the repeated attacks on regions already devastated but not completely subjugated. Bengal was attacked by Bakhtiyar, by Balban, by Alauddin, and by the three Tughlaqs — Ghiyas, Muhammad and Firoz. Malwa and Gujarat were repeatedly attacked and sacked. Almost every Muslim ruler invaded Ranthambhor until it was subjugated by Alauddin Khalji (1301), again temporarily. Gwalior, Katehar and Avadh regions were also repeatedly attacked. Rajputana, Sindh and Punjab knew no peace. In the first decade of the fourteenth century Turkish invaders penetrated into the South, and its population too suffered heavy losses.[19] During campaigns and wars, the disorganized flight of the panic-stricken people must have killed large numbers through exposure, starvation and epidemic. Nor should the ravages of famines on populations be ignored. Drought, pestilence, and famines in the medieval times find repeated mention in contemporary chronicles.[20] Add to this the demographic decline occasioned by the recurring Mongol invasions for almost a whole century.

And yet Habib states that my "evidence for actual depopulation is nil" (p. 39). Has he passed judgement on pages 26 to 156 of my book without reading them? (Habib

p. 2 n. 2). I do not consider him so naive as not to understand the importance of the influence of demographic decline on the economic activity of a country.[21] But apparently he wants to shut his eyes to anything disagreeable to his susceptibilities, and seek refuge in all sorts of untenable interpretations and suppositions.

This brings us to the 'revolutionary researches' of Habib about the economic history of the Delhi Sultanate. His first startling discovery is that the spinning wheel (*charkha*) came to India from Persia and that too in the 13th century. Habib writes that it had "come to Iran in the 12th century". He does not say what it looked like, how it was made, and wherefrom it came to Persia. In India, according to him, "this important mechanical device is referred to first of all, in Isami's *Futuh-us-Salatin* (1350), as an instrument to which women should apply themselves. It, therefore, seems practically certain that the spinning wheel came to India from Iran probably in the 13th century, so as to spread rapidly enough for the kind of statement made by Isami." Thus, according to Habib, it was a novel device introduced in India. But *charkha* or spinning wheel was known in India long before Isami. Amir Khusrau advised his daughter to sit with her back to the door while plying the *charkha*, and Habib himself confesses that "domestic maid-slaves were made to work at spinning" (p. 17), surely not, only after Isami's time. Good quality cloth was manufactured in India from times immemorial. "The skill of the Indian," says Professor Weber, "in the production of delicate woven fabrics...in all manner of technical arts has from very early times enjoyed worldwide celebrity."[22] It is a well known fact that Egyptian mummies dating back to 2000 B.C. have been found wrapped in Indian muslin. Throughout the ancient times, cotton cloth was produced for domestic use. Obviously, its yarn was produced on the spinning wheel device. And yet, according to Habib, India was unaware of the spinning wheel in the ancient times.[23] Therefore, it is wrong to conclude that a sizable expansion in the production of cotton cloths took place because of the immigration of artisans and the introduction of new technology from abroad in the 13th and 14th century. Irfan Habib also claims "it (introduction of spinning wheel) may well be responsible for that large scale use of cloth by ordinary people which the comparison of depictions in ancient Indian sculptures and painting and Mughal-period miniatures so markedly bring out" (p. 9). One may ask how much clothing Kabir, an ordinary man, and a weaver, himself put on after this "central innovation quickened immeasurably the process of spinning yarn".

It is not surprising that for some communal historians suffering from extra- territorial chauvinism, the Persian wheel,[24] the spinning wheel, the dome and the arch all came from lands outside India and the highly developed ancient Indian civilization was unaware of these. It may be pointed out to such writers that the rudiments of the arch and the dome were both known to Ajantan and Buddhist India and one would do well to read E.B. Havell's works in this regard.

The growth of industrial commerce under the sultans was not due to the immigration of a large number of artisans from abroad (for which only the fragile authority of Isami is quoted) and the Indian slave labour, as claimed by Habib. The instances he himself cites are of slaves working as domestic servants (p. 17). Slaves were mainly captured or purchased by rulers for menial services, help in hunting and sport, and service in the army.[25] Surely a few thousand out of the 180,000 slaves of Firoz Tughlaq worked in the royal karkhanas, but there is no evidence to show that the 50,000 slaves of Alauddin Khalji were so engaged. There is no evidence whatsoever of "a process of enslavement of very large numbers of people, so as to provide cheap reserves out of which new craftsmen could be created" (Habib, p .15). However, in spite of demographic decline, the spurt in industry and commerce was there because "the loot from temples and treasuries of Hindu kings, in other words, the wealth lying frozen for decades and centuries, was released into the market,"[26] for providing items of comfort and luxury for the new rulers while the technical know-how for producing such articles was already known in India.

The coming of some scholars, physicians, hermits, unani doctors and assayers of jewels, artisans (*kasiban*) and embroiderers cannot be denied. But if good artisans and architects were available in such large numbers in Central Asia so as to migrate to Delhi "like insects around a lamp", it would not have been necessary for Timur to carry away artisans and architects from India to build his mausoleum at Samarkand.

As Habib somehow manages to bring up the issue of the N.C.E.R.T. sponsored textbooks in his discussion of the economic conditions in medieval India we are constrained to express our opinion on this matter after quoting Habib (p. 34): "The time is surely not distant, when writers wishing to avoid the fate of the N.C.E.R.T. books, would busily exhibit these statistics (in my *Growth of Muslim Population*) to show what terrible straits Indian economy was reduced to by fire and sword under the Muslims rulers."

We assert that the N.C.E.R.T. books are known for their studied bias and fantastic theories and interpretations of writers like Habib and his tribe, and their communal approach in deliberately glossing over the misdeeds of one section of medieval Indian society and repeatedly hammering on the failings of the other.

7.3. *The Mughal Harem*

There is another review of a special brand by A. Jan Qaiser of the History Department of Aligarh Muslim University published in the *Indian Historical Review*, New Delhi, 1991. This is a specimen of how a review may not be written. For it contains sentences like "whom do you think you are bluffing Mr. Lal?" or "what a consistency, Mr. Lal.?" (p. 346). Such is not the language of scholars. Therefore, I ignored Qaiser's review except devoting a page of my *Legacy of Muslim Rule* (p. 171) to take notice of one point . In *The Mughal Harem*, (Aditya Prakashan, New Delhi, 1988, p. 203). I had said that "The large establishment of wives and servants rendered the nobles immobile. No Indian scholars, engineers or travellers went abroad to learn the skills the Europeans were developing in their countries. While people from Europe were frequently coming to Hindustan, no Indian noble man could go to the West because he could not live without his harem and he could not take with him his cumbersome harem to countries situated so far away. Europe at this time was forging ahead in science and technology through its Industrial Revolution, but the Mughal elites kept themselves insulated from this great stride because of inertia. Consequently, the country was pulled back from marching with progress, a deficiency which has not been able to be made up until now."

Reacting to this statement, A. Jan Qaiser in his harsh review of the book observes; "Is Lal really ignorant of the fact that the Indians were being increasingly exposed to a number of European articles of technology and culture brought by the Europeans during the sixteenth, seventeenth and eighteenth century?" (p. 346). The poor man does not realise that he is only confirming my assertion that the Indian nobles were being only exposed (whatever he may mean by the word) to articles *brought* by Europeans. On their own they were incapable of doing anything more.

For Qaiser's information I may add that Professor M. Athar Ali, his colleague in Aligarh, agrees with my contention when he says (in his book *Mughal Nobility under Aurangzeb*, Bombay, 1970, p. 174) that "the ideas of the nobles concerning industry never went beyond Karkhanas or establishments employing artisans at low rates for their needs for luxuries (p. 164)... from the point of view of the Mughal nobility itself chief fault was its failure to change and adapt itself to a new developing situation not only in India, but in the whole world."

Since its publication *The Mughal Harem* has been reviewed in dozens of journals and magazines both in English and in Hindi. A couple of letters from a scholar in California are indeed touching: "I am quite aware of the years of research that has gone into your work and it is very much appreciated," and "My greatest admiration for your work and thanks for all you have given me in my research for understanding and knowledge."

In comparison, A. J. Qaiser's review is dross.

7.4. *History of the Khaljis* and Other Books

My *History of the Khaljis* was first published in 1950. It went through a second revised edition in 1967. A review published in the *Times Literary Supplement*, London, dated December 19, 1968 said, "When this book was published sixteen years ago it took its place at once among the standard authorities... This new edition embodies a good deal of fresh material derived from hitherto unutilised Rajput sources... In its latest form, this book is unlikely to be surperseded." *History of the Khaljis* was mainly my dissertation for the Doctorate degree and was written at Allahabad between 1942 and 1945. The University of Allahabad was then known as the Oxford of India. During the years 1937 and 1945 when I was a student there, Dr. Sir Shafaat Ahmad Khan, Dr. Tara Chand, Dr. R.P. Tripathi, Dr. Ishwari Prasad and Dr. Beni Prasad were some of the great names in the then known as the History and Politics Department. They were all my teachers. Professor Mohammad Habib of Aligarh, was also as good and kind to me as my Professors at Allahabad. Naturally their ideas and views about medieval history left a deep impression on my young mind. Their ideas in turn were influenced by the contemporary Indian political scene which was then in great ferment. Between 1941 when I took the

Master's degree and 1945 when I obtained the D. Phil., the struggle for Indian independence against British rule was at its peak (with Quit India Movement thrown in, in 1942). During those turbulent days it was felt that Hindu-Muslim combined endeavour was most needed to present a united front against the foreign British rule. Allahabad was the home of the Nehrus. Jawaharlal Nehru used to reside in Anand Bhavan when he was not in jail. Mahatma Gandhi also used to come and stay there for days together. Many important meetings of the Congress Working Committee used to be held in Anand Bhavan. The University was at a stone's throw from there. It is no wonder therefore that the Allahabad University became a think-tank for presenting Hindu-Muslim united front. This was one reason why it became a fashion and a tradition in the History and Politics Department not to say a word against Muslim rule in India; everything about it was to be praised. It was an attempt at forging Hindu-Muslim unity with retrospective effect. Naturally, we young scholars of impressionable age learnt about the Muslim rule in India with a definite pro-Muslim bias just as we were taught by our professors. But, I remember, we students used to discuss among ourselves that there was lot of 'white washing' and 'polishing' and *suppressio veri* in what we were taught in the class room.

The Faculty members of the History Department had brought out a number of excellent monographs on medieval Indian history. Beni Prasad's *History of Jahangir*, Banarsi Prasad Saksena's *History of Shahjahan*, R.P. Tripathi's *Some Aspects of Muslim Administration* and Ishwari Prasad's *History of the Qaraunah Turks* were widely read. Ishwari Prasad's *Medieval India* and *Muslim Rule in India* were our textbooks in B.A. and M.A. Tara Chand's *Influence of Islam on Indian Culture* and Mohammad Habib's *Sultan Mahmud of Ghaznin* were highly praised for breaking new grounds. We were recommended lots of books to read. Sir Jadunath Sarkar's *Aurangzib* was avidly read, and also criticised. But those were the days of a different culture not found now among Marxists and progressives. For instance, when there was criticism of some statement of Jadunath Sarkar, it was also acknowledged in and outside the class room (by R.P. Tripathi, for example) that Sarkar was the doyen of Indian historians and "head and shoulders above all of us".

During the early years of my research on Alauddin Khalji which led to the completion of the *History of the Khaljis*, the emphasis was on learning the Persian language. Muslim chronicles, which formed our main source material, were available in that language mainly. The study of Quran, Hadis and other Muslim scriptural literature was not recommended. At this stage there never was even a suggestion to read these and acquaint ourselves with the salient features of the religion of Islam. On the other hand it was often emphasised that the actions of omission and commission of Muslim rulers and nobles had nothing to do with the religion of Islam. We thought as we were told in Professors' lectures and published books — that the tirade of the Muslim ulema like Ziyauddin Barani against the Hindus were the fulminations of a sick mind and the actions of invaders and rulers like Mahmud Ghaznavi and Alauddin Khalji had nothing to do with Islam as such.

But the source materials threw a different hint. The Quran was often quoted by the chroniclers during their spate of abuse against the Hindus. Barani was learned in Islamic scriptures. Mahmud of Ghazni was a scholar of the Quran and Amir Timur prostrated himself before God after he had achieved the great objective of massacring the people of Delhi. Connection between the actions of Muslim rulers and Islamic scriptures was unmistakable. In later years, when I had become acquainted with the fundamentals of Islam through the study of the Quran and Hadis I realized that whatever the Maulanas (and most sufis) had said was not the product of a sick or unbalanced mind but was based on Islamic religious scriptures, and that historical truth could become clearer by discovering the links between the actions of Muslim invaders and rulers, the writings of chroniclers, and the teaching of Islamic scriptures instead of clamping the entire blame on the ulema section of the sultan's court.

In 1945 I left Allahabad and joined the Madhya Pradesh (then known as Central Provinces and Berar) Educational Service and for the next eighteen years or so taught at Government Colleges in Nagpur, Jabalpur and Bhopal. My *Twilight of the Sultanate* was published in 1963 when I was at Bhopal. It deals with the history of the Afghan rulers of the Lodi clan. Sikandar Lodi was an anti-Hindu fanatic, and consequently a true Muslim in the eyes of Muslim chroniclers. I have not failed to write about his bigotry, which was enjoined by his creed, on pp. 192-94 and 287-88 of the *Twilight of the Sultanate*. Else, but for the speciality of his religion, the son of a Hindu mother could not have become so fanatically anti-Hindu. Similar had been the case with Sultan Firoz Tughlaq.

In July, 1963, I joined the University of Delhi as Reader in (Medieval) Indian history

A seminar on "Ideas motivating Social and Cultural Movements and Economic and Political policies during the 15th, 16th and 17th centuries in India" was organised by the History Department of the Delhi University in November, 1965. I presented a paper on "Ideas leading to the impoverishment of the Indian peasantry in medieval times". It had been dinned into our ears that the extreme poverty of the Indian peasant was due to the administrative policies and exploitation of the British rule. I had often wondered if this execrable poverty was the result of a century or so only of British rule, or whether this poverty was of remote past and its origins could be traced back to the medieval period. I found enough evidence to arrive at the conclusion that there was systematic impoverishment of the agriculturists under Muslim rule; to blame the British alone was not right. But such a conclusion was against the current fashion. To find fault with Muslim rule was not in conformity with secular history. After I had presented the paper many delegates spoke to express their views, as is usual in seminars. But Professor Saiyyad Nurul Hasan indulged in "trenchant criticism" of the paper. He was a Marxist, a secularist, and a progressive historian. Such was the clout of this group of historians that they would not brook any disagreement with their mental fixture of only appreciation and praise for Muslim rule in India. I became convinced that until this "gagging of others" was not challenged, their brand of history would go unchecked. Since then I have challenged them in my books.

Later on Nurul Hasan became the Education Minister in the Government of India. Nurul Hasan possessed great qualities of head and heart. He was also a great administrator. Early in his career as Professor at Aligarh he had organized the History Department on a stable footing. When he became the Education Minister he continued the traditions of Maulana Abul Kalam Azad. He had a kind heart and like the great Mughals loved being surrounded by yes-men. Prospective professors thronged round him. Professors of history throughout the country began to be appointed with his consent and approval. He founded the Indian Council of Historical Research. He established the Jawaharlal Nehru University. His proteges took control of the Institute of Advanced Study at Simla and the University Grants Commission at Delhi. The situation is best sketched by Swapan Dasgupta in an excellent article in the *Indian Express* of July 23, 1995:

"Many of those who read history at Delhi in the mid-1970s and later, still bear the ugly scars inflicted by the thought police of *sạrkari* Marxism. 'There are two interpretations of history', a leading representative of the Red Cretin Brigade used to inform his students casually, 'the bourgeois interpretation and the Marxist interpretation, and the Marxist interpretation is the correct one.' The sense of certitude was terribly contagious and ambitious students readily accepted the prevailing dictum: if you read Marx, you will score more marks... The leftists were neither sartorially wild, sexually adventurous nor fanatically anti-establishment. They were boring time servers who lived off the patronage provided by a 'progressive' education minister. They dominated the committees, regulated appointments, set the curriculum, issued monotonously predictable 'anti-fascist' proclamations, hobnobbed with visiting academic dignitaries and travelled on the international seminar circuit. With little original research under their belt, they thrived above all on reflected glory.

"Indeed, being a part of an international Marxist fraternity was central to their existence. If Christopher Hill published an incisive study on the English Civil War, if E.P. Thompson completed a monumental work on 18th century deviancy and if the Ruskin College-based History Workshop undertook a seminar on popular culture, some of the glory would rub off on their progressive counterparts in India. The British Marxists set the standards of history in Britain and this enhanced the reputation of their counterparts in India...

"Whereas the British Marxists established their reputation by crafting their radical concerns their Indian counterparts took cheeky short cuts. It may also explain why substantive research on Indian history has increasingly become the prerogative of British, and a few American and Australian universities. The presiding deities of Indian historiography have meanwhile devoted themselves to writing politically correct text books that present history as chapters of received wisdom. They have also drafted resolutions for the Indian History Congress and written articles in the press on the Ayodhya issue."

The story of their resolutions for the Indian History Congress and their articles on the Ayodhya issue may be briefly recapitulated. A pamphlet entitled "The Political Abuse of History: Babri Masjid — Ram Janmabhumi Dispute" was issued by the Faculty members of the Centre of Historical

Studies, Jawaharlal Nehru University (JNU). It was authored by Professors S. Gopal, Romila Thapar and Bipan Chandra, among others. This "group history", if it was meant to decide the issue of Babri Masjid–Ramjanmabhumi once for all through sheer weight of numbers, failed miserably. Many articles and books appeared to challenge the contention of JNU professors. These were written not only by Hindus but also by Christians (Koenraad Elst) and Muslims (A.R. Khan). Professor A.R. Khan, Department of History, Himachal Pradesh University, Simla, wrote a long rejoinder to the pamphlet. The eminent historians from JNU had repeatedly asserted that Lord Rama's association with Ayodhya was based not on historical evidence but on belief. Dr. Khan asked: "The belief of the Hindus in Rama as an *avtar*, or god, is as strong as the belief of the Muslims in the Quran as a revealed work, as word of God. Can the said exponents of reason dare talk on evidence on the latter?"[27]

Of course, they dare not. But at many sessions of the Indian History Congress they continued to make noise about the Babri Masjid-Ramjanmabhumi. I had stopped attending the Annual sessions of the Indian History Congress a long time back because it had become a propaganda forum for Aligarhian and JNU secularist historians. I enjoyed reading in the newspaper about the goings on at the Congress of 1993 session held at Mysore.[28] The newspaper on 18th December quoted a Professor from Aligarh as exclaiming that "It is to the credit of the History Congress that not a single 'outstanding' historian joined the ranks of the Vishva Hindu Parishad on the Babri Masjid issue". A noted history scholar, on the other hand "alleged that the forum of the Congress was being used as a political platform" (20th December). This is the level to which the Indian History Congress has been reduced by Marxist historians. They have gone by many fancy names like Marxists, secularists, amnestists, progressives etc. Their secular history only means hiding away Muslim fundamentalism or presenting its sanitized version.

In short, the Marxist historians in India derive strength and reputation from works done by foreigners. On their own they have little academic distinction. Their nearness to the establishment has made them academic snobs. They have made the Indian History Congress sessions their propaganda forum. They feel they possess the monopoly of interpreting medieval Indian history. I had a personal experience of this attitude at a U.G.C. seminar on "Urban Rural Relations in Medieval India" held in the History and Culture Department of Jamia Millia Islamia on 7 to 9 March, 1979. Many scholars were invited to this seminar including K.A. Nizami, Irfan Habib, H.S. Srivastava, Lallanji Gopal, Raghuvir Singh, Mushirul Hasan, Iqtidar Alam Khan, Harbans Mukhia, A.B.M. Habibullah, myself etc. etc. At this seminar the junior cadre were more vocal and intemperate. They thought no end of themselves and looked upon others with deep disdain. Once again I became convinced that this group was incapable of doing any substantial research. Irfan Habib is an exception. It must be said to his credit that he continues to work. It is another matter that he and his admirers think that only his secular and pro-Muslim views are the last word on Medieval Indian history.

My *Growth of Muslim Population in Medieval India* was published in 1973. It annoyed some secularist historians in Aligarh. According to them some dark spots of Muslim rule had been brought into focus. But a detailed analysis had to be given bearing on the demographic behaviour of the times. But if Irfan Habib rushed with an adverse review of the book, there were many others who praised it for marshalling such a vast array of evidence in support of my conclusions . During the twenty-three years or so, between the publication of my *History of the Khaljis* (1950) and the *Growth of Muslim Population in Medieval India* (1973), I had not been vegetating. I had been constantly working and growing through learning and experience. I had published the *Twilight of the Sultanate* in 1963 and *Studies in Medieval*

Indian History in 1966. I had edited the volume containing papers presented at the First Asian History Congress held at Azad Bhavan, New Delhi, in 1961. It was published by the Indian Council of Cultural Relations as *Studies in Asian History* (1969). Because of constant pursuit of learning, I had shed many old ideas which had been the product of an impressionable if not very mature mind.

Of this I shall give only one instance. In my *Studies in Medieval Indian History*, I had discussed about the "Factors underlying the loss of Indian independence in the Twelfth-Thirteenth centuries". In this I had repeatedly said that only Kshatriyas or Rajputs fought against foreign invaders. This is what I had said: "A nation exploited by the priestly class...with only one caste set aside for the country's defence...could never be gathered under one banner of a slogan like 'Hindustan in danger'." Again, "... the Rajputs alone fought against the foreign invaders, since the other castes had no obligation to defend the land..." And once again, "Only one caste — the Kshatriyas — was set aside for the purpose of defence against foreign invasions and protection of life and property from internal dissensions."[29]

Equally funny (as they look now) were my observations on the state of Hindu society. "Inside the cities and towns under Hindu rule lived people only of the higher castes. The lower caste people like servants and untouchables like scavengers had their quarters outside the walled city .They came to serve in the city, but could not reside there. The Brahmin cook and Thakur watchman were the only servants who could stay on the premises of the master or go inside his house. It was a very satisfactory arrangement so long as it worked. But when district after district passed into the hands of the Muslims, and Muslims in large numbers began to reside in cities and towns, the shape and form of the latter were completely changed. Not that they treated the menial classes in any way better than the Hindus, but the stigma of untouchability was gradually lost in a Muslim-ruled city. The untouchables served in the cities as before, but now they also lived there. Although the Hindus continued to treat the menials as untouchables and the menial classes continued to remain Hindu, yet in a city under Muslim control the stigma of untouchability was gradually gone and the lower-class people felt better under Muslim rule. The Hindu system had been distasteful to them."[30]

These views had been pressed into my mind by long oral discussions with Professor Mohammad Habib and the writings of Mohammad Habib and K.A. Nizami. The caste system has been considered by these scholars as a very major, if not the sole, cause of the defeat of the Hindus at the hands of the Turks. Professor Mohammad Habib writes, "The conquest of northern India (by Muhammadans), when all factors are kept in mind, can be explained only by one fact — the caste system...the division of the people into smaller water-tight sub-caste groups resulting in the total annihilation of any sense of common citizenship or of loyalty to the country as a whole."[31] Professor K.A. Nizami arrives at a similar conclusion when he says: "The real cause of the defeat of the Indians lay in their...invidious caste distinctions which weakened their military organization. That patriotic fervour in which every citizen instinctively lays his hand on the sword-hilt in moments of national crisis was killed by these caste distinctions. The bulk of the Indian population was apathetic towards the fortunes of the ruling dynasties. No appeal from the Rajput governing classes could possibly receive sympathetic response from the vast mass of Indian population..."[32] I too began to share this view, but later on, on a re-evaluation of facts thought to be unimportant earlier, critical analysis and deeper reflection which grow with age, it appeared to me that the role of caste in the defeat of the Hindus has been given undue importance and emphasis. So that ten years later in my *Early Muslims in India* published in 1984, I wrote as follows: "There is no doubt that caste meant varied interests and divided opinions, but caste after all was a social evil, not a military disadvantage. The Kshatriyas never suffered on account of shortage of numbers on the fields of battle." The mention in the *Shastras* that it was the duty of the Kshatriyas to defend the land, should not lead to the misconception that all others were debarred or disinterested in the defence of their religion and country. Muslim chroniclers do not talk of the Kshatriyas alone participating in battles. They always speak of the 'Hindus', meaning thereby the people as such, fighting in wars. The huge casualties in wars as detailed by the chroniclers also point to the people's resistance to the invaders and conquerors and not only of a small section of the warriors.[33] Indeed Jats, Khokhars and Gakkars, who were not high in the Hindu caste hierarchy, enthusiastically fought against Mahmud on many occasions.

And now, another ten years later, as a result of continuous study, I have arrived at the conclusion in my *Growth of Scheduled Tribes and Castes in Medieval India* (1995) that all castes, all classes of people, resisted foreign invaders and rulers, the lower classes as much as the higher, if not more. How else was this vast country saved from Islamization? How else, among the countries of the East, which experienced the visitation of Islamic armies, India alone could successfully repulse Muslim onslaughts and ultimately do away with Muslim rule slowly but surely? It is because all people, and not only Kshatriyas, put up a perennial resistance to Muslim invaders and rulers to the best of their capabilities.

My studies in the course of years did not remain confined to Persian chronicles; they were supplemented by indigenous source materials like the Rajput chronicles, the vast Bhakti or Vaishnav literature, as well as the plethora of historical works produced by modern scholars on medieval Indian history But the most effective influence was created on my mind by the study of the Quran, the Hadis, the *Hidayah* and other original works on Islamic law. I saw a clear relationship between Islamic scriptures and the actions and policies of Muslim invaders and rulers as faithfully recorded by Medieval Muslim historians. I became convinced that Muslim rule in India derived its inspiration from the dictates of Islamic religion. And in my writings in the nineties I began to quote extensively from these original sources of Islamic law and history instead of only citing from medieval Muslim chronicles. That is how a difference is seen between the *History of the Khaljis* and *Twilight of the Sultanate* on the one hand and the *Legacy of Muslim Rule in India* and other books written by me in the eighties and nineties, on the other. One does grow during the course of half a century if one continues with his studies and I have surely grown. And since I do no believe that "Muslim rule should not attract any criticism. Destruction of temples by Muslim invaders and rulers should not be mentioned and forcible conversions to Islam should be ignored and deleted, etc. etc.", my books are free from such restrictions. I now also apply the same yardstick to medieval Indian history as is done with respect to modern Indian history. If British imperialism was bad for the Indian people so also was Muslim imperialism. Both these sought sustenance from cooperation of indigenous elements but neither of them became indigenous in nature. We in India write the history of British rule not from the point of view of European imperialism but from that of the victims of colonization. I apply the same methodology to the history of Muslim rule. I write about it from the people's point of view rather than from the view of Islamic imperialists. We cannot apply different standards of approach and methodology to different periods of Indian history.

NOTES

1. This is what B.N. Pandey stressed in many seminars and in conversation with S. Kalidas as reported in *The Times of India*, August 22, 1993, on the occasion of his receiving the Khudabakhsh Award for communal harmony from the President of India. "Once Aurangzeb was on his way to Bengal with a retinue of Hindu kings and their wives. When the caravan was about five miles from Banaras, the kings requested a day's halt so that they could bathe in the Ganges and pray at the Kashi Vishwanath temple. Aurangzeb acceded and the kings and their queens went to Banaras. When they returned the maharani of Kutch was missing from the group. A search was mounted and when she was not found, the temple was searched. This revealed a secret flight of steps which led to an underground vault. There the rani was, in a state of shock, her jewellery missing, her clothes torn off... She had obviously been raped. When Aurangzeb learnt this he was very angry. He thought if this can happen to the queen of the maharana of Kutch, who is under my protection, what must be the fate of lesser women! This was not a place of worship, he said, but a den of evil. It was in this context that he ordered the temple to be razed."

This cock and bull story has not been swallowed even by die-hard secularists because of the overwhelming evidence available in the Muslim chronicles about the motives of the Emperor. Aurangzeb was prompted to destroy this and similar other temples in important centres of Hindu pilgrimage to suppress Hindu learning and their practising "idolatry".

2. Mazumdar, *Socio-Economic History of Northern India*, pp. 153-156.

3. Afif, pp. 302-315. Also Carr Stephen, *Archaeology of Delhi*, pp. 292-293 and Thomas, *Chronicles of the Pathan Kings of Delhi*: pp. 292-93.

4. *Maasir-i-Alamgiri*, pp. 51-52.

5. Afif, pp. 379-82: *Zunnardaran kalid-i-hujra-i-kufrund wa kafiran bar eshan muatqid und*. Barani, p. 42, calls the Brahmans as Imams of Hindus and recommends their systematic liquidation. Also Dorn, I, p. 65; Farishtah, I, p. 182 and *Maasir-i-Alamgiri*, pp. 51-52.

6. Barani, p. 273-74; *History of the Khaljis*, p. 87.

7. *History of the Khaljis*, p. 288.

8. Afif, pp. 205-206, 232-233; Barani, pp. 446-450.

9. *Tuzuk*, vol. I, pp. 162-63.

10. *Ibid.*, p. 182.

11. T.P. Hughes, *Dictionary of Islam*, p. 382.

12. *The Times of India*, May 12, 1995. Editorial in the same paper, May 25, 1995. Apology in *Indian Express*, July 25, 1995.

13. *The Times of India*, July 24, 1995.

14. *The Times of India*, Viewpoint, May 1, 1996.

15. *Indian Express*, New Delhi, May 21, 1995.

16. Muzaffar Hussain, 'Lynch law in Iran', article in *Organiser*, New Delhi, May 26, 1996.

17. *The Times of India*, New Delhi, April 22, 1996.

18. This has been done by many colonizers and imperialists. Later in the day European imperialists and colonizers just wiped out major sections of indigenous population in America, Africa and Australia. The "aboriginals" in these continents were reduced to microscopic numbers so that the colonizers began to claim that they were the main inhabitants of America and Australia in particular. So also was tried to be done by Muslims in India who began to claim Hindustan as a country of Islam. Indian resistance, however, did not let any such situation develop in India.

19. K.S. Lal, *Growth of Muslim Population in Medieval India*, pp. 39-42. For copious references to support these figures, the book itself may be consulted.

20. Lal, *Growth of Muslim Population*, pp. 42-44, 217.

21. As Lawrance Stone has pointed out, "The unfounded hypotheses about the beneficent results of early Spanish colonization of Mexico based on purely literary evidence and supported because of national or personal prejudice, collapsed utterly when it was discovered by the demographic quantifiers that the (American) Indian population fell from about 25 million to about 2 million in less than 50 years after Hernando Cortes had first landed." Lawrance Stone in C.F. Delzell (ed.), *The Future of History*, Nashville, Tennessee, 1977, p. 17.

22. Industrial Commission Report, p. 295.

23. For this statement Habib quotes Lynn White Jr. from his article in the *American Historical Review* of April 1960.

24. Probably referred to in the *Mrichchhakatika* (The Little Clay Cart) of Sudraka who lived in Gupta times.

25. K.S. Lal, "The Striking Power of the Army of the Sultanate", *Journal of Indian History*, vol. LV., part 3, December 1977, pp. 85-110 esp. p. 86.

26. K.S. Lal, *Twilight of the Sultanate*, Bombay, 1963, p. 295.

27. *Express Magazine*, February 25, 1990.

28. *Times of India*, New Delhi, December 18-20, 1993.

29. Lal, *Studies*, pp. 117, 119, 120.

30. *Ibid.*, p. 119.

31. M. Habib, *Indian Culture and Social Life at the Time of Turkish Invasions*, published by Aligarh Historical Institute, Lahore (n.d.), p. 6.

32. K.A. Nizami, *Some Aspects of Religion and Politics in India during the Thirteenth Century*, Aligarh, 1961, p. 79.

33. Lal, *Early Muslims in India*, New Delhi, 1984, pp. 39-40.

Bibliography

Original Sources

Abdullah, *Tarikh-i-Daudi*, Bankipore Ms. Text, ed. by S.A. Rashid, Aligarh, 1954.

Abdul Hamid Lahori, *Badshah Nama*, Bib. Ind., 2 vols., Calcutta, 1898.

Abul Fazl, Allami, *Ain-i-Akbari*, 3 vols., vol. I trs. by H. Blochmann and ed. by D.C. Phillot, Calcutta, 1939; vol. II trs. by H.S. Jarret and annotated by Jadunath Sarkar, Calcutta, 1939; vol. III trs. by Jarret and Sarkar, Calcutta, 1948.

Abul Fazl, Allami, *Akbar Nama*, Bib. Ind. Text, 3 vols., English trs. by Henry Beveridge, Calcutta, 1948.

Afif, Shams Siraj, *Tarikh-i-Firoz Shahi*, Bib. Ind., Calcutta, 1890.

Ahmad Yadgar, *Tarikh-i-Salatin-i-Afghana*, Bib. Ind., Calcutta, 1936.

Ain-ul-Mulk Multani, *Qasaid Badr Chach*, Kanpur, n.d.

Alberuni, Abu Raihan Muhammad, *Alberuni's India*, Eng. trs. by Edward Sachau, 2 vols., London, 1910.

Al-Biladuri, *Futuh-ul-Buldan* (written 9th cent. C.E.), trs. in E.D. vol. I.

Al-Kufi, *Chach Nama*, trs. in E.D. vol. I. Also by Mirza Kalichbeg Fredunbeg, Karachi, 1900, Delhi reprint, 1979.

Al-Qalqashindi, *Subh-ul-Asha*, trs. by Otto Spies as An Arab Account of India in the 14th Century, Aligarh, 1935.

Ali Muhammad Khan Bahadur, *Mirat-i-Ahmadi*, Calcutta, 1928; English trs. by M.F. Lokhandvala, 2 vols., Baroda, 1965.

Amin Qazvini, *Badshah Nama*, Ms. Raza Library, Rampur.

Amir Khurd, see Kirmani.

Amir Khusrau, Abul Hasan, *Ashiqa*, ed. by Rashid Ahmad Ansari, Aligarh, 1917.

Amir Khusrau, Abul Hasan, *Tughlaq Nama*, ed. by Hashim Faridabadi, Aurangabad, 1933.

Amir Khusrau, Abul Hasan, *Qiran-us-Sadain*, Aligarh, 1918.

Amir Khusrau, Abul Hasan, *Khazain-ul-Futuh*, see Habib under Modern Works.

Amir Khusrau, Abul Hasan, *Nuh Sipehr*, ed. by Mirza Wahid, Calcutta, 1948.

Amir Khusrau, Abul Hasan, *Miftah-ul-Fatuh*, Aligarh Text, 1954.

Arthashastra, English translation by R. Shama Shastry, Mysore, 1923.

Babur, Zahiruddin Muhammad, *Babur Nama* or *Tuzuk-i-Baburi*, trs. from Turki by Mrs. A.S. Beveridge, 2 vols., London, 1922; trs. from the Persian version by John Leyden and William Erskine as *Memoirs of Babur*, London, 1926.

Badaoni, Abdul Qadir Ibn-i-Muluk Shah, *Muntakhab-ut-Tawarikh*, ed. by Ahmad Ali, Persian Text, Bib. Ind., 3 vols., Calcutta, 1864-67; English trs. by George S.A. Ranking, Calcutta, 1898.

Baihaqi, Khwaja Abul Fazl, *Tarikh-i-Subuktgin* (written 1089 C.E.), trs. in E.D. vol. II.

Barani, Ziyauddin, *Tarikh-i-Firoz Shahi*, Bib. Ind., Calcutta, 1864.

Barani, Ziyauddin, *Fatawa-i-Jahandari*, English trs. by Afsar Begum and Mohammad Habib, Allahabad, 1960.

Barani, Ziyauddin, *Sana-i-Muhammadi*, trs. in *Medieval India Quarterly*, vol. I, pt. III.

Bihamad Khani, Muhammad, *Tarikh-i-Muhammadi*, British Museum Ms.; Rotograph copy in Allahabad University Library; English trs. by Muhammad Zaki, Aligarh, 1972.

Fakhr-i-Mudabbir, *Tarikh-i-Fakhruddin Mubarak Shah*, ed. by Sir Denison Ross, London, 1927.

Fakhr-i-Mudabbir, *Adab-ul-Harb wa Shujaat*, Photocopy British Museum, Add. 165; Hindi trs. in Rizvi, *Adi Turk Kalin Bharat*, Aligarh, 1956.

Fatawa-i-Alamgiri, Urdu trs. by (1) Maulana Syed Amir Ali, 10 vols., Delhi, 1988 and (2) Maulana Mufti Kafil-ul- Rahman, 42 parts, Deoband.

Farishtah, Muhammad Qasim Hindu Shah, *Gulshan-i-Ibrahimi*, also known as *Tarikh-i-Faristah*, Persian Text, Lucknow, 1865.

Firoz Shah Tughlaq, *Futuhat-i-Firoz Shahi*, Aligarh, 1954.

Gulbadan Begum, *Humayun Nama*, trs. as *The History of Humayun*, by Mrs A.S. Beveridge, London 1902, Indian reprint, Delhi, 1972.

Hajiuddabir, *Zafar-ul-Wali bi Muzaffar Wali*, An Arabic History of Gujarat, ed. by Sir Denison Ross, 3 vols., London, 1910, 1921.

Hasan Nizami, *Taj-ul-Maasir*, trs. by S.H. Askari in Patna University Journal (Arts), vol. No. 3, 1963, also in E.D. vol. II.

Hidayah by Shaikh Burhanuddin Ali, Urdu trs. entitled *Ashraf-ul-Hidayah* by Maulana Jamil Ahmad Sukrodvi, Deoband, 1980-88; *Kitab al-Siyar wa al-Jihad*, 2 vol., Mujtabai Press, Delhi, 1331-1332 H. Also see Hamilton under Modern Works.

Ibn Battutah, *The Rehla of Ibn Battuta*, English trs. by Dr. Mahdi Husain, 1953; French trs. as *Ibn Batoutahs Voyages* by C. Defremery and B.R. Sanguinetti, Paris, 1857.

Ibn Ishaq, *Sirat Rasul Allah*, see Guillaume under Modern Works.

Ibn-ul-Asir, Shaikh Abul Hasan, *Kamil-ut-Tawarikh* (written 12th cent. CE), trs. in E.D. vol. II.

Isami, Khwaja Abdullah Malik, *Futuh-us-Salatin*, Persian Text ed. by Agha Mahdi Husain, Agra, 1938. For English trs. see Mahdi Husain under Modern Works.

Jahangir, Nuruddin Muhammad, *Tuzuk-i-Jahangir* or *Memoirs of Emperor Jahangir*, trs. by Alexander Rogers and edited by Henry Beveridge, Delhi reprint, 1968. See also Price for *Tarikh-i-Salim Shahi.*

Jamil Ahmad Sukrodvi, see *Hidayah*.

Kamboh, Muhammad Saleh, *Amil Saleh*, Bib. Ind., 3 vols., Calcutta 1923, 1927, 1939.

Khafi Khan, Muhammad Hashim, *Muntakhab-ul-Lubab*, ed. by Kabir-ud-din Ahmad, Bib., Ind., Calcutta, 1869, 1925.

Khondmir, Ghiyasuddin Muhammad, *Khulasat-ul-Akhbar*, trs. in E.D. vol. IV.

Kirmani, Khwaja Amir Khurd, *Siyar-ul-Awliya*, Urdu trs., New Delhi, 1985.

Minhaj Siraj Jurjani, *Tabqat-i-Nasiri*, Bib. Ind., Calcutta, 1864; English trs. by Major H.R. Raverty, London, 1881.

Mir Masum, *Tarikh-i-Masumi* also called *Tarikh-i-Sind*, ed. by Daudpota, Poona, 1938.

Mufti Kafil-ul-Rahman, see *Fatawa-i-Alamgiri.*

Muhammad Bihamad, see *Bihamad*

Mustaad Khan, Saqi, *Maasir-i-Alamgiri*, trs. and annotated by Jadunath Sarkar, Calcutta, 1947.

Niamatullah, *Makhzan-i-Afghana*, trs. by Nirodbhushan Roy as *History of the Afghans*, Santiniketan, 1958; also B. Dorn's trs., 2 parts, London, 1929-36.

Nizamuddin Ahmad, *Tabqat-i-Akbari*, Bib. Ind., 3 vols., Calcutta, 1927-35; also trs. by B. De.

Otto Spies, see Alqalqashindi.

Padmanabh, *Kanhadade Prabandh*, translated and annotated by V.S. Bhatnagar, New Delhi, 1991.

Price, Major David, *Tarikh-i-Salim Shahi*, trs. under the title of *Memoirs of the Emperor Jahanguer written by himself*, London, 1829; Indian edition, Calcutta, 1906. Also see Price under Modern Works.

Qazvini, see Amin.

Quran Majid, Arabic text with Hindi and Urdu translation, Maktaba al-Hasnat, Rampur, sixth ed. 1976.

Ranking, see *Badaoni.*

Reynolds, see *Utbi.*

Rizqullah Mushtaqi, *Waqiat-i-Mushtaqi*, Photocopy of the British Museum, Add. 11633.

Sarwani, Abbas, *Tarikh-i-Sher Shahi*, trs. in E.D. vol. IV.

Shah Nawaz Khan, Samsam-ud-daula, and his son Abdul Hayy, *Maasir-ul-Umara*, trs. by H. Beveridge and Baini Prasad, 3 vols., Calcutta, 1911-14.

Shihabuddin al-Umri, *Masalik-ul-Absar fi Mumalik-ul-Amsar* (written in middle of 14th cent. CE), trs. in E.D., vol. III; Hindi trs. in Rizvi, *Tughlaq Kalin Bharat.*

Shukraniti, English translation by B.K. Sarkar, Allahabad, 1914.

Timur, Amir, *Malfuzat-i-Timuri,* trs. in E.D. vol. III.

Utbi, Abu Nasr Muhammad, *Kitab-i-Yamini,* trs. by James Reynolds, London, 1858; also in E.D. vol. II.

Wassaf, Abdullah, *Tajziat-ul-Amsar wa Tajriyat-ul-Asar,* also called *Tarikh-i-Wassaf* (written 1327 CE), Bombay, 1877.

Yahiya Sarhindi, *Tarikh-i-Mubarak Shahi,* Bib. Ind. Text edited by M. Hidayat Husain, Calcutta, 1931; English trs. by K.K. Basu, Baroda, 1932.

Yazdi, Sharafuddin, *Zafar Nama,* 2 vols., Bib. Ind., Calcutta, 1885-88.

Hadis

Miskat-us-Sharif by Abdullah al-Khatib al-Umari, Arabic text with Urdu trs. by Maulana Muhammad Umar Bastawi, 2 vols., Rabbani Book Depot, Lal Kuan, Delhi.

Sunan ibn Daud by Imam Daud Sijistani, Arabic text with Urdu trs. by Allama Wahid-uz-Zaman, 3 vols., Aitqad Publishing House, Suiwalan, Delhi, 1985.

Sunan ibn Majah by Imam Hafiz Abu Abad ibn Majah Qazwini, Arabic text with Urdu trs. by Abdul Hakim Khan Shahajahanpuri, 2 vols., Aitqad Publishing House, Delhi 1986.

Jama' Tirmizi, Arabic text with Urdu trs. by Maulana Badiuzzaman, 2 vols., Aitqad Publishing House, Delhi, 1983.

Sahih Muslim Sharif, Arabic text with Urdu translation by Allama Wahid-uz-Zaman, 6 parts in 3 vols., Aitqad Publishing House, Delhi, 1986.

Sahih Bukhari Sharif by Abu Abdullah Muhammad bin IsmailBukhari, Arabic text with Urdu translation by Maulana Akhtar Shahajahanpuri, 3 vols., Atiqad Publishing House, 2 nd reprint, Delhi, 1984.

Sunan Nasai Sharif by Imam Abu Abdurrahman Nasai, Arabic text with Urdu translation by Allama Wahid-uz-Zaman, 3 vols., Aitqad Publishing House, Delhi, 1986.

Foreign Travellers' Accounts

Barbosa, Duarte, *The Book of Duarte Barbosa,* 2 vols., London, 1918-21.

Bernier, Francois, *Travels in the Mogul Empire* (1656-1668), revised by V.A. Smith, Oxford, 1934.

De Laet, John, *The Empire of the Great Mogol,* trs. by Hoyland and Bannerjee, Bombay, 1928.

Della Valle, Pietro *The Travels of Peitro Della Valle in India,* trs. by Edward Grey, 2 vols., London, 1892.

Du Jarric, *Akbar and the Jesuits,* see Payne.

Finch, William, see Foster.

Foster, William, *Early Travels in India* (1583-1619), contains narratives of Fitch (pp. 1-47), Mildenhall (pp. 48-59), Hawkins (pp. 60-121), Finch (pp. 122-87), Withington (pp. 188-233), Coryat (pp. 234-87) and Terry (pp. 288-322), London, 1927.

Foster, William, *English Factories in India* (1618-69), 13 volumes, Oxford, 1906-27.

Ibn Battutah, see under Original Sources.

Major, R.H., *India in the Fifteenth Century*, contains extracts from narratives of Nicolo Conti, Santo Stefano, etc., London, 1857.

Manrique, Fr. Sebatian *Travels of Frey Sebastian Manrique*, trs. by Eckford Luard, 2 vols., London, 1927.

Manucci, Niccolao, *Storia do Mogor*, trs. by W. Irvine, 4 vols., London, 1906.

Mundy, Peter, *Travels of Peter Mundy in Asia*, ed. by R.C. Temple, London, 1914.

Payne, C.H., *Akbar and the Jesuits*, contains in trs. Du Jarric's account of the Jesuit Missions to the Court of Akbar, London, 1926.

Palsaert, Francisco, *Jahangir's India*, trs. by W.H. Moreland and P. Geyl, Cambridge, 1925.

Roe, Thomas, *The Embassy of Sir Thomas Roe to the Court of the Great Mughal* (1615-1619), ed. by William Foster, Hakluyt Society, London, 1899.

Tavernier, Jean Baptist, *Travels in India*, trs. and ed. by V. Ball, London, 1925.

Terry, Edward, *A Voyage to East India*, London , 1655.

Thevenot, Monsieur de, *Indian Travels of Thevenot and Careri*, ed. by Surendra Nath Sen, New Delhi, 1949.

Varthema, Ludovico, *The Itinerary of Ludovico di Varthema of Bologna*, ed. by Sir Richard Temple, London, 1928.

Yule, Sir Henry, and H. Cordier, *The Book of Ser Marco Polo*, 2 vols., New York, 1903.

Modern Works

Abdul Aziz, *Arms and Jewellery of the Indian Mughals*, Lahore, 1947.

Aghnides, Nicholas P., *Muhammadan Theories of Finance*, New York, 1916.

Ahmad see Muhammad Aziz Ahmad.

Ahmad, Aziz, *Studies in Islamic Culture in the Indian Environment*, Oxford, 1964.

Aiyangar, K.S., *Ancient India*, Madras, 1911.

Alavi, Azra, *Socio-Religious Outlook of Abul Fazl*, Idarah-i- Adabiyat-i- Delhi, 1983.

Ali, M. Athar, *The Apparatus of Empire* (1574-1658), OUP, 1985.

Ali, M. Athar, *The Mughal Nobility under Aurangzeb*, Bombay, 1970.

Ameer Ali, Sayyid, *The Spirit of Islam*, London, n.d.

Arnold, T.W., *The Preaching of Islam*, Westminister, 1896.

Arnold, T.W., *The Caliphate*, London, 1924.

Arnold, T.W., and A. Guillaume, eds., *The Legacy of Islam*, Oxford, 1931.

Ashraf, Kunwar Muhammad, *Life and Conditions of the People of Hindustan*, Calcutta, 1935.

Askari, S.M., *A Study of the Rare Ms. of Sirat-i-Firoz Shahi* in *Journal of Indian History*, vol. LII, April 1974.

Bharatiya Vidya Bhavan, see Majumdar, R.C.

Bhatnagar, V.S., see Padmanabh under Original Sources.

Bosworth, C.E., *The Ghaznavids: Their Empire in Afghanistan and Eastern Iran*, 994-1040, Edinburgh, 1963.

Brown, Percy, *Indian Architecture (Islamic Period)*, Third ed., Bombay, n.d.

The Cambridge History of Islam, in two volumes, ed. by P.M. Holt, Ann K.S. Lambton and Bernard Lewis, Cambridge, 1970.

The Cambridge History of India, Cambridge University Press, vol. III, ed. by Wolseley Haig, Delhi reprint, 1958; vol. IV, ed. by Richard Burn, Cambridge, 1937.

Chowdhary, S. R., *Al Hajjaj ibn Yusuf*, Delhi University Press, 1976.

Clarke, Colin, *Population Growth and Land use*, Macmillan, New York, 1967.

Crone, Patricia, and Cook, Michael, *Hagarisme: The Making of Islamic World*, Cambridge, 1977.

Currie, P.M., *The Shrine and Cult of Muin-al-din Chishti*, OUP, Delhi, 1989.

Davis, Kingsley, *The Population of India and Pakistan*, Princeton, 1951.

Day, U.N. *The Government of the Sultanate*, New Delhi 1972.

Devendra Swarup (ed.), *Politics of Conversion*, New Delhi, 1986.

Dorn, Benhard, *History of the Afghans*, being trs. of *Makhzan-i-Afghana*, London, 1829.

Eaton, Richard Maxwell, *Sufis of Bijapur* (1300-1700), Princeton, 1978.

Elliot, H.M., and J. Dowson, *History of India as told by its own Historians*, 8 vols., London, 1867-77; vol. II, with and Introduction by Mohammad Habib, Aligarh reprint, 1952.

Elst, Koenraad, *Negationism in India: Concealing the Record of Islam*, New Delhi, 1992.

Encyclopaedia Britannica

Encyclopaedia of Islam, 1913-38.

Encyclopaedia of Social Sciences, 1949 reprint.

Gage, Matilda Joslyn, *Woman, Church and State* (1893), First Indian Reprint, Voice of India, New Delhi, 1997.

Gehlot, Jagdish Singh, *Rajputana ka Itihasa*, Jodhpur, 1966.

Ghoshal, U.N., *A History of the Hindu Political Theories*, Oxford, 1923.

Gibbon, Edward, *Decline and Fall of the Roman Empire*, 2 vols., Everymans Library ed., n.d.

Goel, Sita Ram, *The Story of Islamic Imperialism in India*, Voice of India, New Delhi, 1994.

Goel, Sita Ram, *Muslim Seperatism*, Revised Edition, New Delhi, 1995.

Goel, Sita Ram (ed.), *Time For Stock Taking* Voice of India, New, Delhi, 1997.

Goel, Sita Ram, *Hindu Temple's What happened to them?*, vol. II: *The Islamic Evidence*, Revised Edition, Voice of India, New Delhi, 1993.

Guillaume, A., *Islam*, 1954.

Guillaume, A., *The Life of Muhammad*, OUP, Karachi, 1987.

Habib, Mohammad, *Sultan Mahmud of Ghaznin*, Delhi reprint, 1951.

Habib, Mohammad, *Compaigns of Alauddin Khilji*, being trs. of Amir Khusrau's *Khazain-ul-Futuh, Bombay*, 1933.

Habib, Mohammad, *Indian Culture and Social Life at the Time of Turkish Invasions*, published by the Aligarh Historical Institute, Lahore (n.d.)

Habib, Mohammad, *Collected Works*, entitled *Politics and Society During Early Medieval Period*, edited by K.A. Nizami, vol. I, 1974; vol. II, 1981.

Habibullah, A.B.M., *The Foundation of Muslim Rule in India*, Revised ed., Allahabad, 1961, first published, Lahore, 1945.

Hamilton, Charles, *Hedaya*, trs. of *Hidayah*, 4 vols., London, 1791; Reprint of vols. 1 and 2, New Delhi, 1985.

Hasan, Zafar M., *List of Muhammadan and Hindu Monuments in the Province of Delhi*, 4 volumes, Government Press, Calcutta, 1916-22.

Herklots, see Jafar Sharif.

Hitti, P.K., *The Arabs: A Short History*, London, 1948.

Hitti, P.K., *History of the Arabs*, London, 1951

Hodivala, S.H., *Studies in Indo-Muslim History*, Bombay, 1939.

Hughes, T.P., *Dictionary of Islam*, W.H. Allen & Co., London, 1885.

Ibn Hasan, *The Central Structure of the Mughal Empire*, Oxford, 1936.

Ibn Warraq, *Why I am not a Muslim*, Prometheus Books, New York, 1995.

Indian Antiquary

Indian History Congress, *Proceedings.*

Ira Marvin Lapidus, *Muslim Cities in the Later Middle Ages*, Cambridge (Mass.), 1967.

Irvine, William, *The Army of the Indian Moghuls*, Indian reprint, Eurasia Publishing House, New Delhi, 1962.

Ishwari Prasad, *A History of the Quraunah Turks in India*, vol. I, Allahabad, 1936.

Ishwari Prasad, *History of Medieval India*, Fourth impression, Allahabad, 1940.

Jafar Sharif, *Islam in India or the Qunun-i-Islam*, trs. by G.A. Herklots, ed. by William Crooke, London, 1875, 1921.

Journal of the (Royal) Asiatic Society of Bengal.

Kane, P.V., *History of Dharmashastra*, 5 volumes, Bhandarkar Oriental Research Institute, Poona, 1946-1968.

Khan, Yusuf Husain, *Glimplses of Medieval Indian Culture*, Bombay, 1957.

Khuda Bakhsh, *Essays, Indian and Islamic*, London, 1927.

Lal, K.S. *History of the Khaljis*, New Delhi, 1980, first published, 1950.
Lal, K.S., *Twilight of the Sultanate*, New Delhi, 1980, first published, 1963.
Lal, K.S., *Studies in Medieval Indian History*, New Delhi, 1966.
Lal, K.S., *Growth of Muslim Population in Medieval India*, New Delhi, 1973.
Lal, K.S.., *The Mughal Harem*, New Delhi, 1988.
Lal, K.S., *Early Muslims in India*, New Delhi, 1984.
Lal, K.S., *Indian Muslims: Who are they*, New Delhi, 1990, 1993.
Lal, K.S., *The Legacy of Muslim Rule in India*, New Delhi, 1992.
Lal, K.S., *Growth of Scheduled Tribes and Castes in Medieval India*, New Delhi, 1995.
Lamb, Harold, *Tamerlane the Earth Shaker*, London, 1929.
Lapidus, see Ira Marvin.
Lanepoole, S., *Aurangzeb*, Rulers of India Series, oxford, 1908.
Levy, Ruben, *The Baghdad Chronicle*, Cambridge, 1929.
Levy, Ruben, *The Social Structure of Islam*, Cambridge, 1957.
Lewis, Bernard, *Race and Slavery in the Middle East, A Historical Enquiry*, Oxford, 1990.
Lewis, Bernard, *Islam, from the Prophet Muhammad to the Capture of Constantinople*, 2 vols., Macmillan, 1974.
Mahdi Husain, *Tughluq Dynasty*, Calcutta, 1963.
Mahdi Husain, *Shah Namah-i-Hind or trs. of Islami's Futuh-us-Salatin*, 3 vols., Aligarh, 1976-77.
Majumdar, R.C. (ed.), *Struggle for the Empire*, Bombay, 1957.
Majumdar, R.C. (ed.), *The Delhi Sultanate*, Bombay, 1960.
Malik, S.K. Brigadier, *The Quranic Concept of War*, with a Foreword by General M. Zia-ul-Haq, Himalyan Books, Indian reprint, New Delhi, 1986.
Majumdar, Suhas, *Jihad*, Voice of India, New Delhi, 1994.
Margoliouth, D.D., *Mohammed and the Rise of Islam*, London, 1905; Indian reprint, with an introduction by Ram Swarup, New Delhi, 1985.
Mazumdar, B.P., *The Socio-Economic History of Northern India* (1030-1194 A.D.), Calcutta, 1960.
Meer Hassan Ali (Mrs.), *Observations on the Mussulmauns of India*, London 1832; Indian reprint, Delhi, 1975.
Mernissi, Faitma, *Islam and Democracy: Fear of the Modern World*, New York.
Mishra, S.C. *Gahba ke Gond Rajya ka Utthan aur Patan*, Jabalpur, 1986.
Moreland, W.H., *India at the Death of Akbar*, London., 1920.
Moreland, W.H., *From Akbar to Aurangzeb*, London, 1923.
Moreland, W.H., *The Agrarian System of Moslem India*, London, 1929.
Muhammad Aziz Ahmad, *Political History and Institutions of the Early Turkish Empire of Delhi* (1206-1290 A.D.), New Delhi, 1949, 1972.
Muir, Sir William, *The Life of Mahomet*, Indian reprint with an introduction by Ram Swarup, New Delhi, 1992.
Mujeeb, M., *The Indian Muslims*, London, 1967.

Mukerjee, Radhakumud, *Economic History of India* (1600-1800), Allahabad, 1967.

Nazim, M., *The Life and Times of Sultan Mahmud of Ghazna*, Cambridge, 1931.

Nadwa ka Sacch, A Pamphlet in Hindi reproducing news reports.

Narain, Harsh, *Jizyah and the Spread of Islam*, Voice of India, New Delhi, 1990.

Narain, Harsh, *Myths of Composite Culture and Eqiality of Religions*, Voice of India, New Delhi, 1991.

Nizami, K.A., *Some Aspects of Religion and Politics in India during the Thirteenth Century*, Aligarh, 1961.

Ojha, Gauri Shankar Hirachand, *Udaipur ka Itihasa*, Ajmer 1928-32.

Om Prakash, *Religion and Society in Ancient India*, Delhi, 1985.

Pant, D., *The Commercial Policy of the Mughals*, Bombay, 1930.

Page, J.A., *A Guide to the Qutb*, Archaeological Survey of India, Memoir 38.

Price, Major David, *Memoirs of the Principal Events of Muhammadan History*, 3 vols., London, 1921. Also see Price under Original Sources.

Qureshi, Ishtiaq Hussain, *Administration of the Sultanate of Delhi*, Fifth ed., New Delhi, 1971, first published, Lahore, 1942.

Ram Swarup, *Hindu View of Christianity and Islam*, New Delhi, 1992.

Ram Swarup, *Understanding Islam through Hadis*, Indian reprint, New Delhi, 1983.

Ram Swarup, *Woman in Islam*, Voice of India, New Delhi, 1994.

Rizvi, Saiyyad Athar Abbas, *Adi Turk Kalin Bharat*, Aligarh, 1965.

Rizvi, Saiyyad Athar Abbas, *Tughlaq Kalin Bharat*, 2 parts, 1956, 1957.

Rizvi, Saiyyad Athar Abbas, *Uttar Timur Kalin Bharat*, part II, Aligarh, 1959.

Rizvi, Saiyyad Athar Abbas, *Muslim Revivalist Movements in North India in the Sixteenth and Seventeenth Centuries*, Agra, 1965.

Rizvi, Saiyyad Athar Abbas, *Shah Waliullah and his Times*, Canberra, 1980.

Saksena, Banarsi Prasad, *History of Shahjahan of Delhi*, Second Impression, Allahabad, 1961.

Sanderson, Gordan, *Archaeology at the Qutub*, Memoir, Archaeological Survey of India, New Delhi, 1912-13.

Saran, Parmatma, *Studies in Medieval Indian History*, Ranjit Publishers, Delhi, 1952.

Sarkar, B.K., *The Political Institutions and Theories of the Hindus*, Leipzig, 1922.

Sarkar, Jadunath, *History of Aurangzib*, 5 vols., Calcutta, 1912-25, reprint 1972

Sarkar, Jadunath, *Fall of the Mughal Empire*, 4 vols., Third ed., Calcutta, 1964.

Sarkar, Jadunath, (ed.), *Later Mughals by Irvine*, 2 vols., Calcutta, 1921-22.

Sarkar, Jadunath, *A Short History of Aurangzib*, Calcutta, 1930.

Sarkar, Jadunath, *Mughal Administration*, Calcutta, 1952.

Shaikh, Anwar, *Islam, The Arab National Movement*, Principality Publishers, Cardiff, 1995.

Shaikh, Anwar, *Liberty*, Humanist Quarterly, Cardiff, 1955.

Sewell, Robert., *A Forgotten Empire* (Vijayanagar), New Delhi reprint, 1966.

Sleeman, Sir W., *Rambles and Recollections of an Indian Official*, ed. by V.A. Smith, Oxford, 1915.

Smith, V.A., *Akbar the Great Moghul*, Delhi reprint, 1962.

Shourie, Arun, *The World of Fatwas*, New Delhi. 1995.

Shourie, Arun, *Eminent Historians, Their Technology, Their Line, Their fraud*, New Delhi, 1998.

Sources of Indian Tradition, Columbia University Press, New York, 1958.

Stephen Carr., *Archaeology and Monumental Remains of Delhi*, Calcutta, 1876.

Thomas, Edward, *Chronicles of the Pathan Kings of Delhi*, London, 1871.

Titus, Murray, *Islam in India and Pakistan*, Calcutta, 1959.

Tod, James, *Annals and Antiquities of Rajasthan*, 2 vols., London, 1957.

Toynbee, Arnold J., *One World and India* (Patel Memorial Lectures), Indian Council for Cultural Relations, New Delhi, 1961.

Tripathi, R.P., *Some Aspects of Muslim Administration*, Allahabad, 1936.

Warraq, see Ibn Warraq.

Wink, Andre, *Al-Hind, The Making of the Indo-Islamic World*, vol. I, *Early Medieval India*, OUP, Delhi, 1990.

Index